Rigorous, comprehensive and admirably lucid, *Gender Identity: Lies and Dangers* is an authoritative and powerful account of the 'gender identity' movement and its devastating impact on women and children. Informed by and building on foundational works by writers like Janice Raymond and Sheila Jeffreys, Lecuona's compellingly argued exposition restores radical feminist analysis to its rightful place at the forefront of understanding the fundamentally political nature of transgenderism.

—Julia Long, author of *Anti-Porn: The Resurgence of Anti-Pornography Feminism*

This is a beautiful book. The prose is elegant, pellucidly clear, and gripping. The reader gets carried along through a very thorough compendium of the present state of the debate and politics surrounding men's practice of claiming something called a female 'gender identity'. There are no dry or boring moments, despite the potential complexity of the arguments. Rather there is a splendidly colourful and persuasive language which makes the book a pleasure to read. Enjoy!

—Sheila Jeffreys, author of *Penile Imperialism: The Male Sex Right and Women's Subordination*

A rigorous interpretation of a feminist tradition that presents the reader with an invaluable analysis and compendium of writers who have challenged the transgender juggernaut. Lecuona's book is remarkable in scope, an impressive contribution in its own right and a dose of political sanity that is badly needed. Her achievement does justice to all those women who walk with her in this critical journey.

—Janice Raymond, author of *Doublethink: A Feminist Challenge to Transgenderism*

It is encouraging to read more and more excellent, well-researched and unapologetically, radically feminist books critiquing the ideology of gender identity. Through her incisive analysis of its reach into Mexico and Spain, Laura Lecuona demonstrates just how globally entrenched this dangerously absurd ideology has become. We should all heed her call to break its stranglehold and "start rebuilding the feminism that was taken from us."

—Bronwyn Winter, Professor Emerita of Transnational Studies and lifelong feminist activist, author of *The Political Economy of Same-Sex Marriage: A Feminist Critique*

Laura Lecuona studied Philosophy at the Universidad Nacional Autónoma de México. An editor and translator specializing in philosophy and social sciences, she has held editorial coordination positions at Paidós Mexicana, Fondo de Cultura Económica and Ediciones SM. As a popularizer of feminism, she is a regular lecturer and writer. In the Spanish-speaking world, she is one of the main referents of the feminist criticism of the doctrine of gender identity.

Other books by Laura Lecuona

Las mujeres son seres humanos (2016)

GENDER IDENTITY

Lies and Dangers

LAURA LECUONA

We respectfully acknowledge the wisdom of Aboriginal and Torres Strait islander peoples and their custodianship of the lands and waterways. The Countries on which Spinifex offices are situated are Djuru, Bunurong and Wurundjeri, Wadawurrung, Gundungarra and Noongar.

First published in English by Spinifex Press, 2024

Spinifex Press Pty Ltd
PO Box 200, Little River, VIC 3211, Australia
PO Box 105, Mission Beach, QLD 4852, Australia

women@spinifexpress.com.au
www.spinifexpress.com.au

Edited by Renate Klein, Susan Hawthorne and Pauline Hopkins
Cover design by Deb Snibson
Index by Aviva Xue
Typesetting by Helen Christie, Blue Wren Books
Typeset in Minion Pro
Printed and bound in Australia by Pegasus Media & Logistics

 A catalogue record for this book is available from the National Library of Australia

ISBN: 9781925950908 (paperback)
ISBN: 9781925950915 (ebook)

 The paper in this book is FSC® certified. FSC® promotes environmentally responsible, socially beneficial and economically viable management of the world's forests.

MIX
Paper from responsible sources
FSC® C008194

In memory of Luisa Fernanda González Molina (1948–2008), who would not let my ears be pierced when I was born and never forced me to play with dolls.

To my sister
To Úrsula and Tenar
To A. G.

CONTENTS

ACKNOWLEDGMENTS

I was introduced to feminism by listening to my mother chatting with her friends. She was part of the team that in the 1980s produced the pioneering series *La Causa de las Mujeres* (The Women's Cause), which was broadcast on Radio Educación, and often they had meals in our house that extended into the night with bottles of red wine. "Today comes La Causa," she would announce to my sister and me. Berta Hiriart, Claudia Hinojosa, Norma del Rivero, Rosamaría Roffiel and Sonia Riquer were loving familiar presences. I had more fun with them than with friends my own age.

I vividly recall the Argentinian edition of *The Second Sex* by Siglo Veinte lying on my mother's night table and of a basket with all the issues of the feminist magazine *Fem* next to the TV. One day, Claudia Hinojosa recommended the book *No es natural,* by the Catalan sociologist Josep Vicent Marqués, and I devoured and underlined it in November 1985, according to my handwritten note on the flyleaf. Thanks to that reading and the atmosphere in that house, always full of women, from a very young age I understood how sexist roles work and how society "manufactures little men and little women."

For the same reason, I never quite understood how it was possible for some people to claim to be women trapped in men's bodies. What is it to be a woman if not having a woman's body? Femininity is something else, of course, independent of the body –

there are men who are feminine and women who aren't. The concept of transsexuality intrigued me, as well as the fact that some men would take such extreme measures to look like what they wanted to be or believed they, deep down, were, but I thought it was something closer to plastic surgery addiction than to transubstantiation. I never paid much attention to it, until one day, in February 2017, I saw the issue of *National Geographic* with a boy with pink hair and clothes on the cover, dedicated to what they called "the gender revolution," and then I came across the news in *The New York Times* that the Boy Scouts organization had finally accepted a nine-year-old girl because she declared herself transgender and therefore she was a boy and her name was not Jodi, but Joe.

I identified with that little girl. I could have been her; at her age I would have wanted to be an explorer too; I never liked to wear dresses and I liked to play football. I said I wanted to be a boy and they even took me to a psychologist, a very sensible one who immediately took away any anguish my parents might have had about my mental health.

If my childhood had taken place in the 2010s and not the 1970s, I would have been an ideal candidate to be treated in one of the gender identity clinics that abound in Canada or the United States and that are beginning to enter Mexico just when other countries, such as Sweden and England, finally aware of the dangers of so-called gender medicine, are already backtracking, and one negligence scandal after another is uncovered. I have good reason to think that my mother, a feminist after all, would not have approached an organization like Chrysallis, Mermaids or the Asociación por las Infancias Transgénero, which promote the idea that girls like the one I was are *trans children,* but rather one like the Agrupación AMANDA or Transgender Trend, which resist, with force, information and reasons, the transgendering, heterosexualizing and normalizing of children with subversive and transgressive potential.

When I was in kindergarten there was a teacher whose given name was Josefina but everybody called Jose, a diminutive that sounded close enough to José. "Why don't we pretend my name is

Josefina and you call me Jose?" I asked my mother one day. With her on one telephone device in her bedroom and me from the living room, I felt delighted as she called, "Hi, Jose, how was school today?" and I imagined being a boy named José. Then I grew out of it, but in that which is called gender nonconformity I have been consistent, insistent and persistent to this day. How fortunate for me that in those days there were no tests in which girls and boys are asked *how they identify themselves* and where they fall on the Barbie versus GI Joe scale.

If, years ago, the trans issue had seemed enigmatic but of little relevance to me, when I read the news about the girl called Joe, my interest was piqued as well as my concern. I devoted the following week to researching in depth. I learned about the violence and intolerance of gender identity activists and, reading some of the authors they attacked and dismissed as *transphobic,* confirmed my intuition that their doctrine went against all feminist teachings and had little logical support. I wrote an opinion piece and put forward my first thoughts on the subject.

Thanks to a friend who, when he read my text, decided to stop being a friend and put me in the activists' sights, I discovered something I had been blissfully unaware of until then: the queer-inspired movement – which that same month had wanted to boycott the inauguration of a feminist library in Vancouver and led a "bloody and violent attack" against the Spanish website Plataforma Antipatriarcado, despite the fact that they had given numerous proofs of support "for the trans community" – had already arrived in Mexico.

For having written that there was nothing transgressive about "maintaining that gender is something like an innate essence that resides not in social structures, but in the mind" and about telling children and adolescents "that the problem is not the sexist society, but their own bodies," I began to experience first-hand the same kind of vicious aggression and harassment that feminists such as Julie Bindel, Germaine Greer, Sheila Jeffreys, Janice Raymond and Rebecca Reilly-Cooper had suffered in other countries.

For a few days I was scared and even anxious about going out in the street. I asked two acquaintances I had in common with the main inciter of the online harassment to intercede on my behalf and tell him to stop (spoiler: he did not stop). The purpose of these attacks is to intimidate the other into repenting and correcting her thinking or silencing her, but I wasn't going to keep quiet and I saw that at this moment in the history of feminism the stakes are high. Faced with the choice of leaving the issue aside or continuing to talk about it, I opted for the latter. That decision has taken its toll on me and has not been easy, but the former does not suit me. I can't imagine myself being quiet, obedient and afraid.

Outnumbering the harassers in number and importance are all the women who at once came to my defense and gave me the support I really needed. I will never forget that the very first were Michelle Morales and Doménica Francke-Arjel. Then came many, many more with whom it has been a pleasure to share virtual refuges and venting. They have provided company, encouragement and a lifeline.

Because of my ideas I lost some friends but gained others. Gudelia Delgado, D. Fernandes, Marisabel Macías, Elisa Melgarejo, and Arussi Unda are just a handful of those who became more than comrades in struggle.

I celebrate the existence of groups such as Las Brujas del Mar, Las Constituyentes MX, the Alianza de Redes Feministas Nacionales, Colectiva Asteria, Marea Verde Sonora or Mujeres de la Sal; therein lies the present and future of feminism in Mexico. Conversations with Yan María Yaoyólotl Castro and Enoé Uranga helped me to understand the first steps of transactivism in this country and to see how the concept of gender identity began to creep in. Reading and listening to Spanish feminists such as Pilar Aguilar, Alicia Miyares and Amelia Valcárcel has given me clarity and energy.

Thanks to Amparo Domingo I was introduced to Women's Declaration International. I joined them and now I am part of a powerful community of feminists from all over the world and of all ages standing up to one of the strongest backlashes this social movement has ever received in its history. I have learned a lot from Katherine Aiken, Maria Binetti, Stefanie Bode, Jo Brew, Kara Dansky, Renate Klein, Sheila Jeffreys, Kathleen Lowrey, Vaishnavi Sundar, Anna Zobnina and many more. For my colleagues at WDI Mexico (Adii, Adriana, Elisa, Fernanda, Raimunda, Susana, Vanessa, Yadira …) I have a very special thank you; their talent and commitment is what inspires me the most.

In these five and a half years, following these debates closely, participating in them, attending webinars, listening to all kinds of women, following their podcasts, their blogs and reading the authors whose books some would like to burn, has been for me a course in feminism more rewarding than any PhD.

There are dear old friends who have been with me through thick and thin. I am also grateful to affectionate people from my time at the Instituto de Investigaciones Filosóficas de la UNAM who are still with me and are very present, such as Isabel Cabrera, Rocío Cázares, Adriana Flórez, Gustavo Ortiz Millán, Francisco Serrano and Margarita Valdés.

A. G., precious company and my first reader, gave me encouragement, love and advice.

A very special thanks to Renate Klein and Susan Hawthorne for publishing the English translation of this book and for their careful reading and feedback. What an honour being in the catalogue of Spinifex Press along with several radical feminists who I look up to.

NOTE ON LANGUAGE

It is important to keep in mind at all times that all women, and only women, are females of the human species, although not all of them embody the archetype of femininity. There are men who are more or less feminine, in the sense that they have some personality traits that are socially and culturally associated with women, or because they wear make-up, have long hair, wear dresses or have some other behaviour that is considered feminine. How great that many of us are rebelling against sexist stereotypes! But feminine men are not women, just as women who wear trousers and don't wear make-up are not, in any sense whatsoever, men. What makes us men or women is a material attribute we call sex, not an ethereal and mysterious essence like gender identity. Our religious beliefs and personal convictions do not affect that fact.

For this reason, and contrary to what is supposed to be politically correct, I do not use *preferred pronouns,* except in textual quotations and moments of free indirect speech. We are told to use them out of empathy, even in the absence of the person alluded to, but it is much more empathetic to speak the truth. I reserve white lies for rare occasions. Using a language that is attached to reality and not to the fantasies or desires of some people is fundamental for the ideas that I present here and to understand these issues, which sometimes seem entangled precisely because of the language traps that are set for that purpose. Preferred pronouns are intended to confuse and manipulate, whereas this book seeks to clarify and explain with arguments and reasons. To maintain that it is false that *trans women* are women and at the same time to refer to some men as *she* is to concede to the other side what it would be up to them to prove and to act as if it were indeed an incontrovertible truth. The issue of pronouns and their implications is discussed at length in Chapter 3.

It is impossible not to employ in this book a number of words and concepts that name supposed realities that I do not believe in (such as *gender identity, sex change, trans children* or *trans women*) or that have a usage that I want to move away from (such as *gender*). I put them in italics now and then – avoiding overuse – to mark my conceptual distance.

On some occasions I use the adjective *queer* to refer to the political movement that is institutionalizing the doctrine of gender identity, and on others, *transgenderism* or some variant. Although queer theory has had an influence on gender identity doctrine, I do not discuss it here, except for the somewhat disjointed set of ideas derived from it that are behind the politics of gender identity. One of the reasons why many people prefer not to approach these issues is that they have heard some queer babble or read a paragraph by Judith Butler and get the impression that the discussions around sex, gender, gender identity and transgenderism are beyond comprehension, but when the padding is removed, they become more understandable and one can make up one's own mind, even if one doesn't have a PhD in Gender Studies or a diploma in queer theory.

I do not set out to demonstrate facts that are already proven true. I make no effort to convince the reader that there is an objective reality, that there are only two gametes, that we reproduce sexually and that humans are a very different species from clownfish. Asking for evidence of what is already known is a distracting maneuver.

Some readers may find it disrespectful that I do not refer to men who assume a female identity as women, or to women who present as *trans men* as men. I hope that by reading this book they will understand that almost everything depends on this seemingly small detail. It is impossible to be congruent if one surrenders to such pressures, which are not humanitarian but political in nature.

INTRODUCTION

This book was born out of a commitment to feminism and to freedom of speech. Both are going through a difficult time, for reasons that will be explained at length in the following pages.

In many parts of the world, legal changes are taking place at unprecedented speed that affect women's political gains and bring about drastic changes in society, not necessarily positive ones. They are taking place surreptitiously, under the pretext that "rights are not up for debate." This uninformed slogan is uttered, and then urgent reforms that pulverize women's rights are fast-tracked behind society's back. If we want to defend these rights and assess whether what is on the table is a conflict of equally legitimate rights, or a conflict between rights and desires, for example, then of course there is a debate to be had. The problem is not the debate, but its absence or its impoverishment.

Discussions around transgenderism and so-called gender identity are often characterized as a categorical disagreement between left and right, progressives versus conservatives, people in favour of human rights for all versus people in favour of human rights just for some, libertarians versus fascists, the sexual diversity community versus people who want to take away their rights, young feminists versus old and middle-aged feminists, the good guys versus the bad guys.

Reality is much less simple. On both sides of this debate there are people from across the political spectrum, feminists from different currents and orientations, lesbians and heterosexual women, gay men and straight men, young people and older people. There are people who consider themselves transgender on both sides as well. The truth is that on both sides there are people who in principle seek the same goals: to get rid of sexist stereotypes. But there is profound disagreement about how to achieve this aim.

There would be much less political disagreement if there were some clarity in the terms used. There would be less disagreement if debate were allowed and different sides were heard, but the problem is precisely that it is not. By framing the issue as a war between pro-rights and anti-rights, between those who are in favour of *trans kids* and those who deny them their identity, a potentially enriching dialogue is suppressed. Instead, we get: "They are transphobic bigots and there is nothing else to say; everyone knows which side to be on, or else." This false and Manichean characterization has precisely the objective of inhibiting the free exchange of ideas.

Some protagonists of this substitute for respectful and rational debate believe themselves to be free of prejudice, convinced that they are on the right side of history. This self-sufficiency closes their ears to any argument or theory that might make them look deeper into the issue and perhaps rethink their position. Dogmatically, they have decided that their opponents' ideas are dangerous, bigoted, hateful or fascist, and should not be paid any attention to. Indeed, they should actively prevent others from coming into contact with these ideas, lest they become infected. By portraying the interlocutor as intolerant, she is denied freedom of speech on the grounds that intolerance should not be tolerated, without even giving her the opportunity to clarify her position and explain how she arrived at her conclusions.

The great concept at the heart of all this is that of gender identity. There are people who seek to break down sexist shackles and defend those who do not conform to sex stereotypes, but they believe that this concept is a trap. I belong to this group and think that, far from being liberating, the idea that people have a gender identity is not only false but counterproductive – it reinforces sexist roles and it is a serious backlash to women's and girls' rights. But to get this point across I need to explain the concept and present some arguments.

The concept of gender identity does not come alone, but in a package: an ideological package favoured or actively promoted by governments, the mainstream media, the entertainment industry and the companies that control social media. For reasons already mentioned, there is wide access to the views of believers on gender identity but little access to the views of agnostics and atheists. In such circumstances it is difficult or impossible for the public to form a free and informed opinion. This book seeks to reduce that imbalance.

I do not claim to be impartial. It would be an unattainable aspiration, and I am not interested in disguising my position, but in making it clear. Nor do I seek to impose it, but rather to persuade in an honest way those who read me. I present the position and reasoning of other parties in their own words, without lying or misrepresenting them, straight from the sources whenever possible, be they books, articles, tweets,[1] lectures, outbursts or TikToks. I criticize not them, but their ideas, and with facts and arguments, not emotional manipulations. It is much more interesting and fun to analyze their discourse than to hurl insults and disqualify them beforehand, as is often the case when believers in gender identity criticize us.

For those watching from the sidelines, it can all be very confusing, starting with the fact that both sides claim to be feminist and also because there is a key concept, gender, which everyone uses in their own way, sometimes with opposing meanings. One of my main aims in what follows is to dispel the confusion. But I did not want to write a book that would be a sterile introduction to the subject and its basic aspects. I do not stay on the surface: I rather dive into the discussions and ideas so that the reader who is on

---

1   Most of this book was written before Elon Musk bought Twitter and changed its name to X on 27 October 2022. For this reason I continue to use the words tweet and Twitter.

neither side is critically involved and has, let's say, an immersive experience. I also tried to bring new reflections, points of view and arguments, even to those who know the subject well and share my position.

Understanding all things related to gender is easier than the language commonly employed would lead one to believe. The first chapter, 'Gender: "It's Complicated"', traces the origins of the current uses of the term, tells a bit of history, and lays the groundwork for further discussion around transgenderism. I wrote it, like this whole book, in such a way that it is very clear to those who are new to these issues but also poses something different and new to those who know them well. I explain the concept of gender identity and argue that replacing the verifiable material category of sex with the unprovable esoteric category of gender identity in laws and policies of secular countries is a serious anomaly, the most damaging consequences of which are set out in detail in the last two chapters. I also present proposals for a way out of certain impassés around the word *gender* and the feminist project of abolishing gender.

The second chapter, 'Three Theories About Transgenderism', also analyzes a concept, in this case that of *transsexuality*, as well as the ideas that feed it and the context in which it arose. Historical background is provided and the main positions (medical-sexological, transgender and radical feminist) are reviewed and schematized to show their weaknesses and strengths. All this helps to put into perspective the agreements and disagreements between the different models and to assess which of the three has the most revolutionary and subversive power. In one section, I take a typical transgenderist allegation (a response to purportedly transphobic statements by Chimamanda Ngozi Adichie in March 2017) and then calmly break it down and highlight its flaws. The same exercise can be repeated with all transgender discourses before allowing oneself to be blindsided by them. It shows that the radical feminist model offers the best explanation for why some people consider themselves transgender and also the most far-reaching solution to their justified nonconformity.

The onslaught of gender identity doctrine and militancy against women begins in the realm of language. With the imposition of invented meanings and a contrived use of words, a whole system of beliefs and a politics are imposed, which bring with them considerable social damage. In the third chapter, 'In the Beginning Was the Pronoun', I argue that it is a very bad idea to give in to black-mail and use so-called preferred pronouns. When we talk about a man in the feminine, we are accepting the interlocutor's conclusion right off the bat. The statement "Trans women are women" is false, and calling a man who claims to have a female gender identity a woman or referring to him as *she* makes us participate in that farce in a condescending way. We are told that it is basic empathy and that it costs us nothing, but this too is false. Truth is not at odds with compassion and, as these pages demonstrate, there is a great deal at stake. It starts with using *their* pronouns and ends with ceding women's spaces and annihilating our sex-based rights.

Chapter 4, 'The Idea of the Transgender Child', recounts when, how and why the concept was created and what political purposes it serves. I argue, yes, that *trans kids* do not exist, but I provide ample arguments and data to support the claim. This, of course, does not mean that there are no children and adolescents who wish to be the other sex or who, influenced by ideas floating around, say they are trans, but the interpretation favoured in this book is very different from that given by the transgenderist and medical-sexological models. To accept that there are trans kids is to accept a set of beliefs that are deeply sexist and to endorse a form of child abuse and a rejection of homosexuality. Numerous studies and life stories show that most children who believe they are *trans* grow up to be perfectly healthy and happy lesbians and gay men if they are left alone rather than being *corrected* by changing their names and selling them the lie that they can transition to the other sex. Promoters of gender identity doctrine claim they question and want to end sexist roles and stereotypes that are instilled through socialization, but at the same time postulate that children who reject those stereotypes are a special category of people who were born with a gender identity that does not match their sex: that is, sexist roles are both a social construct *and* an innate trait (not the only contradiction that will be dealt with in the following pages). Posing the existence of transgender kids instrumentalizes children for the transgender cause and, far from celebrating difference, contributes to its destruction.

To those who ask, "And what is the problem? How does it affect you?" the final chapters give 14 different answers with their respective examples, arguments and evidence. Feminism and women-only spaces (toilets, shelters, prisons) are the main target of transgenderism. Indeed, *feminism* is a word devoid of meaning if we are unable to recognize female oppression because we pretend it's impossible to tell a woman from a man. Women-only spaces disappear the minute a man who claims he's a woman is admitted – but the need for these female enclaves does not fade away just because some theorists declared sex is irrelevant and many people are buying it. The doctrine of gender identity also wreaks havoc on children and young people, on some families, on our ability to study and deal with male violence, on measures to ensure equal representation in politics, on the gay and so-called LGBT community, on the lesbian movement, on some people who have made a *gender transition,* on the partners and wives of trans-identified people, on women's sport, on democracy, and so on. It is particularly damaging to freedom of speech and our aspirations to live in an open and fair society. The institutionalization of an anti-scientific and anti-women doctrine should not only concern feminists, but anyone interested in respect for human beings and their fundamental rights.

Radical feminist arguments and positions are presented here because they are rational, rigorous, have great explanatory power and are based on the observation of reality, and because it is radical feminists who have made the main criticisms of the transgender doctrine. I also draw on the arguments of authors who are not necessarily feminist and who make a valuable contribution. In some respects, I depart from positions that I have observed even in feminists with whom I have important points of agreement. This work distances itself from sectarianism and arises from a curiosity and a concern that have led me to draw from many different sources, although my greatest influence is radical feminism. Perhaps this will lead people who are not familiar with this theory to approach it and adopt some of its arguments and positions.

It will give me great satisfaction if this book succeeds in convincing some people who previously held contrary ideas or were still undecided. However, the main objective is to show the big picture, to provide information and evidence, and to bring some order and clarity to discussions where confusion, personal attacks and lack of sobriety reign supreme.

The best possible outcome will be that, after reading these pages, more people will overcome their fear and dare to speak out.

GENDER:
"IT'S COMPLICATED"

L anguage plays a central role in the debates and controversies
that this book seeks to clarify, and at the heart of all of them is
a word, *gender,* which the different sides claim for themselves and
to which each assigns a meaning to suit their own convenience
or understanding. In such circumstances, it is not uncommon for
confusion and misunderstanding to be the order of the day. In this
chapter I untangle the skein a little, give a brief history of the term,
argue that feminists would do well to abandon the disputed word
(for it is neither bringing clarity nor is it effective in advancing an
authentically feminist agenda, quite the contrary), and give a critical
introduction to the concept of gender identity.

One is not born, but rather becomes,
a pink elephant

Thousands and thousands of pages in books, millions of characters
in tweets, hundreds of blogs, hours of presentations and seminars
have been devoted by feminists to explaining the famous distinction
between sex and gender. In almost every discussion around transgender principles, we try to educate and again and again point

out the confusion between these two concepts and present the umpteenth version of "Sex is biological, whereas gender refers to the norms of behaviour and social expectations imposed on us from early childhood according to our sex." But despite our best efforts, all indications are that the confusion is not only still there, but that the issue is becoming more and more entangled.

And yet the central idea is quite simple. It will always be enriching to read Simone de Beauvoir's *The Second Sex*,[2] a great theoretical feat that lays the foundation for one of the most effervescent periods in the history of feminism, but the heart of the matter is splendidly summarized and explained in the picture book *Candy Pink,* by Adela Turin, with illustrations by Nella Bosnia, published in 1976, intended for readers aged five and upwards.

"Once upon a time, in elephant country, there was a herd of elephants in which the females had large, bright eyes and skin the color of candy pink." These feminine qualities were not gratis: they were due to the fact that the females, from birth, ate nothing but anemones and peonies. They did so not because these flowers were tasty or nutritious, but because their parents forced them to and warned them that if they didn't eat them, no one would want to marry them when they grew up. The female elephants lived enclosed in a fenced garden where the flowers were plentiful. "To make the pink colour come out more, the parents dressed their daughters in pink shoes and pink collar bibs and tied pink ribbons on their tails." Meanwhile, their brothers and male cousins, all of them grey, played and rolled around in the water and mud. One fine day, Daisy decided to rebel. She got rid of her feminine accessories and went off to wander on her own in the tall grass, under the trees, and to wallow in the mud puddles. Her companions watched her in fright and bewilderment until, at last, they took courage to follow her

---

2   In the fourth part of the first volume (chapter 'Childhood'), we find the famous quotation, "One is not born, but rather becomes, woman. No biological, psychic, or economic destiny defines the figure that the human female takes on in society; it is civilization as a whole that elaborates this intermediary product between the male and the eunuch that is called feminine" (Beauvoir, 2011, p. 283).

example. After that, no elephant girl ever wanted to see a shoe again, or eat a peony, let alone enter a fence. "Since then, it has been very difficult to tell the girl elephants from the boy elephants."

The young girl readers of those days who, like the vast majority of girls in the world, had experienced first-hand the different treatment of girls and boys, saw themselves reflected in this story and found in the rebellious Daisy a precious role model. It was clear to them that, despite the social messages, it is not necessary to wear a pink ribbon tied around your tail to be a fully-fledged elephant, and that girls do not have to wear dresses and play with dolls. A female elephant can pull off her ribbon and still be a female elephant, a girl can wear trousers and still be a girl. So, when reading that "one is not born, but rather becomes, woman" years later, it did not occur to them to interpret that Simone de Beauvoir believed that you can become a woman by taking a course to learn how to decorate your house and walk in heels "in a feminine key";[3] their mind was already prepared to grasp the idea behind the literary figure. But it was the 1970s. Half a century later, the brilliant formula that sums up Beauvoir's thought is daily distorted to attribute to the existentialist philosopher ideas completely contrary to the theory she so patiently and brightly elaborated; for example, the idea that in order to become a woman one must learn to *perform* femininity.

For someone who reads her entire book, or at least the chapter that begins with that quote, even in 2023 it is quite impossible to conclude that a man can become a woman or that there are really no natural differences between the sexes, but, for anyone who does not have the time, Beauvoir herself offers a very clear summary that should serve to put an end to any debate on the subject. In 1975, in what was her very first television interview, the host asked her: "You consider that the obvious biological differences play no role in the subsequent behaviour of the individual." The Frenchwoman, clear and forceful, replied:

---

3   Such as those given in 2015 by image consultant Monica Prata at 120 euros per hour to teach "transgender women to walk, dress and talk" (see Sastre, 2015).

I think they can certainly play a role, but the importance given to them comes from the social context in which these differences are situated. It is very important that a woman can be pregnant, have children, something that a man cannot; that is a big difference between the two, but it is not what is the basis for the differences in status, the exploitation and oppression to which women are subjected. It is, to a certain extent, a pretext on the basis of which the female condition is constructed, but it is not what determines it (Beauvoir, 1975).

Without Beauvoir's theory, the course taken by the women's liberation movement, as it was common at the time to call what we now call feminism or, more precisely, radical feminism, would not be understood. The idea that culture, society and education were decisive in the differentiated sex roles for men and women was in the air, at least in the intellectual, university, progressive and left-wing milieu. For feminism, this was the *sine qua non*. Women's liberation was not a movement to break away from biology and nature, but to break the chains of *sexist roles* that limited their development and independence and kept them subordinate to men.

"No one will ever be able to tell us what could happen to a girl if she did not find quite so many insurmountable obstacles placed in the path of her development, solely because of her sex," writes the Italian pedagogue and teacher Elena Gianini Belotti in a book written in 1973, which is still relevant today: *Little Girl: Social Conditioning and Its Effects on the Stereotyped Role of Women During Infancy,* which reads like a series of empirical demonstrations of what Simone de Beauvoir had already pointed out. Gianini Belotti drew on her direct observation of children's behaviour in families, nurseries, pre-schools, primary and secondary schools … but also, fundamentally, on the behaviour of adults towards girls and boys, the way they talk to them, the expectations differentiated according to sex, prejudices that come into play even before the child is born. We want boys to be more lively and more vital than girls, who on the other hand should be calm and passive, she says; even the movements of the foetus are interpreted in this way. The expectations, which are opposite for the two sexes, begin right there, even before the babies are born, and they will never end. "From time immemorial, boys have been conditioned to be active and aggressive and girls to be passive and submissive" (Gianini Belotti, 1975, p. 15). It follows that this is the natural and biological order of things.

But if these traits were so natural, there would be no need to impose them so eagerly; it would be enough to let each person develop their personality freely and discover their uniqueness, without external coercion, spontaneously finding their preferred activities and vocation. Inculcating stereotypes is an active intervention of family, culture and society, and children absorb them: in the words of the English neuroscientist Gina Rippon, babies "appear to be tiny social sponges, quickly soaking up the cultural information from the world around them" (Rippon, 2019, p. xvi).

In her study of femininity, i.e., the sexist roles that many people confuse with the simple fact of being a woman, American journalist and radical feminist Susan Brownmiller, author of the classic *Against Our Will*, recalls:

> Girls were different from boys, and the expression of that difference seemed mine to make clear. Did my loving, anxious mother, who dressed me in white organdy pinafores and Mary Janes and who cried hot tears when I got them dirty, give me my first instruction? Of course. Did my doting aunts and uncles with their gifts of pretty dolls and miniature tea sets add to my education? Of course. But even without the appropriate toys and clothes, lessons in the art of being feminine lay all around me and I absorbed them all: the fairy tales that were read to me at night, the brightly colored advertisements I pored over in magazines before I learned to decipher the words, the movies I saw, the comic books I hoarded, the radio soap operas I happily followed whenever I had to stay in bed with a cold. I loved being a little girl, or rather I loved being a fairy princess, for that was who I thought I was (Brownmiller, 1984, p. 8).

However, not all girls are comfortable being feminine just as not all boys are comfortable being masculine. And usually, if a child rebels and resists being told how to be a girl or how to be a boy, the adults around them make sure to stifle them to bring them back into the fold. This is evident in the most traditional households, but even in more progressive families, prejudices are passed down from one generation to the next, often unconsciously.

A simple and elegant experiment by the BBC illustrates how normal it is for adults to unwittingly treat girls and boys differently based on their preconceived ideas about the sexes. The test involves putting a girl in a blue plaid shirt and trousers and a boy in a dress and a pink jersey, both about one-year-old, then sitting them on a mat filled with toys and asking volunteers to watch them for a while. Observing their interactions with the babies, it is clear that these adults behave differently towards them depending on whether they think it is a girl or a boy. While they put dolls or stuffed animals on the supposed girl's lap, they put the supposed boy on a tricycle and offer him a robot, a car, a puzzle game. All the time these people are convinced that it is the toddler in front of them who shows interest in these toys, and they are only reacting to what the girl or the boy wants. When the experimenters finally reveal the true sex of the baby they looked after, they are surprised and a little embarrassed: "That really astounded me because I thought I was somebody that had a really open mind"; "I automatically went for the pink, fluffy toy because I said it was a girl"; "I've always thought I was rather more open-minded than that and I would think these are children's toys, whatever the gender" (BBC Stories, 2017).

None of this would have surprised Gianini Belotti. Sixty years have passed since she began making her observations and, although the greater participation of women in jobs that were previously denied them might suggest otherwise, the truth is that in the twenty-first century it is still believed that men are from Mars and women are from Venus. In the words of Spanish philosopher Ana de Miguel:

> Contrary to what is often claimed, that there is equality, the culture of inequality, the culture of pink and blue, continues to prevail in the education of our daughters and sons. And [...] we are so familiar with gender norms that we don't even see them, they are invisible, we consider them natural. And if we do see them, we don't know how to interpret them. But they mark us, and very much so [...]. These marks

are going to determine, to a large extent, our (free) choices and our lives (De Miguel, 2015, pp. 56–57).

When it turns out that a seven-year-old girl pretends to play in a beauty parlour, adults jubilantly interpret this as bringing out her natural flirtatiousness and femininity, not seeing that it was they themselves, with their own conditioned reflexes in tow, who instilled these interests in her from a very young age, backed by a whole socio-cultural framework, and thus created femininity in her, just as they create masculinity in a boy.

These cultural trainings are not arbitrary but perform a clear social function. A boy, says Gianini Belotti,

> is expected to become an individual: he is considered for what he *will be*. The girl is expected to become an object: she is considered for what she *will give*. Two different destinies (Gianini Belotti, 1978, p. 25).

The social idea of masculinity is instilled in men, and "that rigid framework that passes for femininity" is instilled in women. And so, by decreeing that women are, by nature, empathetic, maternal and good at teaching, and men violent, authoritarian and good at engineering, the hierarchy in which men occupy the dominant place and women the subordinate one is artificially maintained, with a lot of work and propaganda.

Another author who explains the imposition of sexist roles with great clarity is the Valencian Josep Vicent Marqués, who in his book *No es natural* observes:

> Little people are treated under the permanent – and correct – suspicion that they would not naturally behave as is 'natural'. [...] The differences between men and women are a social product and [...] the process that creates them is discriminatory towards women and at the same time it mutilates the real differences between people, which are not related to sex (Marqués, 1982, p. 56).

It is to this productive social factory of little men and little women that feminists refer when they say that sex roles, or gender in more recent terminology, are social constructs, to emphasize that they are not essential, innate, biological or God-given. And when they insist that sex and gender must be distinguished, it does not mean that sex and gender go their separate ways and that any person, of whatever sex, can choose at will to be *female* or *male* (or, according to some versions, discover it in the depths of his or her being) or renounce it at will. Nor does it mean that *gender* roles are assigned arbitrarily; in traditional households it is well known who gets to help the mother in the kitchen and serve the brothers and the father. Distinguishing between sex and gender, or between sex and sexist roles, means that femininity and masculinity are not intrinsic characteristics of our being that arise spontaneously in women and men, respectively, as secondary sex characteristics arise, but are, to a very large extent, a system of values that are learned and taught at home, at school, in the street, in church, in the community, through games, traditions, cultural and artistic manifestations, religions, customs. But, as has been said many times by feminists all over the world, these inventions are not mere ornamentation, but serve a purpose of social control. They are not playful, removable identities, nor are they catalogues of vocations, clothing and personality traits for everyone to choose a few à la carte. Sexist roles and stereotypes are created on the basis of the inescapable biological fact that it is women who gestate, give birth and breastfeed, to enforce the not so inescapable mandate that in patriarchal societies they play the role of mothers, carers and sexual servants. They are imposed on us and branded on us, even if we don't want them, even if we don't always realize it and even if subtle ways to do it have been discovered.

All these teachings were already quite clear in certain intellectual and progressive circles in the 1960s, 1970s and 1980s, but in the 2020s we find that a trendy ideology has adopted some of the language but has completely reversed its meaning. Based on certain interpretations and vulgarizations of queer theory, in vogue at the end of the twentieth century and still very popular in academia and social media today, we are now told that sex is a social construct, that binaries (such as male/female) are a colonialist invention that has already been overcome, that biology has advanced a great deal and we now know that there are not two sexes, but hundreds of genders, and that gender is the ultimate expression of our inner souls. The pink elephant girl no longer rebels to wander off on her own and wallow in muddy puddles, but finds her fulfilment and her authentic self locked in the fenced garden, obediently eating peonies and waiting for the elephant boy of her dreams. We have returned, enthusiastically and of our own accord, to the fold.

Abolish gender and the word *gender*

The first major linguistic shift was to translate *sexist roles* or *sexual roles* as *gender* and to use *gender* as a word for all occasions. *Gender* began being used to contrast biological sex with the social mandates associated with it, but curiously, unlike the negative connotation of *sexist roles, gender* acquired a certain patina of desirability. Having a gender perspective was a positive thing, and gender equality was the overriding aspiration. Although as early as the 1960s *gender* was used to recognize that between men and women there are not only differences arising from biology but also contingent differences arising from socialization, this explosion of *gender* here and *gender* there was a result of the United Nations Fourth World Conference on Women which took place in Beijing in 1995. The declaration emanating from that meeting commits member states to

> take all necessary measures to eliminate all forms of discrimination against women and the girl child and remove all obstacles to gender equality and the advancement and empowerment of women (Beijing Declaration, Article 24)

and to ensure "that a gender perspective is reflective" in all their policies and programs (Article 38). From then on, government reports and goal statements began to be peppered with these expressions. It was as if by saying *gender* and assuring that a gender approach was being used, they were doing enough to get by and women's rights were magically guaranteed.

It is to be expected, then, that there would be great clarity about what this term means. Indeed, Annex IV of the Report of the Fourth

World Conference on Women suggests that the drafters of the Beijing Declaration were absolutely clear about it:

> 1. During the 19th meeting of the Commission on the Status of Women, acting as preparatory body for the Fourth World Conference on Women, an issue arose concerning the meaning of the word 'gender' in the context of the Platform for Action of the Conference. In order to examine the matter, the Commission decided to form a contact group in New York, with the Commission's Rapporteur, Ms. Selma Ashipala (Namibia), as Chairperson. The Commission mandated the informal contact group to seek agreement on the commonly understood meaning of 'gender' in the context of the Platform for Action and to report directly to the Conference in Beijing. 2. Having considered the issue thoroughly, the contact group noted that: (1) the word 'gender' had been commonly used and understood in its ordinary, generally accepted usage in numerous other United Nations forums and conferences; (2) there was no indication that any new meaning or connotation of the term, different from accepted prior usage, was intended in the Platform for Action. 3. Accordingly, the contact group reaffirmed that the word 'gender' as used in the Platform for Action was intended to be interpreted and understood as it was in ordinary, generally accepted usage (United Nations, 1996, p. 218).

We will search in vain for a glossary in the pages of the global policy document in which UN member states committed themselves to a series of actions to achieve gender equality. Such a glossary would have clarified, for those responsible for implementing these important policies, which is the most common, ordinary and generally accepted use of the word. If somebody does not know, and is therefore in doubt as to what actions they need to take to meet the strategic objective "Develop gender-based methodologies and conduct research to address the feminization of poverty" (Beijing Declaration and Platform for Action, strategic objective A. 4), the problem is theirs alone, because for the rest of the world the definition is more than obvious. According to Alicia Miyares, this use of *gender* introduced confusion and paved the way "for different delegations to adapt the meaning of *gender* to their beliefs or laws and political practices" (Miyares, 2021, p. 119).

The Vatican delegation, a permanent observer state at the UN, requested that the conference report mention its reservations on issues such as family planning or expressions such as "the right of women to control their own sexuality," as it saw a risk of it being interpreted as "a societal endorsing of abortion or homosexuality." Neither late nor lazy, the Holy See also requested the following statement to be included in the report of the Conference:

> In accepting that the word 'gender' in this document is to be understood according to ordinary usage in the United Nations context, the Holy See associates itself with the common meaning of that word, in languages where it exists. The term 'gender' is understood by the Holy See as grounded in biological sexual identity, male or female (United Nations, 1996, pp. 160–162).

If the feminists who participated in the Fourth World Conference on Women and drafted the Beijing Declaration were interested in drawing a distinction between biological facts and socio-cultural mandates in order to end all forms of discrimination against women and girls stemming from biologistic prejudices, what they did was to serve their own heads on a silver platter to the Vatican, which cleverly redefined *gender* as a synonym for *sex* and tied it to "the distinctiveness and complementarity of women and men." Good riddance to the sex/gender distinction. The informal contact group's failure to define clearly and unambiguously a concept so central to the Beijing Declaration has cost us all dearly. As a result, the word has served as the very opposite of what was intended by those who included it more than 200 times in a document that would help achieve *gender equality* worldwide. It backfired through and through.

And so, left to its own devices, the word *gender* took on a life of its own. Many people began to use it because it sounded more inclusive. Why limit it to women? They may be more than half of humanity, but as a subject of study and subject of a political movement they are not enough. In *gender,* on the other hand, there is room for gay men, transvestites, transsexuals, the transgender newcomers and heterosexual men who would like to explore their feminine side and adopt new masculinities. What better way to make feminism acceptable in the eyes of the public than to rebrand it into something that would appeal to men. Gender, or feminism for all. The enthusiasm with which some who today call themselves feminists support prostitution, surrogacy, violent sex and the idea of gender as an identity are clear examples of this U-turn of inventing a supposed feminism whose task seems to consist in pleasing men. In an act of conceptual sleight of hand, the only women-centred theory came to be dominated, like all other disciplines, by men, and from being aimed at ending women's subordination it became a great tool for maintaining it.

On top of everything else, the term *gender* is used in a variety of ways by the same people, depending on the context or the occasion. In the 1990s, it became fashionable to speak of *gender* to refer to feminist theory in general. Nowadays it sometimes has a very different, more psychological usage, which posits gender as a continuum that has the typically feminine on one side and the typically masculine on the other. This is the meaning implicit in the proliferation of *genders,* or in the *gender identity spectrum,* with Barbie at one end and G. I. Joe at the other, with which the English group Mermaids invites girls and boys to locate where they are on the scale. Sometimes *gender* is used instead of *patriarchy,* which is the meaning of the phrase *abolish gender,* which synthesizes the ambitious feminist agenda of ending male supremacy. *Gender perspective* means a feminist point of view. *Gender* can also refer to a recognition of *LGBT people,* to relations between the sexes, to tastes in clothing, to gestures and mannerisms. There are penal codes that sanction *gender-based violence,* although it is much better characterized as male violence against women or indeed rape. Very often *gender* is confused with *sex,* as on forms that ask for your gender, when it is obvious that the relevant information is not how feminine or masculine someone is, but what sex they are.

The Constitution of Mexico and the documents of the National Electoral Institute make this mistake when they use the word *gender* as a synonym for *sex*, for example, when they speak of gender parity. Given the prevailing confusion about these two terms even 27 years after the Beijing Conference, a feminist virtual forum was organized in March 2022 at the National Autonomous University of Mexico under the title 'Necessary Clarifications on the Categories Sex and Gender' (Centro de Investigaciones Interdisciplinarias en Ciencias y Humanidades, 2022).

As if it were not confusing enough that the word has so many loosely related meanings, there is also a glaring lack of conceptual clarity, not only among ordinary speakers, but also among supposed authorities. For example, if we look at UN Women's Gender Equality Glossary we learn, on the one hand, that *gender* "refers to the roles, behaviors, activities, and attributes that a given society at a given time considers appropriate for men and women" and that these "are socially constructed and are learned through socialization processes." On the other hand, the same glossary states that gender identity is "a person's innate, deeply felt internal and individual experience of gender." Beyond the circular definition (the defined term is included in its definition), it is contradictory and extremely strange that what is called gender is an innate experience (which in itself is a contradiction in terms because in order to have experienced it, it is necessary to have lived it) and individual, and simultaneously something constructed, variable according to time and society, which is learned through socialization.

We are talking here about the official tool of the UN Women Training Centre: a glossary from the body that some people might consider the foremost international authority on all things gender ... and even there, the difference doesn't seem to be clear. Not surprisingly, the general public and young aspiring feminists learning about feminism and *gender* on social media are so confused and believe that if they don't understand it, it is because the subject "is complicated." Thanks to these entanglements, when I once told a journalist "We don't have a gender identity," in writing it was translated to, "We can identify as male or female, that is, as masculine or feminine," which is a far cry from the idea I wanted to communicate. And so, when some feminists talk about the goal of abolishing gender, understood as a hierarchical system of patriarchal oppression that keeps women in a socially subordinate place to men, some people interpret this as planning to exterminate people who identify as transgender.

Since transactivists, claiming to have mastered the distinction between sex and gender, speak of the former as socially constructed and the latter as innate, i.e. exactly the opposite of feminists, many women in so-called gender-critical circles think we should *take back* the term and continue to give lessons on the correct way to use it. I don't think this is a good idea; such lectures are doomed to fail because the public gets messages all the time that go the other way. English feminist historian Sheila Jeffreys gives another reason for abandoning the word:

> Radical/lesbian feminists seek to abolish what has been called 'gender' altogether. I am no fan of the word 'gender' and would prefer to abolish it in favour of expressions which refer directly to the political foundation of male domination. Thus I prefer to describe masculinity as 'male-dominant behaviour' and femininity as 'female-subordinate behaviour'. No multiplicity of genders can emerge from this perspective (Jeffreys, 2003, pp. 43–44).

We'd do well to recognize that the situation we find ourselves in with regard to the conflict between women's rights and the demands of men who claim to have a feminine gender identity owes a great deal to this conceptual mess. A key move of the transsexual empire was the invention of the transgender person, which replaces the old-fashioned *transsexual,* and the appeal of transgenderism to some people is largely based on this kind of terminological confusion and the somewhat playful connotations of gender as theatricality in a Butlerian sense. If, instead of *gender identity*, we talked about *stereotyped role identity,* as Jeffreys has suggested in some talks, the concept would be easier to understand and much harder to accept.

Some of the women who insist in reclaiming the word *gender* must think that this term has a feminist genesis. This is not the case at all. One of the first to use it in an ungrammatical and sexist role-related sense was John Money, a psychologist and sexologist who will always be remembered for his failed experiment with Bruce Reimer in 1967, characterized by its lack of ethics from start to finish. When this boy was eight months old, a botched circumcision left his penis mangled; months later, when he was about a year and a half old, Money recommended to his parents that his testicles be removed, he be given female hormones and be "raised as a girl," so that Money could test his theory of psychosexual neutrality.[4] It was not proven, but nevertheless, Money made a successful career of boasting to the contrary and it was a long time before the truth came out, not until 1997.

Money explained:

> Gender role is what you say and do from which other people piece together their own version of your gender identity. Your gender identity is more inclusive than your gender role: it includes ideation, imagery, and an unspoken text that may be known to you alone (quoted in Hodson, 2019, p. 127).

He, for his part, had adopted the sex/gender distinction of psychoanalyst Robert Stoller (author of a book entitled *Sex and Gender: The Development of Masculinity and Femininity*), who coined the concept of gender identity in 1964 and defined it as

> a complex system of beliefs about oneself: a sense of one's masculinity and femininity. It implies nothing about the origins of that feeling (e.g. whether the person is male or female). It has, then, psychological connotations only: one's subjective state (quoted in Di Ceglie, 2000, p. 458).

---

4   More on Money in Chapter 2, and on the famous scandal in Colapinto (2000) and Gaetano (2017).

Thus, the word that some feminists are keen to *reclaim* has its origins in fact in sexology, a misogynist discipline if ever there was one.[5] Moreover, as can be seen, the term was already related to personality, identity, psychology, and its original definition anticipates the transgender notion that it is an intimate attribute known only to the individual. It is clear that its natural place is not feminism. In her introduction to *Gender Hurts*, Jeffreys confirms this:

> The term 'gender' itself is problematic. It was first used in a sense that was not simply about grammar by sexologists [...] who were involved in normalising intersex infants. They used the term to mean the behavioural characteristics they considered most appropriate for persons of one or other biological sex. [...] Their purpose was not progressive: they were conservative men who believed that there should be clear differences between the sexes and sought to create distinct sex categories through their projects of social engineering. Unfortunately, the term was adopted by some feminist theorists in the 1970s. [...]
>
> Before the term 'gender' was adopted, the term more usually used to describe these socially constructed characteristics was 'sex roles'. The word 'role' connotes a social construction and was not susceptible to the degeneration that has afflicted the word 'gender' and enabled it to be wielded so effectively by transgender activists (Jeffreys, 2014b, p. 4).

The American radical feminist Janice Raymond, author of the first book to present, as early as 1979, a feminist analysis of the theory and practice of transsexuality *(The Transsexual Empire)*, also devoted a few lines to discussing the word and its drawbacks. Her argument for avoiding it and using it only with reservations and when there is no other choice complements Jeffreys':

> The word *gender* has certain problems for the feminist critic. It gives the impression that there is a fixed set of psychosocial conditions that determines gender identity and role. When used in conjunction

---

5   In her book *Anticlimax*, Sheila Jeffreys demonstrates how twentieth century sexologists, assuming the role of "high priests who have organised the worship of male power," promoted the idea that sexuality should be "a way of expressing and maintaining male dominance and female submission" (Jeffreys, 2011, p. 1).

with other words such as *gender dissatisfaction, gender discomfort,* or *gender dysphoria,* it conveys that these can only be altered by very specialized therapy and/or sophisticated technical means. Feminists have described *gender dissatisfaction* in very different terms – i.e., *sex-role oppression, sexism,* etc. It is significant that there is no specialized or therapeutic vocabulary of *black dissatisfaction, black discomfort,* or *black dysphoria* that has been institutionalized in black identity clinics. Likewise, it would be rather difficult and somewhat humorous to talk about *sex-role oppression clinics.* What the word *gender* ultimately achieves is a classification of sex-role oppression as a therapeutic problem, amenable to therapeutic solutions. Therefore, I prefer to use the word *gender* and the phrase, *gender dysphoria* and the like, when I am discussing the management of the transsexual issue in the therapeutic and/or technical contexts. However, because of the nature of the subject of transsexualism, there were times, while writing this book, when I found the word unavoidable despite my 'dissatisfaction'. In these places, I indeed used it with reservation (Raymond, 1979, pp. 9–10).

If Simone de Beauvoir could write *The Second Sex* in 1949 without using the word *gender*, and Kate Millett did not need it in 1970 to conceive the radical feminist classic *Sexual Politics*, why can't we live without it? Instead, what Millett employs, as a leitmotif throughout her book, is the trio of concepts *role, temperament,* and *status,* which make explicit the main components of sexist stereotypes and the power relations they help to entrench. Even the 1981 Convention on the Elimination of All Forms of Discrimination Against Women (CEDAW) manages very well without using the word *gender* once.

Nor did the Mexican philosopher and poet Rosario Castellanos need it to explain how to mould women and psychologically amputate them so that they do what is expected of them:

From the moment a woman is born, education works on the given material to adapt it to her destiny and turn it into a morally acceptable, i.e. socially useful, entity. Thus she is stripped of the spontaneity to act; she is forbidden the initiative to decide; she is taught to obey the commandments of an ethics which is absolutely alien to her and which has no justification or foundation other than that of serving the interests, purposes and ends of others (Castellanos, 1973, p. 15).

Because what is important here is the idea, not the word used to express it. The idea that we must get rid of the archetype of women and the hierarchies that keep them in a subordinate position has always been part of feminist theory. It is difficult to fight for Women's Liberation if one thinks that women were born to be submissive and obedient, or to fight against male violence if one thinks that men are violent by nature. In an appendix to her fundamental feminist work *The Creation of Patriarchy*, published in 1986, Austrian-American historian Gerda Lerner writes:

> *Gender* is the cultural definition of behaviour defined as appropriate to the sexes in a given society at a given time. Gender is a set of cultural roles. It is a costume, a mask, a straitjacket in which men and women dance their unequal dance. Unfortunately, the term is used both in academic discourse and in the media as interchangeable with *sex*. In fact, its widespread public use probably is due to it sounding a bit more 'refined' than the plain word *sex*, with its 'nasty' connotations. Such usage is unfortunate, because it hides and mystifies the difference between the biological given – sex – and the culturally created – gender. Feminists above all others should want to point up that difference and should therefore be careful to use the appropriate words (Lerner, 1986, p. 238).

She herself uses the term only ten times in the whole book, so it is not indispensable for communicating her theory. But apparently not all feminists have taken heed of her sensible warnings, and many, like the general public, fall into the widespread confusion.

In her influential article 'Gender: A Useful Category of Historical Analysis', also from 1986, the American historian Joan Wallach Scott argues:

> In its simplest recent usage, *gender* is a synonym for *women*. Any number of books and articles whose subject is women's history have, in the past few years, substituted 'gender' for 'women' in their titles. In some cases, this usage [...] is actually about the political acceptability of the field. In these instances, the use of *gender* is meant to denote

the scholarly seriousness of a work, for *gender* has a more neutral and objective sound than does *women*. *Gender* seems to fit within the scientific terminology of social science and thus dissociates itself from the (supposedly strident) politics of feminism. In this usage, *gender* does not carry with it a necessary statement about inequality or power nor does it name the aggrieved (and hitherto invisible) party. Whereas the term *women's history* proclaims its politics by asserting (contrary to customary practice) that women are valid historical subjects, *gender* includes, but does not name women, and so seems to pose no critical threat. This use of *gender* is one facet of what might be called the quest of feminist scholarship for academic legitimacy in the 1980s. […]

Gender seems to have become a particularly useful word as studies of sex and sexuality have proliferated, for it offers a way of differentiating sexual practice from the social roles assigned to women and men (Scott, 1986).

Interestingly, none of this discouraged feminists, including Scott herself, from using and promoting the word *gender* – quite the contrary.

In universities throughout the west, women's studies departments were replaced one after the other, sometimes soon after their creation, by gender studies departments. To the outside world, this gave the impression that this was a new way of referring to feminism. Some who experienced it from the inside, however, did not share this same opinion. The Spanish philosopher Amelia Valcárcel notes:

Already at the time, the feminist avant-garde had not accepted well that 'gender studies' supplanted feminist studies. I am stating the obvious: that it is perfectly possible to carry out studies that contain the use of the 'gender' variable without feminism appearing in them (Valcárcel, 2019, p. 249).

And Sheila Jeffreys, who in the late 1990s taught about feminism and the construction of sexuality at the University of Melbourne, recalls in her autobiography *Trigger Warning*:

The teaching of feminism in universities had become much more difficult. Women's studies was, in many cases, becoming opaque through using the theory of French male and, mostly, gay academics such as Michel Foucault, whose work was largely irrelevant to women's circumstances. Most of those who taught women's studies were forced to adapt to the rules of a masculine academy to survive. In many places, the name women's studies was changed to gender studies so as not to look too feminist, and post-modern and queer theory was employed to create new forms of language. This had the effect of making many women feel they must not be very bright because they had no idea what 'feminist' academics such as Judith Butler were talking about. This did create a class divide between women. Some feminist research and writing came to resemble the use of Latin in church in the period before the reformation when the vast mass of the population could not read or understand the language. Latin was a form of control. The feminist academy began to move in this direction in the 1990s with the adoption of postmodern language and concepts and was very far from being connected to the liberation of women. Rather it made many women feel inadequate (Jeffreys, 2020, p. 182).

Thus, interdisciplinary gender studies came to decaffeinate and depoliticize feminism and turn it into an elitist, abstract theory, at the service of men and far removed from reality. But is there agreement in that ivory tower on the meaning of the concept whose study is its raison d'être? Judging by Laura Favaro's interviews with 50 academics in this field, not so much. *Gender,* she observes, is

understood in different ways: as socially or discursively constructed (performative model); as an inseparable combination of biological, psychological and social elements (biopsychosocial model); or, to a much lesser extent, as innate subjectivity, evoking notions of sexed brains (psychobiologist model). At times, *gender* is used as a synonym for *gender identity,* usually understood as an internal sense of self as a woman, a man, both, neither or something else, such as 'non-binary' – which, among other possibilities, can be 'plural' ('like having two or more alter egos or personas') or 'fluid' (changing 'over years, months, or the course of the day' (Favaro, 2022).

Therefore, when someone on a university campus announces that they are adopting a gender approach, their listeners or students have little idea of what fate might have in store for them.

Another terminological slippage occurs when one speaks, euphemistically, of *gender-based violence* instead of *violence against women* or the more explicit *male sexual violence against women*. On the one hand, it softens, and on the other hand, it omits the fundamental fact of who usually perpetrates this violence and against whom. This change in language, argues Sheila Jeffreys, throws away years of feminist political analysis of this very serious problem. "Men have nothing in particular to do with sexual violence, it seems. The female sex is removed from sight and hidden under 'all genders' as if there were many" (Jeffreys, 2022, p. 127).

As for the "'nasty' connotations" to which Gerda Lerner alludes, it is worth citing a revealing anecdote. In November 1993, Ruth Bader Ginsburg, who had just received her appointment to the US Supreme Court, "brought gales of laughter" when, at an event in her honour at Columbia University, she told why in the early 1980s, in her litigation on behalf of women before that same court, she began to speak of *gender discrimination* instead of *sex discrimination*:

> I owe it all to my secretary at Columbia Law School, who said, 'I'm typing all these briefs and articles for you and the word *sex, sex, sex* is on every page. Don't you know that those nine men [on the Supreme Court] – they hear that word, and their first association is not the way you want them to be thinking? Why don't you use the word *gender*? It is a grammatical term and it will ward off distracting associations' (Crocker, 1993).

Like a butterfly's flapping wings, Milicent Tryon's pruritus ended up influencing the international politics of the following decades and changed the course of history, not necessarily for the better.

This modest use of the terms has doubled or quadrupled the confusion between *sex* and *gender*, as some people equate this pair of terms with sexuality and biological sex, respectively. This is what seems to be happening in this well-known quote from the American queer theorist Gayle Rubin, written in 1984:

> Feminism is the theory of gender oppression. To assume automatically that this makes it the theory of sexual oppression is to fail to distinguish

between gender, on the one hand, and erotic desire, on the other (Rubin, 2007, p. 169).

Gender, then, is an ambiguous, highly charged and multi-purpose word that confuses more than it explains and gives rise to very serious misunderstandings. If we seek clarity (and we need clarity more than ever), experience tells us that this is not the way to go. We had better recognize that it is a losing battle, not only against transactivists, but with speakers in general. Pondering hard about the ravages of gender is not helping to abolish it, and I don't see why feminists should cling to a term that has its origins far removed from our politics and convictions. It has been shown that the word, since its entry into feminism, has been misleading, and not necessarily by accident. As much as it has worked for some in terms of theorizing, it may be, in view of the chaos of our times, that on balance it has far more problems than benefits.

Almost 15 years ago, with great foresight, Mexican lesbian feminist Yan María Yaoyólotl Castro resigned from the committee of the XI Encuentro Feminista Latinoamericano y del Caribe when she realized that it was not really a feminist congress, but "a genderist and, more precisely, genderist/queer meeting." She made a harsh criticism of the organizers, who were determined to banish certain words, and denounced:

> The content committee considers [...] that the concept of *woman* is essentialist and that the concept of *feminism* is fundamentalist, so it uses the notion of *genderism* instead of *feminism* cunningly, as if they were the same thing, and in the end pretending to substitute the latter (Yaoyólotl Castro, 2008, p. 5).

Today, in retrospect, it is easy to see that she was absolutely right and that these terminological changes were far from innocent.

For all these reasons, I propose that we limit ourselves to using *gender* to quote what other people say or believe and dispense with it in our own discourse and our own analyses. In each case, let us use the words that best describe what we want to communicate. Here are some options as examples:

- *gender* as a system: use *patriarchy* or, as Sheila Jeffreys suggests, *male supremacist society*;
- *gender* as sex in a hierarchical system: use *sexual class* or *sexual caste*;
- *gender perspective*: use *feminist perspective*;
- *gender studies*: use women's studies, queer studies, lesbian and gay studies, as appropriate;
- *gender roles*: use *sex roles* or *sexist roles*;
- *gender stereotypes*: use *sexual stereotypes* or *sexist stereotypes*;
- *gender* as behaviour or character: use *masculinity* and *femininity*;
- *gender-based violence*: use *violence against women, male violence, rape*;
- *gender discrimination*: use *sex-based discrimination*;
- *gender diversity*: simply recall the fact that not everyone is heterosexual;
- *gender equality*: use *equality between men and women*;
- *gender non-conforming person*: use *someone who does not fit into sexual stereotypes or does not enact sexist roles*;
- *gender identity*: use *personality, sex stereotype identity, pink and blue brains, sexed soul*.

The latter needs to be explained in much greater detail. In the next section I will address the concept of gender identity, which perhaps best exemplifies the damage that this terminological havoc has done, and continues to do.

Being a stereotype

Just as the word *gender* began to proliferate in 1995, not always with a clear and unambiguous meaning, now it is the composite term *gender identity* that has become fashionable and is often used as a synonym for *sex*, leading to even greater confusion. Suddenly we women no longer belong to a sex, but are a gender identity. "To be a woman is to occupy, within a patriarchal society divided by gender, the position of the one being dominated by the male gender and having a woman's gender identity," says in an interview Elizabeth Duval, considered a transgender cultural model, and who claims to have a woman's gender identity himself (Maldonado, 2021). So, we have gone from being an objective material reality to something that occurs subjectively in people's minds.

It is clear that feminist teachings have not sufficiently taken hold. The general public does not seem to find it difficult to assimilate the notion, intrinsic to the concept of gender identity, that being a woman or a man comes with a set of predetermined psychological characteristics. Women, for example, are tender, obedient and helpful from birth; we have these personality traits already built into our genes. Some of us naively believed that these retrograde ideas were on their way to disappearing and were only alive and kicking in the most traditionalist households, in some churches and in other cultures, most notably in parts of the Islamic world. However, their renewed popularity in the west in the form of a supposedly transgressive doctrine shows that the common people still believe that women and men have by nature diametrically opposed (or, as the Vatican puts it, complementary) temperaments, that there are some interests and activities proper to women, and others (more diverse and important) proper to men, and that, furthermore, our sex is determined by our inclinations (not by our chromosomes, our sex characteristics, our reproductive capacity).

In other words, being a woman means having a feminine personality and being a man means having a masculine personality, regardless of one's genitalia.

We are going backwards: after a very brief historical period in which a part of the world seemed to be fighting against the most rancid sexist roles, and to understand that sex did not determine our way of being and our capacities, we are now suffering a big backlash and people are swallowing the idea that our ways of being and our capacities determine our sex. If, in the past, conservatives tried to correct the preferences of the boy who liked dolls better than war games to *man him up*, now some who think of themselves as progressive are trying to correct his body to turn him into the little girl he apparently is.

A glance at a toyshop illustrates well the climate in which we find ourselves. To the feminist conviction that toys are genderless and that every child should be free to play whatever they want without anyone trying to correct or dissuade them, toy manufacturers respond that they are not so sure. In order to sell more products, they segment the market: some are aimed at girls and others at boys. In practice, it is as if the toy comes with a factory stamp indicating which sex it is best suited for. Of course, it is sexist stereotypes that determine this suitability: chemistry set for boys, make-up set for girls.

Canadian pop culture and media critic Anita Sarkeesian analyzed the changes over time in Lego construction toys, which encourage spatial memory and are seen as a gateway to mathematics, science and engineering. After being entirely unisex in the 1950s to 1970s, with advertising characteristically non-sexist and emphasizing creativity, imagination and cooperative work, in the mid-1980s the brand began to design games that promoted combat, aggression and conflict, considered the height of masculinity, and to advertise exclusively to boys. "The real reason girls aren't interested in Legos as a whole," Sarkeesian says, "is because for the last quarter of a century the Lego Group has been telling girls repeatedly that bricks are for boys."

In 2012, the company wanted to change course, but what it did backfired. Instead of marketing its toys for girls and boys alike to enjoy, it brought out a special series for girls called 'Friends', in which a group of girlfriends live their adventures in Heartlake City, "a pastel-coloured gender segregated stereotypically female suburban paradise," as Sarkeesian describes it. At last, the Lego bricks are back in the hands of girls … only now it's all about playing at going to the beauty salon, baking cakes, decorating the house, going shopping – activities totally absent in the much more varied and exciting Lego City, aimed at boys. "It seems as though Lego is convinced that boys and girls just naturally have different interests" (Sarkeesian, 2012a).

This contemporary revenge of pink and blue is powerfully captured in the series *The Pink and Blue Projects,* begun in 2005 and still ongoing, by South Korean photographer JeongMee Yoon. Made primarily in Seoul and New York, it consists of portraits of girls and boys, from infants to ten or 11 years old, sitting in their bedrooms amidst their hundreds of pink or blue clothes and other belongings, respectively, as if floating in an ocean of stereotypical consumerism. The sensation when contemplating these photographs is one of profound cloying. Explains the artist on her website:

> The saccharine, confectionary pink objects that fill my images of little girls and their accessories reveal a pervasive and culturally manipulated expression of 'femininity' and a desire to be seen. [...] When I began producing the pink images, I became aware of the fact that many boys have a lot of blue possessions. Customers are directed to buy blue items for boys and pink for girls. [...]
>
> Many toys and books for girls are pink, purple, or red, and are related to make-up, dress up, cooking, and domestic affairs. However, most toys and books for boys are made from the different shades of blue and are related to robots, industry, science, dinosaurs, etc.

And from this consumer-driven segregation of children we are supposed to conclude that girls naturally gravitate towards *femininity* and boys naturally towards *masculinity* and that their preference in toys, clothes and colours is a manifestation of their intrinsic being or, in the more current terminology, their gender identity. It is curious, to say the least, that we have an innate propensity for such artificial things as a hairdryer or a spaceship.

The Supreme Court of Justice of the Nation, the National Institute for Women, the Ministry of the Interior, the Secretariat of Foreign Affairs, the National Council to Prevent Discrimination ... numerous institutions, not only in Mexico but around the world, committed to advancing the transgender cause, present some definition of *gender identity,* which is invariably a more or less verbatim version of that emanating from the Yogyakarta Principles.[6] A particularly creative and variegated example can be found in a communiqué from Mexico City's Council to Prevent and Eliminate Discrimination (COPRED):

> Gender is performative: it is ideas and behaviours that define women and men. You are not born a man or a woman; you learn to be one. Gender identity is the personal and internal conviction of how each person perceives themselves. Trans people may or may not conform in their gender to masculine or feminine. Recognizing the trans reality implies recognizing that, on the one hand, there are stereotypes constructed from a patriarchal system about masculinity and femininity, imposed from the outside, and that people act out, whether we are trans or cis. On the other hand, not all people identify with the gender construction assigned to them at birth, but this does not necessarily imply assuming the identity of the 'other' gender, but rather that each person constructs themselves (COPRED, 2020).

There is much to unravel from these lines, for example the centrality of gender identity to our self-concept, but for the moment let us turn to the original source. The Yogyakarta Principles are a private document that proposes to include both sexual orientation and gender identity among the categories protected by human rights, on the grounds that many violations of these fundamental freedoms, such as extrajudicial killings, torture, arbitrary detention, sexual assault and all kinds of discrimination, are committed toward persons, they say, precisely "because of their actual or perceived

---

6   In her last book, *Doublethink,* Janice Raymond sheds light on the origin of the Yogyakarta Principles and their main instigator: Stephen Whittle (a lesbian who became a *trans man*) "has been credited with almost single-handedly inventing the legal switching of sex with gender identity and is also known for convening a self-appointed group of scholars and activists who came together to draft a set of legal principles relating to transgender, now called *The Yogyakarta Principles.* While not having the authority of a UN convention or declaration, this document has been used as an influential source on gender identity. [… They] have been widely quoted in academic articles, bills, resolutions and reports and serve as a legal basis for making gender into sex" (Raymond, 2021, p. 89; see also Brunskell-Evans, 2020, p. 63, and, for a history of this non-binding but pivotal document, Zobnina, 2020).

sexual orientation or gender identity" (Yogyakarta Principles, 2007, p. 6). To protect a category, it is essential to know what it consists of, how it manifests itself, how it can be distinguished. In this document, which despite not being binding for governments is the main international reference point from which all laws and regulations in the world that have incorporated gender identity are derived, the following definition is offered:

> *Gender identity* [refers to] each person's deeply felt internal and individual experience of gender, which may or may not correspond with the sex assigned at birth, including the personal sense of the body (which may involve, if freely chosen, modification of bodily appearance or function by medical, surgical or other means) and other expressions of gender, including dress, speech and mannerisms (2007, p. 8).

It is not characterized by clarity, but some statements logically follow from Yogyakarta's definition:

1. All people have an internal and individual experience of gender and feel it deeply. That is gender identity.
2. A person's gender identity may or may not correspond with their sex.
3. Sex is assigned at birth.
4. Gender identity includes the personal sense of the body.
5. Personal sense of the body and thus gender identity may involve modification of bodily appearance or function.
6. Gender is expressed in dress, speech and mannerisms (and other things).

At the outset we can see that statement 3 is false. Sex is not assigned to us when we are born: it is determined at the moment of fertilization and is detectable to the naked eye when the baby is born, or even earlier, in ultrasounds or blood samples from the pregnant woman. It is no small matter that the definition of a concept that is supposed to be so important includes a blatant falsehood that would have to jump out at anyone who has not forgotten that words have meaning, but for now let's overlook it and concentrate on statements 1, 2 and 6.

Nowhere does the document give a definition of *gender,* although from its preamble and its definition of *sexual orientation* it is possible to infer that *gender* is basically understood as synonymous with *sex* (all italics are mine in the next paragraphs):

All human beings are born free and equal in dignity and rights, and [...] everyone is entitled to the enjoyment of human rights without distinction of any kind, such as race, colour, *sex,* language, religion, political or other opinion (2007, p. 8).

Respect for sexual rights, sexual orientation and gender identity is integral to the realisation of equality between *men and women* and [...] states must take measures to seek to eliminate prejudices and customs based on the idea of the inferiority or the superiority of *one sex* or on stereotyped roles for *men and women* (2007, p. 9).

Historically people have experienced [...] human rights violations because they are or are perceived to be lesbian, gay or bisexual, because of their consensual sexual conduct with *persons of the same gender* (2007, p. 8).

Sexual orientation [refers] to each person's capacity for profound emotional, affectional and sexual attraction to, and intimate and sexual relations with, individuals of *a different gender or the same gender or more than one gender* (2007, p. 8).

Each person's self-defined sexual orientation and gender identity is integral to their personality and is one of the most basic aspects of self-determination, dignity and freedom (2007, p. 12).

Thus, according to the 29 people who gathered at Gadjah Mada University in Yogyakarta, Indonesia, from 6 to 9 November 2006, all of us have an internal experience of our gender (or sex), which sometimes may not correspond to our sex (or gender). In other words, the internal experience of our gender may not correspond to our gender, which is to say, the internal experience of our sex may not correspond to our sex. In any case, what matters for our personality and dignity is not our sex (or gender), but the gender identity that we define for ourselves. That is, the internal and individual experience of gender as we deeply feel it is above the sex that we, one can guess, perceive when we see ourselves naked in the mirror and which other people may also perceive. (Note how in the Yogyakarta definitions there is a strong contrast between self – gender identity, personal sense of the body – and appearance – expressions of gender, bodily appearance).

If this only meant that our sex is irrelevant to our personality and that men and women have the same human dignity, there would be no problem. However, the very idea that we have a gender identity runs counter to this aspiration for equality and a world without stereotyped sexist roles. This is very clear if we understand *gender* in the feminist way, as the traits that each society considers desirable in, or even mandatory for, people depending on the sex to which they belong (femininity for women and masculinity for men), because then it turns out that we have a deep and individual experience of sexist stereotypes and this seems to deny that such stereotypes are external impositions, social constructs, which also serve to keep us in line and limit our free development. To postulate the existence of a gender identity essential to our personality is to throw away an invaluable body of feminist theorizing and understanding of social relations and to return to the old-fashioned idea that men are made to command and women to obey.

Because let us also ask ourselves what this mysterious inner experience of gender might consist of. How does it feel to be a man or a woman? If you go introspectively in search of that intimate individual experience, you will almost certainly end up with stereotypical ideas about feminine temperament and masculine temperament ("I'm interested in pleasing others and I feel connected to nature, ergo I'm a woman"). Seeing on social media the explanations given by people who, because they are *gender fluid,* feel suddenly female, suddenly male, reinforces the perception that behind the concept of gender identity there are only the crudest stereotypes (but select stereotypes, that is: in their feminine moments they don't feel like mopping the house, but rather like putting on seductive lingerie).

Perhaps the same is true if someone tries to define, for example, *Mexican identity* not as belonging to a nation and a culture, but as a subjective feeling. What might it consist of – a taste for tequila, tacos, mariachi and Frida Kahlo? What would be the indicators that this is specifically a Mexican identity? How would it differ from, say, Swiss or Rwandan identity? Is it possible to feel Mexican while being Swiss or Rwandan, and vice versa? If so, how would a *trans Mexican* know that his or her deep sense of nationality corresponds to Mexicanness and not, for example, Guatemalanness? Similarly, how can a man know that his experience of gender is the same as a woman's experience of gender if he has no direct access to the mental states of any woman, but only to his own? On what basis can he call this very personal experience a *female identity*?

The Yogyakarta definition does not inform us what this internal gendered feeling is like, how it relates to the body, or why it is so important that it needs protection. All it does is mention rather superficial examples of the external correlates of this experience, namely dress, speech and mannerisms. That is to say, the clothes we wear and our way of speaking, while not in themselves our gender identity, express it outwardly.

So, when we see Seo Woo in a pink dress and pink headband in the photo entitled 'Seo Woo and Her Pink Things', we are seeing an external reflection of her inner self. For a colour-blind person it may be more complicated, but the rest of us clearly see someone who, judging by her clothing, has a feminine gender identity, just as in 'Jimin and His Blue Things' we see a six- or seven-year-old creature dressed in jeans and a blue sweatshirt who has, therefore, a masculine gender identity.

It seems that those who met in Indonesia in 2006 realized this unacceptable implication that we can guess someone's gender identity by seeing what they wear, and in the 2017 Yogyakarta Principles plus 10, new writers added a definition that complicates things a bit; they now make explicit how they understand the term *gender expression*

> as each person's presentation of the person's gender through physical appearance – including dress, hairstyles, accessories, cosmetics – and mannerisms, speech, behavioural patterns, names and personal

references [...]; gender expression may or may not conform to a person's gender identity (Yogyakarta Principles plus 10, 2017, p. 6).

So yes, Seo Woo's pink things and Jimin's blue things are part of these children's gender expression, but it may well be that their gender expression does not conform to their gender identity. It is entirely possible that Jimin, despite his marked liking for trains and blue clothes, which are signs of a masculine gender, actually has a feminine gender identity. It is possible that he expresses a male gender because he is forced to and is afraid of being scolded, or just to disorient us.

Thus, although in 2017 a second group of specialists supplemented the original Yogyakarta Principles and gave us more concrete examples of how one can present one's gender (or sex), they still do not tell us what the deeply felt internal experience of which this external expression is a correlate (or not) might consist of.

Given how uninformative the usual definition of *gender identity* is, British political philosopher Rebecca Reilly-Cooper analyzed the concept in search of what features it must have to serve the theoretical purposes of the advocates of gender identity doctrine. She looked for the empirical assumptions behind it, the scientific claims on which it is based, and what would have to be true for the concept to make sense. Her conclusion is that,

> gender identity needs to be a universally possessed, relatively fixed, essential and innate property of persons that is not reducible to their biological sex and not determined by their upbringing and socialization (Reilly-Cooper, 2016a).

There are two options for this property: it is either material or immaterial. If it is material, where does it reside? In the brain? This commits to the existence of male brains and female brains – only there is no scientific evidence that there are male and female brains: there are no proven sex-correlated intellectual aptitudes, behaviours, personality traits that can be attributed to brain differences.

In her book *Gender and Our Brains,* British Professor Emerita of cognitive neuroimaging Gina Rippon reviews all the invariably unsuccessful attempts to find such differences. All the research that has sought to find evidence in the brain that women are, for example, less suited than men to great intellectual or artistic feats has been biased by the researchers' preconceptions and their conviction that men are superior. "There was to be no stone unturned (or skull unexamined) in the hunt for the proof of women's inferiority" (Rippon, 2019, p. 7). Since the eighteenth century, she says, we have been dragging along the notion

> that you can 'sex' a brain, that you can describe a brain as 'male' or 'female' and that you can attribute any differences between individuals in behavior, abilities, achievements, personality, even hopes and expectations to the possession of one or the other type of brain (2019, p. xi).

But in the twenty-first century we know much more about how the brain works, and that idea is crumbling. If there are differences in brains at all, says Rippon, it is because, given their plasticity and malleability, "a gendered world will produce a gendered brain" (2019, p. xix).

The Canadian-born British psychologist and philosopher of science (now teaching at the University of Melbourne, Australia) Cordelia Fine calls *neurosexism* the assumption that inequalities between the sexes can be explained by a difference in the capacities of their respective brains. According to the neurosexist position, if women had to wait until 1978 to formally accede to a seat in the Royal Spanish Academy or until 2019 for a female orchestra conductor to sign a long-term contract with a major record label,[7] it is because, being women, they are less competent than men, and, it goes without saying, it's the natural order of things. Fine agrees

---

7   The first woman to occupy a seat in the Royal Spanish Academy, founded in 1713, was the poet Carmen Conde, in 1978, as already mentioned; 66 years earlier, Emilia Pardo Bazán, whose literary merits no one could dare to doubt, was denied that seat for the third time. The first female conductor to sign an exclusive contract with the Deutsche Grammophon record label, established in 1898, was the Lithuanian Mirga Gražinytė-Tyla.

with Rippon that environment is far more of a determinant than sex in shaping a brain:

> We can't understand gender differences in male and female minds – the minds that are the source of our thoughts, feelings, abilities, motivations and behavior – without understanding how psychologically permeable is the skull that separates the mind from the sociocultural context in which it operates (Fine, 2020, p. xxvi).

Statistical studies of the temperaments and aptitudes of men and women do not reveal significant differences either; even if there is a higher proportion of women or men in such and such an activity or with such and such a faculty, there are also notable overlaps between both groups. "Knowing someone's sex is not a reliable predictor of how well or badly they are going to do on a specific task or in a specific situation" (Rippon, 2019, p. 60). And Reilly-Cooper gives an example: even if you think that women are more inclined to empathize and men are more inclined to systematize, as the British autism researcher Simon Baron-Cohen claims, it does not follow that if you meet someone who is a systematizer, they are necessarily going to be male or that someone who is an empathizer is necessarily going to be female. That a man has a *typically feminine* character trait (without conceding that this is the most appropriate way to describe a character trait) does not in any way mean that his brain is a female one, because men, too, sometimes share those traits. It means that different character traits or personalities can come in male or female bodies alike, and that there are multiple and varied ways of being a man or a woman: it's as simple as that.

However, even if one day it were to be discovered that male and female brains do exist, with clearly marked differences, it would be essential to explain the enigmatic mechanism by which a female brain sometimes comes to be housed in a male body, or vice versa, resulting in a person's sex not matching their gender identity.

As can be seen, the assumption that gender identity is a material property leads to conceptually strange situations that have no scientific basis. The alternative, Reilly-Cooper reminds us, is that it is an *immaterial property*. In that case it has great similarities with what we call the soul or spirit, an abstract, ungraspable and immortal entity, opposed to the body, and considered by some traditions to be a fundamental part of our being. Of course, it is possible to believe that there are feminine souls and masculine souls, and, needless to say, people are entitled to think, for example, "I have a female soul (in a male body)," as well as to hold all sorts of religious or paranormal beliefs. But the rest of the world is not obliged to think the same as these believers, nor is it clear that the soul, as an unverifiable and in all likelihood non-existent entity, needs special legal protections. On the other hand, as Mexican human rights lawyer Andrea Medina (2022) argues, it is a very high risk to let the State meddle in regulating our identity.

For Reilly-Cooper, the crux of the matter is the following: according to the proponents of gender identity, it is essentialist to consider that to be a woman is to have a female body (with a certain reproductive capacity, genital organs, chromosomes ...) and that to be a man is to have a male body. But in what sense is it less essentialist to believe that what makes us women or men is the possession of a feminine or masculine soul? Transactivists and their representatives in institutions should be able to answer this question.

Above all, believers in masculine and feminine souls should tell us why everyone is now obliged to adopt this new metaphysical, unverifiable, paranormal, subjective criterion and abandon the material, perfectly objective, scientific and observable criterion that for thousands of years has served us to clearly differentiate the two sexes that make up humanity and to know their respective roles in the, yes, sexual reproduction of the species. It had better be a very powerful reason, because flouting it can also have very serious consequences nowadays: someone may lose their job, be threatened with death, defamed, denied their freedom of opinion and expression, ostracized, among other punishments imposed on those of us who are still guided by the supposedly obsolete definitions of *man* and *woman, boy* and *girl,* based on sex.

Defining *woman* as "female of the human species" does not mean reducing women to their animality, to their genital organs or to their presumed reproductive capacity (definitions do not reduce, but delimit: think of the definition of *planet* or *person*). Part of the feminist project is precisely to do away with the idea that our personality and our human potential are tied to our possession of one or other genital apparatus. Personhood has no sex. But it is strange that gender identity activists claim to be against something they call *binarism,* because in practice what they are doing is reducing millions of possible personalities to two, and no more than two, great archetypes: the masculine and the feminine. Their catalogue is just as esoteric but much more limited than the Enneagram, which defines nine personality types, and the Zodiac, which recognizes 12 signs and, if we add the variable of the rising signs, several possible combinations.

Feminists have never found it a mystery that there are *feminine* boys and men and *masculine* girls and women, because we do not believe that people's ways of being depend on their sex any more than they depend on the position of the Sun, Moon and planets at the time of their birth. The nebulous concept of gender identity had to be invented by someone looking for an explanation for the completely normal, desirable and harmless fact that there are people who, for whatever reason, break sexist stereotypes. What is not harmless is to be introducing this unverifiable, unscientific and quasi-religious concept into legislation, education and public life with such aggressiveness.

Yes, gender is complicated, but the confusion seems to be largely deliberate, precisely to blur the category of sex, to broaden the definition of *woman* so that all men who choose to do so can enter it without question or obstacle, and incidentally for people to subrogate their ability to think for themselves and delegate their opinions to supposed experts who do understand the jargon and know how to unravel its secrets. However, as I have sought to demonstrate in this chapter, if you strip away the chaff from the obscure and convoluted transgender rhetoric and unpack its claims, it is much easier to detect not only the many falsehoods, absurdities and incongruities, but the misogyny, anti-feminism and conservatism behind the idea that human beings are born with an internal and individual experience of gender.

CHAPTER 2

THREE THEORIES ABOUT TRANSGENDERISM

Where does the idea of there being something called a gender identity and people who are transgender come from and what does it entail for feminism? I will begin by outlining the three main models that are used to explain this phenomenon. As I will show, they are in conflict with each other, although there are several overlapping ideas and parallels between them. None of them is a monolith: sometimes they have internal discrepancies and make considerable shifts over time. Nevertheless, it is possible to sketch out in broad strokes their fundamental ideas. I hope it will be illuminating for anyone interested in understanding the broader context in which the heated debates about the clash of transgenderism and feminism take place. I will call them: 1. The medical-sexological model; 2. The transgenderist model; and – in my view the clearly superior one – 3. The radical feminist model.

1. The medical-sexological model

The medical-sexological model combines endocrinological, psychiatric and sexological theories of transsexuality held by "the conglomerate of medical and other professional practitioners who coalesce to institutionalize transsexual treatment and surgery" (Raymond, 1994, p. xvi). During the years when transsexuality was a theoretical novelty, there were important differences between mental health specialists, who "considered the fantasy of being a woman to be best treated by psychotherapy and surgery to be a 'mutilation'" (Jeffreys, 2014b, p. 23), and endocrinologists and surgeons, for whom the ideal treatment was doing something to the body. Over time, the belief that the *transsexual* male somehow possesses a feminine essence became predominant, and the proposal to solve the mental discomfort with bodily intervention gained acceptance.

The positions of these experts who embodied the system that Janice Raymond called the 'transsexual empire' are therefore included in this model. In focusing on the ideas that ultimately prevailed, I leave out atypical cases of physicians and psychiatrists who on ethical grounds opposed the destruction of healthy tissue, such as Paul McHugh, who in 1992 stated: "We don't do liposuction on anorexics. Why amputate the genitals of these poor men?" (quoted in Jeffreys, 2014b, p. 24).

Despite the unquestionable differences amongst them, the positions included in this model have in common their scientific pretensions, their faith in medical technology, and their search for a cause of transsexuality in the biology or the psyche of the individual, rather than in a social or cultural context.

A diagnosis is born

When hearing the term *transgender person,* what most people think of is some rudimentary version of the medical-sexological model: a woman trapped in a man's body, as the endocrinologist and sexologist Harry Benjamin, author of the 1966 book *The Transsexual Phenomenon* and precursor of this model, would put it. In the same vein, Donald Hayes Russell, of the Law-Medicine Institute at Boston University, proposed this definition in 1968:

> The term 'trans-sexual' refers to a person who is said to believe firmly, in spite of all physical or genetic evidence to the contrary, that he (or

she) is inherently of the opposite sex. The transsexual has a fixed or apparently unalterable belief that he is of one sex 'trapped' in the body of the other (quoted in Raymond, 1979, p. 6).

A trans, transsexual or transgender person,[8] according to this common interpretation, is someone with a somatic or psychological maladjustment, who, in order to alleviate their suffering, longs to *change sex,* through hormones and operations.

And how did psychiatrists 50, 60 or 70 years ago know who qualified for these surgeries? A diagnosis was needed ... but a diagnosis of what? How to justify the removal of healthy organs if there is no palpable illness, but only a vague feeling or a desire? Some ventured possible explanations: the person was suffering from either a hormonal imbalance or a psychiatric disorder. However, neither of these options had been proven (and remain unproven). How did they distinguish between the true transsexual and someone who simply had doubts or mistakenly thought he or she was transsexual? Did the mere desire to surgically change their body determine that someone was transsexual, just as today the irrefutable evidence that one is transgender is the fact that one *claims* to be transgender? Some people thought so:

---

8 Some people attach different meanings to these words. For some, transsexual is someone who has undergone *sex change* surgery or at least takes cross-sex hormones, while transgender is someone who has not necessarily taken steps to *transition* beyond a wardrobe change and is simply convinced that their *gender identity* does not match their *sex assigned at birth*. Most commonly, however, the term *transsexual* is dispensed with and *transgender* is used as if it were its updated version. *Transgender* is sometimes said to be an umbrella term that also includes *non-binary* and multiple *non-normative genders*. In any case, behind these terms always lies the idea that the body and mind are independent of one another and that some people have a gender identity that is dissonant with their body. Here, in the manner of the free indirect speech in literature, I use one or the other word depending on the time and what the authors believed whose positions I am explaining. Sometimes, when I express my own opinions, I italicize them to underscore that I do not believe there is such a thing as a gender identity, that sexist stereotypes are based in genes, or that you can be born in the wrong body. For these reasons, I do not believe in a special category of people that it makes sense to call *trans, transsexual* or *transgender*.

Failing to establish a stable diagnostic framework, Benjamin suggested that the diagnosis required for the surgery could be the request for the surgery itself, arguing that anyone who was sick enough to ask for such painful, ferocious surgery was sick enough to receive it. Not surprisingly, this proposal convinced no one (Ostertag, 2016, Chapter 6).

In the midst of the controversies over the causes of transsexualism, a certain term came in handy. Joanne Meyerowitz, author of a history of transsexuality in the United States, wrote:

> The concept of *gender* was widely adopted, in part perhaps because it did not preclude opposing views of etiology. The gender identity might result from hormones or genes or brain structure, from imprinting or conditioning or other forms of social learning, or from the psychodynamic processes of identification during mother-infant interaction. Participants on all sides of the debate could use the language of gender without undermining their favoured position. Gender then came to dominate the scientific approach to transsexuality, but did not resolve the debates about the causes (quoted in Ostertag, 2016, Chapter 6).

And as Bernice L. Hausman, a scholar of medical technologies writing from a feminist perspective, had noted a few years earlier, it was necessary to construct a "rhetorical system" that postulated the existence of "a prior gendered self necessary to justify surgical interventions" (quoted in Jeffreys, 2014b, p. 27). The invention of the concept brought about the problem. If it could be established within the medical community that a gender identity disorder existed, the causes, even if they had not been found, could remain mysterious for the time being. To diagnose was the priority.

Thanks to the efforts of an incipient transactivism, their discomfort – or their fantasy – became a full-fledged illness. Since 1980, the *Diagnostic and Statistical Manual of Mental Disorders* included *gender identity disorder* as a psychopathological condition, which was what people colloquially known as transsexuals or transgender were afflicted with. This name was retained until 2013, when the fifth edition of the manual (DSM-5) replaced it with *gender dysphoria,* the diagnostic criteria for which are as follows:

A) A marked incongruence between one's experienced/expressed gender and their assigned gender, lasting at least 6 months, and manifested by at least two of the following: 1) A marked incongruence between one's experienced/expressed gender and primary and/or secondary sex characteristics (or in young adolescents, the anticipated secondary sex characteristics). 2) A strong desire to be rid of one's primary and/or secondary sex characteristics because of a marked incongruence with one's experienced/expressed gender (or in young adolescents, a desire to prevent the development of the anticipated secondary sex characteristics). 3) A strong desire for the primary and/or secondary sex characteristics of the other gender. 4) A strong desire to be of the other gender (or some alternative gender different from one's assigned gender). 5) A strong desire to be treated as the other gender (or some alternative gender different from one's assigned gender). 6) A strong conviction that one has the typical feelings and reactions of the other gender (or some alternative gender different from one's assigned gender). B) The condition must also be associated with clinically significant distress or impairment in social, occupational, or other important areas of functioning (American Psychiatric Association, 2013).

Note that DSM-5, despite its scientific patina and the fact that psychiatry is a medical specialty, repeats the misunderstanding that *gender* (apparently used as a synonym for *sex*) is something that, on the one hand, someone *assigns* to all of us at birth (one wonders whether arbitrarily or because of our external genitalia) and, on the other hand, something a person *experiences* (we must assume that one experiences whether one is female or male, just as one experiences a headache or an earache). It also leaves open the possibility of there being more than two *genders* (in case a new type of reproductive cell, in addition to the egg and sperm, was discovered before the launch of DSM-6?).

Here's another definition of *gender dysphoria,* interesting because it emphasizes the most outward and public manifestations of sex or gender: "Literally, a sense of unhappiness […] over the incongruence between how one subjectively understands one's own experience of gender and how one's gender is perceived by others" (Stryker, 2017, Chapter 1). In other words, the gender-dysphoric person suffers because other people don't see them as they see themselves.

Chilean gynaecologist Arlette Adauy and her colleagues explain what a transgender person is in these lines which are an example of succinctness (although after reading them, one may have more questions than answers):

> Gender identity is a person's intrinsic perception of being male, female or some alternative gender. Transgender people perceive themselves to be in the wrong body, because they feel that they are the opposite sex to the biological one. When this incongruence between gender identity and the physical phenotype of the assigned sex generates great distress, anxiety and persistent discomfort, it is called gender dysphoria (Adauy et al., 2018, p. 426).

Sometimes this distress and persistent discomfort motivates a person with gender dysphoria to undergo surgery and hormone treatment to alter the appearance of their sexual organs and secondary sex characteristics, in the false belief that it will change their sex or because they were promised that it would lessen their dysphoria. The Mayo Clinic presents on its website the wide range of operations available today for "some people [for whom] feminizing surgery feels like a natural step," and is "important to their sense of self." Options for feminizing surgery include:

- *Removal of the testicles alone.* This is called orchiectomy.
- *Vaginoplasty.* This is a procedure that may include: removal of the penis, called penectomy; removal of the testicles; creation of a vagina, called vaginoplasty; creation of a clitoris, called clitoroplasty; creation of labia, called labiaplasty.
- *Breast surgery.* Surgery to increase breast size is called top surgery or breast augmentation. It can be done through implants, the placement of tissue expanders under breast tissue, or the transplantation of fat from other parts of the body into the breast.

- *Plastic surgery on the face.* This is called facial feminization surgery. It involves plastic surgery techniques in which the jaw, chin, cheeks, forehead, nose, and areas surrounding the eyes, ears or lips are changed to create a more feminine appearance.
- *Body-contouring.* These procedures may include: tummy tuck, called abdominoplasty; buttock lift, called gluteal augmentation; liposuction – a surgical procedure that uses a suction technique to remove fat from specific areas of the body.
- *Voice feminizing therapy and surgery.* These are techniques used to raise voice pitch.
- *Tracheal shave.* This surgery reduces the thyroid cartilage, also called the Adam's apple.
- *Scalp hair transplant.* This procedure removes hair follicles from the back and side of the head and transplants them to balding areas.
- *Hair removal.* A laser can be used to remove unwanted hair. Another option is electrolysis, a procedure that involves inserting a tiny needle into each hair follicle. The needle emits a pulse of electric current that damages and eventually destroys the follicle (Mayo Clinic, n.d.).

Nobody said looking like a woman when you are a man was easy. The treatment of dysphoria gives lots of work to plastic surgeons, but also to other health professionals.

John Money's legacy

The medical-sexological model owes a lot to John Money, an expert in intersex conditions and a pioneer of *sex reassignment* surgeries, considered "the man who led the fight for the right of transsexuals [...] to obtain hormone therapy and surgery in the United States" (Ostertag, 2016, Chapter 6). This well-known New Zealand-born psychologist and sexologist had concluded that differences in behavioural traits between women and men are due to social imprinting and upbringing, not biology. When they are born, babies are, according to his theory, in a situation of *psychosexual neutrality.* J. Michael Bailey describes Money as "one of the most important scientists of the twentieth century," and, alluding to his experiment with Bruce Reimer, "the intellectual father of reassigning boys with damaged penises as girls" (Bailey, 2003, Chapter 3), while Helen Joyce refers to him, bluntly, as the author of the theory "that if you castrated a baby boy, what you got was a baby girl" (Joyce, 2021, p. 192).

An "agent provocateur of the sexual revolution," as *The New York Times* called him in 1975, Money had founded the Johns Hopkins Gender Identity Clinic in 1966 to freely perform *sex reassignment* operations on both children and adults with ambiguous genitalia (at the time called *hermaphrodites*) and on people considered trans-sexual.[9] The clinic, groundbreaking in the United States, provided the impetus for many more to be founded and served as a model for them. It was, however, closed down 13 years later, after it was concluded that the surgeries conferred "no objective advantage in terms of social rehabilitation" to those who underwent them. In its wake, other clinics also closed down (see Nutt, 2017). Jon Meyer, author of the comparative study that supported this decision, stated at the time:

> My personal feeling is that surgery is not proper treatment for a psychiatric disorder, and it's clear to me that these patients have severe psychological problems that don't go away following surgery (quoted in Witkin, 2014).

Not everyone believed in the validity of Jon Meyer's study, starting with John Money, who had done his own research: according to him, 23 out of 24 patients were certain that they had made the right decision.

Another reason that may have come into play in the closing down of the clinic in 1979 was that Money "had branched out into the realms of child pornography and incest" (Raymond, 1994, p. xii),

---

9   Before the existence of specialized clinics in the United States, American physicians working with *transsexuals* despatched their patients for surgery to Casablanca or Istanbul, or, depending on the budget, to countries such as Denmark, Switzerland or Germany. In Berlin, as early as the 1930s, Magnus Hirschfeld supervised the first documented *sex reassignment* surgeries (and also the first ones intended to *cure* homosexuality; see Ostertag (2016), Introduction and Chapter 1).

something that the revelations of his patient Bruce Reimer[10] and various statements by Money himself confirm. Indeed, if Money had not concealed the truth about the Reimer case, which despite being a failure served to justify thousands of operations (see Raymond, 1994; Slatz, 2022a; Colapinto, 2000, pp. 32–33; Winkler, 2000), the clinic would probably have disappeared much earlier.

The Johns Hopkins Hospital let a few years go by and finally wiped the slate clean – in 2017 it opened a transgender health service and resumed surgeries, now called *gender affirmation surgeries* to reflect the position that gender (understood as sex) is in the mind and, if there is incongruence between it and sex characteristics, some modifications will have to be made to the body. Since this institution had spearheaded these interventions, it could not be left behind now that these practices (which, thanks to Money's perseverance, it had decided to champion when no one else in the United States was doing so), were on the rise.[11]

It is important to underline that, in the whole history of pathologization that defines and is defined by this model, the agents are not only the physicians and sexologists who perform or supervise the operations, but also the patients who request them. In her book *Gender Hurts,* Sheila Jeffreys says, again quoting Hausman:

> It would be wrong, Hausman argues, to see the patients who sought sex changes as the passive victims of the treatments; rather, 'transsexual subjects' played a defining role in the construction of transgenderism, through 'demanding' surgery and drugs that they considered might help them in their aspirations. She says it is 'important' to underscore the agency of transsexual subjects insofar as they forced the medical profession to respond to their 'demands'. Hausman sees the alliance of transgenders with doctors as the defining element in the construction of transgenderism. In 1980 it had led to the inclusion in the *Diagnostic*

---

10   See, for example, John Colapinto's *As Nature Made Him: The Boy Who Was Raised as a Girl,* the result of more than a hundred hours of interviews with him over 12 months.

11   By 2022, there were "more than 60 comprehensive gender clinics in the United States, along with countless therapists and doctors in private practice who are also seeing young patients with gender identity issues" (Bazelon, 2022).

and Statistical Manual of gender identity disorder, which paved the way for treatment. It recognised their desires as a form of mental illness caused by being possessed of an anomalous, but essential, 'gender' (Jeffreys, 2014b, pp. 21–22).

Thus, the medical-sexological model and the transgenderist model have coexisted harmoniously right from the start and have fed back on each other, notwithstanding the paradigm shift which, as we shall see, crystallized in the Yogyakarta Principles.

A biological defect

Gerald Ramsey, an American clinical psychologist who over more than two decades treated "hundreds of transsexuals and other gender dysphoric individuals," falls squarely within the medical-sexological model. He wrote a book that in 1996 was billed as "the first to address transsexual issues in nonmedical language," and could therefore be called the first self-help book for people who believe they are transsexual. To dispel any doubt, the foreword was written by John Money himself. However, Ramsey does not seem to agree with the author of *Venuses Penuses* that babies' brains are a *tabula rasa* when it comes to *gender* and other psychosexual aspects. He considers that "the transsexual phenomenon is, minimally, a psychological birth defect," by virtue of which transsexuals "are not 'normal'," but, "fortunately, with current psychological, medical and surgical advances, they can be rehabilitated" (Ramsey, 1996, p. 142).

It would be a mistake to think that this interpretation is completely outdated and no one would believe it nowadays. Jackie Green, son of the CEO of Mermaids, an organization devoted to the transgendering of children, certainly believes this.[12] He, who

---

12   At the time of writing, Mermaids, an influential English charity founded in 1995, an active promoter of *trans children* and therefore of sexist stereotypes, which lies to teenagers telling them that puberty blockers are harmless, is being investigated by UK's Charity Commission for safeguarding concerns. According to several allegations, it had been offering chest binders (devices that flatten the breasts to give the appearance of a flat chest – often as a preliminary to a double mastectomy – which cause breathing difficulties and lead to serious health problems) to girls as young as 13 even against their parents' wishes (see *The Guardian*, 2022).

at the age of five believed that God had made a mistake because he should have been a girl, and at 13 started taking puberty blockers, explained at 25:

> I was meant to be female and thus had surgery to correct my small birth defect. For a long time I was told I had to play with action men and other 'boy toys' [...], but still I wanted the Barbies and little mermaid toys (quoted in Osborne, 2022).

As Susie Green herself has recounted (see 2017), the person who prevented Jackie from playing with dolls and disapproved of him wearing tutus and dressing up as Snow White was his father (and it was after that that he began to *identify as a girl*), while the surgery he alludes to involved removing his penis and testicles and creating the cavity they call a *neovagina*. It was his mother's gift to him on 16 July 2009, when he turned 16, and the tabloids went into overdrive announcing that Jackie had become "the youngest person in the world to have a sex change" (see Artemisia, 2019). Stories about boys who are *actually girls* and girls who are *actually boys* are heavily relied upon by the tabloid press, which by showcasing them actively participates in the invention of the trans child (see Chapter 4).

Its poor safeguarding of children participating in its online forum is also coming under scrutiny, as it emerged that Mermaids' online moderator often channeled discussions about so-called medical transition and the use of experimental drugs to forums with less oversight (see Beal, 2022). In October 2022, criticism was raining down on this charity, which has had unprecedented influence on British public policy for the recognition of *trans children*. In the midst of all this, it was revealed that Jacob Breslow, one of its trustees, had links to paedophile groups and "a disturbing history of ostensibly pro-pedophile sentiment" (Woulahan, 2022). As several feminists have pointed out, this is not the only case in which close links have surfaced between the movement for the transgendering of children and those who advocate for paedophilia and promote it as a legitimate sexual orientation or identity. It is not surprising because the same arguments that transactivism uses to say that a child can give informed consent to irreversible surgery can also be called upon to say that a child can freely consent to having sex with an adult. In both cases, the legal age of consent gets in the way of their aims and they seek to lower it. And as Meghan Murphy says, "the sordid connection between adult male transactivists and the grooming of minors runs deep, and is only now being reported openly, becoming impossible to ignore" (Murphy, 2022).

Jackie Green, who at the age of 18 reached the semifinals of the Miss England 2012 beauty pageant, would surely also agree with Ramsey that

> like other biological defects, once gender dysphoria is medically or surgically corrected and the individual has dealt with the accompanying psychological damage and concomitant pain, the transsexual should be in a position to lead a 'normal' life in most respects (Ramsey, 1996, p. 143).

Gerald Ramsey makes no secret of his enthusiasm for the power of surgery to cure such a *biological defect,* and especially for what he sees as great progress in that field. Comparing the surgical construction of a neophallus from 1946 onwards with that of the 1990s, he says:

> These early 'penises' were fraught with complications. They were not aesthetically pleasing, had no genital sensation, and were dysfunctional in most other respects. Today's neophallus is light years ahead of these early reconstructions. Surgery can create a neophallus that looks like a penis, through which urination can pass out of the bladder, and which possesses a degree of genital feeling. There is little question that tomorrow promises further enhancements, including perhaps the transplantation of genitals as we now transplant hearts and kidneys (Ramsey, 1996, p. 122).

Anyone who has seen pictures of the end result of a phalloplasty in 2022, skinned forearms included, or read the horror stories circulating online about the many complications it entails, will be amazed that back in 1996 anyone could be so optimistic and found any resemblance between the neophallus and a functional penis.[13] This *gender-affirming* operation is the cruellest example of the false

---

13 Vaginoplasties are not a great success either, in any of its modalities – intestinal, peritoneal, buccal mucosa or penile inversion. They can bring major complications and some patients might require further surgeries; but even if the outcome is acceptable, so-called neovaginas normally require "a lifetime of dilation for maintenance" (Boskey, 2022). This means inserting tube-shaped medical devices – to stretch the tissues and maintain the surgically-created canal – three to six times a day for a total of 120 minutes for the first three months. Then not so frequently; after a year, maybe only once a week. It can be very painful.

promises made to young women who believe that the operating theatre is a necessary step in their search for happiness or their true selves.

In his book *Sex Science Self*, essayist Bob Ostertag, a participant in the gay subculture that flourished in San Francisco in the 1980s, agrees that the results are still disappointing, or at least were still disappointing in 2016, when he wrote the book:

> Early attempts at the surgical construction of penises produced unsatisfying and sometimes horrific results, and despite decades of effort surgeons remain unable to construct anything close to a penis in size, appearance, function or sensation. The techniques available leave visible scarring from skin grafts taken from elsewhere on the body, can involve multiple surgeries, and are expensive, painful, slow to heal, and fraught with complications (Ostertag, 2016, Chapter 8).

The situation has not changed much in the last seven years, except for the increase in demand. As TransLine – a US transgender medical consultation service – acknowledges, "size and appearance are prioritized over erectile capacity, and in some cases over erotic sensation" (TransLine, 2022).

Nevertheless, Gerald Ramsey is convinced that only surgical and psychological techniques can help those he calls transsexuals achieve wholeness, because, while they "may feel 'normal' inside as regards their gender identity, they will not be truly whole until inside and outside match up" (Ramsey, 1996, p. 29).[14]

Bailey, Blanchard, Zucker

Another exponent of the medical-sexological model is J. Michael Bailey, author of *The Man Who Would Be Queen*, a study of *feminine* men. In sharp contrast to Money, this psychologist and behavioural geneticist is quite convinced that femininity and masculinity are behavioural traits that people are born with. Without falling into

---

14 This sales pitch has proved so compelling that by 2022, according to some estimates, the market value of surgeries that supposedly match the body with the mind is estimated to be around two billion dollars in the United States alone, and is expected to reach five billion dollars by 2030 (see Grand View Research, n.d.).

the simplification of the female brain in a male body, he concludes, from the fact that the majority of feminine boys will grow up to be gay men, that it is likely that both homosexuality and transsexuality are genetically determined:

> To say that femininity and homosexuality are closely bound together may be politically incorrect, but it is factually correct, and it has been known for a long time. The idea that some males are 'women's souls in men's bodies' was originally offered in 1868 to explain gay men, not transsexuals (Bailey, 2003, Preface).

Bailey does not define what femininity consists of, but we can get an idea from his examples of supposedly feminine traits in homosexual men (interest in fashion, decorating and dancing, and preference for receptive anal intercourse; see Chapters 4 and 5) and his list of feminine jobs ("waitresses, hairdressers, receptionists, strippers and prostitutes"; Part III) taken up by some transsexual males (whom others might call trans women).

This scientist understands transsexuality in males as having more to do with eroticism than with gender identity. This leads him to adopt the distinction between homosexual transsexuals and autogynephilic transsexuals[15] – a term coined by Ray Blanchard, a Toronto-based sexologist. The first group are men who as children showed a marked femininity and who found themselves sexually attracted to men when they grew up, while the second are rather masculine men who as children did not stand out for their effeminacy and who are sexually attracted to women, although what excites them the most is imagining themselves as women.

People who, adopting transgender language and principles (as several representatives of the medical-sexological model do), consider that these males are actually women, or speak as if they were and use *she/her* pronouns, end up referring to *homosexual transsexuals* not as gay men, but as heterosexual women, and to

---

15　The word *autogynephilia* was created from the Greek words for *self, woman* and *love*. It could be said that the autogynephile is the man who loves the woman he thinks he sees in himself … or the man who experiences sexual arousal by imagining himself as a woman.

autogynephilic transsexuals not as heterosexual men but as lesbian women. This is a classic example of the deliberate confusions resulting from the use of language based not on sex, but on the mental state and fantasies of the person designated by the grammatical subject.

Bailey designed a questionnaire to tell apart autogynephilic and homosexual transsexuals. It asks, for example, "Do you like to look at pictures of really muscular men with their shirts off?," "Were you under the age of 25 or over the age of 40 when you began to live full time as a woman?" and "Have you worn women's clothing in private and, during at least three of those times, become so sexually aroused that you masturbated?" Whoever answers *yes* to the question "Have you worked as a hairstylist, beautician, female impersonator, lingerie model or prostitute?" scores a point in favour of being among the homosexual transsexuals, and whoever has "been in the military or worked as a policeman, truck driver, or been a computer programmer, businessman, lawyer, scientist, engineer or physician" is likely among the autogynephilic ones. Bailey has great confidence in his classification criteria. Cher, one of the *transsexuals* whose stories he tells in his book, apparently talks a lot about sports and automobiles; that is, claims Bailey, enough to indicate that he belongs in the autogynephile category and not in the homosexual one (see Bailey, Chapter 10).

Notwithstanding his avowed biological determinism, Bailey believes that the cultural environment and its degree of tolerance for homosexuality help to define whether a naturally feminine man ends up accepting himself as gay, or living as a transsexual and seeking a surgical *transition* to pass as a woman. Of course, autogynephilic transsexuals are also influenced by their environment; in the words of Alice Dreger, who devotes entire chapters of her book *Galileo's Middle Finger* to Bailey's book (and the scandal it provoked by exposing Blanchard's taxonomy, previously restricted to specialist journals, in a general interest book):

> Whether a man who dreams erotically of becoming a woman opts to
> change sex hormonally and surgically depends upon the interaction of

the individual's body and psychology with the cultural environment. Some of these folks simply fantasize about crossing into womanhood while remaining apparently typical straight men socially their whole lives. They may try to suppress the thoughts, or they may enjoy transsexual erotica, but they limit themselves to thoughts and dreams. Others will occasionally cross-dress for erotic purposes and to enjoy temporarily experiencing a deep feeling of femininity. [...] A few men who experience *amour de soi en femme* do decide to seek medical interventions. Some opt to get breast implants or to take female hormones – to enhance their sense of being a woman and to be socially 'read' as women – while keeping their male genitals. And a few autogynephilic individuals find that they can feel fulfilled only by complete hormonal, surgical, and social transition to women. For those who seek full transition, that's what it takes to feel that they are living an authentic life, true to themselves (Dreger, 2015, p. 61).

Bailey, for bringing Blanchard's typology to the attention of a wide audience, was subjected to a virulent transactivist campaign of harassment and vilification, even though his book is full of respect, affection and compassion for them, and despite the fact that he advocates access to all kinds of feminizing surgeries for homosexual transsexuals and autogynephilic transsexuals alike, which has been a central demand of transgenderism (albeit with a very different language in which the word *autogynephilic* does not appear, not by a long shot). He certainly finds the result much more satisfactory and convincing in homosexual transsexuals, because, according to his determinist theory, they already have a certain femininity from birth and this makes it easier for them to pass as women. Although this author talks about autogynephilia and the erotic motivations behind it without mincing words, for him it is a perfectly respectable sexual orientation and, although he puts homosexual transsexuals in a different category, neither one nor the other receives a negative judgement from him. The problem is that from a strategic point of view, it was not in the interests of the gender identity movement for these issues to be brought out into the open.

Clinical psychologist Kenneth J. Zucker, who directed the Gender Identity Service at Toronto's Centre for Addiction and Mental Health from 1981 to 2015, is arguably a moderate member of the medical-sexological model. This world authority on gender dysphoria in children was, at the American Psychiatric Association, head of the task force for the DSM-5 chapters on sexual and gender identity disorders. Another of his topics of study is male homosexuality; together with Ray Blanchard he has co-authored research articles in an eager search for biological predispositions. One example is the *fraternal birth order effect*, whereby the higher number of older brothers a man has, the more likely he is to be homosexual (speculated to be due to changes in the mother's womb during gestation). J. Michael Bailey claims that this is Blanchard's other major contribution to his field, though not as revolutionary as his taxonomy of transsexual men.

Incidentally, Zucker has co-authored papers with Bailey as well. In one from 1995, they reviewed research pointing to strong associations between stereotypically feminine behaviour in child-hood and homosexuality in adulthood in males. This means that young boys who according to the transgenderist model would be automatically considered transsexual, are highly likely to be homosexual in the future.

In treating children, Zucker's approach, less deterministic than Bailey's, has as its frame or reference attachment theory and takes into account the family and social context. He disagrees with so-called affirmative therapy, which merely validates the patient's own beliefs and discourse, as if these were not influenced by the environment, and as if a six-year-old girl had the capacity to define herself once and for all and make momentous decisions about her health. But

> identity is a process, it's complicated. It takes a long period of time, in a sense, to know who a child really is. A four-year-old might say that he's a dog – do you go out and buy dog food? (BBC, 2017).

When children came to Zucker's office unhappy about being a girl or a boy and wanting so badly to be of the opposite sex, what Zucker did was listen to them and examine each situation on a case-by-case basis, instead of resorting to a prefabricated and easy diagnosis ("Are you a boy and want to be a girl? Then you are transgender"), and to a one-size-fits-all treatment (gender transition for everyone). That is why he understood that a girl who was convinced she was a boy after tragically witnessing her mother being murdered was not because she was a transgender boy, but because, after living through that tragedy, she managed to convince herself that, had she been a boy, she would have been stronger and perhaps been able to save her mother, and that, "by being a boy, she would be safe herself and not be a target of male aggression" (BBC, 2017). Many different paths can lead to gender dysphoria, says Zucker; there is no single cause that explains all cases. "A whole range of psychological issues can manifest themselves in a child's obsession over changing their gender" (BBC, 2017).

For offering this therapy – which takes into account the child's particular situation, looks for the connection between the child's behaviour and underlying feelings, and aims primarily to make the child feel comfortable with their sex rather than to bring about a transition – Zucker was accused of practising *conversion therapy*, and, like Bailey, was subjected to a transactivist campaign of harassment and defamation that culminated in late 2015 with his firing and the shutdown of his gender identity clinic (see Singal, 2017).[16]

The hormone and its henchmen

The medical-sexological model naturally includes clinics, hospitals and health services that endorse or even promote cross-sex hormone therapy for people who claim they are trans, as well as pharmaceutical companies that produce, advertise and market synthetic hormones.

---

16 They then had to apologize and pay him more than half a million Canadian dollars in damages (see *The Canadian Press*, 2018).

There are countries where both surgery and hormone treatment are reserved for those who meet certain requirements, including "persistent, well-documented gender dysphoria" (World Professional Association for Transgender Health, 2012, p. 34), and others where the patient's will is enough if they are of legal age (although in some places, in response to pressure from transgender activism, legal age is not required either).

The Mexico City-based Clínica de Atención Transgénero Integral, with its "interdisciplinary team of specialists with an innovative vision of gender fluidity," provides hormone therapy to those who require it, and defines it thus:

> ... an endocrinological medical treatment that facilitates transition by blocking birth hormones to perpetuate the treatment which substitutes the desired gender (Clínica de Atención Transgénero Integral, 2022).

Fluidity and perpetuity in one place.

For females seeking masculinization, such therapy consists of ingesting or injecting androgens, such as testosterone and anti-estrogens; for males seeking feminization, estrogens, progesterone and anti-androgens are ingested. These hormones alone can have several of the effects sought by those who want to appear to be of the other sex, as they develop some of the opposite secondary sex characteristics. Thus, in females, they cause reversible effects, such as fat redistribution, and irreversible ones, such as beard and body hair growth, deepening of the voice, and enlargement of the clitoris. In males, enlargement of breast tissue, redistribution of body fat, some reduction in strength and muscle mass – in males, unlike females, almost all the effects are reversible. Moreover, a man can spend a lifetime taking estrogen and progesterone and his voice will remain the same, unless he learns to fake it and practices some speech therapy techniques with the help of a speech pathologist, or also undergoes laryngeal surgery. A woman, on the other hand, after only nine months of taking testosterone will have acquired a hoarse voice that will last into old age. As a general rule, if they have already made the *medical transition,* a woman is more likely to pass as a man than a man is to pass as a woman: the visible effects can be much more convincing.

Of course, it is known that giving testosterone does not turn women into men, nor does taking estrogen turn men into women. As Bob Ostertag says, "the idea that gender has a chemical essence, or that taking a pill can cause one's gender to 'transition', are extraordinary claims" (Ostertag, 2016, Introduction). Still, those ideas caught on, and for the pharmaceutical industry they have been highly profitable.

The use of synthetic hormones is not without risks and adverse effects. The Fundación Huésped in Argentina, which works with *transgender* people (and, as stated on its website, does it with support from the Dutch Embassy), acknowledges, for example, that estrogen in the short term can cause weight gain and mood swings in men, and in the long term varicose veins, increased cholesterol, cardiovascular disease and infertility, while testosterone in the short term can cause clitoral pain and increased aggression in women, and in the long term an increased risk of diabetes. There are, however, other effects that are less talked about.

Here is just one example. Aydian Dowling, an American transgender activist who since 2009 has been documenting on YouTube her life and experiences with testosterone (which she started taking at the age of 22), dedicated an episode of her program to explain how orgasms give her severe cramps:

> Eight out of ten transmasculine people that I talk to suffer from some form of this and we don't talk about it enough. [...] The number one reason I'm getting a hysterectomy is because [...], at the very peak, when I orgasm, I experience an extreme cramping feeling, more than just when I used to get menstrual cramping. [...] So, I'm orgasming, I'm at what is supposed to be life's, nature's beautiful pleasure, and it literally feels like someone takes two knives and shoves them into right here [pointing to her underbelly], and twists and turns them. And that goes on from about anywhere from maybe a minute [...] to six, seven minutes. It's very disruptive to the sexual experience; it makes me feel like I don't want to engage sexually, because it's extremely

painful. [...] As the years have gone on, my pain has elevated and dipped, and elevated and dipped, [...] for five or six years now. [...] At first it wasn't that bad, it was just a little bit of pain, a little discomfort, but in the last two years it's gotten more and more drastically painful. At the beginning of this year it's been excruciating and it hasn't just lasted a couple of seconds to a minute or two: it's extended. It's painful, extremely, for about five minutes, and then it tapers down very slowly.

Together with her compatriot Buck Angel, who began transitioning at the age of 28 in 1990, when very few women did, and who suffered from the same kind of pains before having an emergency hyster-ectomy, she decided to open up the discussion to other women who, like them, consider themselves to be transgender men:

A lot of trans men don't want to talk about this, because talking about reproductive health means you're not talking about a penis, you're talking about ovaries, a uterus, fallopian tubes, a cervix, a vaginal cavity. You're talking about female reproductive organs. And so to talk about that and also be confident in your masculinity and your identity as a male person or as a male-identified person can be really hard. [...] I want to be proud about my masculinity and still be proud and ok with me being born into a female body (quoted in Transgender Trend, 2019a).

A Twitter user (@ystriyahysteria) collected responses to Dowling's video; many women said they had experienced the pain (one of them claimed that the acute pain could last up to 24 hours) and were grateful that someone was finally touching the subject and breaking the taboo. As claimed in the Transgender Trend blog (2019a):

The testimonies here expose an arrogance within a medical profession which seems to think it can simply change a female body into a male body and that there will be no problems. [...] Is this just another case of the male body being the default in medicine, and because male transitioners haven't had this problem it's assumed that females won't either? Or is it because of doctors' reluctance to refer to anything which may offend the patient through drawing attention to their femaleness? Either way, young female transitioners deserve the same level of care as any other patient. The lack of awareness among doctors is unacceptable for a medical treatment which is experimental on bodies so young.

And, in addition to the effects of testosterone that some would rather sweep under the carpet, there are the consequences of hysterectomies in women of childbearing age, the most obvious of which is early menopause. But we don't have to worry: the solution is also available in the drugstore, this time in the form of hormone replacement therapy.

Cross-sex hormone therapy usually involves a regular outlay of money for many years for the patient (men up to the age of 55 and women up to 65, according to some recommendations), unless such treatment is covered by social security or health insurance, a goal envisaged by the transgender agenda. It is said that one of the first persons to have administered it is the physician and sexologist Magnus Hirschfeld, founder of the Institut für Sexualwissenschaft (Institute for Sexual Science) in Berlin, a sexological research centre that opened in 1919 and was attacked in 1933 by the Nazi organization German Student Union, which, on 10 May of that year, set fire to much of its rich library, along with thousands of other "anti-German" books, in the historic burning of the Opernplatz in front of 40,000 people in the presence of Joseph Goebbels.[17]

In order for cross-hormone therapy to have the best possible effects in terms of so-called passing,[18] and, let us assume, for his or her mental well-being, the patient should ideally have taken puberty blockers (gonadotropin-releasing hormone agonists, GnRHa) from a very early age, the younger the better. In fact, as Michael Biggs, from the Department of Sociology at Oxford University, recalls in a study on the origins of this intervention, "the crucial advantage of

---

17 According to Harry Benjamin, "the Institute's confidential files were said to have contained too many data on prominent Nazis, former patients of Hirschfeld, to allow the constant threat of discovery to persist" (quoted in Raymond, 1979, p. 152).

18 *Passing* is defined in its Wikipedia entry as "the ability of a person to be regarded as a member of an identity group or category [...] that is often different from their own" (<en.wikipedia.org/wiki/Passing_(sociology), 10 June 2023>).

puberty suppression was creating 'individuals who more easily pass in to the opposite gender role'" (Biggs, 2022). External appearance was what mattered most.

However, suppressing puberty can have very serious effects on a person's development:

> Because sex hormones are systemic – meaning that they act on multiple areas in the body, including the nervous system, cardiovascular system, and skeleton – interfering with sex hormone production can be expected to have multiple and cascading effects on the body (Lesbians United, 2022a, p. 3).

Serious and irreversible consequences include a decrease in bone density (thus an increased risk of osteoporosis and fractures) and a variety of effects on the thyroid, brain, genitals, reproductive system, digestive system, urinary tract, muscles, eyes and immune system. Minors taking these blockers may be at increased risk of depression and suicidal thoughts (see Lesbians United, 2022a, p. 1, and Biggs, 2022).

Neither their serious side effects nor the fact that they do not improve mental health nor diminish the discomforts they are intended to alleviate have prevented puberty blockers from being the treatment of choice for the medical-sexological model in an attempt to *cure* healthy children who do not play stereotypical sex roles. As we will see in more detail in Chapter 4, a boy dressing up as a princess and a girl not wanting to wear dresses and barrettes may nowadays be sufficient criteria for their mothers or fathers – either on the advice of strangers on the internet, at the request of the children themselves, or fearful that their children's somewhat atypical behaviour is a harbinger of homosexuality – to go to the gender identity clinic and ask for this treatment that will interfere with the normal maturation process.

Biggs, in his review of the history of this intervention and the evidence adduced to support it, recalls that the very first "adolescent transsexual" to be treated with GnRHa was a 13-year-old Dutch girl, sexually attracted to women, with an Italian father who had "traditional views on gender" and was very bothered by his daughter's *masculinity*. The girl was given puberty blockers (and then testosterone, followed by multiple surgeries) at the Utrecht clinic that served as a model for gender clinics around the world (see Biggs, 2022).

This is proof that puberty blockers are used for the purpose of heterosexualizing young lesbian girls, i.e. as conversion therapy in the original sense of the term. And over the years they have continued to be used to try to create a heterosexual boy out of a lesbian girl. The US organization Lesbians United did a thorough review of the available literature on puberty-blocking drugs. In the press release announcing the launch of this document, they state that the majority of adolescents diagnosed with *gender dysphoria* are girls and young women, many of whom are likely to grow up to be lesbians. They add:

> Based on these findings, Lesbians United concludes that the prescription of GnRH agonists to treat an actual or perceived mental illness constitutes medical malpractice and a crime against humanity; that parental consent to puberty suppression to treat an actual or perceived mental illness is a form of child abuse; that the widespread practice of administering GnRH agonists to adolescents who have received a gender dysphoria diagnosis is homophobic, sexist, and specifically anti-lesbian, [as is] the widespread practice of diagnosing patients with gender dysphoria with the intent of prescribing or abetting the prescription of GnRH agonists […].
>
> The U.S. medical, pharmaceutical, and psychological establishments are actively subjecting children and adolescents to the horrific effects of GnRH agonists, and willfully ignoring the overwhelming evidence against using these drugs to treat any condition that is not life-threatening. Lesbians United considers this practice to be a form of torture and abuse. It must be stopped. Every medical professional who participated must be held accountable financially, professionally, and socially, and prosecuted to the full extent of the law (Lesbians United, 2022b).

But in the meantime, until that day comes, inventing diseases and miracle cures is still good business. This is why they seek to hide the risks and harmful effects of the supposed cure and resort to all sorts of deceptive practices, such as making false promises to children and instilling fear in parents with the lie that if treatment is not started as soon as possible, there is a high risk that the child will commit suicide. Commenting on this frequently peddled falsehood, Robert Withers, a member of the Society of Analytical Psychology in the UK, says that the actual suicide figures indicate that such a risk is extremely rare among children of these ages who self-identify as transgender and that, where suicidal feelings do occur, co-morbidities such as depression are likely to be present: "It seems naïve in the extreme to suggest that feeling suicidal would be better addressed by puberty blockers than psychotherapy or anti-depressants" (Withers, 2019, p. 149).

Puberty is not the only stage of life that has been pathologized: menopause has also been characterized as a tragedy and a period of physical and psychological disturbances that could do with a cure or even prevention. Parallels to the issue at hand can be found in the following illustrative example, told by American environmental historian Nancy Langston. One obvious common theme is the central role of synthetic hormones and their commercialization, but there are more.

During the late nineteenth century, a popular method for doctors seeking not only to treat the ailments of ageing, but also to halt the ageing process, was to remove the ovaries of women over 40. It later emerged that they could simply give them ovarian extracts, but for that to work they had to be injected, which was not only painful but expensive. In this context, the search for an inexpensive synthetic estrogen intensified, until diethylstilbestrol (DES) was found. In the late 1930s, several pharmaceutical companies petitioned the US Food and Drug Administration (FDA) to approve it as a treatment for this *feminine disease,* even though they were well aware that it could cause cancer, among other serious damage, some of it irreversible. The agency took its regulatory work very seriously and was unwilling to budge. At least not at the time.

Women over 40 were a large group that promised juicy profits. The pharmaceutical companies then hired a lobbyist, mounted an advertising campaign, gave samples to hundreds of doctors to give to their patients, and, in short, created a market for the drug even before it was approved. Along with political pressure, an article by journalist Helen Haberman in *Reader's Digest,* a popular magazine with a large circulation, was particularly effective, announcing to mature women that the help they were anxiously awaiting was on its way and would relieve them of the dreaded ailments that accompany the tragic loss of fertility. The only thing standing between them and the magic elixir was the FDA. Haberman's 'Help for Women over Forty' prompted an avalanche of letters from women pleading with the agency, and with President Franklin D. Roosevelt himself, for approval of the sensational cure. Thanks to all that arm-twisting, in 1941 the drug finally arrived in pharmacies at a very affordable price (see Langston, 2011, Chapter 3).[19]

This example clearly shows that the pharmaceutical industry can be more driven by profit than by a commitment to public health, how far it is prepared to go to achieve its ends, and the drama of government authorities failing to do their job of protecting the population. But even more interesting for the purposes of this book is that it shows how easily healthy people can be convinced that they are sick and need a remedy: just a few simple, thinly disguised advertising techniques and they are duped and ready to go under the knife. The manipulation and deception of women in their 40s and older to make them, of their own accord, enthusiastic advocates of a dangerous substance which, far from curing anything, put their health at serious risk, is the main moral of this story.

---

19 DES had many more uses than *curing* menopause; for example, it was prescribed to reduce the risk of miscarriage (without any evidence that it worked for that) and was used to fatten cattle. Eventually it became impossible to keep turning a blind eye to its high toxicity and its use was discontinued in 1971 (see Langston, 2011, Chapter 3).

Goat testicles and other miracle cures

Finally, another embodiment of the medical-sexological model are the many plastic surgeons who, perhaps willing to use their knowledge and skills to help others, or perhaps because it is a lucrative business and who are they to refuse to do what the client asks, are taking advantage of the fact that in many places the requirements (such as a diagnosis of gender dysphoria) for these major surgeries, advertised as *transgender health services,* have disappeared. There has been a resulting boom in surgical interventions for men claiming to have a feminine gender identity, or double mastectomies, hysterectomies and phalloplasties among young girls who consider themselves transgender or non-binary. These interventions do not serve to cure a disease, but, at best, to fulfil a fantasy or alleviate a psychological discomfort, and even the latter remains to be confirmed in the absence of conclusive studies contrasting risks and benefits, and analyzing long-term outcomes.

Very famous in this group is Miami-based Dr Sidhbh Gallagher, who has a TikTok account aimed at young women seeking to affirm their gender by denying their sex. Reader, do not imagine a physician seriously explaining what this or that surgery involves, its risks, recovery time, possible alternatives to the scalpel … No. This is someone who jokes about and trivializes the issue in a cheerful way, in an attempt to get potential clients to like her. As one 13-year-old girl, whose two breasts were removed by Gallagher a month after she contacted her, put it, "she has a great personality" (see Slatz, 2021).

A savvy marketer and skilled communicator, Gallagher has a slogan that sums up her casual attitude to her *modus vivendi:* "Yeeting the teets." Smiling and with a greedy look on her face, she shows photos of girls with a naked torso and visible scars who have already made use of her services. She assures us that it hurts very little, her requirements are minimal and anyone would think that having a mastectomy or a phalloplasty with her would be less cumbersome and less significant than going to the dentist to get a filling.

Gallagher is not alone in using social media to her advantage and the direct access to clientele it provides. Dr Hugh A. McLean's clinic in Ontario, which treats hundreds of young women seeking a flat chest, boasted 14,000 followers on Instagram in 2020. The image of the handsome surgeon Giancarlo McEvenue wearing a Santa hat, holding up with a mischievous expression a bucket labelled 'Breast tissue' in each hand, accompanied by the caption, "For all you good boys, Dr McEvenue is not bringing gifts, he's taking them away," is famous. In response to criticism for the tasteless joke, he said it was just a relaxed comment to celebrate all the patients who had cosmetic mastectomies during the festive season.[20]

These propagandistic practices are less novel than one might think. Bob Ostertag recounts the case of the notorious John R. Brinkley, a Kansas surgeon who in the 1920s and 1930s made his fortune by allegedly transplanting goat testicles into human males, a procedure that promised to rejuvenate them and restore virility. (Other colleagues did it with monkey testicles.) Advertising his services through a high-wattage radio station he had built for this purpose, he "foreshadowed the role of the Internet and direct-to-consumer prescription medicine advertising" (Ostertag, 2016, Chapter 1). After two decades of deceiving the unwary, Brinkley was banned from continuing to practice medicine, not because he performed totally useless operations, but because he was found to have faked his medical credentials. He is generally remembered, says Ostertag,

> as a huckster and swindler who did not believe in the efficacy of his own surgeries. Yet he can just as easily be understood as a smart guy who realized that there are medical procedures that 'work' because people believe they work, so why not give people what they want? (Ostertag, 2016, Chapter 1).

---

20 But the College of Physicians and Surgeons of Ontario disagreed with the clinic's advertising techniques in general; they said the 'before and after' photos of their young clientele were misleading and showed results impossible to achieve (see Mandel, 2021).

The highly successful Spanish plastic surgeon Iván Mañero, formerly head of the Gender Disorders Unit at Barcelona's Hospital Clínic, also gives people what they want … just not always. It is very revealing to know when this phalloplasty expert honours his clients' wishes and when he does not:

> When it is clear that the patient in front of us is a transsexual man, not many psychological criteria are needed. This person has had this desire since childhood, so the operation only brings happiness for the patient, it increases his self-esteem. You have to imagine that the transsexual man is a patient who looks like a man on the outside, with his beard, his receding hairline, his musculature. In other words, he is a man from top to bottom and was born with a vagina. When a phallus is given to him, that is what he desires. It can be compared to a man who needs a heart and is going to have it transplanted. It is another organ, albeit a sexual one, which may have cultural or religious connotations, but it is still an organ.
>
> Now, when this intervention is aimed at men who have 'gym syndrome', it is different. If the patients are men who look at their penis, see it as small compared to the others and come to the consultation requesting a bigger and thicker penis, in many cases a psychological report is necessary, because the vast majority of the time they don't need anything and the surgeon has to refuse to do an intervention that they don't need.
>
> If the patient is very insistent, he probably has to be referred to a psychologist, because what we have here is a disorder called dysmorphophobia, of which anorexia is a subtype. This pathology […] is suffered by patients who see themselves differently from the way they really are, whether it is the 45 pounds skinny girl who thinks she is fat or the boy who has a normal penis and thinks it is very small. In these cases, a psychological report is mandatory (Mañero, 2019).

Now that he is running his own clinic and a foundation that bears his name, Dr Mañero is rarely forced to refuse to perform this surgery, considering that, as he reports, the most common patient profile today, far more than men with a micropenis or who have had penile cancer or an amputation due to an accident, is the *transsexual man.*

It is not clear what is more admirable about this Spanish doctor: his entrepreneurship, which, as his website boasts, "has established him as one of the best aesthetic and reconstructive plastic surgeons nationally and internationally," or his ability to distinguish at first glance and without a shadow of a doubt between a man looking for an unnecessary operation and a man born in a woman's body.

2. The transgenderist model

In the twentieth century, almost all people who were considered transsexual adopted the medical-sexological model. This model precedes the transsexual individual: indeed it invents the transsexual by seeing illness in behaviours that simply deviate from the, say, set of stereotypes assigned at birth. Masculinity and femininity are not only social constructs: since the Danish painter Lili Elbe entered the operating theatre to remove his testicles under the supervision of Magnus Hirschfeld in 1930,[21] they are also, as the philosopher Janice Raymond would say, surgical constructs. Throughout that decade and until the end of the century, *transsexuals* were mostly men convinced they were women trapped in a man's body. The endocrinologists and surgeons, who promised those who thought they were women on the inside that they would also become women on the outside, were their lifeline. Doctor and patient shared the same yearning: adjusting the outer appearance to match the inner essence.

Depathologization

For a long time, people who considered themselves transsexual were the biggest drivers of what might be called their own pathologization.

---

21 He underwent a total of five surgeries, the last of which was a uterus transplant with complications that led to his death. The acclaimed film *The Danish Girl* is based on his life. Anyone who has seen it and remembers the iconic scene with the dress and the silk stockings will conclude that Elbe, according to the typology of *transsexual* men proposed by Ray Blanchard and popularized by J. Michael Bailey, fits neatly into the group of autogynephiles.

In order to access hormones and *sex reassignment* surgeries, those who believed they had been born in the wrong body required the intervention of experts and therefore insisted that they were sick and in need of medical attention. If so-called gender identity disorder made it onto the DSM in 1980 it was because *trans* people demanded that it be included: otherwise, insurance would not pay for treatment. As Bob Ostertag says:

> Dealing with the medical power structure has been a lifelong priority for transpeople from Lili Elbe to Christine Jorgensen to Reed Erickson to Susan Stryker. As the transgender identity took off in the mid-1990s and was embraced by ever larger numbers of people, more and more queers spent more and more of their lives dealing with doctors, psychiatrists, psychologists, surgeons, pharmacies, and insurance companies. Thus the rise of the transgender identity has swung the interface between queer people and medical authority strongly in the opposite direction it was headed in the 1960s and 1970s (Ostertag, 2016, Conclusion).

It should be clarified that *queer,* for this author, is an umbrella term that includes *transgender, transsexual, trans, gay* and *lesbian* (see Ostertag, 2016, definitions) and in this quote he alludes to the fact that the gay and lesbian movement had fought in the 1960s and 1970s to remove homosexuality from the DSM, thus stopping it from being considered a mental illness, a goal achieved in 1973.

The transgender tendency to want medicalization moved gradually downwards at the end of the twentieth century until a paradigm shift took place: throughout the first two decades of the twenty-first century, a common demand of the *transgender rights movement* has been depathologization: no longer to consider them to be suffering from a mental illness, a goal reflected in the Yogyakarta Principles, which in number 18, 'Protection from medical abuses', state:

> No person may be forced to undergo any form of medical or psychological treatment, procedure, testing, or be confined to a medical facility, based on sexual orientation or gender identity. Notwithstanding any classifications to the contrary, a person's sexual

orientation and gender identity are not, in and of themselves, medical conditions and are not to be treated, cured or suppressed (Yogyakarta Principles, 2007, p. 23).

On gender identity ideologues' lips, however, *depathologizing* seems more of a rhetoric than effective action. It does not mean putting an end to breast implants, genital surgeries and hormone treatments that turn the *transitioned* person into an almost lifelong medical patient, but to stop calling the supposed mismatch between sex and *gender identity* a disorder, to make these treatments entirely optional, and to make a slight shift in focus. It is no longer a matter of correcting a mental problem, but of appeasing the torment caused by the dissonance between genitalia and *felt gender,* or between what other people can see and what one imagines oneself to be.

A guide from the Basque Government states:

Transsexual people do not demand care because they suffer from a pathology or disorder, but because of the social obstacles they encounter in the free development of their most fundamental rights and because of the pain and anguish with which these difficulties fill their lives (Administración de la Comunidad Autónoma del País Vasco, 2016, p. 29).

It may be inferred that in order to overcome social obstacles, it is often necessary to do something to the body: surgery and hormone therapies are considered a right that the state should guarantee, as they are supposed to reduce discomfort. Sometimes, to make the argument sound more convincing, it is claimed, albeit without evidence, that these procedures not only bring relief, but in some cases are a matter of life and death (see Brunskell-Evans, 2020, pp. 50–56).

However, it is flatly rejected to make the medical interventions a requirement to change the box on identity documents and to be treated, for all intents and purposes, as someone of the opposite sex:

No one shall be forced to undergo medical procedures, including sex reassignment surgery, sterilisation or hormonal therapy, as a requirement for legal recognition of their gender identity (Yogyakarta

Principles, Principle 3: 'The right to recognition before the law', pp. 11–12).

Despite the fact that these changes have been pushed for several years and crystallized into law in some countries, the bulk of society still associates transsexuality or transgenderism with body modifications and ignores the fact that only a small percentage of people who now call themselves transgender have done little more than change their wardrobe and pronouns. This assumption was shared, for example, by the neighbour of English journalist and broadcaster Shon Faye:

> When someone learns that a person is trans, their first instinct is usually to ask details about that person's surgical status. When my mother told a next-door neighbour, who'd known me since I was a child, that I had transitioned to live as a woman, his first instinct was to ask when I was due to undergo surgical genital reconstruction. I don't believe he realized how invasive his question was – particularly in asking my mother, of all people, about the genital configuration of her daughter (Faye, 2021, p. 66).

Specifically, when people think of *trans women* they imagine that they are men who have shed their penis and are therefore now women because the absence of a penis makes a woman (the idea of her as an incomplete human being is as present in transgender discourse as it is in the social treatment of women). The reality is that, according to some estimates, only five to 13 per cent of men who declare themselves to be women have had genital surgery (see Nolan et al., 2019). In other words, 87–95 per cent of the *trans women* in question have an intact penis and testicles. Passing or not passing, this is often lost sight of.

Despite the reality reflected by the statistics, trans people are still expected to do something to their bodies, says Miquel Missé, who has participated in the international campaign Stop Trans Pathologization. In her book *A la Conquista del Cuerpo Equivocado,* a powerful critique of the medical model and all that persists of it in the transgenderist model, she writes:

Nowadays, in the 2020s, corporal modification is expected of trans people. That is to say, trans people's right to have surgery is defended, celebrated and applauded. We value and respect the trans person's ability to achieve the 'tailor-made' body they desire.

Society has learned that being a trans ally means supporting their battle against their bodies or for their identity, a fatal dichotomy. Anything else is labelled transphobic. If you were to say to a trans person 'I hope you will be able to reconcile with your body in this process and don't need to go under the knife' you will be seen as a total jerk, right up there with the people who'd like to see us exterminated.

[…] Passing unnoticed as a trans person is highly valued in society, and can even save a person from the wrath of transphobia in many situations. That's why I say that passing has become the trans ideal.

[…] Trans people don't like to look trans – call it interiorized transphobia, call it survival – and this discomfort exposes the weakness of passing as supposed trans empowerment. Passing, in fact, is the opposite of empowerment, it is having to remove all traces that indicate that we have lived a gender transition, that our bodies have a history different to those of cis persons, as if looking trans were the most horrible thing that could happen to us (Missé, 2018, Chapter 6).

This last idea is well reflected in a tweet with which Mexican *transgender* MP María Clemente García Moreno seeks to offend a rival representative with whom he had participated in a TV debate: "Is it me or is Teresa Castell so operated on that she's the one who looks trans? I look more natural than her, don't you think?" (@MariaClementeMX, 2022). In two lines he manages to mock both middle-aged women, for whom beauty mandates are particularly merciless, and trans-identified males who don't have so much passing as he believes he has.

Like Missé, a sector of transgenderism also rejects the "pathologizing category" of gender dysphoria and any attempt to psychiatrically diagnose someone who is convinced that their *gender identity* does not correspond to their *assigned sex at birth*. But in the same sector there are also those who, without rejecting it altogether, do not think that *gender dysphoria* is the unequivocal sign that someone is *transgender*. Among the latter is Faye, who describes gender dysphoria as an experience many trans people have to deal with, which can be alleviated with medical intervention, but states that it is, however, not a necessary condition for being trans (see Faye, 2021, p. 67).

So, what is the necessary condition, the reader may ask. The answer is that there is none. In the third decade of the twenty-first century, being trans is having the feeling that one is trans; and for the rest of the world to know one is trans, one has only to declare it. What's more, "I am a woman" may state a fact, but it can also be a performative speech act and turn the speaker into a woman.[22] Reality is created while it is spoken. This authentic linguistic abracadabra, together with the strictly elective character of surgeries and hormones, constitutes the basis of *gender self-identification* or self-ID.

Transformations of the body are still, for many, desirable and sought after, and some would consider them indispensable; only their purpose is not to cure anything: it is to affirm an individual in his or her self-perception. But what is the point of affirming one's self-perception if the birth certificate or identity card contradicts it? Until recently, in order for an individual's official identity documents to state their desired sex and not their actual sex, the authorities had to confirm he or she was indeed a *trans person* who was committed to his or her new identity. Depending on the time and country, there had to be some requirements, which could include surgery, hormone therapy, *living as someone of the other gender* for a few months, or a diagnosis of gender dysphoria signed by an expert.

---

22   In his lecture series *How to Do Things with Words,* British philosopher of language J. L. Austin introduced the classification of performative speech acts. They consist of linguistic expressions which do not describe or record anything, have no truth value, and the issuing of the utterance is the performing of an action – some kind of action is being done by the person who utters. Austin's own examples are "I name this ship the *Queen Elizabeth*" as uttered when smashing the champagne bottle against the stem or "I give and bequeath my watch to my brother" as occurring in a will (see Austin, 1975, p. 117). To say "I name …" is to name, to write "I bequeath …" is to bequeath. This simple characterization inspired the American philosopher Judith Butler to propose her theory of gender performativity, which has had a huge influence on the current version of the transgenderist model.

With *transgender* people guaranteed access to technologies that promise them a body consonant with what they consider their *gender identity* if that is what they wish, transgenderism turns its back on the medical-sexological model and repudiates it, but, as can be seen, only half-heartedly. Total repudiation would mean patricide. Having a body more or less similar to that of the opposite sex remains a possible overwhelming drive which, with a little help from the power of words, becomes a right – a health care right, to be precise.

The transformation of the body is also at the heart of the campaign for the recognition of so-called trans kids and for free access to puberty blockers, which is somewhat paradoxical. On the one hand it is claimed that *sex reassignment* surgery, sterilization or hormone therapy should be optional for adults, but, on the other hand, if, faced with a child who has embraced a transgender identity, someone resists putting them on the path of corporal modifications, worried that it might render them sterile and cause other health problems, he or she will be accused of conversion therapy, as they have recently done with the Spanish psychologist Carola López Moya (see Coronado, 2022). What for the adult is a simple option, for the child and teenager seems to be the only conceivable approach. Alicia Miyares and Amelia Valcárcel sum it up eloquently: "For children, puberty blockers; for children, hormones … and for me, a wig" (Feminario Valencia, 2022).

This fact may seem very strange considering that even the Yogyakarta Principles, non-binding but always wielded by trans-activists to pressure governments to replace the category of *sex* with *gender identity* in their legislation, stipulate that states shall

> take all necessary legislative, administrative and other measures to ensure that no child's body is irreversibly altered by medical procedures in an attempt to impose a gender identity without the full, free and informed consent of the child in accordance with the age and maturity of the child and guided by the principle that in all actions concerning children, the best interests of the child shall be a primary consideration; [and] establish child protection mechanisms whereby no child is at

risk of, or subjected to, medical abuse (Yogyakarta Principles, 2007, Principle 18, 'Protection from medical abuses', p. 23).

Despite the forcefulness of this principle, the recognition of *transgender children* and their access to hormone blockers and surgeries is a key point of the transgender agenda driven by these same principles. The big move in the Yogyakarta Principles is that they underhandedly introduce the problematic concept of gender identity, which, despite its unverifiable status, or precisely because of it, is used to demonstrate or defend whatever is suitable.

The recognition of *trans children* works in tandem with depathologization and self-ID, which means that, without further ado and without the need to prove anything, all official documents of *transgender* citizens must state the sex to which they wish to belong – or to which they *feel* they belong – even if their chromosomes, reproductive organs and secondary sex characteristics tell otherwise. It is of paramount importance that the rest of the world participates in the identity illusion of those who consider themselves to be trans.

And if, in the past, to convince the world that one was of the other sex or *gender* one had to pretend, now the arsenal to persuade others that one is a woman despite male genitalia, or vice versa, includes not good arguments, but sophistry, falsehoods, contradictions, emotional blackmail, and sometimes harassment, aggression and cancellation. As the English writer J. K. Rowling, who has experienced it first-hand, says, "Violence is not a bug, but a feature of this authoritarian movement" (Rowling, 2022).

In several parts of the world, the demand has already been abided by to eliminate all non-administrative requirements altogether, and even these have to be extremely simple and carried out as quickly as possible. If a man comes to the civil registry window to request an expedited change and declares "I am a woman," his word is the law and no one dare question it. He is not looking to be respected as a proudly feminine man, but to be legally recognized as a woman. Moreover, it may be that his *gender expression* is masculine to a fault. That has nothing to do with it. What he is asking for is for his identity papers to correspond to the sex to which he is convinced he belongs, and for them to be issued to him,

> … any request for psychological, psychiatric or medical testing, or the requirement to undergo reaffirmation surgeries or hormone treatments, is a violation of human rights as it is invasive and pathologizing. Nor is it reasonable to ask for other requirements that serve as proof of an individual's gender identity, since self-perceived gender identity should not be subject to external scrutiny (Organization of American States, 2020, p. 20).

It makes perfect sense not to demand external scrutiny of a personal feeling that is impossible to verify or demonstrate empirically, and to abandon the search for an objective criterion to determine whether someone belongs to a category whose reality no one has been able to establish.

If until a few years ago a diagnosis of gender dysphoria was the minimum requirement to give someone with a penis, testicles and XY chromosomes an identity document stating that they are a woman, today the mere suggestion that in order to grant such legal recognition it would be appropriate to have a criterion merits moral condemnation. Woe betide anyone who does not blindly believe, not only that this person is in possession of a gender identity that is in conflict with their sex, but that their sex is, in all the possible meanings of the verb *to be,* what they say they are. The possibility that they say this out of ignorance or malice is excluded, as if in the transgenderist model there is no room for falsehoods or lies.

All this gives gender identity the extraordinary character of being an intimate, unverifiable and highly personal conviction that nevertheless demands universal recognition and acceptance. All other people are obliged to have faith, literally, and not only to have it, but also to profess it, for example by using the *preferred pronouns.*

Thus, the sex box in the official records begins to state something quite different, namely gender identity, and sex becomes non-existent or irrelevant. Similarly, everyone is obliged to know, even if they didn't get the memo, that *woman* no longer means female person. Now a woman is someone who claims to have a feminine gender identity … so those of us lifelong women who lack that and don't believe in stereotypical souls will have to find another word to name ourselves.

Bruce Jenner (now Caitlyn Jenner), who won the gold medal in the decathlon at the 1975 Pan American Games and the 1976 Olympics,[23] former race car driver, father of six children, is a *transgender woman,* i.e. a subclass of women, such as Asian women, young women or autistic women. What's more, even though he announced it at the age of 65, Jenner has always been a woman. In every possible sense. A woman by decree. A woman, full stop. So, everybody has to call him a woman, or else.

The Holy Office

"Trans women are women" is the dogma of faith of transgenderism. "Trans women are trans women," on the other hand, far from being a truism, is a transphobic and hateful statement. Nigerian writer Chimamanda Ngozi Adichie did not know this when she was interviewed on the occasion of the launch of her book *Dear Ijeawele, or a Feminist Manifesto in Fifteen Suggestions,* and when asked whether in her opinion a *trans woman* was "any less of a real woman," she replied:

> When people talk about, 'Are trans women women?', my feeling is trans women are trans women. I think if you've lived in the world as a man with the privileges that the world accords to men and then sort of change, switch gender, it's difficult for me to accept that then we can equate your experience with the experience of a woman who has lived from the beginning in the world as a woman and who has not been accorded those privileges that men are. I don't think it's a good thing to conflate everything into one, I don't think it's a good thing to talk about women's issues being exactly the same as the issues of

---

23 It would be misleading to say that in the male category, not because Bruce Jenner was not a man, but because women do not compete in the decathlon: its equivalent today is the heptathlon and before 1981 it was the pentathlon.

trans women. What I am saying is: gender is not biology, it is sociology (Channel 4 News, 2017).

All hell broke loose, and social media went for the jugular. At the time of these statements, in March 2017, momentous changes were taking place in the transgenderist model. New axioms and new prohibitions were coming up. That time, thanks to the punishment of Adichie – and of anyone who sought to defend her – we learned that trying to qualify the statement "Trans women are women" was anathema; it was like daring to challenge the immaculate conception back in the thirteenth century. Missé, writing around the same time, that trans people's bodies "have a history different to those of cis persons" (Missé, 2018, Chapter 6), a mirror image of Adichie's statements, was dangerously close to heresy.[24]

Readers tempted to concede a point to the charismatic author of *Americanah,* better think twice. In a piece entitled 'Why Chimamanda Ngozi Adichie's Comments About Trans Women are Wrong and Dangerous', Jarune Uwujaren asserts:

---

24 One of the first to point out the importance of this bodily historicity was Janice Raymond when she wrote:

> No man can have the history of being born and located in this culture as a woman. He can have the history of *wishing* to be a woman and of *acting* like a woman, but this gender experience is that of a transsexual, not of a woman. Surgery may confer the artifacts of outward and inward female organs, but it cannot confer the history of being born a woman in this society (Raymond, 1979, p. 114).

She elaborated on this years later:

> It is this female reality that the surgically-constructed woman does not possess, not because women innately carry some essence of femininity but because these men have not had to live in a female body with all the history that entails. It is that history that is basic to female reality, and yes, history is based to a certain extent on female biology (Raymond, 1994, p. xx).

Robin Morgan pointed to this very thing in a famous speech at the Lesbian Feminist Conference in Los Angeles in 1973:

> No, I will not call a man *she*; thirty-two years of suffering in this androcentric society, and of surviving, have earned me the title *woman; one* walk down the street by a male transvestite, five minutes of his being hassled (which *he* may enjoy), and then he dares, he *dares* to think he understands our pain? No, in our mothers' names and in our own, we must not call him *sister. We know what's at work when whites wear blackface; the same thing is at work when men wear drag* (Morgan, 1973, p. 220).

Adichie failed to recognize that it is not her place to tell trans women who they are or how they live in the world. The feminist movements of our time have been historically weighed down by gender essentialism, cissexism, transphobia, and a belief that trans people are not who they say they are but who they are violently pressured to be.

You cannot fix your mouth to say you are an ally to trans people if you think Adichie's decision to talk over trans women was appropriate. You cannot claim to shed tears for the trans women out here being killed while defending Adichie's belief that trans women aren't really women (and yes, that's what she said) because that belief upholds such violence. You cannot talk about trans people as if we're talking points or theoretical concepts and ignore our own words about our experiences with gender and call that allyship. Trans people are working, living, and speaking before your eyes about who we are and what we need – stop looking to cis feminists to dictate how you see and support us.

In short, you need to listen to trans people more than you need to speak for or about us. Anything else is further marginalizing a group of people who cannot afford to be further marginalized (Uwujaren, 2017).

Gender identity policing serves an important educational role. These words of Uwujaren, who introduces himself as a Nigerian-American writer and feminist and a non-binary trans person, encapsulate several transgender principles that anyone who does not want to arouse divine wrath must keep in mind. They are also paradigmatic of the rhetoric now prevalent among exponents of the trans theory with which we are concerned. Unpacking them will immerse us fully in the ideology that, from the university to the market, from the specialized book to the showbiz magazine and from the drag show to the Supreme Court, has come to permeate almost all social spheres.

Uwujaren's statements can be grouped into three categories. In group 1 are factual assertions that can be verified; in group 2, moralistic assertions and accusations that seek to curtail other people's freedom of speech and thought; in group 3, rules that must be followed by anyone who aspires to the title of trans ally:

Group 1, factual assertions

1a Feminist movements are transphobic.

1b Feminist movements are gender essentialist.

1c Trans women are a highly marginalized group of people.

1d Trans women are being murdered.

1e There are groups or individuals who violently pressure trans people to be who they are not.

Group 2, moralistic assertions

2a Talking about trans people means claiming to speak for them or telling them who they are.

2b Anyone who does not fall into the category of *trans woman* should refrain from speaking, conversing or theorizing about trans women.

2c If trans women are murdered it is partly the fault of those who are not fully convinced by the statement "Trans women are women."

Group 3, the good ally's rules

3a A trans ally has an obligation to listen to and believe what trans women say about themselves.

3b A trans ally should not listen to cis feminists.

3c A trans ally must actively support trans women and help them meet their needs.

3d A trans ally must condemn anyone who talks about trans women without themselves being trans.

3e A trans ally should sympathize with trans people.

3f A trans ally must believe that a trans woman is literally a woman.

Let's scrutinize these claims with the attention they deserve.

1a: Feminist movements are transphobic

Given that *transphobia* is systematically attributed to anyone who does not subscribe to gender identity ideology, there is no point in trying to disprove this assertion. However, it is striking how hard some feminists want to prove that they, unlike others, are not transphobic. Sooner or later, in the eyes of the transgenderist model, we will all be transphobic, because the only alternative is total submission, and feminism and submission to the dictates of men do not go together.

1b: Feminist movements are gender essentialist

It is easy to demonstrate the falsity of this assertion. A central struggle of feminism is to break down sexist stereotypes and the belief (and its many practical ramifications) that to be a woman is to be *feminine*, that is, to conform to the stereotype of womanhood, which is what others call gender. The label *gender essentialist* much better describes people like Theryn Meyer, a South African-born, Canadian-based *transgender* male whose beauty and feminine appearance have made him an internet celebrity. In an interview, controversial Canadian psychologist and self-help author Jordan Peterson, intoning an ode to passing, says to him: "Obviously you're doing everything in your power to present yourself to the world in a manner that makes you easily categorizable," and Meyer responds:

> Absolutely, and I guess I don't necessarily even think of it that way. I don't think 'I want to be seen as a woman, so I'm going to do all these things to be viewed as a woman' – I do all these things because I *am* a woman, I do all these things just because it comes naturally to me, and the end product happens to be a subject that in people's minds is easily registerable (Peterson, 2016).

Theryn Meyer feminizes himself to the point of near-perfect passing. With the videos and photos in which he displays his femininity in a markedly sexualized way, he is an example of what Missé calls "an individualist and even neoliberal turn in gender transition in which the body becomes the object of consumption" (Missé, 2018, Chapter 6). But, if we are to believe Meyer, the reason he goes to all this trouble is not a desire to look like a woman, but the prior possession of an inner feminine something that moves him. If women paint their eyelashes, pose with their mouths half-open and throw their hair back in a sexy way, it is because it is in their nature; it's their inner essence showing.

This is what several representatives of today's predominant trans model think and say without blushing, the same ones who accuse us feminists of being essentialists for maintaining that being a woman or a man is a material reality determined by our genes and our reproductive capacity. It is necessary to clarify that knowing that only women can gestate does not mean believing that our only function in life and what makes us women is getting married, getting pregnant and having children. On the other hand, those who base their discourse on the existence of a supposed gender identity implicitly accept that people possess an essence that is masculine, feminine or somewhere in between, but an essence nonetheless.

Now, if recognizing that there are two sexes and two gametes because our species reproduces sexually is tantamount to essentialism, so be it.[25] That does not mean that we should start doubting a truth that is confirmed every time an egg cell meets a sperm and of which every human being on earth is living proof. The burden of proof, moreover, is not on us, but on those who claim that sex is a spectrum and that there are more than two sexes. When they show us a third gamete we can talk.

1c: Trans women are a highly marginalized group of people

It is true that historically, men perceived as feminine (however they identified) have suffered discrimination and marginalization, more so at certain times and in certain places, but today, with much of the industrialized world ostentatiously embracing the gender identity agenda, and in light of the millions of dollars that the transgender project commands (see WLRN, 2017; Bilek, 2018; and Still, 2021), *highly marginalized* is perhaps not the most accurate description of such a group. In Chapter 5, I will address the money issue in more detail.

---

25 For a thorough philosophical discussion of sex and essentialism, see Kathleen Stock, 2021, Chapter 2.

1d: Trans women are being murdered

With unusual frequency, the gender identity camp trots out the claim that men who identify as trans have a very high risk of being murdered and that their life expectancy is 35 years. The truth is that several authors have shown, statistics in hand, that this is, thankfully, untrue (see Herzog, 2019; Lee, 2018; and Still, 2022a). In fact, in places like the United States, the rate of violence against them is lower than against the general population (see Vigo, 2017).

However, for the *argumentum ad misericordiam* to have any effect, it is necessary to manipulate the figures, for example, by extrapolating the numbers from Brazil, where such violence is most dramatic, to other parts of the world, and omitting the important fact that the vast majority of these murder victims have been engaged in prostitution. Shon Faye acknowledges the latter when he writes that most murders of trans people are not "the result of a random 'hate crime' from strangers. The victims are usually trans women, and the killers are men who desire sex with them" (Faye, 2021, p. 144).

In this context, it is worth mentioning that one of the main struggles of radical and abolitionist feminism is precisely to end prostitution, which in the words of Spanish sociologist Rosa Cobo is "an extreme form of inequality and exploitation" and "one of the new barbarities of the twenty-first century" (Cobo, 2017, p. 13), while transactivists enthusiastically support the prostitution system.[26]

---

26   This is an open secret. Abolitionist feminists such as the British journalist Julie Bindel or the Mexican lawyer Teresa Ulloa have seen the same characters attacking them with the same strategies from the pimp front and from the transgender front. Sometimes this fraternity rears its ugly head, as on 6 July 2022, in the Mexican Chamber of Deputies, when María Clemente García Moreno, a *trans* male who holds a federal deputation, interrupted a session of the VII Latin American and Caribbean Congress on Human Trafficking and Migrant Smuggling claiming that the words of the speakers (for example, these of Ixchel Yglesias González: "One cannot understand human trafficking for the purpose of sexual exploitation without understanding that this is a way of supplying a globalized demand for prostitution") were hate speech. The climax came when Sonia Sánchez, a spokeswoman for Latin American abolitionist feminism, told him that "no woman is born a whore" and this man shouted back: "I am a woman, and I was born a whore, and I like it. Big deal" (see Slatz, 2022c).

But let us dwell for a moment on the overused figure of the life expectancy of 35 years and its original source, which gives us an idea of how far the manipulation goes and where it begins. In a 2015 report by the Inter-American Commission on Human Rights on the situation of "lesbian, gay, bisexual, trans and intersex persons in the Americas," we read:

> Latin American organizations report that the life expectancy of *trans women in the region* is between 30 and 35 years of age. According to the data collected by the IACHR, *80% of trans persons killed* during a 15-month period were 35 years of age or younger. The IACHR has received consistent reports showing that trans women who are sex workers are particularly vulnerable to community violence, including killings by individuals, their clients, illegal armed groups or gangs (Inter-American Commission on Human Rights, 2015, p. 15; italics mine).

The chosen wording leaves some questions open, but for reasons of space I will concentrate on what I have italicized. This report by a principal and autonomous organ of the Organization of American States, carried out with financial support from the Arcus Foundation, UNAIDS, the Netherlands and the governments of other countries, is extrapolating the age of 80 per cent of the murdered *trans* people to the totality of *trans women* in Latin America. Moreover, if we assume, as this paragraph implies, that a large number of the murdered *trans* people were engaged in prostitution, it is not valid to infer that all *trans people* engaged in prostitution have a life expectancy of 35 years, because the figure does not take into account all those who, although engaged in prostitution, are not murdered, but only those who unfortunately are. And not even in the extraordinary and tragic case that all *trans women* in prostitution in Latin America were killed between the ages of 30 and 35 could it be said that this young age is the life expectancy of all *trans women* in Latin America, unless 100 per cent of them were in prostitution.

From what happens in one subset of all Latin American *trans* people alive or dead (in this case, the subset consisting specifically of the 80 per cent of Latin American trans people who died or were murdered in a certain period), one cannot draw conclusions about what happens in another very different subset (in this case, all trans women in Latin America), let alone extrapolate it to a much broader set, for example, all trans people in the world. But perhaps statistics are not the strong suit of the Latin American organizations that sent their figures to the IACHR, nor of those who use these data to lecture trans allies.

1e: There are groups or individuals who violently pressure trans people to be who they are not

I am not sure who this statement alludes to, but I see at least five possibilities:

- Those who, believing that sexist stereotypes stem from the natural order of things, reject femininity in men or masculinity in women, and want to *correct them*. This is the opposite of the feminist position, as demonstrated in the previous chapter.
- Those who require people who consider themselves trans to undergo medical procedures to issue a certificate stating that they are of the other sex. Although it is often mentioned as an unacceptable requirement, I have found no evidence of authorities in western democracies requiring *trans* adults to undergo genital surgery. One country where some people are forced to undergo *sex change* is Iran, where homosexuality is punishable by death, and to avoid that fate gays and lesbians resort to the operation (see Hamedani, 2014, and Membrado, 2015), so it is they who, by being forced to *change sex* and heterosexualize themselves, are violently pressured to be who they are not. On the other hand, and as the experience of de-transitioners demonstrates, it is possible to argue that it is often gender identity activists and advocates acting in tandem with the techno-medical complex who drive young people to surgery.
- Those who seek some criteria for considering a person, even a minor, as a candidate for *gender affirmation* surgery or cross-sex hormone therapy. One demand of transgenderism is that there

should be no requirement for this other than a desire for surgery and informed consent.

- Feminists who do not accept self-ID, i.e. the position that a man who says he is a woman is a woman, just because he says so. The serious implications of this position for women's rights will be discussed in Chapter 5.

- Feminists who, by saying that the statement "Trans women are women" is false, are supposedly denying *trans women* their identity. The latter is a very obvious fallacy: why does the fact that other people do not share your convictions threaten your identity? It has to be a very fragile identity that depends on what other people think. Shon Faye echoes this fallacy when he talks about "how exhausting and demoralising it can be for trans people to have their identities and human rights be the subject of toxic and noisy debate" (Faye, 2022, p. 10). The debate in question, in which this book is embedded, is not whether people who claim to be transgender have human rights; no one, at least no feminist, doubts that. From my point of view, which I share with a growing group of radical feminists and gender-critical people, what is on the table are *women's human rights*, and it is unfair to try to prevent feminists from defending them against the onslaught of a movement that wants to take them away from us. And, by the way, if the debate is toxic, it is largely due to the virulence with which transactivists respond to anyone who does not subscribe to their doctrine. Nothing illustrates this better than the horribly misogynistic insults and threats of death and rape that the creator of Harry Potter has received since, in an ironic tweet, she criticized a newspaper headline referring to women as "people who menstruate" (see Reilly-Cooper, 2020).

2a: Talking about trans people means claiming to speak for them or telling them who they are

Adichie is criticized because she is dishonestly interpreted as claiming to speak on behalf of *trans women*, just when byzantine discussions about the meaning of *woman* are the order of the day for men to tell us, once again, who we are, in search of loopholes that will allow *trans women* to get into the category women and thus speak on *our* behalf. It is not uncommon to see men claiming to be women who think they have that right, and, unfortunately, it is not uncommon to see women ceding their place to them.

In an emblematic episode, the *Revista de la Universidad de México* released its special issue 'Feminisms' in November 2019, and they could think of no one better to present it at the Guadalajara International Book Fair than the trans-identified male comedian and influencer Ophelia Pastrana. In front of an almost all-female audience, he had no qualms about defiantly blurting out: "Who here is a woman? Raise your hand. I'd like to ask them a question I get asked all the time: how do you know?" (Cultura UNAM, 2019). To pose obvious questions as if they were profound metaphysical enquiries is also a good example of the sophistry that characterizes the doctrine of gender identity. How do you know you are a woman? Why is there something rather than nothing?

Inviting men to speak on behalf of women has become commonplace. Most recently, actor Dylan Mulvaney, who in his TikTok videos vividly presents to his nearly eight million followers the childish caricature of what he believes it means to be a woman, was invited by the business magazine *Forbes* to participate in a conversation on 15 September 2022 at the tenth Annual *Forbes* Power Women's Summit in New York (see *Reduxx*, 2022).

Uwujaren speaks of *cis feminists*. When someone defines women who are not men as cis or cisgender (which in transgender parlance means that your gender identity is in sync with the sex you were assigned at birth), they are trying to tell us who we are. This Nigerian-American, along with battalions of transactivists, insists on describing us this way even though it is an insulting label and, as Rebecca Reilly-Cooper says, "I feel [it] does not accurately describe me, nor many other women I know" (Reilly-Cooper, 2015). Double standards run rampant in the transgenderist model.

2b: Anyone who does not fall into the category of trans woman should refrain from speaking, conversing or theorizing about trans women

The statement "Trans women are women" speaks of both *trans women* and women; however, for transgenderism only men who identify as women have the right to comment on it or determine its truth value. Women do not.

At this moment in the history of feminism it is of the essence to talk and theorize, yes, about *trans women* and their invasion of women-only spaces and of our political movement, but also about the misogynistic doctrine that, under the false pretext of promoting transgender rights, is being imposed on a large part of the globe and in all spheres. How can they expect us to remain silent and stand idly by when women's sex-based rights, which were not graciously granted to us, but are the result of the struggle of several generations of feminists, are hanging in the balance?

2c: If trans women are murdered it is partly the fault of those who are not fully convinced of the statement "Trans women are women"

Emotional blackmail, in all its possible versions, is very characteristic of transactivism, both in social media and in political forums, books, interviews, media in general. Above all, it is extremely effective. A great many women keep their opinions on these issues to themselves, and even doubt their own minds, for fear of sinning in word or thought. Accusing us of provoking murders or suicides because we don't subscribe to transgenderism, or because we believe that being a woman and being a male who for whatever reason claims to be a woman are different experiences, is its most blatant form. As Faye acknowledges, "trans sex workers around the world are often at most risk by the very same men to whom they sell their services" (Faye, 2021, p. 144). What a sad irony that it is precisely gender abolitionist feminists, who are almost all also abolitionists of prostitution and seek to end such violence, who are blamed.[27]

3a: A trans ally has an obligation to listen to and believe what trans women say about themselves

Unless someone has fallen into the traps of transgenderist language, it is clear that this first commandment translates as follows: "A woman has an obligation to listen to and believe what men say about themselves." In other words, a woman who wants to be a trans ally (a usual way of gaining male approval) has to think the same as men who call themselves trans, and adopt their point of view.

One of the ways violent husbands exert dominance over their wives is to control what they think. There is a strong resemblance between the two situations. In her powerful and insightful book *Loving to Survive*, American psychologist and radical feminist Dee Graham proposes the thesis that women, in places where male violence in all its varieties is pervasive, have found survival strategies very similar to those of some hostages toward their captors, as if women as a whole suffered from a kind of societal Stockholm syndrome in relation to men as a whole: "Like hostages who bond to their captors, women bond to men in an effort to survive" (Graham, 1994, p. xiv). Part of this dynamic is precisely that we see the world from their point of view:

> Because women's survival depends on knowing how things affect men's moods, we come to experience the world from men's perspectives. Eventually, we are no longer aware of our own feelings, thoughts, and moods: we are only aware of theirs (Graham, 1994, p. 165).

---

27   It is no coincidence that Janice Raymond and Sheila Jeffreys, two of the authors most cited in this work as the theorists who have most clearly seen the threat to women posed by transgender ideology, have not only written books denouncing the violence of prostitution (*Not a Choice, Not a Job: Exposing the Myths about Prostitution and the Global Sex Trade*, and *The Idea of Prostitution* and *The Industrial Vagina: The Political Economy of the Global Sex Trade*, respectively), but both have been very active and longstanding participants in international campaigns for the abolition of prostitution.

When a man, even if he presents himself as a non-binary or trans feminist, demands that we listen only to him and his kind because he wants to force his own perspective of the world on us, he is acting like a typical abuser.

3b: A trans ally should not listen to cis feminists

Another way in which violent men exert their domination over women they consider their property (their wives, their girlfriends, their allies) … is to isolate them from the world: to force them to cut family and friendship ties, to *forbid* them to see their friends, to prevent them from having a life of their own outside the castle of purity in which they want to lock them up. They monitor their thinking, their relationships and their actions. A wife who has little contact with the outside world reduces her chances of access to worldviews other than those of her husband. Forbidding women to listen to feminists is a way of tying them to this master-slave relationship. Like controlling husbands, gender identity activists, determined to make women listen to them and nobody else, respond with violence, threats and blackmail when a woman does not obey. It should come as no surprise that part of their *modus operandi* is also to suffocate feminism – to put an end to this emancipatory movement and deny women their freedom of thought, freedom of speech and freedom of assembly is an infallible way of isolating them from any perspective other than the male one. "Women's physical and ideological isolation means that we have few reminders of our own perspectives or even of the fact that there might be such a thing" (Graham, 1994, p. 166).

3c: A trans ally must actively support trans women and help them meet their needs

This mandate has a high compliance rate. Political parties, supreme courts, human rights commissions, anti-discrimination councils, embassies, city halls, universities, midwives associations, women's ministries, organizations with *women* or *feminist* in their names, LGBTIQ+ groups, Facebook mothers' groups, media, police departments, professional associations, theatres and cinemas, sports clubs, department stores, large corporations, small and medium-sized businesses go out of their way to show the world that they are the greatest trans allies and that they help people who come under the trans umbrella to meet all their needs. Indeed, all their desires.

In Mexico City, long pastel pink and blue flags have hung down from the façade of the Antiguo Palacio del Ayuntamiento and the Teatro de la Ciudad. The President of the Supreme Court of Justice of the Nation pronounces the words "We have to respect the rights of *todos, todas* and *todes;*[28] we have to recognize their identity" (Mederes, 2022). A television station that for many years made it a condition for gay and lesbian actors not to come out, today informs the public that

> a transgender woman is a woman who was identified as a man at birth, but who has transitioned, that is, who has undergone certain changes to adapt to the female form in which she feels inside (Noticieros Televisa, 2021).

Clothing stores, university faculties and spas decide that in order to send the message that everyone's identity is recognized there, it is necessary that the dressing rooms, bathrooms and saunas be *for all genders,* that is to say, unisex. There is no shortage of ways to virtue signal one's wokeness and inclusiveness. Long live all diversities, except that of thought and belief.

In laws all over the world, the vague and ethereal concept of gender identity, invented by people who needed an explanation for the fact, apparently unusual to them, that *feminine* men and *masculine* women exist, is replacing the material concept of sex, and with the disappearance of sex, women's specific rights disappear as well. This introduction into laws and official documents of an intangible esoteric idea reminiscent of phlogiston, that hypothetical substance with which the ancient alchemists tried in vain to explain combustion, is the institutional way of satisfying the political needs of transgenderism. The capture is almost total.

---

28   *Of everybody* in inclusive language.

Individuals also comply with the third commandment, especially so-called liberal feminists. They too have embraced the transgender agenda and from their podiums or desks they religiously play their role as trans allies, even if in the process they throw women and girls under the bus. When they occupy positions of power, they never miss a chance to demonstrate the extent to which they have adopted the male perspective. The trans ally par excellence is Irene Montero, since January 2020 head of the Spanish government's Ministry of Equality, whose main mission has been to push through, whatever the cost, self-ID laws and other measures dictated by international transgenderism, which multiple feminist voices have seen as a serious offensive against women's rights (see Confluencia Movimiento Feminista, 2021a). "Trans Law will be law" is her slogan.

3d: A trans ally must condemn anyone who talks about trans women without themselves being trans

Every time a woman blacklists another woman, accuses her of hate speech for exposing the dangers and lies of transgenderism, or calls her a TERF, she is doing the dirty work of the thought police and acting as an informer. She will say in her defence that TERF *(trans exclusionary radical feminist)* is nothing more than a neutral description, when in fact it is a misogynistic slur with even more negative baggage than *witch* or *feminazi*. As Canadian feminist Meghan Murphy puts it:

> The term, TERF, is itself a deliberate manipulation, intended to reframe feminist ideas and activism as 'exclusionary', rather than foundational to the women's liberation movement. In other words, it is an attack on women-centred political organizing and the basic theory that underpins the feminist analysis of patriarchy (Murphy, 2017).

Moreover, the insult is often accompanied by calls for violence, as in phrases such as "I punch TERFs," "TERFs can eat my (female) dick" or "Die in a grease fire, TERF," which can be seen in memes, tweets, graffiti or on T-shirts. In the following dialogue between two gay gamers on Twitter, the word is the trigger for a very serious threat:

> Joe Glass: Ugh, just learned there's a TERF conference coming to Cardiff this month [face vomiting emoji].
>
> Huwpazombie: What the absolute fuck? Is it in a building that would be a loss if it got burned down?
>
> Joe Glass: Not sure yet. It's not been confirmed which hotel is hosting it.[29]

They were alluding to the FiLiA Women's Rights Conference, scheduled for late October 2022 in the Welsh capital, the main annual gathering of the European feminist movement. Someone will say that these tweeters were just joking, but what would happen if you put *indigenous people, black people, deaf people, immigrants, Jews, Muslims, retired people, gays* or *trans women* in that dialogue instead of TERF? Would it be acceptable? Would they get away with it? It's unlikely. Apparently horrible things can be said about *TERFs* which nobody would say about groups of marginalized people. It is very clear that this slur serves to deny the women so described their humanity and to make violence against them seem justifiable or at least a laughing matter. People usually think twice before expressing their hatred for a group of people so openly and in full view of the world, but so-called TERFs seem to be the exception. This smear has led many men to openly flaunt their contempt for women and their desire to kill them – and to be applauded by some women.[30]

None of this matters to the ally. *Misgendering* is, in her eyes, an unforgivable crime, but these genuine incitements to violence she can overlook. An obedient collaborator, she believes that by pointing the finger at others and calling for their heads, she saves herself. Demonizing radical feminists is the first step in justifying

---

29 The authors of these tweets deleted them after criticism but the screenshot survives; it can be seen at @TheAttagirls (2022).

30 This misogynistic and dehumanizing use is extensively documented on the website terfisaslur.com.

violence against them. This is achieved by calling them TERFs and by putting a scarlet letter, T, on their chests.

TERF is not a description: it's a stigma. In this age, characterized by the obsession with likes in social media and popularity, no one wants to be perceived as an *exclusionary transphobe*. One has to be on the right side, and the best way to show one's philias is to condemn the supposed phobias of those other people and not wanting anything to do with them.

3e: A trans ally should sympathize with trans people

As noted above, those who haven't gone deep into these issues imagine that people who are considered trans have the impression of living in the wrong body and that this is the source of great suffering. The familiar complaint of being "denied their identity" can also catch someone unawares and make them believe that this must feel awful. It is good to sympathize with those who suffer, but a little scepticism is not contrary to empathy. It is one thing to put yourself in other people's shoes and another to be taken for a ride by them.

Much of what comes out of the mouth or keyboard of a gender identity activist, whether it is Irene Montero or an anonymous troll on Twitter, is false, misleading and grossly manipulative. And they are not harmless lies: to begin with, they can have very serious consequences on people's health; thousands of children have taken the path of puberty blockers, hormones and surgery because of them. Their falsehoods harm the rights of women and girls and yet they have been enshrined in law; they have been embraced by major local, national and international institutions and agencies; they are part of the basic education curriculum in several countries; they are dogma of faith on university campuses and revealed truth in newsrooms … Overcoming the multiple harms of this collective deception will be a long and costly job. It is already late, but the longer we let it go on, the more damage will have accumulated and the more regrettable and long-lasting the consequences will be.

Uwujaren tells the trans allies that they cannot be empathetic if they defend "Adichie's belief that trans women aren't really women" because that is why they are being killed. With lies and emotional blackmail he tries to force them to believe, but does he succeed in making them harbour that belief? Or, rather, is he in fact making them suppress, out of guilt, their critical thinking and denying what is before their eyes? The truth is that we can sympathize with people who call themselves trans without necessarily sharing – or endorsing – their dogmatic worldview. Compassion and solidarity are compatible with diversity of thought.

In principle, nothing should prevent empathy from extending to other groups, but do we, for example, have the same compassion for the millions of women who, because they are uncomfortable in, and displeased, with their bodies due to beauty mandates, spend money and risk their health to make themselves more pleasing to the male gaze? They in many ways resemble the conventional thinking about *trans* people, and the metaphor of the wrong body is just as valid and timely in their case, but outside of their loved ones, not many people shed tears for them, even though some die in the process through medical malpractice.

And they are not few in number. In July 2022 alone, two women in Tijuana died after undergoing surgery by "impostors of the specialty" of plastic and reconstructive surgery, who weren't properly trained nor authorized (see EFE and Telemundo, 2022). In January 2022, a healthy woman from Murcia who entered the operating room for liposculpture came out "with around 30 perforations of between 0.5 and 2 centimetres in organs such as the kidneys, colon, intestine or liver" (García, 2022). In Colombia, 21 women died between January and December 2016 from a cosmetic procedure (see Portella, 2022), while, in the same country, between 1 October 2015 and 30 September 2016, 14 *trans* and *gender-diverse* people were murdered (see Transrespect versus Transphobia, 2016). The purpose of presenting these figures is not to engage in Oppression Olympics, but to anticipate the claim that Uwujaren, when he writes about shedding tears, is thinking of murdered *trans women*. Fair enough. It is also worth asking how many women, out of rejection of their bodies, put themselves in the hands of charlatans and end up losing their lives. Of course, in both cases the victims are too many.

But no one believes that women who seek breast augmentation or reduction, gluteoplasty or *intimate surgery* – the "improvement of the appearance and function of the female genitalia, repairing a congenital malformation or beautifying the area" (see Clínica Saint Paul, 2021) – were born in the *wrong body*. It is assumed that when they go to reduce their waistline and enlarge their breasts and hips, they do so in full exercise of their freedom and are therefore not worthy of compassion. Have we delved into the motivations of the woman who goes to the surgeon to have an hourglass figure made? This account by Rafaela Martínez Terrazas, a medical surgeon with a clinic in the city of Culiacán, in northwestern Mexico, gives us an idea:

> Many times they come with a boyfriend who pays for the surgery. And I have several gentlemen who call me and say: 'Hey, doctor, I'm going to send a girl for you to operate her'. One man called me and said, 'So-and-so is coming to you. Please fix her for me. You know how I like them. Don't do as she likes, it is me who paid you' (Pressly, 2021).

Also very illuminating are the words of this man who moves in the drug trafficking circuits and has paid for the surgery of two women:

> Men compete with each other for women. Your wife is someone who will be at home taking care of your children. The other women you have are more like trophies. It's mostly wishing to have a woman who has undergone plastic surgery: the morbid desire to see bigger buttocks, larger breasts. Maybe a friend says to you: 'Hey, my friend wants to have her breasts, buttocks or nose done. She's looking for a sponsor'. And if the man is attracted to her, yes, he sponsors her (Pressly, 2021).

These beauty practices involving the use of a scalpel are, in the words of Sheila Jeffreys, "a severe form of mutilation of women's bodies. However, it is a practice that fits the rules of beauty as required under male dominance, and is thus not regarded with horror" (Jeffreys, 2005, p. 149). This explains why there is more pity for a man who makes the drastic decision to change his body shape because he *was born that way* or has a special gender identity, than for a woman who does the same because, in her mind, she is worthless without a man by her side and only by being beautiful will she be loved and respected.

Janice Raymond makes a direct comparison between men who *transition* in order to look feminine and women who resort to surgery to better conform to the femininity expected of them (see Raymond, 1994, pp. xiv–xv). Although in the first case it is usually expressed as "a search for one's true identity" and in the second as "wanting to look prettier," the material act is the same. It is possible that this double standard reveals that, deep down, even the trans ally who describes herself as feminist knows that *trans women* are men and that she still has a deeply internalized idea that men are superior and more worthy of our attention and commiseration.

Young women who have *detransitioned* and recount how the lies of transgenderism hurt their bodily integrity and mental health are another group who deserve our solidarity. They are not so different from all other women, victims of the same idea that femaleness "is pathology enough to physicians," as lesbian feminist detransitioner Max Robinson observes (2021, p. 47). Not only do they apparently not deserve our sympathy – they are even blamed and shamed for what they submitted to:

> It is coercive to deliberately activate shame in a woman who has been made vulnerable through an incredibly misogynistic society in order to convince her that removing healthy tissue will solve her emotional problems, whether it's two pounds from her thighs or the flesh of both breasts (Robinson, 2021, p. 52).

However, detransitioners, like radical feminists or gender-critical people, are often targeted by transactivists, because their life stories contradict the trans discourse head-on. Does empathy for them have to stop, just as support from what they considered their community stops, the moment they stop believing they are trans?

In Chapters 5 and 6, I will write more on detransitioners, as well as on women prisoners who have to live with violent offenders who identify as women, sportswomen who lose opportunities because of males entering the female category, so-called trans widows, and other direct victims of the gender identity doctrine, for whom feminists' empathy is perhaps a little more justified than for the men who have harmed them.

3f: A trans ally must believe that a trans woman is literally a woman

The 'woman trapped in a man's body' narrative was given a very bold twist by stipulating that a male body can be a female body despite appearances and all evidence to the contrary. They say it with much conviction: "There are girls with a penis and boys with a vagina" (or, as seen on stickers and graffiti, "There are girls with dicks, guys with vaginas and transphobes without teeth"). The woman no longer dwells just inside in the form of femininity or the feeling or desire to be a woman: she is now also outside, in plain sight, as she has always been. Don't let the penis and testicles cloud your vision; remember that, as the Little Prince says, what is essential is invisible to the eye. If a person with male genitalia claims to be a woman, *she is a woman* and her genitalia are *female*, because, repeat after me, trans women are women, trans women are women, trans women are women.

Not content with imposing on his would-be allies the obligation to believe that trans women are women, the Nigerian-American *non-binary trans person* who berated Chimamanda Ngozi Adichie warns them that they must believe that they are literally women. No nuance here.

The ally who says, "To me, trans women are women in a very important sense," "Trans women also belong in feminism because we should consider them women," "Trans women are women because they transitioned to be women," "Trans women are women even if they were born men," "Trans women are women because they also suffer male violence," "Trans women should be treated as women for all purposes" fails the test, because, unbeknownst to her, her words still give away what she thinks. Her true beliefs come to the surface, and they are the wrong beliefs. Her duty as an ally is to believe with total conviction that trans women are women, not *in one sense,* but in every possible sense of the word *woman.* This person doesn't have a vulva? Oh yes, she does! This person doesn't know what it's like to suffer from menstrual cramps? Oh yes, indeed she does! This person hasn't experienced growing up and living as a woman in a patriarchal culture? Of course she has, because she is a woman, full stop! Any aspiring trans ally who dares to ask for evidence of these assertions is doomed to fail.

As Raymond says, when they claim to be women in every sense of the word, they want us to suspend our disbelief, not as we would gladly do during the two hours of a film or a play, but permanently and as if it were a moral imperative (see Raymond, 1994, p. xxiii). Because in the end what is being sought is not rights for a marginalized group in society. If that were the case, the right to be free from discrimination on the basis of what is called gender expression, i.e. appearance, mannerisms and dress, would be more than enough, and in the countries where self-ID laws are now being promoted, this right is already in place and warranted. But no – the real aim is to kill everyone else's freedom of speech and thought. Transactivists want to control our mental states and they don't even try to conceal it it.

It is now commonplace to cite *1984,* but for anyone who has read George Orwell's dystopia, it is impossible to overlook the profound similarities with the transformations we are witnessing in the first decades of the twenty-first century:

> Don't you see that the whole aim of Newspeak is to narrow the range of thought? In the end we shall make thought-crime literally impossible, because there will be no words in which to express it. Every concept that can ever be needed will be expressed by exactly *one* word, with its meaning rigidly defined and all its subsidiary meanings rubbed out and forgotten. [...] Every year fewer and fewer words, and the range of consciousness always a little smaller. Even now, of course, there's no reason or excuse for committing thought-crime. It's merely a question

of self-discipline, reality control. But in the end there won't be any need even for that (Orwell, 1961, p. 52).

There is an important group of people who, although they consider themselves transsexual, do not agree with this identitarian doctrine and do not believe themselves to be of the opposite sex – they know very well that they are women with a masculine presentation or men with a feminine presentation. The *trans women* who say that trans women are *not* women are among them. Many of them are from a generation that did not grow up with the idea that sex is not a material reality but a state of mind, at a time when the medical-sexological model and the transgenderist model ran side by side. US journalist Michelle Goldberg calls them "the apostates of the trans rights movement" (Goldberg, 2015).

Their criticisms of transgender politics sometimes coincide with those of radical feminism, and they realize that gender self-ID carries with it dangers for women; other times their criticisms stem from personal experience. Helen Highwater, for example, asserts that the rallying cry "Trans women are women" condemns *trans women* to failure:

> It's a lie that sets us up to be triggered every time we are called 'he', or 'guys' or somebody dares to suggest that we have male biology. Even a cursory glance from a stranger can cut to our very core. The very foundations of our self-worth are fragile (Goldberg, 2015).

After radical feminists, gender-critical people and detransitioners, these apostates are the thought-criminals that transactivists harass the most, to the point of silencing them or breaking them down. The movement that claims to defend trans rights does not allow its own people anything but total and absolute conformity either. They regard them as traitors to the cause and treat them particularly mercilessly.

One of them is Canadian Jenn Smith, a History and Political Science graduate. He was nine years old when he started wearing women's clothes in the 1970s. Now as an adult, he thinks those urges had something to do with the rejection and violence he suffered as a foster child. He, like many people regardless of their political affiliations, is concerned about the transgendering and medicalizing of children who do not conform to sexist stereotypes, which he sees as a serious infringement of their rights. He has genuine empathy for children like the one he was and is determined to protect them.

But transgenderist spokespersons on social media, mainstream media and universities falsely paint him as a conservative with "dangerously transphobic ideas" who spreads hate speech and attacks *queer* and *trans* children (see Lloyd, 2020). On 23 June 2019, Smith gave a talk at the University of British Columbia. Days before, dozens of people had demonstrated to demand the cancellation of the event. "Jenn Smith's views are so repellent and so outside of the norms of acceptable discourse on trans issues," said Mary Ann Saunders, a researcher at UBC who considers himself a trans woman and who was deeply troubled that Smith would be speaking out loud such unacceptable ideas in a campus classroom (Vikander, 2019).

Nevertheless, the university decided to go ahead, not without charging the organizers extra security fees and not without making psychological support services available to students who might be put at risk by Smith's words or by his mere presence a few hundred metres away (see AMS of UBC, 2019). On the day of the lecture, three protesters showed up and attempted to boycott it, without success (see Justice Centre for Constitutional Freedoms, 2019).

With presentations suspended at at least six universities, Smith claims to be one of the most censored speakers in Canada. In an article in which he draws comparisons between the methods of transactivism and those of the Synanon Church, in particular the dubious therapeutic technique known as 'The Game', he recounts this personal experience with the pink and blue flag community:

> When I, as a transgender person opposed to child indoctrination and the destruction of women's safe spaces and programs, began speaking out, I was immediately attacked quite viciously by numerous transactivists, who engaged either knowingly or unknowingly in a textbook example of 'The Game'. They hurled non-stop insults at me, insulted every aspect of my appearance and identity. They said I was

fake, pathetic, a dirty old man, and pounded me relentlessly with one personal insult after another – classic gaming. When it became clear to them they had finally upset me emotionally and that I did not appear to be resisting anymore, they then suddenly changed tone and assured me that if I just came to a realization that I was wrong and they were right, that I too could be a real, beautiful, genuine trans and we could all triumph against trans oppression together. This latter stage of rebuilding is standard in Synanon-styled behavior modifying cults. It was when they began rebuilding me after tearing me down, that I realized that I was in fact being 'gamed' by these people. When my tone changed, the insults came at me fast and furious again (Smith, 2017).

Scenes like this and others out of *Lord of the Flies* usually take place not on a desert island, but on social media, sometimes before the eyes of bystanders who watch the cruel spectacle undaunted, and sometimes in private chat rooms, such as Q Chat Space. The habitat of everyday gender identity activism is not the Mount Carmel Center but digital platforms: Tumblr, TikTok, Twitter … This is where they connect and organize to spread their cultist ideology, find followers, push their demands and especially to silence, intimidate, psychologically destroy and get anyone who dares to dissent sacked at work.

A troubled relationship with truth

In September 2022, a small scandal unfolded in Mexico City that is a fully fledged portrait of transactivism and its institutional penetration. With slogans such as "Hate speech is not free speech," "Our lives are not up for debate," "No TERF on air," and "We are the trans resistance and here we are," a group of people demanded the dismissal of Renata Turrent, host of a political talk show broadcast on a public television channel, Capital 21 (see Aquino, 2022). Her fault was that she had two guests that transactivists consider undesirable: Mauricio Dimeo, who champions what he calls a gender-critical masculinity, and Itzel Suárez, who also takes a stance against sexist stereotypes.

A few weeks earlier, Dimeo was going to take part in a round-table discussion on the subject of *masculinities*, organised by Suárez, as part of the Feria Internacional del Libro de las Universitarias y los Universitarios book fair, but it was cancelled at the last minute because cyber-transactivists mobilized to demand that Universidad Nacional Autónoma de México (UNAM) exercise this act of censorship. Why our highest house of studies obeyed the orders of some anonymous people and accepted their version of the events without further investigation is a mystery. Turrent chose these two guests precisely to talk about so-called cancel culture, to challenge the fact that it is not possible to criticize the idea that gender is an identity and to give Dimeo the opportunity to present his feminist-inspired proposal so that men in general stop seeing women as sexual objects for male consumption.

But lo and behold, the same two or three people who had been at the forefront of the protest that culminated in the suspension of the round table on masculinities at UNAM called for Turrent's head (and also, curiously, that of Mercurio Cadena, a guest they were mistaking for a host) and for the officials responsible for the broadcast to be sanctioned.

Their protest statement (Red de Resistencia y Disidencia Sexual y de Género, 2022) contains lies and fallacies such as those analyzed in detail in Uwujaren's rebuke of Adichie. There are false and hyperbolic accusations (Dimeo "is a leader" of the LGB Alliance, an "extremist group" that "has connections to American right-wing homophobic groups and even supports conversion therapy for all LGBT+ populations"),[31] unsubstantiated insinuations ("Hate speech

---

31 The Mexican chapter of the international organization LGB Alliance (founded in 2019 to promote the rights of lesbians, gays and bisexuals) denied from the start that Mauricio Dimeo was part of it, a claim that *Animal Político* had reproduced, accompanied by defamations (and on the alliance's website you can read its responses to different rumours spread by transactivists: lgballiance.org.uk/facts). Far from apologizing or rectifying, this news outlet repeated the falsehood in another article a week later. It is worth mentioning that for its various publications on the case, it has had as its only source the alleged network, whose leader is Eme Flores, a famous bully who presents himself as non-binary.

towards trans people is not innocuous, it is not harmless, and for many the risk goes far beyond an intellectual debate"), appeals to pity ("From what we have experienced firsthand, we sense that most of the trans community lives in fear"), blatant lies ("The media does not regard trans people as valuable human beings worthy of being heard") and outright tantrums (Turrent "let out a derisive laugh at the mention of feminist academic Judith Butler"). But the crux of the matter lies in these loaded words: "Trans women belong in women's struggles and feminisms." Put bluntly, feminism is for men.

To appreciate the troubled relationship between transactivism and truth, it is illuminating to contrast what the unitary group called the Network of Sex and Gender Resistance and Dissidence claims Dimeo said with what Dimeo actually said. When asked for a final brief comment, the panellist stated:

> This proposal of gender-critical masculinity is also for the benefit of men themselves. The ability to manage our emotions, the ability to integrate ourselves into domestic work in order to be self-sufficient adults, implies a full development of our humanity as men and not as mere sexual predators (Capital 21, 2022).

But read what that *network* alleges: "At the end of the show, Mauricio suggested that trans women and other transfeminities are sexual predators." This talent for distorting words and twisting facts is the hallmark of transactivism.

At the time this chapter is being written, Mexico City's Council to Prevent and Eliminate Discrimination is investigating these allegations, the influential news outlet *Animal Político* continues to limit itself to reporting the transactivist version, and the 16 or 17 people who protested on 28 September in front of Capital 21 threaten to return every Wednesday to demonstrate as long as "Cadena and Turrent continue to host the channel" and to keep open "the corresponding administrative processes so that those who made use of public funds to disseminate discriminatory speech are punished" (Aquino, 2022).

They lie, we know. What is alarming is that people and institutions from whom one would expect a little more insight believe them and are frightened by their actions, threats and tantrums. Almost by reflex, the most important university in Latin America cancels an activity at a fair dedicated to books and reading, and *Animal Político* adopts a biased and uninformed version of easily verifiable facts, while several other media outlets reproduce the same partial information, all taking for granted the serious accusations without taking the trouble to confirm the basic data ... These are not small things. I share Amelia Valcárcel's curiosity about this phenomenon, which plays so much in favour of the transgenderist cause: "The problem that has come to almost obsess me is not that some heads produce damaged goods. No. The problem is why others buy them" (Valcárcel, 2019, p. 250).

I have a hypothesis. Statements like the one from the above-mentioned *network* almost always follow the same template. Their greatest effectiveness lies in the fact that they hurl, as if shot with a machine-gun, fiery accusations, and it's all very overwhelming for the brain. The people who write these accusations have plenty of time, but those who receive them at their desks have backlogs and various other worries. Just unravelling the meaning of their long and convoluted pages can take a couple of hours, plus the time it takes to work out how true or worthy of consideration their claims are. For those who work from dawn to dusk, it is difficult to always follow Spanish politician Carmen Alborch's sound maxim: "Even if an expression sounds good, we must always be sure what it means and what it contains" (quoted in Valcárcel, 2019, p. 249). Surely, several of the dazed recipients of these arcane memos read them diagonally, panic, and comply with the transactivists' demands before the matter escalates. It is easier and quicker to pick out a scapegoat than to stop and take the time to understand what is going on. The institutional capture we are undergoing is greatly aided by something as mundane as the laziness and mental confusion that reading such complaints and suggestions can produce in anyone. Muddle and conquer.

I also have a very simple proposal: let's start ignoring them and stop acting as if these complainers were the ultimate authority. It is possible to brush aside the anonymous cyberbullies and we can (still) stand up to the authorities when they act undemocratically. There are universities with even more transgender presence than UNAM where there are nevertheless healthy outbreaks of anti-establishment rebellion. At Cambridge, for example.

Athena SWAN is a programme that was set up in the UK to encourage women who wanted to study mathematics, engineering or for some other scientific degree at a higher education institution. Like anything that sounds vaguely feminist and has the word *gender* sprinkled into its mission statement, it was at some point expanded to include male students and faculty who say they are trans. One of its purposes was "tackling the discriminatory treatment often experienced by trans people." The clause was slipped in and no one complained. But in 2021, the wording in their gender equality charter was changed slightly. Now the idea was "fostering collective understanding that individuals have the right to determine their own gender identity, and tackling the specific issues faced by trans and non-binary people because of their identity." Sounds about right, but if we stop to think, as Alborch suggests, about what the nice phrase means and what it contains, we will notice that the change is not minor.

A group of academics at Cambridge University did stop to think. Unlike several universities that were ready to sign up and endorse the new wording, this one put the brakes on because faculty members realized that forcing them to uphold unquestioningly that people "have the right to determine their own gender identity" was tantamount to introducing thought-control and enforcing gender identity ideology. Arif Ahmed, Professor of Philosophy, voiced his objections:

> A university should absolutely not be 'fostering collective under-standing' on controversial issues but encouraging open debate. [...] Academic freedom is our fundamental value. What kind of university

tramples on free speech for the sake of corporate virtue signaling? (Ellery, 2022).

Thanks to the academics who spoke out, Advance HE, the organization that manages Athena SWAN, will be forced to review the proposed changes.

Let's hope that UNAM officials stop and think the next time a mob demands that they go against academic freedom and that Capital 21 channel sets an example and does not give in to blackmail. Let its actions speak and show us that it values, above virtue signalling, freedom of expression and the rights of audiences, such as the right to "receive content that reflects the ideological, political, social, cultural and linguistic pluralism of the nation," the right to "receive programming that includes different genres that respond to the expression of diversity and plurality of ideas and opinions that strengthen the democratic life of society," or the right to "receive programming that respects human rights, the best interests of the child, gender equality and non-discrimination" (AMDA, n.d.). By the time this book is published, it will surely be known whether the channel stood up to censorship attempts or allowed itself to be extorted.[32]

In the next section, we will see what the supposedly discriminatory, transphobic and hateful discourses consist of and what are the "reactionary and anti-rights positions" held by radical feminists and gender-critical people, on whom much of the toxicity of this debate falls and who are the most hated, harassed and targeted by transgenderism, cancelled by universities, made redundant by corporations and ignored by the mainstream media. In view of the deliberate distortions of those who have granted themselves the exclusive right to talk about all things transgender, it is good practice to reach out to them and get to know in their own words what they think and why they are so concerned that the transgenderist

---

32   Now we know: unfortunately, Capital 21 apologized publicly for the "transphobic discourses" and regretted "the declarations of one guest, who denies the existence of trans and non-binary gender identities" (*El Financiero*, 2022b).

model in its twenty-first century version is being adopted almost universally and is serving to undo, one by one, all of the policies created to protect the rights of women and girls.

3. The radical feminist model

The radical feminist model (and let us note that *radical* in this case means going to the root of the issues and not 'extremist') could be called simply feminist if it were not for the fact that a large group of women who describe themselves as feminists prefer to adhere to the transgenderist model. This name is also meant to do justice to the radical feminists who, in the 1970s, were the first to realize that a transgender politics was incompatible with feminism. Among them were Janice Raymond and Sheila Jeffreys, visionaries who very early on saw the big picture and decades ago warned us of what was coming. It was incipient at the time, but it eventually exploded and we are now suffering the consequences and its scope to a degree that even they could not have predicted.

For the purposes of this book, as a definition of *radical feminists*, this one from another pioneer, Robin Morgan, American poet, novelist and journalist, leader of the wave of the feminist movement that began to rise up in the United States in the late 1960s, will suffice. She is someone who, by the way, also saw it coming:

> What radical feminists have in common [...] includes a stubborn commitment to the people of women, the courage to dare question anything and dare redefine everything, a dedication to making the connections between issues, a sobering comprehension of the enormity of this task [...] and perhaps most importantly of all, *radical feminists share an audacious understanding of this politics' centrality to the continuation of sentient life itself on this planet.*
>
> This is no hyperbole. Women constitute the majority of the human species, so the female condition is hardly a marginal or minority issue. Furthermore, all the ills that afflict humankind – from pollution to war to poverty – impact first and worst on women, who are also the last to be consulted about solutions to these problems (Morgan, 1996, p. 7).

Neither in 1996 nor in 1973, when a man tried to crash a lesbian feminist conference in which Morgan was to give the keynote address, was there any need to specify that what all the members of the people of women have in common is their sex. It is obvious that when Morgan speaks of them and the commitment that unites radical feminists, she is thinking precisely of human females.

For radical feminism, the category of *sex* is central because it is where women's specific oppression derives from; sex, not femininity, is the distinctive character that makes half of the human race a group with a specific history and set of experiences. It is their sex that makes them the main victims of rape and sex trafficking. This is best expressed by Dominican activist and researcher Raquel Rosario Sánchez when she asks:

> How do men know who to harass in the street? How do families know who to give all the burden of care to? How do museums know which artists should be hegemonic and which artists to under-represent? (Sánchez, 2018).

Similarly, how did the Islamic fundamentalist group Boko Haram know who to abduct on 14 April 2014 from a school in the city of Chibok in northeastern Nigeria?

> There were 276 people kidnapped. Who and what were these 276 people? […] Do you think the guerrillas were asking each of the 276 kidnapped girls and adolescents if they wanted to be treated like women? Let's be clear: they were kidnapped to be raped repeatedly and to give birth to babies for their kidnappers. Accessing their female bodies was a fundamental part of the terrorist act, as it is in any armed conflict in which the biological sex of women and girls is used as a weapon of war against themselves (Rosario, 2018).

It is important to point out that one does not need to be a radical feminist to share this position or some of its principles. In fact, as has already been seen and will be confirmed in the following pages, there are people who, despite considering themselves transgender, have some ideas closer to the radical feminist model than to the transgenderist model, just as there are health professionals who act within the medical-sexological model without fully sharing its values. Anyone can realize the seriousness of the situations that feminists are denouncing by all the means at their disposal and join, from their own place, the struggle that seeks to confront this whole series of harms and injustices.

Agreements and disagreements

Before going fully into the radical feminist model, let me review the path from the medical-sexological model to the now predominant transgenderist model, embraced, not always with full awareness, by some of the most powerful layers of society. Fourteen crucial *moments* in this ideological journey can be identified. In the table opposite, I mark with a tick which of the three theories or models of transgenderism presented here accept or are content with the principle that emerges from the moment in question. I use the following initials:

- MS for the medical-sexological model,
- TG1 for the transgenderist model in a first phase,
- TG2 for the transgenderist model in a second phase, and
- RF for the radical feminist model.

The separation of the transgenderist model into two parts serves to indicate the ideological trends prior and post the demand for depathologization, which is when a paradigm shift occurs.

When viewed schematically, it becomes clear that the medical-sexological model and the transgenderist model almost always walk hand in hand, despite an apparent temporary break. From moment 3 to moment 8, transgenderism rides on whatever the medical-sexological model determines. At moment 9, they part ways, but only temporarily. From moment 10 to moment 13, it is the medical-sexological model that adapts to whatever the transgenderist model dictates. At moment 14, what we see is a consummated marriage between the two. The one point on which they are not together, that of depathologization, is also the only one, apart from the simple factual observations of 1 and 2, on which the transgenderist

From the medical-sexological to the transgenderist model	MS	TG1	TG2	RF
1. Certain behaviour is observed in some people, namely a deviation from what is expected of them because of their sex; feminists call these expectations *sexist roles* and *stereotypes*.	✓	✓		✓
2. People who deviate from such expected behaviour are rejected by society and suffer distress, and it is important to alleviate it.	✓	✓		✓
3. Some sexologists and psychiatrists conclude that this behaviour, whether it has biological or mental causes, is pathological and needs to be remedied, and people with this behaviour accept or even encourage this version. (This can be seen as the invention of the transsexual person.)	✓	✓		
4. Sexologists, endocrinologists, psychiatrists and plastic surgeons, motivated in part by their patients' requests, invent and experiment with various supposed remedies. Two prevail: a) helping the person to adjust to the sexist roles of the opposite sex (*living as a man* or *living as a woman*) and b) adopting a body more similar to that of the desired sex (hormonal treatment and surgery). The result of these procedures, whose efficacy is trusted without being tested, is misleadingly called sex change or gender transition; radical feminism would call it the surgical construction of the transsexual person.	✓	✓		
5. As these are not minor procedures, and in order to avoid accusations of negligence, it is necessary to establish criteria to determine who does have the alleged condition, and therefore is a candidate for treatment, and who does not.	✓	✓		
6. Even without any clarity about the causes of the alleged malady, the medical-sexological model blindly stipulates the existence of an abstract category called gender identity, just as physicians of antiquity postulated the existence of the four bodily humours.	✓	✓		
7. This makes it easier to name the behaviour considered pathological: *gender identity disorder,* later softened as *gender dysphoria,* and defined as a mismatch between biological sex and gender identity.	✓	✓		

From the medical-sexological to the transgenderist model	MS	TG1	TG2	RF
8. It is determined that, in view of social rejection, people whose gender identity conflicts with their sex need, in addition to treatment, legal recognition (such as a *sex change* certificate), to pass as people of the other sex and, as these people are usually homosexual, be able to marry. (This was before same-sex marriages were accepted.)	✓	✓		
9. In a total paradigm shift, the transgender movement determined that deviating from sexist roles is not pathological, does not need a cure and should be stopped to be called gender dysphoria to reflect that it is not a mental illness. The characterization of the trans person as someone who is "trapped in the wrong body" is also beginning to be rejected. Interestingly, this is what radical feminists have always claimed.			✓	✓
10. However, the concept of gender identity, whose existence had been stipulated in order to categorize the supposed disease that transgenderism now, in this second phase, considers non-existent, is retained.	✓		✓	
11. The transgender movement doesn't dispense with an optional access to treatment, even though it is recognized that there is no disease to be cured.	✓		✓	
12. After depathologization, since there is no disease to diagnose, it no longer makes sense to ask for diagnostic criteria. Wish and informed consent become the only requirements to allow someone access to hormone treatment and to undergo surgery.	✓		✓	
13. The transgenderist model is interested in maintaining the legal recognition of *trans* persons as the sex (or *gender*) of their choice. Since gender identity mismatch is impossible to prove objectively and is no longer considered a disease, and therefore diagnoses cannot be requested as proof, the only criterion for such recognition should be the person's own statement.	✓		✓	
14. The existence of transgender children is stipulated and their full legal recognition and access to puberty blockers, hormone treatment and operations is demanded with the only requirement of informed consent.	✓		✓	

model agrees with radical feminism. This is no coincidence. It is a fundamental point, which opened up to the transgenderist model the possibility of a divorce from the medical-sexological model, which in the end did not happen, and of an alliance with the radical feminist model, which also failed.

If transgenderism had committed patricide and discarded, along with pathologization, all that pathologization implies for people who do not act out sexist roles, the disagreement between radical feminism and transgenderism would be much less serious today. They might even be able to unite in an effective campaign to do away with sexist roles and stereotypes, which do so much harm, and work side by side in the radical task of abolishing gender. But such a union was prevented by the fact that transgenderism clung, in an at first glance incomprehensible way, to a concept created expressly to give a name and treatment to a disease that today several of its own representatives recognize as non-existent.

In order to pathologize children with supposedly atypical behavior for their sex and thus invent the utilitarian concept of transgender children, and in order to continue to have access to operations and treatment covered by health insurance or public health and legal recognition as the other sex, it was necessary to preserve the fiction of a gender identity. The transgenderist model thus stands on a theoretically unstable ground where something can be true and not be true at the same time. It is a disorder or dysphoria in order to justify medical care and to block puberty for girls and boys, but it is not a disorder or dysphoria in order to prevent anyone from asking for any kind of proof, and for the free choice of legal sex (self-ID) to be enforced.

Bob Ostertag, writing about the disagreements within the trans-gender movement, observes:

> The bitterness in the confrontation over whether transgender people are 'really sick' comes from the fact that the outcome of this debate carries a price tag, in that it heavily influences the question of whether hormones and surgeries for transgender people are covered by health insurance (Ostertag, 2016, Introduction).

The medical-sexological model has no qualms about adapting to the new transgenderist principles. If supposedly depathologizing people who consider themselves trans does not prevent them from continuing to queue in gender identity clinics for treatments, then everything is fine. As long as people want to modify their bodies, whether or not they call themselves ill is of little consequence to endocrinologists, plastic surgeons and psychologists who subscribe to the affirmative approach, which consists of validating what the clients or patients think about their own discomfort and giving them the treatment the clients or patients themselves determine, without taking into account possible risks.

Of course, there are psychologists and psychiatrists who are more committed to the health and well-being of the patient than to ideological fashion. Examples of this are the whistleblowers at the Tavistock Clinic who were concerned about what they interpreted as an eagerness to *heterosexualize* gender non-conforming children and a tendency to prescribe puberty blockers hastily and without having delved deeply enough into each individual patient's history (more on this in the section 'The great negligence' in Chapter 4). In this respect, they do not adhere to the medical-sexological model, although they sometimes embrace some of its concepts and may come to believe that, in certain extreme cases, body modifications are justified.

Janice Raymond and the critique of the medical model

Judging by what gender identity activists say about Janice Raymond, author of *The Transsexual Empire*, this radical feminist must be the main cause of people who consider themselves transgender being forced to "undergo medical procedures, including sex reassignment surgery, sterilisation or hormonal therapy," coercions condemned by the Yogyakarta Principles. No one would think that the first voice raised to deplore them was that of this feminist who some have accused of nothing less than believing that "transsexuals ought to be eradicated on moral grounds" (Synnøve Økland Jahnsen quoted in Raymond, 2021, pp. 213–214). Who would have imagined that this *transphobe* par excellence was making a harsh criticism of the technomedical empire that created the supposedly ill transsexual person, passing and the narrative of the wrong body several years before Spanish sociologist Miquel Missé, was born.

Missé, who represents what she calls a radical trans activism, says in *The Myth of the Wrong Body* that these are expectations that weigh on the trans person to authentically look like someone of the other sex:

> In the short term, passing solves many things, but in the long run it is not exactly our friend: passing will haunt us all our lives and we will always have to feed it. And what does passing eat? Bodies! (Missé, 2018, Chapter 6).

Janice Raymond, who inaugurated this critique, had written 39 years earlier, in 1979, that

> the baptism of 'passing' behavior that is conferred upon the transsexual, plus the administration of exogenous hormones, along with constant requests for corrective polysurgery, turn him into a lifelong patient (Raymond, 1979, p. 181).

If Missé wished in 2018 that "all the time spent on medical solutions to transsexuality would be devoted to fostering empowerment, visibility and bodily self-esteem" (2018, Chapter 5), Raymond had already pointed out years earlier how problematic it is to tie these people to "medical-technical solutions," as they destroy

> integrity and the potential of transsexuals to deal with their problem in an autonomous, genuinely personal, and responsibly social way. The transsexual becomes a kind of acolyte to his doctor and psychiatrist, and learns to depend upon these professionals for maintenance (Raymond, 1979, pp. 180–181).

Missé claims that the category of transsexual was born in the 1950s along with "the whole arsenal of medical treatments to treat our 'disease'" (2018, Chapter 6), just as Raymond argued at length that *transsexual* was a category created by doctors using as therapy those hormonal and surgical techniques, which were already possible in the 1930s but were refined in the 1950s.

The transsexual empire that Raymond denounces is not very different from the body thieves to whom Missé directs her justified reproaches. Despite the profound similarities in their approaches and analyses, Missé, born in 1986 in Spain, never quotes Raymond, born in 1943 in the US, and has, in all likelihood, never read her. It would not be unusual, since one of the main tasks of gender identity activists is to ensure that people do not read or listen to their detractors and instead buy the manipulated and distorted versions that they are interested in selling.

So much has been done to distort Raymond's work that this Professor Emerita of Women's Studies and Medical Ethics created a website to make the original text of *The Transsexual Empire* freely available to anyone interested in learning her position directly from the source and to debunk the myths that have been created around her position. It says there:

> Transsexual and transgendered persons are entitled to the same human and civil rights as others. Recognizing these rights, however, does not mean that we must accept that hormones and surgery transform men into women and women into men; or that persons who self-identify as members of the opposite sex are what they subjectively claim to be. [...]
>
> Any dissent from [this view] is said to come from a transphobic cast of mind that is hateful and discriminatory – not from a different viewpoint at odds with the ideology that those men who identify as trans women are actually women and those women who identify as trans men are actually men.
>
> [Trans activists have set up various websites, blogs and tweets] not only to criticize opposing viewpoints but also to distort the words and work of anyone who dissents from transgenderist orthodoxies.
>
> Unfortunately, transgender activists often resort to scurrilous and defamatory claims about their critics (<janiceraymond.com>).

We have already seen that it is easier for them to cancel their opponents by lying and deceiving than to hold a rational discussion. The aforementioned case of Capital 21 allowed us to witness how, by means of blatant lies, a group with the word *dissidence* in its name is devoted to destroying the careers and peace of mind of people who dissent from it, and how the media, failing in their social responsibility, reproduce this single view *ad infinitum.*

In her critique of the medical-sexological model, Raymond devotes several pages to making a rigorous analysis of John Money's ideas, which, as she concludes, amount to pseudometaphysics rather than science. This founding father of transsexualism ends up creating "a new theory about the social 'nature' of sex-role differences that is just as immutable as older biological natural law theories" (Raymond, 1979, p. 64).

The attachment to stereotypes, according to Raymond, is present from beginning to end in the medicalization of transsexuality by promoting the idea that dissatisfaction with social norms around *gender* can only be remedied by manufacturing a body of the opposite sex:

> What takes place is a surgical construction of body appearance that is brought in line with the body stereotype of what a masculine or feminine body should look like in a gender-defined society; e.g., in a woman, a big bust, a curvacious figure, a small frame, etc. (Raymond, 1979, pp. 3–4).

In the years when the transgenderist model and the medical-sexological model were one and the same, doctors' criteria for determining whether someone was a *true transsexual,* and therefore a candidate for hormones and surgery, was their ability to pass as someone of the other sex even before they supposedly became one:

> 'Passing' standards evaluate everything from an individual's feminine dress, to feminine body language, to so-called feminine positions in intercourse. Most clinics require candidates for surgery to live out culturally-fabricated opposite sex behavior and roles for periods of six months to two years (Raymond, 1994, p. xvii).

This was like prescribing stereotypes of womanhood (or manhood) as a preliminary to the operation, after which the transsexuals would fully embody femininity or masculinity. In Raymond's view, this reinforcement of sexist roles to achieve *acceptable* and *permissible* behavior is a method of control and, in fact, a form of social engineering (see 1979, pp. 132–133, p. 137). The medical institution and the gender identity clinic function here as the gatekeepers of sex roles and as guarantors of the established order. Bernice Hausman calls them gender managers.

Here, too, the radical feminism of the 1970s anticipated criticisms that 50 years later are still brewing within transgenderism itself. The following quote from Shon Faye, the author of *The Transgender Issue: An Argument for Justice* (2021), is a perfect example of how the transgenderist model sometimes seems to be on the verge of making a definitive break with the medical-sexological model and adopting an abolitionist stance on what some feminists still call gender. But in the end it closes off that possibility:

> The entire trans healthcare infrastructure emerged in the course of the twentieth century under the mantle of the highly patriarchal field of psychiatry. Institutionally, doctors came to understand hormone treatment and surgery as a means to police the parameters of what they deemed was or wasn't an 'acceptable' trans person – and, by logical extension, the boundaries of gender itself. When medical transition was first devised as a technology, its primary purpose was not to help the trans patient, but to control and manage gender variance in society while leaving the gender binary intact. Movement between the two sexes could be made possible by hormones and surgery, but the semblance of two mutually exclusive categories, male and female, would remain. In order to sustain this fixed binary, cis people created paternalistic, prejudiced requirements that trans patients had to meet in order to merit health care (Faye, 2021, p. 72).

Shon Faye thinks he is taking a revolutionary stance, but if anyone is leaving what he calls *binarism* intact, it is the conservative movement he champions. His commitment to queer-inspired doctrine and terminology prevents him from seeing that what is needed to achieve the more just, free and joyful world he claims to dream of is not to deny the (inevitable, morally neutral and product of millions of years of evolution) reality that there are two sexes, but to do away with the patriarchal idea that human beings are defined by a gender essence, nature or identity, which can be masculine or feminine, and which in *cis* people is consistent with sex and in *trans* people is not. He does not realize that, by maintaining that a feminine man is a woman and a masculine woman is a man, both the medical-sexological model that he believes he repudiates and the transgenderist model in which he inscribes himself are doing away with true *gender* dissidence. A real death blow to the despised *binarism* would be to stop limiting the range of interests, aptitudes, roles and temperaments which are socially acceptable only if one belongs to one sex and not the other, not to pretend that the sexes are not a biological reality but only a more or less arbitrary theoretical category.

Faye is not only committed to the transgenderist concept that reduces personhood to two major types, feminine and masculine, but also to the transgenderist practice of condemning feminist authors without having bothered to read or understand them. Despite the important substantive overlaps between his argument and Raymond's work, he describes her as "the pioneer of anti-trans radical feminism" (Faye, 2021, p. 246). Once again, we have a double standard: if a radical feminist says it, it is bigotry and transphobia, but if one of his own says it, it is a bold anti-establishment critique.

The radical feminist model offers a real way out of the constraints of what is called gender; it is also a personal liberation that is part of a collective struggle, unlike the false and individualistic solution of exchanging stereotypes so that everything stays the same. There is no place in the radical feminist model for transgendering a feminine and possibly gay boy to surgically turn him into a '*heterosexual woman*' who conforms beautifully to the sexist canon and possesses so much femininity and passing that she can even be a beauty queen. The radical feminist model, on the contrary, allows for a possibly gay boy, and possibly not, who is given the freedom to explore his tastes and interests and to shape his personality without having to limit his play because someone deems it inappropriate for his sex, and who will never come to reject his body to the point of wanting to amputate it.

Comparing her experience with that of her sister, Missé recalls:

> In our adolescence we were, by the prevailing social standards, two very masculine girls. Today my sister is a very masculine adult woman and I'm a not-so-masculine transman. In a way, we both occupy an intermediate space, a gray area. [...]. The question is: why did I have a gender transition and she didn't? (Missé, 2018, Chapter 2).

In her response she alludes to rigid ways of thinking about what it means to be a woman, and concludes that each of them found different survival strategies. She adds:

> The choices we make are based on many complex factors, conscious and unconscious, our beliefs, things we've learned, our self-esteem, our connections, our desires.
>
> Just one note: because I truly felt that I was a man, I felt the need to modify my body. She never did, and I dare say she had a much healthier relationship with her body than I did. And I think it is because when she rejected the trans narrative, she also rejected a specific subjectivity that linked her identity to the modification of her body. (She managed to thwart the attempt to steal her body whereas I was cleaned out) (Missé, 2018, Chapter 2).

In her frontal critique of the medical-sexological model and in her recognition of the place of social teachings about what it means to be a man or a woman in her own acquisition of a trans identity, Missé is much closer to the radical feminist model than to the transgenderist model. However, she gets stuck at point 10 of the table presented above, by retaining the concept that was invented to categorize a supposed illness that she, in her depathologizing stance, does not recognize as such. Her discourse doesn't need this concept at all. But by retaining the idea that we possess a gender identity, by validating essentialist pairs such as *cis* and *trans,* and by describing personality traits as feminine or masculine without distancing herself, she remains to some extent trapped in the same narrative that, when she began her *transition,* did not allow her to see other possibilities beyond medical treatment. "I felt like something was taken from me, like I was robbed of the possibility of experiencing my body any other way," she laments (Missé, 2018, Prologue). Taking away possibilities is precisely what is sought by those who, under the pretext that radical feminists spread hate speech and with the power of their words abuse trans people, prevent others from listening to them and thus deny them access to liberating interpretations. Raymond says:

> Defining and treating transsexualism as a medical problem prevents the person experiencing so-called gender dissatisfaction from seeing it in a gender-challenging or feminist framework. Persons who think they are of the opposite sex are therefore not encouraged to see this desire as emanating from the social constraints of masculine and feminine role-defined behavior. Thus a man who is emotional or nurturing is encouraged to think of himself as a woman instead of as a man who is trying to break out of the masculine role. A primary effect of defining transsexualism as a medical problem is to encourage persons to view other persons (especially children) who do not engage in normative sex-role behavior as potential transsexuals. Ultimately transsexual surgery reinforces social conformity by encouraging the individual to become an agreeable participant in a role-defined society, substituting one sex role stereotype for the other. The medical solution becomes a 'social tranquilizer' reinforcing sexism and its foundation of sex-role conformity (Raymond, 1994, p. xvii).

Radical feminists were among the first to point out that the medical establishment was transforming healthy individuals into chronically ill ones. They were not paying lip service to depathologization; rather, they were determined to put an end to the practice of correcting behaviours which, in their model, were entirely normal and, in fact, positive. Only from the point of view of gender managers and the guardians of sexist roles can a boy with character traits described as feminine be fodder for psychiatrists. A gender identity clinic only makes sense to someone who does not consider it normal and healthy for some girls to reject stereotypical femininity. Feminism does not want to add, as Raymond would say, more "medical victims to sex-role conformity" (1994, p. xxiv). For this reason, the radical feminist model seeks full and total demedicalization. But the word *demedicalize,* says Arnoldo Kraus, a Mexican physician interested in medical ethics, does not exist, so we need to invent it:

Medicalize, according to the Royal Spanish Academy Dictionary, means 'to equip a place so that it can offer a medical service'. Medicalizing, in addition to equipping, involves other actions: weaving plots in order to provide drugs to the sick even though they do not need them, and weaving scenarios to turn healthy people into sick people. […] There is no such word as *demedicalize*: it is necessary to create it. *Demedicalize*: 'Action aimed at disempowering doctors and technology and pharmaceutical companies whose aim is to promote the medicalization of life for financial gain' (Kraus, 2017).

The transgenderist model, which took several decades to demand this half-hearted depathologization that means continuing to go to the pharmacy every month to fill scripts and finding money for double mastectomies and facial feminization surgeries, continues to accuse radical feminists of being anti-trans. Them of all people: the women who from the beginning were able to see that medicalizing was not the best way to go, the only ones who have proposed a model about transsexuality or transgenderism whose validity has been demonstrated, whose predictions have come true, which has great explanatory power and which does not resort to abstract concepts with no material correlate.

We have never seen protesters shouting "We are the trans resistance and here we are" in front of a clinic that performs unnecessary and irreversible operations on children, but we will surely continue to see them trying to boycott conferences of feminists concerned that children are having the same thing done to them that the body thieves did to Miquel Missé.

The problem is elsewhere

As we have seen, the medical-sexological model speculated about the possible causes of a behaviour it considered deviant in order to correct it and looked for them in individuals. It never found any causes, but nevertheless its exponents believed they had found a way to correct the atypical behaviour. From their point of view, it was revolutionary to no longer repress behaviour considered feminine in men and masculine in women, but to give the men and women in question the possibility to *mutate* into women and men respectively instead. With this simple rearrangement, the anomalous behaviour ceased to be a deviation and everything fell into place. The end (conformity to sex roles) justified the means (hormones and extreme surgeries).

Radical feminism starts from a very different premise. Here, no one needs to *transition* because no one is out of place. The problem to be solved is not the girl who does not conform to stereotypes, but the very claim that she must conform to them. The evil is not in the brain, the genes or the person, but in the sexist society in which the person is educated and develops: in that hierarchical social system based on what some feminists call patriarchy and others still want to call gender to contrast it with sex (despite the confusions to which this gives rise; see Chapter 1). The causes, then, are not biological or psychological, but social, so it is not the body or the mind, but society, that needs to be corrected and changed:

> While biological and psychological investigations seek different causes, they both utilize the same theoretical model – i.e., both seek causes within the individual and/or interpersonal matrix. In such investigations, social, political, and cultural processes tend to be relegated to a subsidiary or nonexistent role, because the model focuses attention on individual or interpersonal gender differences and similarities rather than upon the gender-defined social system in which transsexual behaviors arise. For example, psychological theories measure a transsexual's adjustment or nonadjustment to the cultural identity and role of masculinity or femininity. They seldom question the social norms of masculinity and femininity themselves (Raymond, 1979, pp. 43–44).

But radical feminism does question those social norms, and ending them is a central part of its struggle. In them, and not in hormones or brain structures, feminism finds what causes in some people the wish to change sex and conceptualize it as a necessity. In a gendered society, "norms of masculinity and femininity generate the desire to be transsexed" (Raymond, 1979, p. 16). These same norms cause women to occupy an inferior place in a male supremacist society.

In a world without this hierarchy and not governed by stereotypes of femininity and masculinity, personalities would not be problematic. Girls would not be brought up to be modest and complacent and boys would not be brought up to be violent macho men. It would not occur to anyone that they were born into the *wrong body* – neither to men who resist stereotypes of masculinity nor to women who are uncomfortable in the corset of femininity.

In the world radical feminists dream of, there would be no men wanting multiple cosmetic surgeries to pass as women and no women hating their sexualized bodies and desperately seeking to escape imposed femininity. Teenage boys would not be learning from pornography how to relate to their partners, nor would pimps be able to profit from the sexual exploitation of women. Drug traffickers' girlfriends would not be going to have their waists reduced or their breasts enlarged at those men's request.

Of course, if such a project were to become a reality, there would be losers: for one thing, men would no longer have the prerogatives they enjoy today, and the profits of the sex industry and the medical-technological complex would be drastically reduced. Educating in feminism and telling children that their bodies are not the problem doesn't make money. That is why there is so much opposition, and it is so vicious.

So, the radical feminist model coincides with the medical-sexological model only in the simple observation that some people deviate from sexist roles and suffer distress that it would be important to alleviate (points 1 and 2 of the table), and from then on they are irreconcilably separated. Radical feminism does not share the astonishment of sex scientists towards *transsexuality* because it is not in the least intrigued by the fact that not everyone obediently complies with sexist mandates. The question is why more people don't rebel like that. A woman who is not feminine or a man who is not masculine are not phenomena whose causes feminism is interested in delving into, because for feminism it is the most normal thing in the world: just another result of an unjust and limiting social order. Women know that the obligation to act out externally imposed roles causes great discomfort. That is why there are so many conscientious objectors. Radical feminists are the original gender non-conforming people, the non-binary *avant la lettre*.

Of course, no one who shares feminist principles would think that the suffering caused by not fitting into behavioural roles constructed by a sexist society is a *biological defect*, nor that in order for this discomfort to diminish it is necessary to *surgically correct* the body of the afflicted person, as Gerald Ramsey and others who subscribe to the medical-sexological model do. Although the radical feminist position is not necessarily at odds with the search for some individual psychological relief, it argues that the ultimate solution lies in the transformation of society through collective struggle – that is, the solution lies in the feminist movement.

In fact, the existence of this movement, which was very vibrant in the years when Janice Raymond was writing *The Transsexual Empire*, explains, according to her, why many more men than women wanted to change sex:

> Women have had a political outlet, that is, feminism, which has helped change the distribution of power for women in society and challenge sex role rigidificaton. There has been no comparable 'men's movement' which has confronted, in an organized and political way, masculine gender roles, male sexual identity, and manhood standards (Raymond, 1994, pp. xiii–xiv).

Logically, many women throughout history would have preferred to be men, not because they believed they had an aura of masculinity, but for the simple reason that men enjoyed freedom and women didn't. Many of them dared to wear trousers in times when it was unusual, or even adopted a masculine identity, but not because they possessed a man's soul or a *fluid gender*, but because they wanted to do something forbidden to them, for example, playing a sport (like Pakistani squash player Maria Toorpakai in the first decade of the twenty-first century), loving a woman (like Spanish teacher Elisa Sánchez Loriga in the late nineteenth century) or to practice a profession (like Irish surgeon Margaret Ann Bulkley in the first half of the nineteenth century). In many countries, the feminist struggle has opened up possibilities for women that were previously completely forbidden to them, and as a result they no longer need to pass as men to pursue their intellectual or professional interests.

The radical feminist model also has a profound discrepancy with the transgenderist model, even after the latter's ostensible momentary break with the medical-sexological one, as both of them reinforce the sexist stereotypes that the women's liberation movement has struggled to banish. The fact that transgenderism so enthusiastically embraces the belief in an innate gender identity is proof that the difference is not just one of form. Although transactivists claim to question sexist roles, in practice they exalt them and make the fight to eradicate them impossible since they consider them inherent to our being. The very idea that *gender* can be played with is offensive to women who know that it has been the cause of their oppression as a sexual caste.[33] Clearly there is no coincidence of interests. Raymond comments on this incongruence between the pretence of trans discourse and the reality of transactivism:

> Transsexualism is said to be a radical challenge to gender roles, breaking the boundaries of gender and transgressing its rigid lines. But if the transsexual merely exchanges one gender role for another, if the psychiatric and medical experts demand that transsexuals pass in the opposite gender role before they can undergo surgery, and if the outcome of such a sex reassignment is to endorse a femininity which, in many transsexuals, becomes a caricature of much that feminists have rejected about man-made femininity, then where is the challenge, the transgression, and the breaking of any real boundaries? (Raymond, 1994, pp. xviii–xix).

And when one sees gender identity activism in action, the violent way its supporters silence feminists, the misogynistic abuse that is

---

33 In preferring *sex caste* over *sex class,* I follow in the footsteps of Sheila Jeffreys, who explains her choice of terminology as follows:

The term *sex class* can be problematic because it implies that women could move out of their *class,* in the same way that individual working-class people could change their class position by becoming embourgeoised. The term *caste,* on the other hand, is useful [...] because it encapsulates the way in which women are placed into a subordinate caste status for their lifetime (Jeffreys, 2014b, p. 5).

their daily bread, their male entitlement in disregarding a whole body of radical feminist theory, the zeal with which they invade the spaces that women have built for themselves, their indifference to women's concerns and their stubbornness in eliminating women's sex-based rights, it is difficult to believe that they are interested in challenging sexist roles. Not in the least. In their actions and their way of taking what little is not theirs, the sexual hierarchy remains intact. Of course, they demonstrate a very limited understanding of sexist stereotypes: they reduce them to their most superficial manifestations, such as dress, adornment, mannerisms and the way they speak or walk, as any glance at transgender influencers on social media confirms (see for example Izea, 2022; Teen Line, 2018; Valero, 2020).

If an unflagging struggle of feminism has been to try to eradicate sexist roles, it is easy to understand that the concept of being a walking stereotype is completely alien to it. No matter how much a man may gesture and talk the way women are supposed to, how much make-up and ultra-feminine clothes he wears, and so on, to a congruent radical feminist that man will never be a woman – indeed, to anyone who does not suffer from extreme levels of self-delusion; people who berate others for denying that *trans women* are women often give away by their actions and priorities that they don't believe it either. For a radical feminist, neither hormones nor surgery make a difference, as she has never thought that women are defined by low testosterone or the lack of a penis. She knows, like people in general, that it is not possible to change sex; at best, some procedures can only alter the external appearance of the sexual organs and disguise certain secondary sex characteristics.

The radical feminist, finally, also does not believe that people have an innate, deeply felt internal and individual experience of gender, so it would be very odd of her to accept the existence of such a thing as a special category of people with a gender identity discordant with their sex, i.e. being trans in its canonical definition. By the same token, the radical feminist does not believe that there are people with a gender identity in harmony with their sex, i.e.

that they are *cis*. Of course, rejecting the category does not mean believing that there are no people who think they belong to it; the radical feminist denies that there are trans people, but is well aware that there are people who consider themselves trans.

In addition to this theoretical and conceptual objection to the idea that there are transgender or transsexual people, there is a serious political objection to the belief that a man who claims to feel like a woman and to possess a mysterious halo of femininity should be considered a woman in public life (the latter objection will be dealt with in Chapter 5).

Gender-critical feminism

Not just some feminists, but a great many people, men and women, consider themselves, without necessarily being feminists, gender-critical. These people largely share the radical feminist model and have imbibed the theory but reject the label, perhaps in part because they (mistakenly) associate it with extremism. Their objections to the transgenderist model centre on self-ID, for all the dangers this poses to women's rights, and on the recognition of so-called transgender kids, as they clearly see that a child cannot give full informed consent to treatments and operations that may harm their bodily integrity, fertility and future sex life, and they are concerned that safeguarding is being neglected on so many fronts.

Several of the feminists fighting against what they call female erasure fall into this subdivision of the radical feminist model. Many of them can be seen taking to the streets in Spain and England, countries where discussions on these issues are very present in the public sphere despite the fact that transgenderists are working hard to silence them. The so-called Trans Law promoted by the head of the Ministry of Equality, in Spain, and the proposed changes to the Gender Recognition Act of 2004, in the UK, have led to a public debate and an exemplary feminist political mobilization in recent years. The opposition of organized women to the legislative changes pushed by the transgender lobby in these and other countries is admirable, but in these pages the focus will be on some theoretical positions of critical gender feminism and its similarities and discrepancies with radical feminism.

One difference between gender-critical feminists, as they call themselves, and various exponents of the radical feminist model is that, as can be seen from the description, they still find it useful to use the concept of gender, and are interested in *reclaiming it,* even if it designates something they are fighting to abolish. In their public presentations, writings and social media discussions, they spend time patiently explaining the distinction between sex and gender. In Chapter 1, I set out reasons why it would be a good idea to forget about the term *gender* and stop using it in our theorizing, so in the following pages I will focus on another, much more important, discrepancy between them and the radical feminist model. This is that, judging by their discourse and some of their actions, gender-critical feminists believe that there are indeed people who truly are transgender, as opposed to people who falsely claim to be trans. On the other hand, these gender-critical feminists do not believe that there is such a thing as cis people. They reject this category outright, saying that gender is oppression and no woman identifies with her oppression.

Like radical feminists, they are politically opposed to gender self-ID and are well aware of the risks to women's rights and protection if a man can simply declare himself a woman and be recognized as such in the eyes of the law. But unlike them, they believe that some people who consider themselves trans should have documents that identify them as people of the other sex (because "they really are trans") and that, ideally, the rest of us should be kind enough to refer to them by their preferred pronouns.

This position has three undesirable consequences, in my view:

1. It allows for the concept of gender identity to creep in.
2. It introduces a distinction between true trans and false trans.
3. It obliges one to accept the requirements for someone to be recognized as a person of the other sex.

What distinguishes true trans people from false trans people, according to them, is the presence of gender dysphoria. This is highly problematic because, as shown above, this disorder is tied to the belief in a gender identity, that is, a belief in feminine souls and masculine souls. But in their discourse, gender-critical people do not accept that there is such a thing, because they know that it is a concept fuelled by sexist stereotypes. However, gender dysphoria, both in its psychiatric and more colloquial definitions, is based on the supposed existence of a person's innate, deeply felt internal and individual experience of gender. The latter concept has no place in the position of these gender-critical feminists, even if we assume that such an experience is not innate but acquired: they, who have mastered the sex/gender distinction, know that this description plays on the ambiguity of *gender* and also know that we women do not recognize ourselves as women by virtue of some deep, internal experience of femininity. There is a theoretical inconsistency here; one cannot accept gender dysphoria if one does not also accept gender identity.

But sometimes their guideline for knowing who the true trans people are is not the diagnosis of gender dysphoria: they know it by exclusion: false trans people are those who need gender self-identification in order to be officially recognized as such; true trans people are the others. Therefore, true trans are those who do pass the test, which, as we have already seen, may consist of having undergone hormone treatment or operations or having lived for a certain period of time *as someone of the opposite gender.*

Their acceptance that some people are trans leads them to participate in the reinforcement of sexist roles by making it a requirement to live *as someone of the desired gender* or to acquire some semblance of the other sex, as well as pathologizing the *trans* condition. Talking about *real trans people* puts them, on the one hand, in the position of acting as watchdogs of sexist stereotypes and on the other hand leads them to the idea that transsexuality is a disease (only those who are sick would be trans and the rest would be impostors). Like Jordan Peterson, they accept as trans those who strive for it and obtain enough passing.

This acceptance that there are real trans people seems to be motivated by empathy for this subset of those who declare themselves to be trans. It is also because gender-critical people want to appear moderate and are interested in conceding some reason to their opponents. If they think that this will win them the sympathy of a part of the *transgender rights movement,* the reality (in the form of accusations of transphobia, abuse and cancellations) proves them wrong. And this is to be expected, because nowadays one of the main demands of transgenderism, as we have already seen, is *depathologization*, which is otherwise tied to gender self-ID ... which gender-critical feminists do not accept either. Most ironically, more than one transactivist will end up accusing them of being the ones who force some people "to undergo medical procedures [...] as a requirement for legal recognition of their gender identity," as the third Yogyakarta principle condemns.

In all these respects, gender-critical people are closer to the medical-sexological model than to the radical feminist one, except at the point where the latter almost overlaps with the transgenderist model in its second phase. As illustrated by the table on pages 119–120, gender-critical people who believe that there's such a thing as true transgender people do not fit comfortably with point 9, precisely where the new transgender paradigm and the radical feminist model converge.

In order to recognize that some people suffer for being the sex they are and wish they were the opposite one, it is not necessary to cling to the concept of gender, let alone the diagnosis of gender dysphoria. The radical feminist model, as we have seen, has a better explanation for this suffering and offers better ways out. This model, inspired by a solid theory, has at its core women's sex-based rights, which are entirely incompatible with the supposed right of some people to be treated according to a legal fiction (i.e. as women if they are men, or as men if they are women), whether they meet such and such requirements or not.

In addition to giving rise to a number of theoretical inconsistencies, when gender-critical feminists insist that some people are true trans or suffer from gender dysphoria, and thus for them the possibility of changing their legal sex should remain open, it leads to political contradictions. These will be addressed in Chapter 5.

For now, let us dwell on what happens when one, trying to be nice and empathetic, gives in to blackmail or extortion and uses the preferred pronouns of people who believe in the sublimated sexist fabrication called gender identity.

CHAPTER 3

IN THE BEGINNING
WAS THE PRONOUN

If pronouns are gendered in a grammatical sense, they now seem to be gendered as well in that other sense that is confused with sex, feminism, stereotypical roles, identity. Focusing on these morphemes will serve as one more example of the enormous influence that gender identity activism has achieved in society at large in a very short time, and also to further analyze the central role that language has played in the various victories of transgenderism.

Grammar as identity

Pronouns, as we know, are short words that are used to replace nouns, noun phrases or the name of a person, and whose referents are named or understood within a specific context, especially to avoid repetition. Personal pronouns in English include *I, you, he, she, it, we, they, me, her, us, them.* We see it in social media accounts, but it has also become fashionable for company or institutional staff to specify their *preferred pronouns* along with their name and position on electronic signatures or business cards. Like almost everything related to gender identity ideology, it began in the English-speaking world and has been spreading to the rest of the planet through social media, mass media, advertising, propaganda, universities, transnational companies and lobbying groups.

It is as if pronouns have suddenly acquired the status of honorifics. Some find it important to address people by their hard-earned professional or academic titles, but almost no one would consider it a matter of life and death. Nowadays it would seem that pronouns *are* a matter of life and death. Not using a *trans* or *non-binary* person's preferred pronoun, and thus reminding them that the rest of the world does not see them as they see themselves, can make them feel invalidated and *trigger* them, that is, causing them some degree of emotional distress that, if repeated, can eventually lead to suicide. Or so activists say, to convince us that we must be aware of their needs and be very careful never to make the mistake of using, for example, *he* for someone whose preferred pronoun is *she*.[34] "One of the most important parts of non-binary identity is the identification of each person with a pronoun that is comfortable for them and that does not fall into the male and/or female gender binary," explains a news story in *El Heraldo* (Mata, 2020). "Using someone's correct pronouns is also a way to show you respect them and helps create an inclusive environment. It signals that the person matters to you," asserts Len Meyer (whose pronouns are *they/them*) in the Planned Parenthood of Illinois website.

Until recently, when meeting someone, the introduction "My name is so-and-so" used to suffice. Now in certain circles it would not be unusual for people to *offer their pronouns* when they introduce themselves.[35] The largest "lesbian, gay, bisexual, transgender and queer" civil rights lobbying organization in the United States, the Human Rights Campaign, suggests that to begin a conversation everyone should say "Hi, my pronouns are _____. What are yours?" American evolutionary biologist Colin Wright poses an analogy to underline how absurd this trend is:

---

34   Here is a manual for understanding the importance of respecting people's pronouns: <uwm.edu/lgbtrc/qa_faqs/why-is-it-important-to-respect-peoples-pronouns>.

35   With the proliferation of *genders* came a proliferation of neopronouns. In English the list reached 78 at last count (*Bob Cut Magazine*, 2021).

Imagine a similar request from the American Federation of Astrologers encouraging everyone to begin conversations with, 'Hi, I'm a Sagittarius. What's your sign?' To respond with your own star sign would be to operate within and signal your tacit agreement with the belief system of astrology (Wright, 2022).

In the past, for the sentence 'My pronouns are …' to have any meaning, the only possible way to complete it was *I, me, mine, myself*. The Colombian writer Carolina Sanín, who does not mince words, points out bluntly and without fear of cancellation:

The phrase 'my pronouns' is already the ridiculousness of arrogance and tyrannical childishness. No, my friend: language is neither yours nor mine. Language aspires to name reality, and 'my pronouns' is the most basic way of imposing on another what to say by bending to your desire. To believe that one has 'one's own pronouns' is the delirium of private property, and it is pure megalomania. A generation (or three) of spoilt brats who, if anything, know the possessive adjective *my* and the possessive pronoun *mine* (Sanín, 2022).

Every speaker knows which of the personal pronouns is relevant each time, because, in addition to having linguistic skills, we recognize at first sight, with a very high degree of accuracy, the sex of the person, even if they are dressed and regardless of the type of clothing, and therefore we know whether the appropriate pronoun is *he* or *she*. On the other hand, in various circumstances, it could be considered rude, in the presence of someone, to speak of them as if they were not there, using a third person pronoun instead of their name. When addressing someone, it is still common to use *you,* which lacks a grammatical gender.

But of course, nowadays many conversations take place on social media or forums that are digitally recorded, so that, at least in theory, there is always the possibility that the person in question, even if they were not present when they were talking about them, will eventually find out. That is why their presence is not necessary for people who have already been lectured or reprimanded, or have seen how those who do not comply are attacked, to feel morally obliged or coerced to use the pronouns that someone else claims to prefer, in order to avoid them experiencing possible future suffering or offence, or to lead by example. Every opportunity is, apparently, a good opportunity to educate the rest of the world.

Thou shalt not misgender

The name of the offence committed by using a pronoun other than the one preferred by the person in question is *misgendering*. Using *he* or masculine nouns and adjectives to refer to a man who claims to identify as a woman is nowadays considered, in *progressive* circles, a serious offence, literally verbal violence, something much worse than calling a woman a *whore,* a *feminazi* or a *TERF.* Anyone who for some reason uses the *wrong* pronouns (wrong in an upside-down world, i.e., those that correspond to their sex) will be accused of committing a hate crime. If this happens on social media, it is common to tag the National Human Rights Commission in order for it, we must assume, to take action and scold or show a yellow card to the offender.

One of the reasons the pronouns game has become so popular is that it facilitates activism: it is tempting to feel that, by the symbolic act of announcing whether one wants to be called *he* or *she,* by making a point of not misgendering people who claim to identify with the other sex or neither, and by making sure that others do not do so either, one is doing one's bit to end the injustices of the world. This virtue signalling is also very convenient for companies and public institutions: why implement effective policies against sexual harassment in the office if you can require staff to put their pronouns in their email signatures and enrol them in a course to learn how to use *gender-inclusive language* and become trans allies into the bargain?

For those who identify themselves as non-binary, that is, those who consider they don't belong to either the male or the female category, in English it is common to use the plural pronoun *they*,[36] because, unlike *he* or *she*, it has no gender marker, although it introduces a number disagreement. (Of course, there are precedents of this singular usage of *they* in English when the sex of the person referred to is unspecified or is irrelevant to the context, as used throughout this book.)

In Spanish, a language in which *they* does have grammatical gender (*ellos*, masculine, and *ellas*, feminine), the difficulty has been solved by inventing neutral pronouns, some of them unpronounceable, for example *elle, ellxs or ell@s*, with which nouns and adjectives must be made to agree by giving them the corresponding ending in *e, x* or @. Spanish also has definite neoarticles, such as *le, les, lx, lxs*, which, in conjunction with noun and adjective endings in *x* or *e*, are used to refer to people whose identity falls under the trans umbrella. These novel endings are also used interchangeably as a way of avoiding the generic masculine.

But this dual usage, for people who identify as non-binary and for mixed-sex groups of people, brings the supposedly gender-inclusive language closer to the generic masculine, which in Spanish serves to refer to both male individuals and to collectivities composed of men and women, for it is a gendered language in which the masculine is always the default. It doesn't even have an equivalent for *child/ children, parent/ parents, sibling/siblings*, so, for example, to refer to both parents, it is most common to use the word for *father* in plural *(padres)*. The default masculine, however, doesn't only dwell in language, but in our minds. Invented and imposed words and particles, which do not arise organically from the speakers, are not enough to transform this reality.

Incidentally, neoarticles as *le* and *les* or *lxs* end up doing something that gender-inclusive language in its feminist origins sought to combat, namely the omission of women in discourse:

---

36   The online version of the *Oxford English Dictionary* already includes this meaning of *they*: "2. 1 [Singular] Used to refer to a person whose gender identity does not correspond to the traditional binary opposition of male and female." As of September 2019, Merriam-Webster also includes it.

> In the search for recognition of the rights of a little more than half of the population, women, naming them becomes imperative and an act of justice. History, a history built from the patriarchal gaze, has hidden and denied them, but they have always been there ...

urged Claudia Guichard Bello in a more or less recent manual (but prior to the arrival in Mexico of the *non-binary* category) on non-sexist communication (Guichard, 2015).[37] The feminine *a* and women are as lost in the traditional generic *o* as in the modern generic *x* or *e*.

All Spanish-speaking women in history endure real misgendering on a daily basis, and although many of us are critical of sexist biases in the use of language and seek ways to turn them around, it doesn't cause us identity crises nor is there any record that it has led any of us to suicide. In addition to a lifetime of dealing with sexism in our language, some of us are accustomed – especially if we have short hair, don't wear make-up and prefer comfortable trousers and shoes (in other words, if we don't perform femininity) – to sometimes being greeted "Good afternoon, Sir" or "gentleman" by clerks, shop assistants or waiters. It can be annoying, yes, but it would never occur to us to demand the dismissal of the distracted employee.

Misgendering someone who identifies as trans is another story.

Proportional punishment

In November 2018, Canadian Meghan Murphy, founder of the website *Feminist Current,* was suspended from Twitter, which for a journalist is a work tool, for having replied in a tweet "Yeeeah, it's him" in allusion to Jonathan – *Jessica* – Yaniv, a character who became famous for the complaints he filed in Canada against 16 women in charge of small home-based waxing businesses, some of them immigrants, for refusing to wax Yaniv's genitals, male to be precise, even though he claimed to be a woman (see Murphy, 2019).

---

37   According to a Google Trends search, in Mexico the *non-binary* category took its first steps in 2018.

The pronouns game is not limited to social media and business cards. Also in 2018, Peter Vlaming, a French teacher at a Virginia high school in the USA, was fired for insubordination after refusing to use male pronouns for a female student who shortly before had begun to identify as transgender (whom Vlaming did refer to by her preferred boy name). According to a newspaper report, he was obliged to use the girl's preferred pronouns under school rules and the state's Department of Education code of ethics (see Sorto, 2019).

In Mexico, too, we rebuke sinners. On 30 July 2019, a Starbucks barista wrote 'Ofelio' instead of 'Ophelia' on a disposable cup, even though the aggrieved person had specified: "I am a trans woman. Use feminine pronouns with me, please." The influencer complained on Twitter to his many followers, blasting the coffeehouse chain. "We are thoroughly investigating what happened. We do not tolerate any act of discrimination," they replied at 11:08 p.m., a few hours later; the matter could not wait until the next day. Mexico City's Council for the Prevention and Elimination of Discrimination had acted with greater alacrity: 23 minutes after Pastrana's tweet, its staff had already been on hand to provide information on how to report this and other acts of discrimination. In the end, the offender was fired, although it is worth mentioning that Pastrana would have wanted the company's response to be different. "What you have to do is educate," he explained.

The demand not to misgender has also reached the courts. In September 2017, at Speaker's Corner in London's Hyde Park, a group of feminists was beginning to gather for a meeting later in the day to discuss proposed changes to legislation that would affect the rights of women and girls. Some transactivists were hanging around. Sixty-year-old Maria MacLachlan was videotaping her colleagues with her camera. The atmosphere was festive; some were singing, others were dancing. Then a 26-year-old male over six feet tall, who calls himself Tara Wolf, rushed at Maria, wrestled with her, snatched her camera and, along with another man, punched her. During the subsequent criminal trial, which took place in April 2018, a judge warned MacLachlan that she should say *she* when referring to Wolf for the simple reason that he wanted that pronoun to be used in reference to him (see Finlay, 2019).[38] MacLachlan's own account of what transpired exemplifies what can happen when someone is forced to use pronouns that correspond, not to the person's sex, but to their fantasy of themselves or the image they would like to project:

> I was asked 'as a matter of courtesy' to refer to my assailant as either 'she' or as 'the defendant'. I have never been able to think of any of my assailants as women because, at the time of the assault, they all looked and behaved very much like men and I had no idea that any of them identified as women. After he was arrested, the defendant posted vile misogynistic comments on his Facebook page that no woman would ever make. He was also aggressively intimidating a woman on a picket line, shouting obscenities at her. In what sense is this person a woman?
>
> I tried to refer to him as 'the defendant', but using a noun instead of a pronoun is an unnatural way to speak. It was while I was having to relive the assault and answer questions about it while watching it on video that I slipped back to using 'he' and earned a rebuke from the judge. I responded that I thought of the defendant 'who is male, as a male'.
>
> The judge never explained why I was expected to be courteous to the person who had assaulted me or why I wasn't allowed to narrate what happened from my own perspective, given that I was under oath (in Moss, 2018).

Stephen Wood, also known as Karen White, a British *transgender* convicted rapist and paedophile, served part of his sentence in a women's prison, during which time he raped at least two inmates. The following words came out of the prosecutor's mouth during the

---

38 That was even before the Judicial College's *Equal Treatment Bench Book* included this instruction: "It is important to respect a person's gender identity by using appropriate terms of address, names and pronouns. Everyone is entitled to respect for their gender identity, private life and personal dignity." This imposition of preferred pronouns earned them serious criticism from feminist advocates who were concerned that women who had suffered sexual violence would be required to refer to their rapists as women if they claimed to identify as such. There appear to have been adjustments in response to these criticisms, although, in the view of Maureen O'Hara and other legal scholars, they remain insufficient (see O'Hara, 2022).

trial in 2018: "The defendant would stand very close to her, touch her arm and wink at her. Her penis was erect and sticking out of the top of her trousers" (Evans, McCann and Rudgard, 2018). In this quote it is transparent how the demand to adjust pronouns to the *gender identity* of the subject clashes head-on with reality.

Besides some prosecutors and social media vigilantes, others who have become adept at *respecting pronouns,* either out of conviction or to avoid the barrage of criticism that would otherwise await them, are the media. A newspaper may run headlines such as "San Pedro will seek improvements for the weaker sex," describe as romance a relationship of abuse and power between a 39-year-old man and a 14-year-old girl, or encourage its readership to speculate about the death of a young woman victim of femicide. But misgendering? Never ever.

A misdemeanour akin to misgendering is what is called *deadnaming,* which consists of calling a person who is considered transgender by the name they were baptized with or known as previously, a name that is already dead, so to say. Until April 2023, Twitter considered it hateful conduct and punished offenders by shutting down their accounts. (One wonders why remembering the maiden name of a woman who adopted her husband's surname when she got married, or the married name of a woman who got divorced, do not qualify as deadnaming.)

Given that deadnaming is as serious as misgendering, it would be unthinkable that *El Sol de México,* in a July 2021 article about the person who now goes by the name of Ophelia Pastrana (Ávila, 2021), would add to the description "physicist, economist, technologist, YouTuber and comedian transgender woman from Colombia naturalized Mexican," the harmless and historically important fact that his name used to be Mauricio. Unfortunately, it is even more unthinkable that, one day, newsstands will no longer display tabloids showing pictures of half-naked women in sexy poses next to images of dismembered corpses. This clear double standard makes it difficult to believe that non-sexist journalism is the real motivation. "Journalism that reports from an egalitarian and sensitive perspective on the different areas of public and private life" – which will be achieved when "those who work in the media have banished sexism from their minds and hearts" (Valle, Hiriart and Amado, 1996, p. 81) – does not seem to be the ultimate goal.

The odd significance of pronouns acquired overnight lends itself to jokes and puns.[39] Comedy could not overlook the hypocrisy of some zealous guardians of their prescribed usage. *SuperNature,* the stand-up special by British comedian Ricky Gervais released in May 2022, features the following fictional dialogue between a woman concerned about the risk that any man can now, with the power of his self-identification, enter women's locker rooms or bathrooms, and an ally who defends the presence there of men who claim to be women:

Oh, they want to use our toilets.
Why shouldn't they use your toilets?
For ladies!
They *are* ladies – look at their pronouns! What about this person isn't a lady?
Well, his penis.
Her penis, you fucking bigot!
What if he rapes me?
What if *she* rapes you, you fucking TERF whore?

Gervais upset a lot of people, not because of his sexist jokes or jokes which, in this age prodigal in phobias, many would consider *Islamophobic* or *fatphobic,* but because of the *transphobic* ones (see Holmes, 2022). There were angry reactions, but it's a bit more difficult making life hard for the creator of *The Office* than for a freelance journalist.

Crime reporters also endeavour not to misgender. That is why it is now more common to read news stories about 'female rapists' or 'female child abusers', and why at first glance the proportion of

---

39 Mr Menno's *The Gender Pronouns Song* is unbeatable (<www.youtube.com/watch?v=Xetogrd3n4Y>).

female murderers seems to have risen inexplicably.[40] Between July 2019 and December 2021, the UK feminist organization Fair Play for Women highlighted ten headlines in which the words *woman* or *female* had been used to describe men claiming to identify as transgender women, mostly sex offenders, without the stories making it clear that they were not actually talking about women (see FPFW, 2022). Often the only clue the reader has, apart from an inkling that there is something fishy going on, is the mugshot of the perpetrator accompanying the story. The pictures do not lie.

To misgender or not to misgender

"Thou shalt not misgender" weighs so heavily on the conscience of people that more than a few feminist authors who are openly critical of transgenderism and who have endured the inevitable harassment, for some reason obey this major commandment. This does not prevent them from being accused of transphobia, of course, or from suffering all kinds of reprisals, but they obey anyway, at the risk of confusing their readers with this incongruity and forcing them to ask themselves whether these women share the transgenderist postulates after all.

Spanish writer Rosa María Rodríguez Magda, in her 2019 book *La mujer molesta,* mentions *trans* author Sandy Stone and "her text *The Empire Strikes Back: A Posttranssexual Manifesto*" as the origin of something which she calls *transfeminism* (Rodríguez, 2019, p. 64). This care not to misgender the founder of transgender studies has not prevented Rodríguez Magda from suffering silencing attempts (see Gallego, 2021), nor has it stopped some tweeters

---

40 A glance at the websites Reduxx (<reduxx.info>), Women Are Human (<www.womenarehuman.com>) or They Say This Never Happens (<theysaythisneverhappens.tumblr.com>) confirms what the statistics indicate: violent crimes committed by men who claim to identify as women are at least as frequent as those committed by old-fashioned men (see Freedman, Stock and Sullivan, 2020). The explanation should be obvious: it is not because they identify as *transgender,* but because they are males.

from describing her as "a philosopher with a clearly transphobic discourse."

US journalist Abigail Shrier, who has made a major contribution to raising awareness of the damage that gender identity ideology inflicts, particularly on young girls, also makes her own disclaimer in the very first lines of *Irreversible Damage*:

> I take it for granted that teenagers are not quite adults. For the sake of clarity and honesty, I refer to biologically female teens caught up in this transgender craze as 'she' and 'her'. Transgender adults are a different matter. I refer to them by the names and pronouns they prefer wherever I can do so without causing confusion (Shrier, 2020, xv).

After the American Booksellers Association sent Shrier's book in a promotional shipment to its members, it was forced to apologize:

> This is a serious, violent incident that goes against ABA's policies, values, and everything we believe and support. It is inexcusable. We apologize to our trans members and to the trans community for this terrible incident and the pain we caused them (quoted in Carlisle, 2021).

The fact that a stream of girls, influenced by transgenderism and driven by their own rejection of their sexually objectified bodies, are flocking to plastic surgeons to undergo wholly unnecessary double mastectomies is nothing compared to the shock experienced by a trans Brooklyn bookseller when he excitedly opened the ABA box and the first book he pulled out was *Irreversible Damage*. Shrier's respect for preferred pronouns has done nothing to appease her many detractors.

British philosopher Kathleen Stock, at the beginning of her book *Material Girls,* clarifies: "I've made the decision to use preferred pronouns for trans people in a way that tracks their gender identity and not their sex" (Stock, 2021, p. 12), and in Chapter 6, in which she goes through a series of solid arguments against pronoun hype, aware of the apparent incongruity she defends her decision thus:

> I normally use 'he' and 'him' for trans men, 'she' and 'her' for trans women, and 'they' and 'them' for non-binary people, where preferred.

> Most of the time, I choose to immerse myself in a fiction about sex change for trans people, where it seems they would wish me to. (I choose to make an exception for trans women who assault or aggress women) (Stock, 2021, p. 209).

Despite this concession, months after the publication of her book, constant harassment, protests and pressure led her to resign from her post at the University of Sussex, where she had been ostracized by her colleagues for her stance on trans issues. Stock called the whole experience "medieval" (see Adams, 2021).

Not even Irish journalist and mathematician Helen Joyce, such a fine arguer and for whom logic is second nature, dares to disobey the pronoun mandate in her brilliant work *Trans: When Ideology Meets Reality*.[41] Yet anyone who sought an interview with her to understand and listen to her position risked being declared guilty by association:

> Anyone who gives me any kind of platform at all, even mentioning my book exists, can expect to get a torrent of people saying they are transphobic, that they are bigoted, that they are driving people to suicide, that they are racist, bizarrely (in Hastings, 2021).

In May 2022, Australian philosopher Holly Lawford-Smith achieved what seemed impossible in a climate of transgender censorship and institutional capture: she published a book about the feminist critique of gender identity ideology with an academic publisher, Oxford University Press, despite protests and not one, but two open letters from "deeply concerned" groups of people questioning the decision to publish it. The signatories of one of the letters – authors,

---

41   Helen Joyce stopped playing the pronoun game in 2023. On 28 April, during a 'pronoun debate' in a conference organized by the Irish-based organization Genspect, which "provides support for individuals and families impacted by gender distress," she explained:
> So I too have moved. [...] As I wrote more and more, and as I talked to people, I'm like, you know, this is just a man. The things that this person is doing [...] are just so masculine that the story makes total sense if I describe this person as a man and no sense at all if I describe him as a woman. [...] So more and more I found that I was confusing myself and confusing other people when I used anything except sex-based pronouns.

reviewers, translators and readers who claimed to be "associated with Oxford University Press and its reputation" – set themselves up as an editorial board and laid out a series of requirements, including "the due diligence of consultation" with experts in transgender studies and, if it went ahead with publication, proposed some "steps for accountability" to compensate for the damage their reckless act might cause, such as "donating a portion of the book's profits to supporting transgender rights organizations" and other measures, always "in consultation with transgender rights activists and transgender scholars" (Weinberg, 2022). The publisher responded to this blackmail in a way that should be an example to all media outlets that allow themselves to be intimidated by transactivist demands for censorship. In addition to confirming that the book would be published, it stated:

> We recognise that there is considerable and passionate debate about some of the positions held by gender-critical feminists and their perspectives on a variety of issues. We are confident that *Gender-Critical Feminism* offers a serious and rigorous academic representation of this school of feminist thought. [...]
>
> We will continue to represent a wide range of feminist philosophy in our publishing and a wide range of books on philosophy and gender, featuring authors who are trans and gender non-conforming. The press does not advocate through its publications for any particular views, political positions or ideologies. Equally, what we publish is not reflective of – nor influenced by – the personal views of our employees (Brown, 2022).

However, in order to publish with such a prestigious publishing house, Lawford-Smith – a thinker convinced that we must base our speech on the material reality of sex and not on the fiction of gender identity – had to compromise, making some *small* sacrifices that nevertheless compromised the internal congruence of her work;

for example, when talking about some men, she had to *respect their preferred pronouns.*[42]

Unlike Rodríguez Magda, Stock, Shrier, Joyce, Lawford-Smith and many other women who, in texts or conferences, use the grammatical feminine and *she/her* pronouns when referring to men who claim to identify as women, I have decided, as already seen and commented, not to engage in this fiction. In doing this I follow in Sheila Jeffreys', Janice Raymond's and many other radical feminists' steps. This, of course, does not prevent me from recommending that all these other authors be listened to and read, nor from recognizing the importance of their work. We can learn a lot from all of them, regardless of how much their positions coincide with our own. If I bring them up now, it is because they illustrate the degree of observance of the transgender commandments that exists even among feminists who stand up to their ideology. It is, of course, up to each individual to decide whether to abide by the preferred pronouns or not, although it is clear that doing so is not in all cases an entirely free decision.

These authors are also a clear example of the fact that their kind and empathetic compromise does not remove their stigma or free their works from the automatic accusation of hate speech that allegedly endangers an oppressed minority. The people they want to ingratiate themselves with do not appreciate their gesture; only total submission to the ideology of gender identity and its commandments could exonerate them. How worthwhile, then, is this infidelity to themselves and this concession to the essentialism of sexist stereotypes?

---

42 She recounts this from the fiftieth minute onwards in the video by Women's Declaration International, 2022. Lawford-Smith's experience is also an example of the relentless transactivist harassment of those who dare to defend women-only spaces (see Bartosch, 2021).

How hard can it be?

Why make a fuss over using the preferred pronouns and talking about some people the way they want us to talk about them? It is supposed to be a simple courtesy, a politeness:

> Using the correct name, gender and pronouns with people is about manners. It's about letting someone know that you respect who they are, and it's really not that hard getting it right and respecting other people's pronouns (Stonewall, 2019).

So states a document to celebrate Pronouns Day produced by Stonewall, Europe's largest 'LGBT rights' organization and one of the main driving forces behind institutional transgenderism in the UK.

Funny that, if the issue here is good manners, the reactions to that particular alleged lack of politeness are so extreme. Are those who do not say "thank you" and "please" harassed with the same viciousness? If a waiter does not say "Good afternoon," does it merit a complaint to the National Human Rights Commission? It is clearly not about being polite and courteous. In fact, people on social media and some columnists accuse us not only of not being sweet and nice, but of something that sounds much more serious (although its meaning is not entirely clear): denying trans people their identity.

The assumption is that by not saying *she* to a man who wants to be seen as a woman we are discriminating against him. The reality, however, is that by insisting that we *respect pronouns* we are not being asked to refrain from discriminatory treatment of people who claim to identify as trans, but rather we are being pressured to treat them in a deferential way ... and if we don't, if we don't acquiesce in whatever they wish, we are being mean. We are made to believe that being kind and empathetic is about adopting *their* point of view, about seeing them as they want others to see them. As Julia Long says, "it's not about kindness or courtesy; it's about submission, and the naming of these pronouns is about colluding with this pretense that there is such a thing as transgenderism" (Long, 2020b). In short, we are required to participate in a fiction, as Kathleen Stock rightly says; she, as we saw, willingly engages in the white lie, but why should the rest of the world be forced to do the same? Some of us do not want to contribute to this collective deception.

And how true is it that saying Karen to Stephen and talking about him in the feminine costs us nothing? An author using the pseudonym Barra Kerr, in her influential article 'Pronouns are Rohypnol', which has been removed from the internet several times, offers decisive arguments against this transactivist imposition of *preferred pronouns*. Kerr says:

> One of the biggest obstacles to halting the stampede over women's rights is the pronoun and preferred name 'courtesy'. People severely underestimate the psychological impact to themselves, and to others, of compliance.

To illustrate this impact, the author brings up the Stroop effect, which can be defined as "a semantic interference produced by the automation that our brain carries out when learning to read." To measure the interference, there is a psychological test consisting of reading names of colours that are written with letters of other colours, which "produces a delay in processing [...], increases reaction time and favors errors." While

> the right hemisphere of the brain tries to say the color because this is where the functions for thinking and remembering in images are located [...], the left hemisphere insists on reading the word, as it is related to linguistic ability, reasoning, writing. So, this exercise causes a right-left conflict (INB, n.d.).

By using preferred pronouns, we cause ourselves some cognitive interference. They are, says Kerr, like Rohypnol, a drug with a powerful hypnotic effect. She continues:

> They change our perception, lower our defences, make us react differently, alter the reality in front of us. They're meant to. They dumb us. They confuse us. They remove our instinctive protective responses. They work.
>
> Forcing our brains to ignore the evidence of our eyes, to ignore a conflict between what we see and know to be true, and what we are expected to say, affects us.

Using preferred pronouns does the same. It alters your attention, your speed of processing, your automaticity. You may find it makes you anxious. You pay less heed to what you want to say, and more to what is expected of you. It slows you down, confuses you, makes you less reactive. That's not a good thing.

But bad as it is forcing women – very well trained since a very young age to be attentive of the needs of others and disregarding our own – to be more concerned with the *misgendering* of others than with our own cognitive dissonance, the damage is not just to ourselves. "The problem for us is that it's not you, it's us that are compromised," Jo Brew told Holly Lawford-Smith, commenting on the concessions she had to make to get her book published by Oxford University Press (see Women's Declaration International, 2022).

To prove that having those *simple kindnesses* of not *misgendering* or *deadnaming* is not trivial, Kerr proposes a very simple experiment: to restore sex-based pronouns and the original names in transgenderist articles and comments that we come across:

> If those small acts of preferred pronoun compliance are truly meaningless concessions […], given as a courtesy to others at no cost to you or to other women, then this private exercise will change nothing, cost nothing, affect no-one. […] Nothing *should* change, should it, simply with the alteration of pronouns and names? You already know the actual sex of the subject you're reading about. Pronouns, male or female, add no incremental information. How can they in any way alter your perception, or influence you when you already know all the facts? […]
>
> Cognitively, you should be immune to the effects of such linguistic cross-dressing. Pronouns are irrelevant, so you concede them easily, because they have no power to influence you, since you already see clearly. Yes? […]
>
> But try the experiment. Translate pronouns and references back to male. Insert *dead names* or use surnames. […] Read it a second time. And be honest with yourself. Do you feel differently, on reading it this way? Do you react differently? How's your anxiety? Are you angrier?

Do you feel more scared? Is your sense of injustice alerted? [...] You may discover that, despite yourself, you have a viscerally different reaction to what is before your eyes.

In many circumstances in life, it makes a huge difference to women what sex the other person is. Hearing footsteps behind us walking down a deserted street at night, for example, finding out it's a woman can mean the difference between relief and dread. It is not the same when other women see us naked and when men see us naked. Forcing us to use the wrong pronouns is a cheap but effective psychological ploy: the white lie interferes with our perceptions. "Same story, same players, same core knowledge. Different pronouns, different reaction." That's why some of us refuse to play the game and engage in this fiction. Kerr concludes:

> I feel like I owe it to myself and I absolutely owe it to other women. And more than anything, I owe this to girls. I don't want to play even the tiniest part in grooming them to disregard their natural protective instincts. Those instincts are there for a reason. To keep them safe. They need those instincts intact, and sharp.

Male violence against women and girls is the big issue that drew me to feminism almost four decades ago. By relying on the sex of the subject to determine which pronoun I use, what I am doing is declaring myself in favour of women and girls, as I've always done.

The prevention of vice

I'm an atheist, but because of social commitments or out of affection for other people, I have had to go to some Catholic masses throughout my life. On those occasions, I do not cross myself on entering the church, I do not use the kneeler, I do not pray, I do not answer in chorus "conceived without sin" and I do not receive communion. I could perhaps pretend to be a Catholic and move my lips in the litanies, but I see no point and fortunately no one has ever thought of asking me to do so. In other words, nobody suggests that I follow the rituals and nobody tries to impose their faith upon me.

We are in the twenty-first century and in liberal democracies people are generally quite tolerant of other people's beliefs. It is not uncommon to have friends with different religions, and before the advent of social media it was still conceivable to have a rational dialogue with people who had different or even opposing ideas to one's own. The rise of gender identity activism broadly coincides with the polarization brought about by social media, but its intolerant and authoritarian style seems to be inspired by other political-religious movements.

In a reversal of the rights that Afghan women had won back since the fall of the Taliban regime in 2001, on 7 May 2022, nine months after the Taliban's return to power, they ordered women to resume wearing head-to-toe veils in public. To protest against these conditions, female presenters and journalists from three television channels disobeyed and on the day the measure came into effect, they went on camera with their faces uncovered.

Their contempt could not last long: the Taliban immediately issued an ultimatum, to them and to the TV networks. A spokesman for the strict Ministry for the Propagation of Virtue and Prevention of Vice declared: "The decision is final and there is no room for discussion on this issue." If a woman fails to comply, she will be automatically dismissed; "if they don't, we will talk to those responsible." The unassailable order was that "They will have to cover their face when they are in front of a man who is not a member of their family, to avoid provocation." After resisting, the rebels finally had no choice but to obey and cover their faces (see *Profile*, 2022).

The parallels with the subject of this book are obvious. Several examples show how the Ministry for the Propagation of Pronouns and Prevention of Hate Crime imposes its will. The female presenters who initially disobeyed the Taliban order are like women who do not profess their identity faith and do not play the pronoun game. The same female presenters who, in a second instance, wore the veil under protest, are like feminists who reluctantly agree to say *she* to a man so that they will not be banned from social media or have their publishing contract cancelled.

Gender identity activists have a habit of accusing us (to our employers, our publishers, the government agency of the moment) when in their view we misbehave, as the Afghan ministry in this example threatened to "talk to those responsible" if women presenters did not cover their faces the next day.

Both groups accuse women of causing, through their actions, what may happen to others: whether they are supposed to provoke *uncontrollable sexual desire* by wearing their heads uncovered or triggering some man by not calling him *Ma'am;* both are about making us responsible for someone else's behaviour and emotional well-being.

But the key phrase here is "There is no room for discussion on this issue." The accusation of hate speech, with the accompanying slogan "Trans rights are not up for debate," is central to the survival of this movement. Nothing threatens it as much as freedom of speech.

Calling a spade a spade

The imposition of pronouns is quite contrary to freedom of speech and freedom of thought. The very fact that *misgendering* is in some places considered a hate crime makes this clear. According to transgenderist discourse, when someone does not use someone else's preferred pronouns, the only possible motivation is hatred and the aim is to harm them. There is no other explanation. This idea that if I disagree with you it means I hate you is one of the great evils brought about by social media.

Actually, misgendering is dangerous for transgenderism insofar as using sex-based pronouns denotes that we do not believe that a man can be a woman no matter how much he claims to feel like one. It is as simple as that. When an interviewer asked Kellie-Jay Keen, "What do you have against trans women?," she replied, "I don't, I just don't think they're women," in the best summary of this debate there could be (Sky News, 2018).

They are right that our beliefs are dangerous, but not because they cause suffering, but because their ideology does not stand up to feminist analysis. If you don't believe in being born in the wrong body and in stereotypical souls, you can't possibly believe in transgender principles. This ideology crumbles when it is put black on white. Tucking the discourse into convoluted rhetoric and confusing people is part of the job; the other part is to prevent radical feminists and abolitionists from being heard at all costs, so that people, naturally confused, cannot clarify their ideas.

Calling *he* a man who says he identifies as a woman is a refusal, a woman saying *no* to him. That's what they like the least. It's a resounding "No, thank you," like the one uttered by American weightlifter of Mexican descent Sarah Robles at the Tokyo 2020 Olympics when the medallists were asked to comment on what they thought of a male's participation in the female category of their sport. *No, thank you, I'm not going to pretend Laurel Hubbard is a woman; No, thank you, we don't want men invading our space; No, thank you, I'm not playing the game, I'd rather say what I believe and describe what my senses perceive.*

One activist who insists on the importance of language reflecting reality, and who doesn't care the least about being liked or not liked, is the aforementioned Kellie-Jay Keen (or Posie Parker), the brain behind some *provocative* signs and billboards with a black background and white letters with the dictionary definition of the word *woman*. Although she doesn't have a history of rigorous feminist formation, this housewife, who a little earlier, in February 2018, was summoned for questioning by the police for tweets in which she criticized, in her words, "the current pro trans ideological climate," with her unwavering energy and commitment has become emblematic of the British feminist movement, and also, unsurprisingly, one of the people most demonized by those who don't like us calling a spade a spade.

In September of the same year, after one of those billboards in Liverpool was removed in response to a complaint from trans ally Adrian Harrop, Keen was interviewed face-to-face with him. He thinks she is appropriating the term *woman* and excluding *trans women* from the definition. When the presenter asks if by using the language she uses Keen is not being "deliberately provocative," she answers: "No, I am being deliberately truthful in an age when it doesn't seem feasible that people can just speak the truth." And when Harrop accuses her "transphobic campaign" of "making transgender people in Liverpool feel unsafe and unwelcome in their own community," she replies:

> A dictionary definition on a billboard makes men feel unsafe? [...] We knew when we put the billboard up that chaps like yourself would think that they could control what we think and what we say; we know this, and that's why we did it. It's absolutely time that women are allowed to talk about ourselves, our spaces, our rights, and our legal rights without men like you telling us that we are not allowed to speak (Sky News, 2018).

British radical lesbian feminist Julia Long also stresses the importance of calling things as they are and of using language based in reality when talking about the irreconcilable conflicts between transgenderism and feminism, in order to illuminate instead of obscuring. She understands the relationship between language and thought, as well as the crucial role of language in maintaining systems of oppression. "The relationship between the words we use and the lives we live is, to borrow Andrea Dworkin's phrase, an umbilical one" (Long, 2020a). She, like many others who have been observing it for years, sees transgenderism as part of the war on women, a very serious attack on our rights and spaces. It seeks, she says, an elimination of women's presence and voices in the public domain:

> One of the very central ways in which this situation has been achieved is through language, because the transgender movement [... has created] a very bizarre ridiculous nonsensical language [...] which

in a very short space of time has become not just established but thoroughly, increasingly normalised, and also increasingly supported by the full weight of the law and the state, and for them is a kind of a linguistic triumph. [...But] none of these terms stand up to even the slightest scrutiny, because they are all based on fictitious concepts: the notion of *gender identity*, for example, or the notion that you can be born in the wrong body, or the notion that you can change from one sex to another. [...] So, through language, we now have a whole set of nonsense concepts that have achieved the status of reality, such as *trans woman, trans man, non-binary, the transgender child* or *transgender rights, transphobia* (Long, 2020b).

It seems to her a total lack of strategy, as well as an incomprehensible incongruity, that so many feminists who call themselves gender-critical adopt, out of a desire to be kind and empathetic, the vocabulary invented precisely to enthrone gender. It is as if they were doing the ideological work of the enemy and validating their fictions.

As women who are experiencing this attack, we need to be very clear about the language that we use, because if we speak the language of transgenderism, what we do is to reinforce these concepts even if we are critical of them. [...] Using simple but clear language that names men as men [has] always been a central part of feminist understanding: that we see where the men are and what they are doing in the world and who they are doing it to. [...] If I refer to someone as a *trans woman*, I am saying that that individual is a type of woman [...]; the adjective is suggesting that that person is part of a subgroup of women [...]. I would refer to that same individual as a man who demands that we pretend that he is a woman. I think that is a far more precise way of stating who that individual is, what his behaviour is, and what his impact is on women. That description reveals [...] he believes he is entitled to dictate how I speak; it reveals male force and coercion. Behind these word demands there is a force that if we don't comply there could be very serious consequences for us. It reveals psychological abuse, because he is demanding that we pretend that something is true when it isn't true; [...] and it reveals the male will to violate women's boundaries, because he is pretending he's a woman and wants us to pretend he's a woman so that he can access our spaces, our communities (Long, 2020b).

Pronouns are only the beginning. You start by saying *she* out of politeness and end up denying what your eyes see, compromising your own ability to think clearly, and surrendering feminism in the process. If feminists who resist gender identity activism and risk so much to defend women's sex-based rights capitulate to such verbal imposition, what message are they sending to those who are sitting on the fence?

CHAPTER 4

THE IDEA OF THE TRANSGENDER CHILD

The last decade has seen the invention of a category: the transgender child. In practice, this is tantamount to pathologizing completely normal behaviour in perfectly healthy children. Many people, with good intentions but not enough information, support measures that are sold to the public as attention to the children's health and well-being, and recognition of their identity. In the following pages I review what lies behind the idea that some children need to go through a gender *transition* and discuss the consequences of the false promise implicit in that term.

In search of innocence

Transgenderism's most effective propaganda campaign is the invention of so-called transgender children. For the movement committed to spreading and enforcing this agenda, the concept of a transgender child serves to establish the belief that one does not become trans, but is born one, and to support the thesis that *gender identity* is an essential part of our being. To argue that a gender identity that is out of sync with our body is innate is a tactical decision of current transactivism, not a fact obtained from available evidence.

The inspiration for this can be found in the gay and lesbian rights movement, which has in the last decades favoured the view that *sexual orientation* is innate (although many lesbians and gay men disagree).

As is well known, same-sex marriage has dominated the lesbian-gay roadmap[43] at least since the 1990s, when the AIDS crisis and the strong anti-gay backlash it had brought with it were beginning to be left behind. Various voices within the lesbian-gay movement itself were opposed to focusing the struggle on it, not necessarily for religious reasons or because they believed that marriage should consist entirely of the union of a man and a woman. The more revolutionary sector of that movement saw marriage, as lesbian feminism still does, as an institution to be abolished, regardless of the sexual configuration of the couple. In the words of Sheila Jeffreys, "Marriage is not on the agenda of lesbian feminism, because it symbolizes and constructs women's subordination" (2003, p. 150). Despite these dissenting voices and their sensible arguments, this aim prevailed in the struggle of what would become known years later as the LGBT movement. From April 2001, when the Netherlands was the first country to legalize same-sex marriage, to July 2022, when Andorra followed suit, the number of nations allowing two people of the same sex to marry totalled 33.

Those who fought for equal marriage saw it not just as an end in itself, but as a fundamental step towards full social acceptance of same-sex couples and, by extension, of lesbianism and male homosexuality. But to achieve this goal it was felt necessary to introduce an exculpatory element. As it seemed that it was not enough to recognize their human condition to consider them worthy of respect and subject to rights, it was necessary to prove their *innocence*. As early as 1973, when homosexuality was removed from the *Diagnostic and Statistical Manual of Mental Disorders* in

---

43 Back then, the acronym LGBTIQ+ was not in use, and gays and lesbians were at the centre of the movement, unlike today's landscape, where the transgender agenda is all-embracing.

response to the 1969 Stonewall riot in New York and years of lesbian and gay activism, it was no longer considered a pathology and was understood as a simple *sexual orientation,* as valid as heterosexuality, albeit much less common.

In the eyes of the public and the psychiatric profession, gays and lesbians were no longer mentally ill. Wonderful that they no longer carried that stigma. But even if there was no longer a need to *diagnose* and *cure* homosexuality, there was still an eagerness to find its causes. If these were not a dominant mother or a "hidden but disabling fear of the opposite sex," as psychiatrists trained in psychoanalysis in the 1940s and 1950s believed (see Pillard, 1997, p. 226), then what? For several decades they have looked into genes, evolutionary mechanisms, hormones, brain structures ... No hypothesis has been conclusive. The optimism of the Austrian endocrinologist Eugen Steinach in 1919, when, based on a series of experiments with removed and transplanted rat ovaries and testes, he concluded that "the question of the biological basis of homosexuality has been definitively solved" (quoted in Ostertag, 2016, Chapter 1), was entirely unjustified.

But why so much insistence on assigning this or that cause for this human behaviour of perhaps a minority but by no means unusual sexual orientation?

"Knowing there are scientists who are spending huge amounts of time, money and effort in an attempt to ascribe a biological basis to our sexual orientation makes me [...] feel like a specimen under a microscope as opposed to a person deserving of rights and respect," complains lesbian feminist Julie Bindel (2020), echoing the sentiments of countless fellow activists. Others, however, do not share this unease. Biologist Garland E. Allen writes:

> Many gays and lesbians have welcomed the genetic, or at least biological, explanation of homosexuality as one way of bringing about greater understanding and acceptance – both within the gay community and from the larger society. The implications of the genetic research are that [...], if homosexuality can be shown to be inborn, and therefore beyond the individual's control, then perhaps it will be

viewed as more natural and thus less stigmatised. Gays, lesbians and their parents can feel less 'guilty' that homosexuality was *caused* by a dysfunctional or disturbed family. 'It's not my fault' is supposed to be a liberating conception (Allen, 1997, p. 263).

Allen, like Bindel, takes a dim view of this tendency to rely on biological causes to gain acceptance for a minority group. He considers theories of genetic determinism to be double-edged swords and reminds us that in Germany, in the 1920s and 1930s, homosexuality, although punished, was already considered a trait that could be explained by genes. It would not be unthinkable that in an atmosphere of totalitarianism and outright rejection of homosexuality, genetic engineering techniques would be sought to eliminate it. Indeed, as Bob Ostertag says,

> the belief that sexual deviance is biological did not confer on sexual minorities in Hitler's Germany the [anticipated] protections [...]. When the Nazis came to power, the idea that sexual minorities were 'born that way' and could not be changed became the rationale for rounding them up and putting them in concentration camps (2016, Chapter 7).

Historically, the feminist movement has contributed an important critique of the biologistic explanation of sexuality. According to the radical feminist analysis, and as the experience of very many lesbians confirms, lesbianism can be a choice.[44] Julie Bindel (2014) herself states:

> I made a conscious and happy choice to be a lesbian and reckon that when we have less anti-gay bigotry, more people will be free to do so. But when I use the word *choice,* I don't mean in the same manner that you choose your cereal. Rather, I am suggesting that if we were not

---

44 The experience of Sheila Jeffreys and other feminists active in the women's liberation movement in the 1970s and 1980s is exemplary. Jeffreys recounts this in her autobiography, *Trigger Warning* (Spinifex Press, 2020). Heterosexuality, on the other hand, is a social imposition that subsists with the help of a large cultural propaganda machine. For an analysis of *compulsory heterosexuality,* see Rich (2018). For a critique of heterosexuality as an institution, see Jeffreys, 2011, Chapter 6, and 2022, Chapters 1 and 4.

under such extreme pressure to be straight, and if we did not fear the inevitable prejudice and bigotry, we might be more open to falling for someone of the same sex.

In the 1970s, not only lesbians, but also some gay activists, favoured the interpretation that homosexuality can be chosen.[45] Believing oneself to be the victim of a biological destiny did not fit well with a struggle that claimed to be revolutionary. However, despite the fact that the search for the *gay gene* and for a causal explanation has proved utterly futile, in the long run the exculpatory biological interpretation prevailed: they are born that way, it is inevitable, they are not to blame; *therefore* it is wrong to discriminate against them. It is curious to show such a strong conviction that there must be a biological cause, even if one cannot point to one with the slightest certainty. But this outcome is not surprising considering that the movement, although made up of men and women, was dominated by men, who were much more likely to believe in the biological version. As Marilyn Frye puts it:

> It has generally been the political policy of the male-dominated gay rights movement to *deny* that homosexuality is chosen, or worthy of choice. In the public arena that movement's primary stance has been: 'We would be straight if we had a choice, but we don't have a choice' supplemented by 'We're really just human, just like you'. The implication is that it is only human to want to be straight, and only too human to have flaws and hang-ups. While apologizing for difference by excusing it as something over which one has no control, this combination of themes seeks to drown that same difference in a sentimental wash of common humanity (1983, p. 149).

---

45 Anyone surprised by that statement might find the following fact enlightening: Australian academic Lorene Gottschalk interviewed three generations of lesbians and asked them whether they believed their lesbianism had a biological cause. Her study found that among those who became lesbians in the 1950s and 1960s, the biological explanation was predominant; those who embraced lesbianism in the 1970s and early 1980s believed they had chosen their sexuality; and finally in the 1990s, a return to the biological explanation could be perceived. This indicates that there is a relationship between the prevailing cultural beliefs of a given era and the way people interpret their own experience (see Gottschalk, 2003).

Judging by its results, saying that one is born homosexual was, from a strategic point of view, a very wise move which, besides allowing same-sex marriages in many countries, avoided at least three serious prejudicial and discriminatory implications: if it is a choice, why not choose heterosexuality instead? (with the help of so-called conversion therapies if they find it difficult); if it is something they choose, nothing prevents society from continuing to condemn them and see them as degenerates; if it is not innate but acquired, gays and lesbians can recruit and pervert the youth.

Thus, although, as Bindel says, immutability has never helped black people, Jews or women to save themselves from intolerance and oppression (see 2020), the idea that they should be tolerated because they were born that way and there is nothing to be done about it was central to the equal marriage project. They were *innocent victims* and aroused compassion rather than rejection. The nascent LGBT movement found a way to harness this experience for its new venture, transgenderism. The idea that transsexual people were born that way had to be resurrected and reinforced. For that, it was not enough for adults to claim that they had perceived a mismatch between their gender and their sex since they were kids – transgender children would be the required living proof, the younger the better.

An idea is born

The condition of possibility of so-called trans children is not a gene, an imbalance in hormones, a difference in brain structure, nor of course a female soul in a male body or vice versa, but an idea, a discourse, the bizarre belief that some children were assigned the wrong gender at birth, the one that does not correspond to their gender identity, and that the only thing that can alleviate their plight and spare them some suffering is a transition, whether social, legal or medical.

As the editors of the volume *Inventing Transgender Children and Young People* write, "the *transgender child* is not a naturally occurring figure external to current discourses and practices but is brought into being through gender medicine and transactivism" (Moore and Brunskell-Evans, eds., 2019, p. 26). But to say that trans kids are a discursive invention, a fabrication without a material correlate, does not mean that there are no children who one day arrive and announce to their parents or their classmates that they are transgender; that there are no people who from a very young age are especially resistant to fulfilling sexist roles; that there are no diagnoses of *gender dysphoria* in minors, or that their suffering is fictitious. There are no trans children in the sense that the discourse behind this misleading label is false, deceitful and fraudulent. Trans children do exist, but on the same plane of reality as indigo children do.

"An Indigo Child is one who displays a new and unusual set of psychological attributes and shows a pattern of behaviour generally undocumented before," is offered by way of definition in the book *The Indigo Children: The New Kids Have Arrived,* which features contributions from an adult indigo, a life empowerment coach, a visionary and healer, and other experts. Published in 1999, it had sold 250,000 copies by 2006, and sparked a publishing craze that yielded good returns for the industry: almost every self-help imprint had a title to teach parents of these children how to be sympathetic to them and how to value and treat them. Then came films, lectures, radio interviews, courses, seminars, special schools and variants (such as the *crystal children*). One infallible way to recognize who falls into this classification is to look at their aura or colour emanation, which should be indigo blue, but as this luminous halo is invisible to most people, one can only rely on behavioural observations. Some of the most common behaviours among indigo children, according to the editors of the aforementioned foundational work, are:

- They come into the world with a feeling of royalty (and often act like it).
- They have a feeling of 'deserving to be here', and are surprised when others don't share that.

- Self-worth is not a big issue. They often tell their parents 'who they are'.
- They simply will not do certain things; for example, waiting in line is difficult for them.
- They often see better ways of doing things, both at home and in school, which makes them seem like 'system busters' (nonconforming to any system).
- They seem antisocial unless they are with their own kind. If there are no others of like consciousness around them, they often turn inward, feeling like no other human understands them. School is often extremely difficult for them socially (Carroll and Tober, 1999, Chapter 1).

What's more, these children of light, more empathetic and creative than their peers, have a unique awareness and know they are special: "They seem to spiritually 'know who they are', and report it to their parents very early! [...] Believe us, they know they are different!" (Carroll and Tober, 1999, Introduction). Jasmine, interviewed in 2006 for a report in *The New York Times,* has the same impression – she always felt different from other children and found the *indigo* designation reassuring. Her godmother confirms this: "I always knew there was something different about her. Then when I saw something about indigos on television, I knew what it was" (Leland, 2006). But not everyone feels at liberty to comment on this, because there are people with no connection to magic who are scared by it. We could perhaps call those people who don't understand the spiritual dimension of children with an indigo-blue aura *indigophobic.*

There was no shortage of sceptical voices that recommended caution in the face of this esoteric phenomenon and branded it a hoax, such as the Argentinian paleontologist Carlos A. Quintana, author of the article 'Niños índigo: una doctrina contraeducativa y pseudocientífica' (Indigo children: a counter-educational and pseudo-scientific doctrine) and the book *Niños índigo. ¿Fraude o realidad?* (Indigo children: fraud or reality?), in which he warns about hoaxes that confuse reality and fiction, of which the *children of the new Millennium* are a paradigmatic example:

An even more damaging variant of the spreading of pseudoscience for society is when there's the intention of incorporating false knowledge into the educational system so that it can be taught to our children as if it were true. In this way, the deception is more effective because it relies on passive actors – the teachers – who multiply the imposture by giving a false veneer of seriousness to the subject due to their status as education professionals. Meanwhile, the scammers line their pockets more efficiently (Quintana, 2007, p. 7).

The tuition fees paid by some families who sent their children to schools specifically for *indigo children* in 2002 were as palpable and material as the money being pocketed by some plastic surgeons and the pharmaceutical industry on the back of *transgender children* in the 2020s. The idea that there are children with an indigo aura who are more empathetic and creative than their peers and are at the next stage of human evolution cannot be substantiated empirically, nor does it have any scientific credibility. The prevailing view today is that this is quackery.

Although the rise of this trend took place at the beginning of the twenty-first century, the fact that 20 years later you can buy a copy of *I Am an Indigo Child – Hear My Words,* by Sasha Brisk, or *Empowering Your Indigo Child: A Handbook for Parents of Children of Spirit,* by Wayne Dosick and Ellen Kaufman, to mention just a couple among several titles on the market, is a sign that there are still gullible families who think they will find answers in this typology about what to do with a child who despairs when he or she has to queue, among other uncommon characteristics.

"I call them Indigos because that's the color I 'see'. [...] I look at people's life colors to learn what their mission is here on the Earth plane – what they're here to learn, what their syllabus is," says Nancy Ann Tappe, who presented herself as a psychic and synesthetist, and was the first promoter of indigo children (in Carroll and Tober, 1999, Introduction).

And how can we know who to call trans children? Hershel Russell, a trans-identified Toronto-based registered psychotherapist who "over the years [has] been a 'Transition consultant' for many trans people, of a wide range of genders," gives us a hint:

> A mother of a gender diverse kid asked her eight-year-old, 'So how can you know that you're really a boy?' And the child said, 'I know way down deep, where the music plays'. And I think that's so precise! It's not rational: it's profound, it's beautiful, it's deep. That's how we know what gender we are and very young children know that.[46]

Both experiences, that of indigo children and that of trans children, are equally subjective and unverifiable, and their adherents, instead of providing clear explanations and definitions, spout esoteric metaphors.

In order to believe in indigo children, one has to buy into the whole new age paraphernalia and let oneself be convinced that these kids have an indigo *aura* and other qualities that supposedly make them special and superior, despite having traits that are not difficult to find in any child, or else abstractions open to any interpretation. In the same way, to believe in transgender children one has to buy the whole transgender ideological package and let oneself be convinced that there are girls with penises and boys with vaginas because sex is in the brain and not in the genitals ... and sometimes we find male brains in female bodies and vice versa ... and this is something that nobody can verify except for oneself through introspection ... and it can be known with full certainty at very early ages ... and so on.

In that sense, there is no such thing as an indigo child, nor a transgender child. It all comes down to attributing to people some vague traits mixed together from unsystematic sets of confused, unscientific and sometimes contradictory beliefs. Both doctrines

---

46 The quote is taken from the BBC (2017); the information about Hershel Russell is from her website: hersheltoronto.ca. In case anyone would like to argue that this statement is not reflective of more serious positions within the gender identity movement, Russell co-authored an article published in 2013 in the peer-reviewed *International Journal of Transgenderism*, 'Attachment and Shame in Gender-Nonconforming Children and Their Families: Toward a Theoretical Framework for Evaluating Clinical Interventions'. Thus, she is anything but an improviser and can be considered a model of transgenderism.

take advantage of the public's unsophistication, and they certainly cash in on it. As Argentinian-Canadian physicist and philosopher Mario Bunge says,

> the credulous outnumber the sceptical. Moreover, the counterfeit is often more profitable than the genuine thing. This is true even for the sciences. Suffice it to recall the commercial success of *alternative* medicine and psychoanalysis (Bunge, 2017).

The problem is that the transgender hoax has gone much further than the indigo children fraud. Indigo children were a business for a few lecturers, book authors, unscrupulous psychologists and school owners, but it never occurred to anyone that these children should, for example, undergo treatment to match the colour of their skin to the colour of their aura.[47] But transgender children's promoters argue that, for the future social and emotional well-being of transgender and non-binary children, if their innermost sense and personal experience of gender do not match their body, "seeking medical treatment so that their body more accurately reflects their sense of gender" is of the essence (Brill and Pepper, 2022, p. 340). And such medical treatment does not come cheap; hormone therapy alone can represent almost a lifetime expenditure. The pharmaceutical industry, plastic surgeons and in general the techno-medical complex, as Jennifer Bilek calls it, are cashing in on a popular but unprovable idea that subsists and spreads on fear, ignorance and credulity. In this sense, while the belief in indigo children is not entirely innocuous, its dangers pale in comparison to those arising from the belief in trans children.

The lucrative notion of the wrong bodies does not sell itself. To spread it around the world, gender medicine and transactivism have had key allies in international organizations, national and local governments, the executive, legislative and judicial branches, educational and health institutions, the media, the entertainment

---

47   It is worth mentioning, however, that Carlos A. Quintana warns of possible negligence in concluding that a child is indigo and not simply hyperactive (and he is not the only author to note a high rate of children with ADHD in this group).

industry, human rights commissions – a monumental infrastructure that the experts in indigo children, who made money but ultimately fended for themselves, never in their wildest dreams could have imagined. There was indigo propaganda, but it was not ubiquitous or as lavishly funded as transgender propaganda. There was no eight-season reality show tailing an indigo child, as there is one devoted to the private life of Jazz Jennings, "diagnosed with gender dysphoria by age four," and his vicissitudes as a *trans girl*.[48] Indigo sceptics were not condemned and demonized, and no one claimed that pointing out such new millennium quackery was hate speech, or implied that anyone who did not play along would be driving indigo children to suicide. Above all, there is no record of any country having pushed for laws seeking recognition of indigo children, unlike what is happening in various parts of the world with so-called trans children, for whom gender self-ID policies already in place for adults are being sought.

Free development of personality

Isn't it ironic that the movement that has taken us back to the 1950s in terms of recreating sexist stereotypes wants us to believe that it is interested in favouring the free development of the personalities of children who are rebelling against these stereotypes? On the one hand, they repeat feminist discourses about the famous distinction between sex and gender (which is why some people think transactivists are feminists, when in fact they are quite the opposite), and even give the impression that they agree that we should challenge stereotypes and allow girls and boys to play with prams or dolls equally. But it is very confusing because, on the other hand, when it comes to explaining what the signs are that a girl or a boy is trans, they invariably resort to stereotypes and go no further.

---

48 The show, *I Am Jazz*, premiered in 2015 and its eighth season began to air in January 2023. The average number of viewers per episode in the United States hovered around one million (Wikipedia entries for Jazz Jennings and for *I Am Jazz*, accessed August 2023).

And they can go no further – as we have already seen, stipulating that there is a gender identity makes sexist roles and stereotypes an essential and inescapable part of our being.

Perhaps the most honest answer to the question of how to tell if a child is trans can be found in a pair of stories written and illustrated by Patricia Murube Jiménez and published in 2017 by the Spanish association "for trans youth and families" Chrysallis. The first is *Cinco diademas para Matilda* (Five Tiaras for Matilda), about a four-year-old boy (the story describes him as a girl) who "puts on her mother's shoes, looks in the mirror, sees herself … and smiles." Matilda is very angry that the adults around him want to repress his tastes. Of course, the story does not portray them as narrow-minded persons who cannot conceive of a boy wanting to wear a tiara, but as people incapable of seeing "the little girl inside her." But then the parents wake up and agree to give him the longed-for tiaras. The interpretation is not that they finally realized that there is nothing wrong with a boy wearing such a hair ornament, but a very different one:

> They have finally realized that she is a girl! And for her fifth birthday they have given her the five tiaras they always denied her. At long last, they let her wear the clothes she always wanted, they don't correct her when she talks and they tell her that she looks pretty. A few days have passed and for Matilda everything has changed. Her classmates call her by her name. She goes to school with a glitter backpack and to ballet class in a fancy tutu.

To put it another way, in order to give him permission to wear head-bands and tutus to ballet class, Matilda's parents first had to be convinced that their son was in fact their daughter. In the world of *transgender* children and youth organizations like Chrysallis, there is no other option, and among the families who embark on the belief that their children are trans, there are many who, like Matilda's, are unaware that a boy can wear a crown of flowers in his hair and that this is okay. Susie Green, who from January 2016 to November 2022 was chief executive of Mermaids – a British charity "supporting trans, non-binary and gender-diverse children, young people and their families since 1995" – could not bring herself to buy her son a dress, no matter how hard he begged, before he was diagnosed with gender dysphoria at the age of seven.[49]

For blue-brained girls there is a story too, by the same author and also published in 2017. It is called *En la piel de Daniel* (In Daniel's Skin) and goes like this:

> Miss Simona is worried … Is her classroom a zoo? Her most unruly pupil, in one way or another, drives her crazy. The one whose skirt is torn and who doesn't like to wear pink. The one who at carnival dresses up as a Comanche or a cowboy and at Christmas wants to be a fireman. […] Berta, the one who takes off her hairpin first thing in the morning – maybe she's not a girl. At home, for a few days now mum and dad have understood this, and have gone to school to explain what's going on. 'Berta is a boy! It seems complicated but it's very simple. He said it when he was very young, but we didn't know how to listen to him, and finally we understand what we couldn't see before. Berta is Daniel!'

And with that, Miss Simona is reassured. Now everything fits together: the girl who plays football and scores goals is a boy. Why didn't she realize this before?

Don't imagine that explanations of this phenomenon aimed at an adult audience are very different from the infantilized versions of this influential Spanish association. Developmental and clinical psychologist Diane Ehrensaft, author of the book *The Gender Creative Child*, claims that to know if a child is transgender, you just have to listen to them and let them tell you in their own way. This self-awareness of transgender children can occur very early in life, according to experts in the field, and is irrefutable. In a lecture to mental health professionals on 26 February 2016, Ehrensaft said that even preverbal children know how to communicate their gender. By way of demonstration, the co-founder of the Child and Adolescent

---

49 She unashamedly confesses this in a TEDx Talk (see Green, 2017). Susie Green famously took her son on his sixteenth birthday to be castrated in Thailand because it was forbidden in England; of course she prefers to call the procedure *sexual reassignment surgery* (see Artemisia, 2019).

Gender Center at the University of California, San Francisco, gave an example:

> I have a colleague who is transgender. There is a video of him as a toddler – he was assigned female at birth – tearing barrettes out of then-her hair. And throwing them on the ground. And sobbing. That's a gender message.[50]

As can be seen, hair accessories come up a lot in these stories. There are other elements that recur again and again. Miranda Yardley, who despite presenting himself as transgender has a critical view of gender identity ideology, set out to find the common denominators and discourses around *transgender children*. In a series of stories published in the British press between 2009 and 2017 about children who wanted or claimed to be girls, these commonalities were apparent: preference for pink, long hair, princesses and dresses, toys *for girls* (Yardley, 2017). If you can get a believer in transgender children to say how they know a boy is a girl or vice versa, they are unlikely to point to anything other than stereotyping or esoteric vagueness.

If a boy plays being a princess, has more girl friends than boy friends, likes to wear dresses and wants to grow his hair long, it won't take long for the verdict to be pronounced: he is trans, and something must be done about it. The feminist approach to such a boy would be simply to support him in his tastes and explorations without instilling sexist ideas and, if he is being bullied or criticized, to explain, to him and his schoolmates, that toys and clothes are unisex and there is nothing wrong with a boy playing a princess. Instead, the approach of self-help books, organizations such as Mexico's Asociación por las Infancias Transgénero or Spain's Chrysallis, as well as transgender children and professional bodies, is to convince the boy that his tastes in clothes and games indicate a discrepancy between his body and his mind (or playing along if it was he who,

---

50   On the 4thWaveNow website you can read a critical note about her talk and links to the symposium in which it was framed – Clinical Essentials for Increased Understanding of the Diverse Transgender Community.

influenced by his environment, began to harbour such ideas).[51] But worry not – there's a solution: gender transition. If radical feminism, developmental psychology and common sense recommend helping the child to accept their body, their sex and their way of being as normal and positive, the prevailing transgenderist model and gender identity activism reinforce the idea that there is something wrong with the body and it may eventually need to be changed.

Transgender rhetoric is fluid and misleading; there are those who deny that the discourse of the wrong body is an integral part of this doctrine (and claim, for example, that "the intention is not to regulate bodies, but for children and adolescents to have the freedom to grow up").[52] In characterizing their positions, I rely not only on their often contradictory statements and declarations, but also on their actions and the beliefs that logically follow from them. It is patently incongruous to tell self-declared trans teenage girls that their bodies are perfect and there is nothing wrong with them, while at the same time celebrating those who undergo unnecessary double mastectomies and show off their new flat chests and scars on TikTok as if they were badges of honour. If they truly believed that the body was not the issue, Rachel Levine, US Assistant Secretary for Health (who is also "the first openly transgender four-star officer" in the nation's uniformed services), would not call to "support and empower these youths" by giving them unlimited access to "gender-affirming care" (Kornick, 2022; Schemmel, 2022), which famously consists of administering puberty blockers and cross-sex hormones and subjecting them to unnecessary surgeries on the false promise that they will eventually change their sex.

And if the champions of gender identity really thought that children who don't fit in with sexist stereotypes should be encouraged to be who they are and not be made into something else, it would be impossible to understand the vitriol with which English poet Rachel Rooney was attacked after the publication of her picture book

---

51 Playing along is the so-called affirmative approach.
52 Statement by Tania Morales, "lawyer, mother of a trans youth and director of the Asociación por las Infancias Transgénero" (in González, 2020).

My Body Is Me, illustrated by Jessica Ahlberg, which invites readers aged three to six to love their bodies and appreciate all that they can do. Written to counter the explosion of children's picture books that, like those from Chrysallis above, promote the idea that someone can be trapped in the wrong body, *My Body Is Me* is a book in verse in which all kinds of young people, including those with physical or sensory disabilities, can find themselves reflected. The characters play, have fun and move their bodies. With charming simplicity and without fuss, Rooney and Ahlberg break down sexist stereotypes and communicate how natural it is for a girl to dress up as a robot, or a boy as a fairy. Their messages of acceptance, such as, "Bodies are different, children are too" or "You're born in your body, you don't have a spare, so love it, hug it, treat it with care," seemed subversive and unacceptable to transactivists and trans allies who were quick to accuse their author of making "terrorist propaganda," being a "transphobe" and having a "hateful world view" (see Rooney, 2021).

Rooney had been on the transgender movement's radar since 2018, when she began expressing ideas contrary to gender identity doctrine on Twitter, but in 2019, when her picture book was released, a campaign of harassment and intimidation was unleashed, damaging her career and her health. People in the circle in which she moved, that of children's literature and children's books, swallowed the lies and joined in the attacks. Finally, on 3 June 2020, the writer announced on Twitter:

> Due to sustained bullying received from within the children's publishing industry for speaking out on gender issues, I am withdrawing from public life as an author for the sake of my mental health, [although] as an autistic woman & special needs teacher I will continue to speak out for autistic youth caught up in this shitshow (Rooney, 2020).

Her account of the unpleasant experience reveals how these increasingly common smear and harassment campaigns against those who dissent from gender identity ideology can affect a person, which is ultimately what it is all about – to make her give up her forbidden ideas and turn her into a scapegoat to serve as a lesson to others. It also illustrates the intolerant nature of such persecution. Rooney continues:

> I am pretty exhausted. I haven't recovered from the industry abuse and treatment I've been receiving for over two and a half years, and I've not written anything significant since it began. Poetry had been my livelihood and my way of staying sane yet now I associate it with trauma. I've lost a good deal of respect for publishing and for a number of influencers, organisations and activists within it. I'm disappointed that hardly anyone who knows me spoke out in my defence though I understand why they might have chosen not to. But I am grateful for the increasing numbers of people in the industry who are brave enough, despite the inevitable attacks, to engage tentatively but intelligently on gender issues and around matters of free speech. At times, gender ideology reminds me of a religion. As an atheist child growing up in a strict Catholic household, I received physical and psychological 'corrections' at home and school for not stating my belief in God and for refusing to repeat the mantras or to attend church. There are parallels to be drawn (Rooney, 2021).

Why do gender identity activists find it abhorrent to invite children to be comfortable with the body they have and the body they are? It is a mystery. It might seem that suddenly they find satanic messages hidden in innocent-looking texts. Readers of my generation will remember that, according to legend, some rock songs concealed some devil-worshipping content; to detect it you had to play the LP backwards, turning the turntable anti-clockwise. Maybe those who accused Rooney of being a terrorist are reading *My Body Is Me* backwards and for that reason, in a message of love and acceptance, they find nothing but hate and rejection. Let's not rule out this hypothesis for lack of a better one.

But the more important question for society as a whole is, what is more conducive to the free development of a child's personality? Allowing young people to explore their tastes and interests on their own without labelling these as feminine or masculine – which has been the feminist position since the second wave and had its most influential moments in the 1970s – or keeping a close eye on whether a boy likes *girl stuff* or a girl *boy stuff* in order to, at the first sign that *their gender does not match their body*, push them into *social transition* and then refer them to the endocrinologist or transgender care centre – as do those who claim to be advocates for *trans children* and call for procedural reforms to allow minors to have "the right to choose their gender on their birth certificate"?

Ministry of Magic Administrative Services

Once spread in popular culture, the false beliefs that 1) some children are born in the wrong bodies, 2) this condition makes them especially vulnerable to discriminatory acts, and 3) the only solution to the problem is for them to transition socially and physically, the next step is to facilitate that transition by getting its legal recognition expedited. Enshrining the concept of transgender children into law is the key to its full legitimization.

The model of these legislative initiatives and reforms is practically the same all over the world: they follow almost verbatim the familiar arguments and definitions emanating from the Yogyakarta Principles, and simply make the necessary adjustments to local legislation. For this section, the main example I use will be the 'Guidelines to Guarantee Human Rights in the Administrative Procedure for the Recognition of Adolescents' Gender Identity' in Mexico City. They were issued by the head of government, Claudia Sheinbaum, on 27 August 2021, after a couple of years of intense transgender lobbying in the legislative, executive and judicial branches.

The rhetoric with which the gender identity lobby pushes these kinds of measures exploits the same confusions and ambiguities that characterize such discourse elsewhere. In the bills and laws resulting from these pressures, the words *sex* and *gender* are used interchangeably, *trans rights* are equated with the rights of gays and lesbians, *transgender* children and adolescents are considered a particularly vulnerable group "that should enjoy reinforced protection from the State" (CDHCM, 2021), false statistics are cited and taken out of context, it is taken for granted that there is something called gender identity that develops between 18 months and three years of age and consists of a "deeply felt internal and individual experience of gender," sex is spoken of as something *assigned* at birth, people are assured that they have the right to have their self-perceived identity legally recognized, and, in the case of measures informally known as transgender children's laws, the narrative of the male minds in female bodies and vice versa as something innate is assumed without question.

Even people with a background in transactivism, such as Miquel Missé, view with concern this essentialist addition that the new category brings with it:

> My feeling is that the debate on minors has allowed discourses about transsexuality that some trans activists had been contesting to make a strong comeback. At times, it seemed that we had succeeded in establishing that experts on trans issues could not be psychiatrists, endocrinologists and surgeons. That was basically what the struggle for trans depathologization was all about. With the advent of the category 'transgender minor' came the return of medical experts, the discourses around sex in the brain and the innateness of transsexuality (Missé, 2018, Chapter 5).

The "recognition of self-perceived gender identity" is presented as an extension of the right to a name and identity, and as something done in the best interests of children and adolescents. Justifications such as "The access to an administrative procedure to obtain a birth certificate in accordance with one's gender identity is part of the exercise of the right to a free development of personality," "The State should not assign an identity to each person, but rather recognize the identity with which each person identifies," and "Trans children and adolescents have the right to exist according to the identity they have in their minds"[53] are accepted axiomatically, without even

---

53 The first is taken from González (2020); the second, from a call by Mexico City's Council to Prevent and Eliminate Discrimination to local deputies to "recognize trans children and allow the change of their birth certificate through administrative channels" on 9 August 2021, and the third, from a letter that the Instituto de

stopping to think, not only about their truth value, but about what they mean or the consequences they may bring with them. These stipulations come in social cascades,[54] without plural democratic discussion or intellectual filtering, straight from the non-binding Yogyakarta Principles, through the Inter-American Commission on Human Rights and other international bodies, to bureaucratic guidelines in the Mexican capital. We are assured that "allowing them to change their birth certificate through administrative channels would contribute to the formation of healthy and happy children" (Copred, 2020) without giving any reason or saying how or why. Suddenly, without further explanation, "the right to one's own name, legal personality and nationality" (Registro Nacional de Población, 2020) is translated into the misleading right of children to "rectify their birth certificate with their chosen name and self-perceived gender" (González, 2020).

To rectify, according to *The Concise Oxford Dictionary of Current English* (9th ed., 1995), is to "adjust or make right; correct, amend." In the case of the birth certificates of *trans children,* the information which needs to be corrected or made right is that which was entered in the sex (or *gender*) box at the time of going to the registry office. Up to now, a simple correction of data, for example a mistake in the surname, was a not too cumbersome procedure. But when it comes to trans children, it is not a question of correcting a typo, but of introducing a lie: by decreeing that the girl is a boy or the boy is a girl, a false piece of information is made official in this important identity document, and so the white lie becomes a legal deception.

The concept of sex rectification follows from the equally fallacious concept of *sex assigned at birth.* The only people who can claim they were *assigned a sex* (or, in this case, a *gender* would perhaps be more accurate) at birth are babies with a disorder of

---

Liderazgo Simone de Beauvoir sent in October 2019 to the Gender Equality and Administration and Procurement of Justice Commissions of the Mexico City Congress when a couple of bills on *trans children* were being studied.

54   Social cascades according to Cass R. Sunstein will be briefly considered in the next chapter.

sexual development. English lawyer Claire Graham, an intersex/DSD advocate, explains the context in which this term arose:

> Some boys were born with micropenises. [...] Sometimes the doctors would decide that the boy's penis wasn't adequate enough and he would never be able to grow to be a man. [...] What they would do then is remove the boy's penis and testicles and create a 'neovagina' and the boy was told he was a girl and would be raised as a girl. That's what we mean when we talk about assigned sex, because it's not the baby's sex – it's not their biological sex, but they have this sex assigned to them, that they will live their life as. I think it's really unhelpful for other people to use this language. If that happened to you, you would want and need words that describe that unique thing, and applying that language to everyone else when the rest of us had a simple observation of our genitals I think it is really cruel to those people, who should be able to say that they were assigned, that this is what happened to them (Graham, 2021).

These kinds of rather cosmetic operations, arising not from an interest in the life and health of a child, but from very narrow ideas of what bodies should look like and what it means to be male and female, are frowned upon in intersex activist circles, who "tend to be against unnecessary medical interventions, particularly for children" (Graham, 2019).[55] Tumblr user Intersexunicorn agrees with Graham's assessment:

> It's been a terrible erasure of intersex identities with these labels: FAAB = female-assigned at birth, MAAB = male-assigned at birth, etc. First, *assigned*.
>
> This was a word for intersex children. A child was born ambiguous and was assigned a sex with scalpels and sutures ... *Assign* is a verb, meaning something physical happened. Someone did something physical to you.

---

55 Fortunately, such operations on babies are now considered contrary to their human rights. This does not prevent them from continuing to be performed in Mexico – and several other countries – whenever genital ambiguity is detected, according to the organization Brújula Intersexual (Arena Pública, 2018).

[…] The problem is that intersex people have been trying repeatedly to drop the term *intersex genital mutilation* and just go with the gentler term *assigned*. But with trans people taking this away from us, now we have to go back to it.

We're trying to be subtle and just blend in with society but if trans people keep trying to take our traumatic experiences as a fun label, then we just keep finding ourselves buried deeper and deeper as ashamed people who should never be spoken about.

What was done to me should be something that no human being should ever be subjected to, and is why I lobby that it should never happen to any person ever again (Intersexunicorn, n.d.).

Once again, gender identity activism is appropriating other people's experiences in order to feather their own nest. They take the term out of context and try to make us forget that sex is determined at the moment when the egg is fertilized by the sperm and that it can be detected by blood tests after nine weeks and by ultrasound at 12 weeks of pregnancy. Those who, on the assumption that this is the polite or politically correct way of putting it, blithely talk about the *sex assigned at birth* to babies who have not undergone intersex genital mutilation, seem to ignore the fact that the sex of a newborn child is obvious with a degree of accuracy that is close to 100 per cent. Furthermore, if we all had our sex assigned at birth, this leaves a question – who is supposed to do the deed? The midwife? The obstetrician? The parents? The head of the newborn nursery?

One possible answer can also be found among the Chrysallis educational resources, which have already been so illuminating. According to the story *La gran equivocación* (The Big Mistake), by Ana Castro Ortega and Patricia Murube Jiménez, it is the doctor who assigns the sex of a newborn baby, but with the indispensable help of some fairies who talk in his ear. Sometimes the fairies are very busy, and a novice, more prone to make mistakes, has to take over the task. On one occasion, the inexperienced fairy on duty,

> because she was so nervous, didn't take a good look and thought that the baby was a boy, because she only looked at his little body, forgetting to look where she had been taught so many times that she should

look, which was in the brain. That's where birth fairies have to look in order to know if someone is a girl or a boy, because that's the most important part of the body.[56]

We have seen how associations for transgender children teach kids to identify their *gender* based on their taste in clothes, games and hair accessories. Now we see how they explain to them the origin of the possible discrepancy between their sex and the way they are. It is not uncommon for a children's book to present fantasy worlds, but when it is known that these books are being used to deceive their very young readers and present fantasy as reality, there is much to criticize besides their graphic and literary quality. If preschoolers are no longer led to believe that storks deliver babies, why are they told that sex can be chosen and that it is a matter of identification? Why do we keep feeding them sexist stereotypes and reinforcing the idea that children have to fit into certain sexist moulds – and if they don't fit, it means that someone made a mistake when *assigning* them their sex? The problem takes on another magnitude when adults are also expected to live in this fairytale world and we are forced to participate in the deception if we do not want to pay the consequences and be banished from society.

In order for people to believe that, prior to the rescuing administrative measures (i.e. the falsification of the birth certificate), these children were denied their right to identity and their right not to be discriminated against, the trans lobby needs the invaluable support of the media, members of which often simply copy and paste the press releases and very rarely dare to include feminist voices that call for caution and reflection and warn that laws for transgender children are entirely counterproductive and detrimental to the very minors they are supposed to benefit.[57]

---

56 All Chrysallis stories quoted in this chapter can be found on their website: <chrysallis.org>.

57 Two examples of the media collusion with transgenderism. Julian Vigo revealed that the English newspaper *The Guardian,* which over the years has given virtually no voice to more than one side of the debate, received USD $250,000 from the Open Society Foundations in 2019 alone, with the express mandate to publish

Wealthy as well as powerful, this lobby also has its own media. A year before the guidelines issued by Mexico City's head of government, a bill to allow minors (under the age of 18) to *rectify* their birth certificates in an express manner and without any questions asked, was held up in the local Congress, Presentes Agency (whose logo is a letter *P* on a rainbow flag) published an article entitled 'Niñeces trans necesitan protección y el Congreso de CDMX se la niega' (Trans children need protection and the Mexico City Congress denies it to them) (González, 2020). To communicate that, if one wanted to change from *female* to *male* or vice versa in the sex box of the birth certificate by means of a simple procedure, one had to be at least 18 years of age, the article states:

> Today, in order to have access to their birth certificate, trans children and teenagers and their families are subject to a pathologizing, stigmatizing, slow and costly trial where a judge is finally the one who accredits the gender identity of the minor.

They paint a bleak picture, but it might help, to put it in perspective, to know that it is a total falsehood that these minors lacked access to their birth certificate, and that by "pathologizing, stigmatizing … trial" they mean that some psychological tests were required before an official document would state that a girl is a boy or the other way around.

Reading the testimony of Luis (who "discovered his identity at the age of 13, when he found the definition of the term *trans*"

---

articles in favour of the doctrine of gender identity (Vigo, 2020). In Mexico, the digital outlet *Animal Político*, which claims to put "citizens at the centre, privileging a dialogue with them," addresses trans issues without any impartiality or dialogue with dissenting voices. Claudia Ramos *(Mala Madre)*, head of analysis, advisor and wife of the director general, puts in her Twitter bio: "I don't accept transphobic speeches, don't insist." On 27 July 2022, Lydia Cacho – a renowned Mexican journalist who uncovered a political-business network of child prostitution – wrote a tweet that some considered transphobic. Ramos responded with these words to it: "I have two trans people at home and that is all the more reason why I know that what you are doing is called transphobia." This may give us a clue as to how *Animal Político*'s editorial line is defined in relation to the themes of this book. As can be imagined, Cacho received a barrage of attacks, besides Ramos' scolding, and, having learned her lesson, she soon deleted it and days later did penance.

and, after telling his family, "they decided to start the legal path to change the identity of someone who, until then, was recognized as a girl") makes one think that perhaps, for such a transcendental decision, instead of only making it a condition that the minor be at least 12 years old and "state that he/she perceives him/herself as having a gender different from the one stated in his/her original birth registration" (Gobierno de la Ciudad de México, 2021a), it was not such a bad idea to ask for a professional opinion. Luis said:

> It was very nice because I felt very identified with this definition of what trans was and it felt nice because I could finally name what I felt. I told them about it and we started to look for ways in which I could live as a man (Noticias IMER, 2020).

Would it be awfully pathologizing and stigmatizing to ask a 13-year-old girl what "living as a man" means to her[58] before setting in motion a series of interventions that may be irreversible and never even lead to the promised destination?

Because on top of everything else, we must attribute magical powers to the bureaucratic procedure, which in the eyes of transactivists and allies – more enthusiastic than clever – becomes the only possible solution to school bullying and social discrimination suffered by boys who do not comply with the expected masculinity and girls who are insufficiently feminine. Beyond alluding to their distress at being *misgendered* or called by the name on their birth certificate, no one takes the trouble to explain convincingly the causal relationship between a document with altered data and the ultimate remedy to bullying. When a mild-mannered boy is called a *sissy* or *faggot* by his classmates, do the insults stop the moment he produces the document that makes it official that he is not a faggot, but a girl with a penis?

---

58 I was asked such questions by a psychologist when I was six years old and it wasn't a bad experience; in fact, I found it liberating to understand that in order to do the things I liked to do, there was absolutely no need to be a boy.

If we are to believe Mexico City's Council for the Prevention and Elimination of Discrimination, this tiny *rectification* breaks down all barriers so that *transgender* minors have

> the guarantee of a life free of violence and discrimination, and rights as elementary as being called by the names and pronouns they identify with, travelling, going to school, going to the doctor or taking part in a sports class (Copred, 2021).

So why don't we extend this administrative magic to the four million Mexican children and adolescents living in extreme poverty, or to the 340,000 girls between 15 and 19 years old and 5,000 under 15 who give birth in this country every year? Surely, they could do with state institutions guaranteeing them some rights even more pressing than the right to identify themselves with this or that pronoun.

Child safeguarding

As feminists we are not only sceptical about the efficacy of *rectifying* birth certificates to magically solve the suffering of children who feel different from others because they are encumbered by the straitjacket of sex roles or because they have an uncomfortable relationship with their bodies. We are convinced that there are ways to solve what could be interpreted as a child's *gender dysphoria* that do not consist of making false promises and telling lies as big as the one that human beings can change their sex. We also call for serious measures to be taken to put an end to bullying, not just bullying of these children specifically, but of anyone and for any condition: ethnicity, skin colour, possible disability, weight, height, sex, appearance, hair length, etc.

We believe that classrooms should be a place where sexism is combated and stereotypical roles and limited ideas of what it is to be a man or a woman are challenged. However, the idea of transgender children, by enthroning sexist roles and considering them intrinsic to our personality, does the opposite. It does not help young students to shed that straitjacket, but rather tightens it even further.

In different parts of the world, schools are teaching pre-school and primary school students that gender identity is their authentic self and that is why there are girls with a penis and boys with a vagina. In this way they actively participate in the social construction of the transgender child, whose tastes in clothes and toys indicate that his or her body is out of sync with his or her mind, and whose birth certificate must therefore be corrected first, and then his or her body – in the reverse order of yesterday's intersex babies.

The UK, the United States and Canada are among the pioneers of these practices, which in a relatively short time have spread to other countries.[59] One of them is Spain, where the group Docentes Feministas por la Coeducación (Feminist Teachers for Coeducation, Dofemco) was founded in response to alarm from a number of female teachers at all stages of education, according to one of its members, anthropologist Silvia Carrasco. On the one hand, the teachers perceived an increase in sexist attitudes and mentalities among students, and on the other hand, they felt that they were being robbed of coeducation, "an instrument of feminism to achieve a fairer society from school as a mission of education for citizenship." Under the label of *coeducation,* the transgender/queer movement was making proposals for teacher training and raising awareness among students "that had nothing to do with coeducation, but quite the opposite," because they see "gender as a felt identity, regardless of the sexed body, when gender is the main instrument of patriarchal oppression, which defines women as inferior and justifies their subordination at the hands of men" (Carrasco, 2022).

---

59   The documentaries *The Call is Coming from Inside the House* and *This Is Not a Drill: The Indoctrination of Gender Ideology in Schools,* by the creator known as Skirt Go Spinny, expose how this is happening in the United States, with multiple examples of *queer* teachers who boast on their social networks that they have taken the transgender crusade into their own hands. On the British website Transgender Trend (a treasure trove of resources to help families who, when a child announces he or she is *transgender,* decide to try alternatives to the affirmative approach), there is a section devoted to critically documenting social transition practices in US schools. The author of one contribution calls the whole thing a "quirky educational experiment" (Anonymous, 2016).

Faced with this situation, which began to be observed in 2014, Dofemco makes ten demands to educational administrations and institutions, teachers' unions and political parties. The first two are a clear response to the energetic revenge of the pink and blue brains against feminist theory.

We demand:

1. The development and promotion of authentic coeducation, free of manipulation and transgender propaganda. Gender identity ideology has distorted and replaced the objectives and strategies of coeducation, which, we recall, are:
   - Guaranteeing an education free of androcentrism and machismo for children.
   - Educating children in fair relationships, based on equality and respect.
   - Eradicating attitudes and values that underpin violence against girls and women.

2. The withdrawal of the *trans* educational guides produced by the Regional Ministries of Education themselves and of the materials of the educational unions and transactivist associations, since they:
   - Deny that biological sex is a reality that defines us as women and men, and confuse students by mixing and misrepresenting the concepts of sex and gender.
   - Deny and censor the specificity of women's bodies and their biological cycles.
   - Reinforce and perpetuate harmful sexism and sexist stereotypes.
   - Include age-inappropriate pornographic content and normalize pornography and prostitution.[60]

In Mexico, although this hijacking of education has not been made official, there are organizations that are seeking entry into schools,

---

60 Available at dofemco.org. In November 2021, this same organization held the international congress La Ideología de la Identidad de Género en las Aulas (Gender identity ideology in the classrooms), where it was widely documented that "under pressure from the transgender lobby, [...] ultra-conservative content contrary to rational education based on science and on the principles of education [to achieve] equality between women and men" is being distributed in schools. All this and much more information can be found on the website dofemco.org.

albeit through the back door. The Asociación por las Infancias Transgénero (Association for Transgender Children), for example, has an action protocol "aimed at preschool, elementary school, middle school and high school, as a tool to guide the actions of their authorities and teachers when registering cases of trans* children and adolescents," in which indoctrination in transgender language and ideas is disguised as a call for "respectful and inclusive coexistence." They aspire to make these norms compulsory and, to go no further, their first request is that school authorities include "in the curriculum for students the approach to trans* and non-binary gender identities." They also provide counselling to families interested in

> requesting the adoption of the [feminist] protocol in each school and, if necessary, filing a complaint with the Council to Prevent Discrimination and the different human rights commissions involved (Asociación por las Infancias Transgénero, 2018).

These rules are intended to contribute to the

> recognition of self-perceived name and gender on school lists, exams, report cards, sports competitions and, crucially, in the use of bathrooms and locker rooms (Asociación por las Infancias Transgénero, 2018).

In other words, if a high school male teenager (14–18 years old) one fine day announces that he identifies as a girl, his female classmates will not only have to speak to him with female pronouns, but accept him in their competitions and, "crucially," in their bathrooms and locker rooms, where they may be naked and more vulnerable. If they don't comply, human rights commissions will be called in to defend him. If we remember that men are consuming pornography at younger and younger ages (see Chiappe, 2022), and that the phenomenon of boys and adolescents who rape is becoming even more notorious (see Clark, 2021), it becomes abundantly clear that it is not women's and girls' human rights that matter to promoters of transgenderism.

It is claimed that instilling these *inclusive* ideas in the classroom contributes to an atmosphere of tolerance and acceptance. What it does in fact is create a climate contrary to critical thinking, in which dissenting or even asking questions is forbidden, and doing this at an age, such as puberty and adolescence, when the need to fit in and belong is stronger than ever and therefore these teenagers are more inclined to believe the same as the majority of their peers.

American researcher Lisa Littman observed that in her social circle many young girls were suddenly beginning to identify as transgender, and later found out that in clinical settings it was being noticed that more and more teenagers and young women in their 20s were seeking help to deal with their *gender dysphoria*. Littman then undertook a descriptive and exploratory study based on a survey of parents (91.7 per cent of whom were mothers) who perceived in their children (82.8 per cent of whom were daughters), with an average age of 15 years and no history of gender nonconformity, signs of what she characterized as *a rapid onset of gender dysphoria* (ROGD).[61] These girls were part of groups of friends in which several or all of them began to consider themselves transgender at about the same time. Another element present was an intensive use of the internet and social media before children came forward with the idea they had a transgender identity.

Littman's observations were consistent with another new phenomenon – a reversal in the demographics seeking professional help for gender dysphoria. Whereas in 2009 and 2010, 40 boys and 32 girls consulted the Gender Identity Development Service (GIDS) at the Tavistock Clinic in England, in 2018–2019 there were 624 boys and 1,740 girls. This amounts to an increase of 1,460 per cent for boys and 5,337 per cent for girls in less than a decade (Transgender Trend, 1 July 2019). In the United States, between 2016 and 2017, the number of plastic surgeries to change the appearance of secondary sex characteristics in women (they call them *gender affirmation surgeries*) quadrupled: if in 2016 there were 1,759 men and 1,497 women, in 2017 there were 2,483 men

---

61   Littman is careful to insist that this is not a diagnosis, but a possible way of understanding a social phenomenon in search of an explanation.

and 5,821 women, representing an increase of 41 per cent and 289 per cent, respectively (American Society of Plastic Surgeons, 2017). This is an unprecedented phenomenon for which there should be an explanation, and we as a society have the duty to seek it.

The typical transgender response is that this is due to greater social acceptance of transgender people, but this explanation is not convincing, for several reasons. First, nothing similar happened when same-sex marriage was passed – the numbers of lesbians and gay men in the population have always remained very uniform. Secondly, the demographic reversal, the fact that there are now many more trans-identified women than trans-identified men, also needs to be explained. Thirdly, women in their 30s and older have not seen the same explosion that is so evident among teenage girls and young women. And finally, don't gender identity activists themselves say that transphobia is a serious social problem and that *transphobic hate crimes* are the order of the day?[62] Aren't transgender children's laws supposed to prevent these minors from having to suffer the ubiquitous irrational fear of people who were assigned the wrong sex at birth? So, where's the greater acceptance?

Littman wondered whether this sudden gender dysphoria in adolescents might not be influenced by the environment; whether it might not be due, for example, to social contagion, understood not in the sense of infectious disease, but as "the spread of affect or behaviours through a population" (Littman, 2018, p. 4) and mutual influence among people of the same age, terminology that is now academically established and does not entail any value judgement. This physician and researcher sees clear similarities in rapid onset gender dysphoria and the spread of anorexia among female peers:

> There are many insights from our understanding of peer contagion in eating disorders and anorexia that may apply to the potential role(s) of peer contagion in the development of gender dysphoria. Just as friendship cliques can set the level of preoccupation with one's body,

---

62 This may well be true, since refusing to participate in the fiction of gender identity is transphobia in the transgender universe, and *misgendering* and saying that men cannot be women are transphobic hate crimes.

body image, weight and techniques for weight loss, so too many friendships cliques set a level of preoccupation with one's body, body image, gender, and the techniques to transition. The descriptions of pro-anorexia subculture group dynamics where the thinnest anorexics are admired while the anorexics who try to recover from anorexia are ridiculed and maligned as outsiders resemble the group dynamics in friend groups that validate those who identify as transgender and mock those who do not. And the pro-eating disorder websites and online communities providing inspiration for weight loss and sharing tricks to help individuals deceive parents and doctors may be analogous to the inspirational YouTube transition videos and the shared online advice about manipulating parents and doctors to obtain hormones (Littman, 2018, p. 34).

Littman's revelations about the influence of social media on the adoption of transgender identities raise a red flag and offer a glimpse into the workings of the machinery. Respondents were asked what kind of advice their children had received from people they communicated with online. Here are the answers:

Adolescents and young adults had received online advice including how to tell if they were transgender (54.2%); the reasons that they should transition right away (34.7%); that if their parents did not agree for them to take hormones that the parents were 'abusive' and 'transphobic' (34.3%); that if they waited to transition they would regret it (29.1%); what to say and what not to say to a doctor or therapist in order to convince them to provide hormones (22.3%); that if their parents were reluctant to take them for hormones that they should use the 'suicide narrative' (telling the parents that there is a high rate of suicide in transgender teens) to convince them (20.7%); and that it is acceptable to lie to or withhold information about one's medical or psychological history from a doctor or therapist in order to get hormones/get hormones faster (17.5%) (Littman, 2018, p. 20).

Don't think for one moment that Littman was spared the charge of transphobia. Controversy erupted and the usual scenario of misrepresentations, personal attacks and hyperbolic false accusations was repeated. The journal that published her study yielded to political pressure to review the methodology and analysis and demanded that the author made a series of "corrections" (it is worth mentioning that after the revision none of her results had changed). Her article is measured and thoughtful, born out of genuine concern for the harm that may be inflicted on young people through an inaccurate diagnosis:

> The findings of this study suggest that clinicians need to be cautious before relying solely on self-report when adolescents and young adults (AYAs) seek social, medical or surgical transition. Adolescents and young adults are not trained medical professionals. When AYAs diagnose their own symptoms based on what they read on the internet and hear from their friends, it is quite possible for them to reach incorrect conclusions (Littman, 2018, p. 37).[63]

This sounds very reasonable, but it goes totally against the axiomatic principle that "trans children know who they are; they don't 'feel it', they don't 'believe it': they *know* who they are and they experience themselves that way," as Janet Castillo, legal coordinator of the Mexican transgender ally association Litigio Estratégico en Derechos Sexuales y Reproductivos (Ledeser) asserts (see Nochebuena, 2022).

Littman was accused of bias for having interviewed only parents and not their children – when the purpose of her study was to offer precisely that point of view, which in the current climate is rarely taken into account. It was also claimed that she had sought out only conservative or anti-transgender parents – when in fact 88.2 per cent of respondents believe "that transgender people deserve the same rights and protections as others" in their country – and it was implied that the study's findings "could be used to discredit efforts to support transgender youth and invalidate the perspectives of members of the transgender community" (Wadman, 2018).

The authority on trans children who claims that an 18-month-old baby who tears barrettes out of her hair is communicating in her own way that her gender does not correspond to her *assigned* sex at birth (because at that age they do not yet speak but they already

---

63 On the Littman *affair*, see also Shrier (2020, pp. 25–39) and Vigo (2021).

understand an abstract concept better than most adults) commented on Littman's paper:

'I would have rejected this manuscript outright for its methodological flaws and also its bias', says Diane Ehrensaft [...], who treats transgender young people as a clinical psychologist and has reviewed scientific papers for journals. Its implication that gender exploration 'is simply a fad whipped up by peer influence' should not be taken as authentic, she argues. 'It negates the experience of many transgender youth' (Wadman, 2018).

Lisa Littman's information and hypotheses shake the foundations of transgender doctrine and tactical principles such as the insistence on innate nonconformity between a person's *gender identity* and their *sex assigned at birth*. In that sense, the outrageous reactions and attempts to invalidate her paper, not necessarily with facts and arguments, are understandable. Almost four years after its publication, the decision to close the Tavistock GIDS by the spring of 2023, announced on 28 July 2022, vindicates Littman. And not only her: it vindicates all the people, especially feminists, who, in a climate of demonization of their critical stance on transgenderism, have denounced the haste with which children who do not fit into the prefabricated sexist moulds are labelled as trans and pushed down the uncertain path of *transition*.

The great negligence

Tavistock's GIDS, the only clinic in the UK dedicated exclusively to children and adolescents "experiencing difficulties in the development of their gender identity," favoured puberty blockers over psychotherapy – better to alter the body than address the underlying psychological issues. Their model was based on the so-called Dutch protocol, created in the late 1990s by two Amsterdam-based endocrinologists who came up with the idea that gonadotropin releasing hormone (GnRH) agonists could be used to stop sexual development before it started. This would prevent children considered trans from going through the difficult changes of puberty, with the aim of making it easier for them to pass as someone of the other sex in the future. Together they founded a gender identity clinic and, as Swedish journalist Kajsa Ekis Ekman puts it, "in so doing, started something of a revolution" (Ekman, 2022, p. 128).

The GIDS launched their trial with 13-, 14- and 15-year-olds in 2010; prior to that they did not administer blockers to anyone under 16 years old. To make their idea more palatable, they claimed that GnRH agonists treatment was reversible and presented it as a harmless pause button that would allow more time to explore one's identity and decide whether or not to transition, even though this contradicted their research protocol, which stated:

> It is not clear what the long-term effects of early suppression may be on bone development, height, sex organ development, and body shape and their reversibility if treatment is stopped during pubertal development (quoted in Biggs, 2020).

A paediatrician on the study team acknowledged that there were serious risks:

> If you suppress puberty for three years the bones do not get any stronger at a time when they should be, and we really don't know what suppressing puberty does to your brain development. We are dealing with unknowns (quoted in Biggs, 2020).

More is known now about the effects of hormone blockers on the brain: they can obstruct its development and impair memory and other brain functions:

> A Brazilian case study of a boy who was given puberty blockers for two years and four months concluded that his IQ had diminished: 'A global IQ reduction is observed. At the end of 28 months of treatment, speed processing and memory remain lower than before GnRHa treatment'. Shockingly, the boy's mental development did not simply stagnate – it actually deteriorated (Ekman, 2022, p. 204).[64]

---

64   The quote is from the study by Maiko A. Schneider et al. (14 November 2017), 'Brain Maturation, Cognition and Voice Pattern in a Gender Dysphoria Case under Pubertal Suppression', *Frontiers in Human Neuroscience*.

The aforementioned Lesbians United report, which is highly recommended for those who want to be fully informed and get the raw data stripped of sentimental rhetoric, confirms this: "Evidence suggests that GnRH agonists may have long-term consequences for intelligence and memory in children and adolescents" (2022a, p. 8).

After four years of this trial at Tavistock, the blockers were not shown to cause any significant difference in psychosocial activity, but instead there was a higher incidence of self-harm and, among girls in particular, more emotional and behavioural problems, as well as greater body dissatisfaction. Arguably, puberty blockers worsened mental health and exacerbated *gender dysphoria*. Michael Biggs found signs that the latter was precisely what was being sought:

> Puberty blockers were the first stage on the predestined path to cross-sex hormones. After four assessment interviews, a child of 12 would be consenting in effect to a life of drug dependence and the loss of fertility and the probable loss of sexual functioning. Because the 'treatment' was intended to enhance the child's desire to change sex, it naturally exacerbated her or his gender dysphoria. 'Worsening behavioural and emotional symptoms of dysphoria', the Health Research Authority notes cheerfully, 'would therefore not in itself be unexpected' (Biggs, 2020, p. 11).

This is why those who attended the clinic left with a diagnosis of gender dysphoria and a prescription for puberty blockers under their arm, despite their ineffectiveness for what they were supposed to do and despite the risks. Clearly, no interest in the health and well-being of the children was guiding the decisions. The results of the trial did not serve, as they should have, to stop such treatment, but quite the opposite. In fact, it is now known that inhibitors were prescribed to children as young as ten years old (see Manning, 2017).

By July 2022, when the decision was finally taken to close it, the GIDS had long been in crisis and had moved from scandal to scandal. Over 17 years, staff members at this National Health Service (NHS) clinic had expressed concern about the unethical nature of some of its practices. They found it problematic that, instead of trying to understand the difficulties the children were experiencing, they preferred to affirm their beliefs and their own diagnoses without question (this is called the *affirmative approach,* which has become almost compulsory in several countries: if a child thinks they might be transgender, you have to affirm their belief, otherwise it is *conversion therapy*). Sometimes two appointments were enough for them to be prescribed puberty blockers as the solution to all their ills, because all their ills were reduced to a catch-all diagnosis: in three years, 35 doctors resigned because they saw that too often, and not always accurately, children were diagnosed with gender dysphoria whose problems lay most likely elsewhere (see Donnelly, 2019). The criteria for diagnosis were the least important because, as Biggs notes, "the condition in practice is defined by the patient's wish for endocrinological and surgical interventions" (Biggs, 2022, p. 348).

The first one to see the red flags at GIDS was psychiatric nurse Sue Evans, an associate professor at Tavistock in those years. In 2005, she noted hasty medical assessments and the influence on the clinic's policies from transgender activist groups, such as Gendered Intelligence or the aforementioned Mermaids. In February 2019, an internal report by board member David Bell warned that patients were suffering long-term harm because GIDS was becoming politicized and bowing to pressure from transactivists. Around the same time, a group of parents had sent the board a letter expressing concerns about the speed with which their children were being assessed and conclusions drawn.

People outside the clinic were also concerned that perfectly healthy children were being medicated without justification and on the basis of a prefabricated diagnosis. One of them is British philosopher Heather Brunskell-Evans, who since 2015 has been at the forefront of an intensive campaign to defend the rights of children who are uncomfortable with gender stereotypes, rights that Tavistock violated with impunity with nobody stopping them:

> The GIDS offers physically healthy and phenotypically normal children and young people dangerous, off-label drug treatment with life-long deleterious consequences on the basis of a child's subjective feeling,

for which there is no scientific test or where clinical diagnosis is based on the child's self-report. [...] In the context of the UK legal system which enshrines the myth that transgenderism exists, all children are now being taught that they and their brothers, sisters and friends may have been born in the wrong body (Brunskell-Evans, 2019, p. 37).

In December 2020, the lawsuit against Tavistock by Keira Bell, a young detransitioner (someone who regrets having transitioned and no longer assumes a trans identity), was a decisive blow – she had gone to the clinic seven years earlier, at 16, and had been prescribed puberty blockers after brief trivial conversations with social service workers in which she said she believed she was a man, not a woman. At 17, she was prescribed testosterone, and at 20 she had a bilateral mastectomy. Like a growing number of detransitioners, Bell argued that when she went to the Tavistock she was too young to accept such interventions and had been given misleading information; they should have challenged her more, she claimed. On that occasion the High Court ruled that before the age of 16 it was difficult for someone to give informed consent because they did not understand the long-term risks.[65] The following day, the NHS stopped puberty blocker treatments for children under 16.[66] During the trial it emerged that the clinic lacked statistics on the ages of the children who had been prescribed them and did not know how many had a prior diagnosis of autism, which is a common co-morbidity with *gender dysphoria.*

---

65   This decision was overturned by the Appeal Court in September 2021, but in June 2022 the NHS confirmed that, implementing advice from the Cass Review, it would stop routinely prescribing puberty-suppressing drugs to children and adolescents (see NHS England, 2023).

66   In June 2020, Finland had already broken with World Professional Association for Transgender Health 'Standards of Health' (see Society for Evidence-Based Gender Medicine 2021b); in February 2021, Anova, the trans healthcare centre of the Karolinska Hospital in Stockholm, Sweden, ended the practice of prescribing puberty blockers and cross-sex hormones to minors with *gender dysphoria;* as of August 2023, Norway is under pressure to follow suit, and it seems that Denmark is also taking a more cautious approach (see Lane, 2023). This only proves that in transgenderism, as a global phenomenon, what happens in some countries has an impact on others.

In June of the same year, a BBC report revealed that several GIDS staff members had long expressed fears to their superiors that they were harming children for life through hasty treatment decisions, but were ignored. All of these whistleblowers had observed that some parents brought their children to the clinic because they were homophobic: "Some parents appeared to prefer their children to be transgender and straight, rather than gay, pushing them towards transition," which again demonstrates that transgendering a child often functions as a genuine conversion therapy. One of the informants reports that she had to deal with the case of a young girl who, after announcing that she was a lesbian, was rejected by her family and bullied at school, and then suddenly changed her mind and came out as trans. She even stated: "My mum wants the hormone more than I do." The psychologist spoke to senior officials, but they still ordered the girl to be referred for hormone treatment (BBC News Night, 2020).

In March 2022, an independent investigation commissioned from paediatrician Hilary Cass revealed that there was no quality control of treatment and, when children came to GIDS, other health problems were overshadowed by a focus on gender identity issues (Cass, 2022). Patients were prescribed drugs without sufficient evidence about their benefits or information about their harms. Finally, in July 2022, it was confirmed that the clinic would be closing in a few months and was to be replaced by regional centres in existing children's hospitals that would provide a more holistic care, not only focused on gender identity.

Let us hope that this landmark decision will set a precedent for all transgender clinics around the world that apply the same affirmative approach as the Tavistock did and allow themselves to be infiltrated by gender identity ideologues. The organization Transgender Trend welcomed the decision and explained very well what the root problem is:

> The separation of gender dysphoria into a specialist area has led to the profound failings of a service which has replaced normal levels of care with a fast-track medical transition service for 'trans kids'.

The separation of these children into their own clinic, away from other pediatric services, has helped to promulgate the idea at the heart of child transition activism: that these children are somehow 'different' to other children and fall outside normal understandings of child development and normal standards of safeguarding and patient safety. Separation from all other pediatric services has allowed lobby groups to put pressure on an already ideologically captured management team and NHS Trust.

In no other area of paediatric care have unqualified political organisations been allowed to influence treatment protocols for children (Transgender Trend, 2022).

The role of GIDS was instrumental in the invention of so-called trans children. Its influence is not limited to the UK, but extends to other countries that, under the same pressures of the powerful global lobby of gender identity ideologues, repeat the same script and *modus operandi*. Its extinction, while necessary and welcome, will not reverse all the damage done, nor will it mean the end of the harmful idea that there is such a thing as trans children, which it helped to solidify. However, it may well be seen as a clear sign that we are closer to the end. The tide is turning.

The right to deceive

The existence of trans children was stipulated to reinforce the notion of an innate transgender identity and set up a juicy and immoral business that profits from children's suffering and raises false expectations into the bargain. The invention of *trans kids* serves, in turn, to make more acceptable to the public the idea that some men are women, and that their female identity, according to this narrative, is not something these men have created in their imagination and out of their desire, and influenced by their environment – and possibly by their porn consumption – but a congenital condition. This is how they were born, they say, and therefore we must pity them.

The Tavistock scandal reveals a series of very serious medical malpractices and procedural anomalies at the heart of which are the pressures of a group with well-defined political interests. They are clearly not those of the main victims, that is, the young girls who in all likelihood will move from puberty blockers to cross-sex hormones and later on to unnecessary surgeries on a well-worn pathway of self-harm by proxy.[67] Considering that those pulling the strings of this movement are mostly adult males, it is particularly scandalous that children, and especially girls and young women, are being driven to mutilation and sterilization to pave the way for some men bent on having everyone participate in their self-deception and be recognized as women in the eyes of the law.

The use of language plays a crucial role in all of this. It is essential to translate euphemisms into more realistic terms that make transparent who the actors are and what their intentions might be. The sweetened and misleading "Trans children are no longer denied their identity and now have access to specially designed health services" sounds very different from the crude but frank, "Many girls who have learned to hate their bodies are being psychologically manipulated and forced to self-amputate in order to advance the transgender political agenda and enrich the technomedical complex in the process." The first sounds nice, precisely to hide the fact that we are faced with a medical scandal of giant proportions. Is it possible to conceive of a less empathetic form of political use of children, one more contrary to their human rights? Most of these teenagers who are being carried off by transgenderism are lesbians who, in their learned misogyny, prefer to assume a false heterosexual male identity rather than recognize themselves as women who love other women. To promote this under the banner of LGBT rights is cruelly brazen.

In Mexico, promoters of special laws for transgender children claim that these administrative reforms do not seek to facilitate hormone treatment because the person seeking a sex change on

---

67 For a discussion of cosmetic surgery as self-mutilation by proxy, see Jeffreys (2005).

the birth certificate "is not obliged to start or undergo any hormone treatment" (Asociación por las Infancias Transgénero, 2020). What they conveniently do not say is that when a child, convinced of being a girl trapped in a boy's body or a boy trapped in a girl's body, goes through a social and then a legal transition, everything is already set up so that taking the next steps is much easier than retracing the previous ones. In fact, social transition consists of making the rest of the world a participant in our fantasy of being a person of the other sex and becoming more and more immersed in this false belief, which then comes to dominate the whole of our lives. The so-called progressive social-legal-hormonal-surgical transition is a path from which, once embarked upon, it is very difficult to turn away, as the figures indicate and as the experiences of the so-called detransitioners, to whom a section of Chapter 6 is devoted, demonstrate.

The majority (an estimated 80 per cent) of children with a condition that some call gender dysphoria overcome it over time without any intervention; that is, if as children or adolescents they say they feel or wish they were the other sex, as adults they end up forgetting the matter and accept the reality of their natal sex if nothing is done about it. Sexologist James Cantor compared 11 studies, carried out between 1972 and 2013, which looked at the rate of persistence of a trans identity:

> Despite the differences in country, culture, decade, and follow-up length and method, all the studies have come to a remarkably similar conclusion: Only very few trans-kids still want to transition by the time they are adults. Instead, they generally turn out to be regular gay or lesbian folks. The exact number varies by study, but roughly 60–90% of trans-kids turn out no longer to be trans by adulthood (Cantor, 2016).

This also confirms that rebellion against sexist dictates in childhood can be an indicator of homosexuality in adulthood, something already sensed by some of the parents who take their *effeminate* sons or *tomboyish* daughters to gender clinics to be heterosexualized, as observed by all the whistleblowers at the Tavistock.[68]

Even the World Professional Association for Transgender Health (WPATH), a group which promotes and lobbies for the *gender-affirmative approach*,[69] acknowledged in its 2012 edition that *gender dysphoria* in childhood most often disappears:

> Gender dysphoria during childhood does not inevitably continue into adulthood. Rather, in follow-up studies of prepubertal children (mainly boys) who were referred to clinics for assessment of gender dysphoria, the dysphoria persisted into adulthood for only 6–23% of children. Boys in these studies were more likely to identify as gay in adulthood than as transgender. Newer studies, also including girls, showed a 12–27% persistence rate of gender dysphoria into adulthood (WPATH, 2012, p. 11).[70]

In contrast, most young people who begin a *transition,* whether social or medical, persevere and keep identifying as trans. Biggs notes that now, because puberty blockers are so readily available, it is more common for parents to treat a *masculine* girl or a *feminine* boy as the other sex, "which guarantees that the child will experience the onset of puberty as catastrophic and thus demand endocrinological

---

68   In the documentary *Transgender Kids, Who Knows Best?* a father recounts how his son, who "ran like a girl," attended a camp for children who do not fit sexual stereotypes to *socially transition*. Upon returning from the camp, which judging by the images included a cabaret dress-up workshop and a beauty pageant, he was no longer, in the father's words, a boy who runs like a girl: he was a girl who runs like a girl! His relief is visible, because a boy with delicate features is a mistake of nature, but a girl trapped in a boy's body is the most normal thing in the world and it is scientifically proven. For him, in that instant, everything fell into place (see BBC, 2017).

69   The aforementioned Stephen Whittle, one of the first signatories to the Yogyakarta Principles and part of the team who wrote them, presided WPATH from 2007 to 2009.

70   In the new edition, released when this book was almost finished, there is also the recognition that it cannot be known whether a prepubescent child who identifies as transgender will continue to do so in adulthood: "Gender trajectories in prepubescent children cannot be predicted and may evolve over time" (WPATH, 2022, S. 67).

intervention" (Biggs, 2022, p. 360). And then what? The process continues:

> Almost all children who start puberty blockers then go onto cross-sex hormones, suggesting that desistance after medication is very rare. This may of course reflect the increased certainty of the persisters at this stage. Or it may be that it is simply too difficult to consider or admit to a change of mind (Transgender Trend, n.d.).

It is to be expected that after you have followed the transgender script of forcing everyone to refer to you using your *preferred pronouns,* announcing to friends and acquaintances that you are trans, and getting your name and sex changed on official documents, going back can feel like a personal failure. Even worse if you have already started hormone treatment and started a GoFundMe campaign to pay for a bilateral mastectomy.[71] The steps of a transgender journey are, unsurprisingly, just like lies: one leads to another. It's not easy to admit one's mistakes, especially when an identity was forged around them, hoisted as a source of utmost pride and, as is now de rigueur in the age of social media, trumpeted to the world. Kajsa Ekis Ekman explains it well:

> A 13-year-old who remains a child while their classmates begin to develop has rooted their entire identity in their body. The body becomes a project, and that project is sex change. The ongoing contact with health services, the injections and appointments, are a constant reminder of the young person's identity as a trans teen, which in most cases is complemented by membership of an online community founded on trans identity. [...] The more one invests and sacrifices, the harder it usually is to backtrack (Ekman, 2023, p. 136).

Thus, the change in the sex box on the birth certificate may be no more than the starting signal.

---

71 It's hard to know the exact number, but thousands upon thousands of young women eager to get rid of the most visible signs of their sex go to this crowdfunding platform to raise money for their *top surgeries* (bilateral mastectomies) or *bottom surgeries* (phalloplasties – creating mock penises with large amounts of their own skin taken from their forearm, calf, thigh or some other part of their body).

But there is another reason why it is very naïve to think that children who have already made the social transition will be content to change their documents without wanting to proceed to change their bodies. One justification behind the insistence that birth certificates should record the *gender identity* of people unhappy with their sex is that otherwise people would realize that they are in fact male or female. In the words of Mexico's Supreme Court Justice Norma Lucía Piña Hernández:

> If a comprehensive adaptation of gender identity is not allowed through the issuance of new identity documents, trans people would be forced to show a document with data that would reveal their status as a trans person, without full recognition of the person they really are, generating a tortuous situation in their daily lives, or one that undoubtedly and decidingly could affect their emotional or mental state and, hence, their right to comprehensive health (SCJN, 2018).

Although Minister Piña's argument overlooks the fact that we humans have a highly developed ability to perceive sex characteristics at a glance, no matter if the person is dressed or wears heavy make-up, the need for a changed birth certificate is rarely stated that clearly. According to Piña, people who identify as trans do not want to look like trans or for others to perceive their true sex. The intricate and euphemistic explanation that each person has the right "to have the attributes of personhood noted on the various registers and to have other identification documents which match the identity definitions each person has of herself" (SCJN, 2018) can be rephrased as the unambiguous, "People who consider themselves trans have the right not to let others know the truth." Unless we speak plainly, we cannot have the necessary discussions. If we use straightforward language, without the usual convolutedness, it is more difficult for people to recognize what is being put forward as a right and much easier to perceive that what we are dealing with might be a conflict of rights, to say the least. Of course, that is precisely what is being sought by transgenderism; obscure and mystifying language serves to obscure and conceal the underlying issues.

Because the right we should be talking about is not the invented right to have others recognize our fictitious *gender identity,* but something much simpler and incontrovertible: the right of everyone not to be discriminated against because of their appearance. But if we look at the current discussion, it suddenly seems that in order not to discriminate against young girls who don't want to wear dresses and prefer to wear their hair short, what is needed is to decree that they are in fact young boys. Read these statements by 17-year-old Iker, who would like to be recognized as a boy and refers to herself in the masculine grammar gender:

> Having my birth certificate with my name and gender would help me to reduce the social anxiety I suffer from at school. I always get very nervous in class when the teacher announces roll call. And if I had my birth certificate with my name and gender, my only concerns would be, like any other student, about getting good grades, and I wouldn't have to worry all the time about how people will react if the teacher makes a mistake or having to hear murmurs when this happens because it has happened so many times. I would be a lot calmer because the teacher, *not knowing that I am trans, would not have to discriminate against me* and I would not have to be worried about my grades being at risk because of something that I cannot really control, such as my gender identity (González, 2020; italics mine).

Of course, the teacher should not discriminate against Iker for any reason, but if he does, the best solution is definitely not to force the young girl and the people around her to live in an upside-down world. Resorting to the myth of trans kids is like capitulating to the schoolyard bullies who pejoratively call the effeminate child *faggot, sissy* or *little girl.* Now, if the effeminate boy doesn't want to be bullied, he knows what he has to do: identify himself as a girl and live a life of deception. That is exactly the idea that is being communicated here – now every child who does not fit sexist stereotypes will be pressured to transition; otherwise, their bullying will be justified.

But what do we as a society want to do: instil in schools respect for difference, as embodied by gays and lesbians, and in general by people who do not conform to sexist stereotypes, or do we want to give in to the bullies and join the chorus that considers a boy who does not pass the masculinity test as a girl and a girl who refuses to be feminine as a boy? For someone who is not seeking to impose an ideology, but to prevent discrimination and stop bullying, the answer is crystal clear.

It has been shown that a major motivation for having an altered birth certificate is to be able to pass more easily as someone of the other sex in the belief that this will avoid bullying. Evidently, the onset of puberty does not contribute to these aims, as it is at this stage that secondary sex characteristics develop and girls and boys begin to look less similar to each other. A boy immersed in the lie of being a girl, reinforced every day by the adults around him, will not want the truth to come out any day in the form of chest hair or an Adam's apple.

For this is what puberty inhibitors are all about: stopping the onset of menstruation, the growth of beards, voice changes, thus facilitating appearances and increasing the likelihood of success with cross-hormones and surgeries. No girl as determined to pass as a boy as Iker (or as convinced that she is a boy) is going to want her breasts to grow and be noticeable through her school uniform.

Miquel Missé, perhaps one of the most authentically revolutionary and radical voices within transactivism, in her aforementioned *The Myth of the Wrong Body* makes a very strong criticism of the groups of families of *trans children* in the Spanish context, but the same experiences can be observed in other countries. She accuses pro trans civil society organizations of having "somehow colonized trans politics." She recognizes that with their lobbying strategies they have conquered public opinion but she does not look favourably upon their strategy to have children tell their life stories on television, which is one of the best vehicles for their characteristic emotional blackmail. Missé says that showing them on every home screen "is the opposite of the discourse they promote that at any moment these children can change their minds," because how do you change your mind when you have appeared in five hundred newspapers, magazines, reports and documentaries saying that you are the first transgender kid in your school, or the first trans kid to change their ID card, or their health card, in your autonomous community?

Missé also criticizes the obsession with the discourse of so-called passing, whether it concerns minors or adults. When these organizations

talk about trans visibility, gender euphoria, or that there are no wrong bodies, they always use trans children with a 'perfect' passing, who look like regular everyday children that no one would ever suspect to be trans. And that's a big lie because it generates a false idea of social acceptance. As a strategy for increasing sensitivity I'd say it's poor, because what I want is for society to let us look trans, not to applaud us only once not a trace of being trans remains. So creating the narrative that we are winning social acceptance because people are melting over these beautiful and perfect trans children is cheating ourselves (Missé, 2018, Chapter 5).

This is the same deception Michael Biggs points to when he says:

Taking GnRHa early in puberty promises a more passable resemblance to the opposite sex, and this is why it proved so fascinating to television audiences. It is no coincidence that media coverage of transgender youth focuses on those who suppressed puberty at a young age, most famously [Jazz] Jennings (Biggs, 2022, p. 360).

All transgender objectives are part of the same machinery. The falsification of birth certificates to reflect *the gender identity of trans children* is not innocuous: as well as being instrumental to officializing a harmful lie that is far from being morally justified, it has the purpose of facilitating hormone treatments for minors, even if it is not stated in the guidelines or put as a condition. It is no coincidence that Mexico City's Unidad de Salud Integral para las Personas Trans (Integral Health Clinic for Transgender People) was inaugurated by the Head of government, Claudia Sheinbaum, on 1 October 2021, barely a month and four days after she herself issued the guidelines for the *rectification* – that is, falsification – of the birth certificates of children over the age of 12. In less than a week, the clinic was attended by "twenty people seeking to begin hormone treatment for gender reassignment, two of whom were minors." Moreover, a reporter "spoke with staff, who commented that young people are the ones who request services the most" (Vargas, 2021).

On their agenda, nothing is isolated from the rest, and they are insatiable. Luis Tirado Morales candidly admits this when she says:

> It fills my heart to think of all those little faces that know that they will no longer be invisible; that the state recognizes their existence. But it is also a call to continue our struggle; we have unresolved issues regarding non-binary children and kids under 12, and 30 states [haven't adopted laws for trans children]. But still here we are: trans* children, teenagers, young adults and adults; our blood families and our families of choice. Because this struggle is extremely complex and it is full of intersections, and, come to think of it, it is only us and our vision of a possible future (Tirado Morales, 2021).[72]

It is worth mentioning that children under the age of 12 have already been ticked off the to-do list. On 15 June 2022, the Supreme Court of Justice agreed to the request that even children and adolescents under the age of 12 can obtain a birth certificate reflecting their *self-perceived gender identity* in Mexico City through a simple and quick administrative procedure, not an amparo lawsuit, as before, which is more cumbersome and costly. Are the transactivists on the street, in the university, on the public service payroll, in the media, happy? Not quite. One of the complaints is that the court's sentence

---

72 Luis' mother is Tania Morales, Head of the Asociación por las Infancias Transgénero. Tania had arrived at the Mexico City Women's Parliament in 2019 with the sole purpose of promoting a transgender children bill, which she carried already fully drafted into her portfolio from day one, and which became the first initiative to supposedly emerge from that parliament to be passed on to the Mexico City Congress. At the age of 13, Luis told her mother that she was a lesbian, but shortly afterwards she read *This Book is Gay*, by Juno Dawson, who defines himself as a trans woman (and is the author of the famous statement, "A lot of gay men are gay men as a consolation prize, because they couldn't be women"), and shortly afterwards Luis decided that, on second thought, she was not a lesbian, but a trans boy (see Flores, 2021).

uses the word *minor* to refer to children and adolescents because that means they are deemed "persons subordinated to a secondary hierarchy" (CDHCM, 2022). Another reproach, more fundamental, is that it leaves open the possibility "for civil registries to request a medical expert opinion […] to determine the mental and emotional maturity of minors" (Nochebuena, 2022).

Indeed, some media and institutions involved in the transgender agenda seem very annoyed that someone might be interested in "verifying the degree of psycho-emotional development and personal autonomy" of a child, and determine whether he or she is giving, or is able to give, informed consent to a decision that can completely change the course of his or her life. It makes no difference that the Supreme Court established that these medical expert opinions are brief interviews with a civil registry authority in accessible and friendly language, in the form of a conversation, with the possibility for children to speak whenever they wish, and following the same requirements as other legal procedures involving a minor (see Lobo, 2022).

The movement for the transgendering of children does not like any requirements. They claim that a self-declaration of gender is a revealed truth and as such deserves absolute respect; any attempt to limit or regulate it is heresy. What comes out of a child's mouth, no matter how small she or he is, is unquestionable. The possibility of her or him making decisions that go against their own good is non-existent. These gender identity activists and trans allies only pay lip service to child protection. For them, the stages of child development are an old relic that can be thrown away. Children are little adults and to say otherwise is adultcentrism.

Mexican institutions, one after another, show signs of being taken over by this movement and of looking only after their own interests. Yielding to pressure, with more haste than reflection and without paying attention to more than a tiny sector of the citizenry, they have given legitimacy to harmful fictions such as gender identity or transgender children. Completely sold on the abstruse discourse to which they committed themselves, and without it crossing their minds that it would be a good idea to check it against reality, they turn a deaf ear to the warning words of people concerned about the safeguarding of children, in a shocking neglect of their democratic obligation.

Following the announcement of the closure of GIDS, Kemi Badenoch, UK Minister of State for Equality from 2021 to July 2022 and Minister for Women and Equalities from October 2022 onwards, described the political landscape in which decisions affecting women and children are being made today. Among the obstacles to finding the truth and the best course of action, she pointed to pernicious groupthink among public servants and a toxic atmosphere created by social media vigilantes, in this case advocates for the transgendering of children:

> The reason it took this long for the Tavistock to be shut down is that activists succeeded in creating an environment in which critics and journalists felt unable to interrogate the dogma that youngsters should be able to medically transition in the way overseen by Tavistock. The treatment of these women [Lucy Bannerman, Kathleen Stock, Maya Forstater, Allison Bailey and others who know that biological sex is real and dare to say it] showed the heavy price to pay and many people including members of Parliament on all sides of the house simply didn't want to get involved (Badenoch, 2022).

In Mexico, as in so many other parts of the world, we are immersed in the same poisoned atmosphere in which people are afraid to speak out and prefer to watch from the sidelines. But those who are silent now, with their omissions and their apparent indifference, give more and more power to this movement, which represents a noisy minority of the citizenry. Let us learn from the experience of those who are already backing out. A public discussion in which freedom to say what one believes is guaranteed and from which the most critical feminist voices are not excluded is indispensable, one that places the health of minors and their right to free development of personality and bodily integrity at the centre. It would be fair, indeed necessary, to exclude from this conversation those who have a clear conflict of interest, such as individuals and groups who receive personal or economic benefits from the fiction that trans children exist.

To end the suffering of children who do not fit into sexist stereotypes, what we need to do is to combat such stereotypes, not to enthrone them as transgenderism does. The problem lies in society, not in bodies, even less in children. Ways will also need to be found to redress the damage already done and to prevent further harm. To do this, the first thing that needs to happen is to end the lies once and for all, and to stop and take the time to think about the different consequences (psychological, social, medical) of this deception, in the short, medium and long term, for all children, not just those who have *transitioned*. Sex does not change, neither by a speech act nor by undergoing hormone therapy or surgery. There are no minds trapped in wrong bodies; there are manipulated minds trapped in false and misleading beliefs. Says Canadian philosopher Kira Tomsons:

> We commit a moral wrong to children when we deliberately allow them to form false foundational understandings of the world around us that we know to be false. In doing so, we violate the trusting relationship they place in our hands. [...] We fail to practice epistemic virtue when we encourage children to believe false things and deliberately try to keep them from finding out the truth (Tomsons, 2020).

But for transgender ideologues, it is more problematic calling these children *minors* than lying to them.

Long live the children who refuse to repeat sexist scripts. The answer to their natural sense of not fitting into limiting stereotypes, and to much of their discomfort about believing that their bodies are inadequate, can be found in feminism. It consists in offering them a listening ear and understanding – not to stifle their explorations but to support them, and speaking truthfully to them; not to seek to mould them by sacrificing their own health and bodily integrity and to encourage them to deceive others – but most of all themselves.

CHAPTER 5

FEMINISM AND WOMEN'S SPACES

Transgenderism is an invasive movement that seeks to occupy the places that women, in a world tailor-made for men,[73] have built for themselves. By branding itself as feminism, this type of men's rights activism is the perfect Trojan horse, aiming to destroy feminism from within and even appropriating lesbianism, the ultimate male-free space. Other areas to which some men are demanding access include women's bathrooms and locker rooms, the female category in sports, so-called gender quotas in politics, awards specifically created for women, shelters for female victims of male violence, women's hospital wards, and women's prisons. Of course, the feminist defense of these spaces does not specifically seek to exclude *trans women,* but men in general. Nevertheless, since the strategy to infiltrate them is to call oneself a woman, anyone who denounces this entryist tactic, or simply prefers to take off her swimming costume away from the male gaze, is accused of transphobia. Women are then forced to conceal the discomfort

---

73 For anyone interested in the extent to which males are effectively the measure of all things, I recommend the book *The Invisible Woman* by the English writer and broadcaster Caroline Criado Perez.

that this marking of territory causes them. Reciting "Trans women are women" will not make this true by force of repetition, nor will it make people really believe it. Since – unless one is self-deluded – it is impossible to believe it, most of the time this slogan achieves something quite different: it makes women understand that they had better act as if they believe it.

Feminism

Just as *gender* can be understood as one thing and its opposite, the word *feminism* has been manipulated and emptied of content, to the extent that today some women can passionately dedicate themselves to destroying everything feminism has fought for and still call themselves feminists. With the onslaught of transgenderism, we are experiencing very dramatic consequences of this trend, which were already evident when Women's Studies or Feminist Studies were rebranded as Gender Studies in universities for marketing reasons.

Some women wear the green scarf symbolizing the fight for the right to abortion, but sign agreements to legalize reproductive exploitation without batting an eyelid. They go to demonstrations to protest violence against women, but they defend pornography and prostitution, which are two of the main manifestations of the very same violence. The truth is they do not defend women's bodily autonomy, but the prerogative of males to access female bodies. They call for women-only spaces on public transport to avoid sexual harassment, but scorn those they call TERFs for saying that women need toilets that men cannot enter. They are alarmed by female genital mutilation in distant countries, but welcome mastectomies and phalloplasties for *trans boys* in their locality. They propose a month to read books written by women, but pretend not to know what a woman is. They create a literary prize to promote fiction written by women, but they give it to a man who started cross-dressing at the age of 16. They despise bearded feminists, aka woke *cis* men,[74] but they welcome *women with penises* to their movement. And in the midst of all this, rape and femicidal violence are on the rise. Their inconsistencies are blatant, but they themselves do not seem to perceive them. Logical reasoning is another casualty in this war.

Amelia Valcárcel calls this invasion coming from within *the supervening agenda of feminism*. "Some years ago, not many," she says, "I observed how the feminist canon was being penetrated by another kind of discourse" (Valcárcel, 2019, p. 247). That discourse was an imposture, but it ended up prevailing:

> Suddenly the serious problem for women in a society that was unfair to them was binarism, for example the binarism of public toilets. They were, by their even existence, a serious attack on gender/sex fluidity. [...] The problem was not the job interview, or the lack of a job, nor the caring responsibilities, nor the increasing precariousness. No. It was semantic violence. [...] But the requirement was to be able to call it 'feminism'. Not by any other name, but precisely 'feminism'. [...] If it was excessive to say that this was feminism, or authentic feminism, it was enough to claim that it was 'the other feminism' [...]; feminism was plural.
>
> A complete falsehood. Feminism has always been a field of debate because it has grown up with debates, but, once it sets its agenda, it shuts them down. [...] Let's not forget another characteristic of this Trojan horse – verbosity. Knowing that feminism is debate, and it always has been, the aim was to sneak in the notion that the debate itself, without further data or knowledge, was feminism. In other words, it was enough to debate. And this already showed the last root in the sophistry that these approaches displayed. Debating was the rhetoric of sophistry after sophistry, without paying attention to cause or method, with the sole intention of stirring up waters (Valcárcel, 2019, pp. 259–260).

In the midst of this burlesque, when a young woman begins to take an interest in feminism and starts looking for a group to join or some introductory reading, she is likely to be taken for a ride. What

74 For the concept of the bearded feminist, see Klein, 1983.

predominates today in universities, gender sections in bookstores, magazines, mass media, social media, is the imposture that has cut off feminism's political roots and whose subject is now totally blurred. The newcomers are not presented with a congruent and combative feminism, but rather a fun pretence with glitter and sequins, misogyny-friendly, which opens the doors to anyone who *feels like* a woman, and ends up adapting their political agenda to that of a movement with very different interests.

This is a faux feminism that sits well with the oppression of women, which gives the impression of not knowing who it is working for. These so-called feminists seem to happily embrace the utilitarian place assigned to them by males. They are more interested in policing the use of pronouns than in eliminating all forms of discrimination against women and girls. They go out of their way to follow the commandments of the trans ideologue just as a middle-class woman in the 1950s would have followed the good wife guide to the letter.

Chilean lesbian theorist Margarita Pisano coined the term that describes them better than any other: *regalonas del patriarcado*, that could be translated as *patriarchy's pets:*

> Daddy's pet is in solidarity with women only insofar as they remain within the symbolic order of femininity. [...] The pet does not detach herself from the already disturbed and violent masculine/feminine relationship. The favorite daughter syndrome is one of the most difficult points to work on in and among us. [...] For the feminist pets, it is much more important to be accepted by the male collective than to be recognized by women. [...] The tactic of the male hegemonic group to neutralize any political and cultural project that threatens the dynamics of domination consists of taking over the discourse, co-opting leaders and making the collective and its transformative logic invisible (Pisano, 1995, pp. 4–6).

In her article entitled 'Qué es una terf y cómo identificarla?' (What is a TERF and how to identify her?), Chicana political analyst Estefanía Veloz states: "It is clear that a person who deserts the male gender assigned at birth is the greatest affront to the phallocentric patriarchy that exists." In one fell swoop she thus wants to erase the entire theoretical corpus of radical feminism and decades of feminist work. With a conjuring trick of identification, any one man alone achieves more than thousands and thousands of pages do, and more than the dedication of thousands and thousands of women to the feminist cause.

Veloz reveals through every pore that her understanding of the debate around transgenderism does not come from a direct reading of any feminist author, but from the distorted gloss given by some members of the male collective:

> A trans-exclusionary feminist will always say that gender identity is an invention of the oppressive system of biological sex, the only criterion that can define women. In this respect, it can be said that these feminists reduce being a woman to a biological category and deny the cultural component of the construction of a feminine identity. Here, trans-exclusionary feminists contradict themselves again, because if one of the arguments is that a woman is a woman because she was raised that way from childhood, then genitals would not matter, but if according to them genitals are the most important thing, is a trans woman who modifies her body to have a vagina not a woman? A trans-exclusionary feminist would say no, and that would completely expose what underlies her contempt for trans women: their inability to gestate (Veloz, 2022).

It is easy, but intellectually dishonest, to attribute to someone the opposite of what they actually say and then claim that they contradict themselves. No feminist has ever said that women are reduced to their biology or that the most important thing is their genitalia. Mexican anthropologist Marcela Lagarde sums it up splendidly when she reminds us: "We are not only biology, but we *are* biology" (CEIICH, 2022). It is not a disjunction, it is not one or the other; the cultural does not cancel out the biological. Is it necessary to explain once again that we are not born with sexist roles already programmed into our genes and to clarify that this does not mean that genes do not exist?

It is also striking that Veloz believes that radical feminists deny the cultural component in the construction of femininity (or a feminine identity, as she calls it), when anyone can confirm that radical feminists never tire of insisting on this (for example, by explaining over and over again the distinction between sex and gender). But of course, when you falsely characterize a position, you can say whatever you like about it and draw whatever conclusion you want (e.g., TERFs despise trans women because they can't gestate). It's unclear what impoverishes the discussion the most, the blatant lies or the spitefulness.

In this climate of demonization of radical feminists, to which patriarchy's pets contribute so much, it would be extremely rare for a radical feminist collective to have access to funding. Resources for civil society organizations working for women are controlled by groups such as Fondo Semillas, who make it a condition for those interested in accessing this money to support *sex work* (which does not mean supporting women in prostitution so that they can move to decent jobs, but perpetuating the system that forces them into prostitution), and nodding their heads in agreement with the mantra "Trans women are women." In other words, if a recent university graduate wants to work in one of these groups, what she needs is not to be a feminist, but a *trans ally*. Fondo Semillas claims to fight sexual discrimination, but a lesbian who doesn't believe there's such a thing as a lesbian with a penis (i.e. straight men who call themselves women) will have the door slammed in her face.

If anyone dares to question any of the multiple other feminisms, they are accused of pulling out the feminist card. "Who are you to decide whether I am a feminist?," they say. But that is not the point. Feminism is not defined by you or me: it is defined by feminism itself, which has a very solid history and theory. So, what does feminism say?

Just as in 1979 Janice Raymond saw what the transsexual empire represented for women, in 1993, in her book *Women as Wombs,* she realized the great threat to our freedom posed by reproductive technologies. In it she rigorously criticizes the positions in favour of women's reproductive exploitation that were being incorporated into this gelatinous feminism:

> 'Don't call your position feminist' has become one of the ten commandments of sexual and reproductive liberalism. This convoluted prohibition effectively says that feminists cannot dare to articulate what feminism means because if we do we are mouthing a single, correct-line, exclusionary feminist position. Articulating what feminism means, however, seems not exclusionary but honest. If we do not articulate what feminism means, what does feminism mean? And then we can debate what feminism means, rather than how dare we think we can say what feminism means! (Raymond, 1993, p. 93).

We have been stuck for a long time in the "How dare you say this is not feminist!" when what we should have been doing is articulating what this movement means, and what its legitimate struggles and ethical and political principles are.

The lack of clear definitions and this refusal to debate the fundamentals has led to legislation being pushed through in the name of feminism and progressivism that is openly contrary to the interests of women as a caste, and allows the championing of anti-feminist causes. What we have witnessed over the last few decades is not an internal struggle between feminists, but a full-blown invasion of feminism by forces indifferent or contrary to its raison d'être. It is urgent to reclaim feminism.

And there is an urgent need to return to a women-centred movement. The presence of just one man in feminist groups completely changes the dynamics and priorities. Just as in a classroom or social gathering women have a protective tendency (the result of a lifetime of training in femininity) to focus on them, care for them, pay more attention to them, agree with them and go out of their way for them, in feminist organizations they unconsciously make males the focus of their concerns. Even if they don't intend to, men mostly come to feminism to cause trouble. On target, Australian biologist and feminist researcher Renate Klein calls this "a modern version of the old, old script called 'men dividing women'" (1983, p. 413). In 1983, writing about the "men-problem" in Women's Studies, whereby males usurp power in an environment that was created by and for women, Klein observes:

> There are many ways in which men have been able to 'penetrate' Women's Studies with a considerable degree of success, and sadly, it seems one of the results of their increased presence is often a correlative division among women who invariably find that they are obliged to compete with each other in the presence of the still authoritative and powerful sex (Klein, 1983, p. 415).

Four decades have gone by, and this male penetration has reached its highest expression with the help of a magic wand: the concept of gender identity and the substitution of the bearded male feminists of yesteryear with the still more destructive and powerful bepenised female[75] feminists of today.

How many stories do we know, for example, of Facebook groups, even mothers' groups, in which a plot similar to this one unfolds:

> They are all very calmly talking about issues related to motherhood (or lesbianism, reproductive autonomy, care work, male violence …).
>
> Enter a man who flaunts a feminine gender identity.
>
> He becomes the focus of attention, the birthday boy.
>
> Some women say that he has no business being there and that if they could please get back to the group's issues.
>
> Others ask that he be allowed to stay because they need to have empathy and be inclusive.
>
> Some remember what the purpose of the group is.
>
> Others accuse them of being TERFs.
>
> A pitched battle breaks out.
>
> The troublemakers are removed from the group.
>
> Those who remain devote themselves to comfort the male and remind their fellow feminists of the importance of being inclusive.
>
> He remains the focus of attention.

---

75 That's right: not content with the appropriation of the word *women*, now they are claiming femaleness; remember transgenderism is biological denialism. "The identities of transwomen can be affirmed within a Beauvoirian framework, because trans women are (or are becoming) female," argues King's College's Matilda Carter in a paper published in *Hypatia*, "a journal of feminist philosophy" (2022, p. 385).

One of the first documented instances of this intrusion into feminism by men who claim to be women took place at the West Coast Lesbian Feminist Conference in Los Angeles in 1973. It was attended by 1500 women from all over the United States, some from Canada and even France. Organizers had not slept for days, finalizing details of accommodation, childcare, entertainment and everything else needed for a gathering that big. Robin Morgan was to give the keynote address, and recalls that on the night of registration and arrival, all hell broke loose,

> caused by the gate-crashing presence of a male transvestite who insisted that he was 1) an invited participant, 2) really a woman, and 3) at heart a lesbian. (It is, one must grant, an ingenious new male approach for trying to seduce women.) The conference promptly split over this man. More than half the women there Friday evening demanded that he be forced to leave an all-woman conference; others […] defended him as their 'sister'. Some women left the conference for good, and returned to their home states in disgust. The situation was exacerbated when he insisted on performing during the entertainment. He apparently wished to embark on a nightclub career and thought this was a fine place to begin, what with both controversy and press at hand. But the genyoo-ine-real-women-lesbian entertainers present were not amused when they were asked to cede their place on the program to this man in drag. By the time I arrived, this was the issue of the conference – the one around which all hostilities and divisions magnetized. It was incredible that so many strong, angry women should be divided by one smug male in granny glasses and an earth-mother gown (he was easily identifiable, at least – he was the only person there wearing a skirt).
>
> I sat up half the night revising my speech so as to include the issue, trying to relate it to the points I was already endeavoring to raise, attempting to show how male 'style' could be a destroyer from within (Morgan, 2014, pp. 209–210).

The next day, in her speech, Morgan questioned whether the obligation to be compassionate meant that they were once again defending male supremacy, but now embodied in men who wear heels to glorify sexist stereotypes and parody the oppression of women.

Another telling example of the mess brought about by men who feel entitled to violate women's boundaries with the excuse that they are feminine on the inside is offered by Australian writer, political activist and aerialist Susan Hawthorne. She recalls:

> I was a member of Melbourne's Women's Circus when in April 2000 a transwoman wrote and asked if he could join the Women's Circus. The circus was formed in 1990 in order to work with women who had suffered from sexual abuse or rape. I joined in 1994. Circus is a place of physical and emotional trust. There is bodily intimacy in balances, in double aerials acts. There is one balance in which the flyer puts her head between the legs of the base; there are aerials movements that involve hands between thighs or on breasts. This takes trust. Over the next six months, his application was talked about by members of the circus. To my knowledge no other applicant was ever accorded this privilege. It was a privilege because in the past, membership was either accepted or denied. In his case there were clear boundaries for denying it. He was not a woman who had been subjected to sexual abuse or rape (Hawthorne, 2020, p. 225).

Even though his membership should have been denied from the outset, it took more than a year for his application to be withdrawn. In the meantime, the circus was divided, and Hawthorne, who spoke out about the issue and objected to allowing a man in a place created by and for women, was punished by exclusion: "I no longer felt welcome in a place where previously I had felt at home [...]; I had lost an entire community, friends and a fabulous way of keeping fit" (Hawthorne, 2020, p. 226).

Sadly, many women who call themselves feminists fail to understand that women need male-free spaces – and that men cannot be women however much they aspire to. "Cruel and unsympathetic though it may seem, women should not automatically accept all those who do not wish to be male as being *ex gratia* females," declares Australian writer Germaine Greer (2000, p. 76). Do not think that gender-critical feminism is absolved of performing this kind of subordination acts as second nature. In Renate Klein's words, "rare is the woman who tells a man to 'get lost' [...] and clear off women's space" (1983, p. 418). Some lesbian feminists, such as American activist Joey Brite or British researcher Julia Long, have observed how these dynamics are at work in various circles of women opposed to transgenderism who nonetheless welcome with open arms a few men who identify as women. Because they themselves know they are not women and disapprove of self-ID and other features of gender identity ideology, in these groups those men are considered allies ... and the same dynamics described above are set in motion.

In her article 'A Meaningful Transition?', Long points out that the presence of these men has the effect of inhibiting critical thinking and imposing a certain use of language. For example, in some prominent British feminist groups, although they know you can't change your sex and are fighting against proposed legislative changes to make self-ID a legal reality, they insist that they defend the rights of transgender people and use female pronouns and the term *trans woman* when referring to some men who claim to identify as such:

> Paradoxically then, much of what is written and spoken in the name of British gender critical feminism in fact does the ideological work of transgenderists for them, promulgating their fictions as legitimate and valid through speaking their language (Long, 2020a).

Those who, like this anti-pornography activist, denounce such political inconsistencies and refuse to call these men women, are accused of being provocative, disrespectful and cruel. All of this prevents others from speaking out. Long recalls:

> In 2018, two men, Kristina Jayne Harrison and Debbie Hayton, between them, spoke at a third of all A Woman's Place UK (WPUK) events between them. Billed and introduced as 'transwomen', their speeches were greeted with great enthusiasm, often surpassing the reception given to female speakers. Harrison's talk at a WPUK meeting in Hastings remains the second most popular of all the talks on WPUK YouTube channel, with an astounding 23,000 views (most of the talks garner around two or three thousand) (Long, 2020a).

While opposed to self-ID, both Harrison and Hayton – who, incidentally, claims that the motive for his transsexuality was autogynephilia (see Hayton, 2020) – have defended the supposed right of men to be treated as women and to enter women's spaces. The greatest hypocrisy, Long points out, is that it is they who are handed the microphone at the events of the feminist organization A Woman's Place and not, for example, their wives. Women whose partner is a man who one day decided that he is actually a woman are colloquially called *trans widows,* who are another collateral damage of gender identity (see Chapter 6), among other reasons because, oddly enough, even after the husband's transition, they are still the ones who are mainly responsible for the housework and the children. They also have an extra conjugal duty: taking care of the husband's new psychological needs in his transition. Long alludes to them when she says:

> It is strange, given their name and declared mission 'to ensure women's voices would be heard', that WPUK chose to offer regular speaking opportunities to men who put their wives into this position, rather than to the women themselves (a woman's place is staying at home while her *transwoman* husband holds forth at women's meetings?) (Long, 2020a).

Not only Long says so. Before the explosion we are now witnessing, Christine Benvenuto wrote a memoir to recount what her husband's sudden transformation into a *trans woman* meant for her life and that of her children more than a decade ago, and there she mentions the women who swarmed around her spouse to support him in his search for identity, without much consideration for what she might be suffering:

> From Tracey's cheerleaders I learned that in the new political correctness, female solidarity is out. A man in a dress is in. Among women who consider themselves feminists, a man who declares himself a transsexual trumps another woman any day. Women, feminists, Jewish feminists, rushed to embrace Tracey. I found it peculiarly painful (Benvenuto, 2012, p. 62).[76]

---

76 Indian filmmaker Vaishnavi Sundar is currently working on a film about trans widows: *Behind the Looking Glass.*

If radical feminists stress the need for a women-centred feminism and for this social movement to be a male-free environment, it is because they are well aware that men invariably hog the microphone and everything ends up being about them.[77] It happens, as we have seen, even in gender-critical environments, but the clearest and most pathetic example of this sociological phenomenon is the substitute for feminism which, devoting body and soul to the transgender agenda, has no qualms about turning its back on women and women's rights.

The W word

We are expected not only to accept that some men are women, but also assume that we are *the other*. Simone de Beauvoir analyzed it well:

> She is simply what man decrees; [...] She is defined and differentiated with reference to man and not he with reference to her; she is the incidental, the inessential as opposed to the essential. He is the Subject; he is the Absolute – she is the Other (Beauvoir, 2012, p. 18).

And when he is the Woman, she is the cis woman, the person with a vagina, the menstruator, the cervix-haver. First they appropriate the word we use to name us and next they take over our spaces and our movement.

Inclusive language that excludes women and gender identity-based language that seeks to erase sex prevail in news and other reflections on these issues. And whenever our views are mis-represented or we are subjected to character assassination, we have no right of reply because, if we have already been branded

---

77 Does this mean that men cannot be feminists? No. A feminist-inspired movement of men standing up against male violence against women is urgently needed ... One doesn't see many hands raised, but what happened to Mauricio Dimeo gives us an idea of the animosity faced in the current climate by the few groups of men interested in questioning masculinity and doing something about it (different from invading women's spaces). Robert Jensen's writings will be useful to them (e.g. *The End of Patriarchy. Radical Feminism for Men*, Spinifex Press, 2017).

as transphobic, it is decided in advance that anything we say will be hate speech. Not even someone with J. K. Rowling's fame and money is safe from such accusations or from rape and death threats if she even dares to insinuate that such language is dehumanizing and degrading. One of the tweets that made the celebrated writer a target of transactivism ironized the title of an op-ed about a more egalitarian world for *people who menstruate*: "I'm sure there used to be a word for those people. Someone help me out. Wumben? Wimpund? Woomud?" (Associated Press, 2020b).

On 30 July 2020, less than two months after the storm that Rowling's vindication of the word *woman* sparked, the Women's Parliament of Mexico City discussed via Zoom a bill against obstetric violence that spoke of women *and pregnant people*. Only two parliamentarians (Adriana Lecona and Adriana Leonel de Cervantes) opposed this latter formulation on the grounds that, as so many feminists have pointed out, such expressions contribute to the legal erasure of women, as well as being unnecessary, given that, as everyone knows, only women can become pregnant.

During the interventions of these two objectors, their female colleagues rolled their eyes, made fed-up comments, looked at their cellphones or ostentatiously ate peanuts. But lo and behold, in that Women's Parliament there was a man who claims to identify as a woman (how else could he have joined a women's political body?) and who refers to females as *corporalities with vulvas*. At some point, he wrapped himself in the trans flag and then put it in front of his screen. That was the cue for at least seven women to display rainbow-colored LGBT flags or pastel pink and blue trans flags in the background of their Zoom rectangle (despite the fact that their own internal rules prohibit the display of banners or posters).

Thus, on that day the Women's Parliament gave a graphic demonstration of how so many women are conditioned to obey men, and how transactivist pressure groups infiltrate or influence our legislative bodies and institutions.

Playing into the hands of gender identity activism by using their language and adopting their point of view prevents a clear perception of the capture of feminism that is taking place right under our noses. For example, it is easy to understand why women are uncomfortable with the presence of men in places where they are naked if this is said in plain language. The opposite is true if it is manipulatively turned around like this: "There are cis women who, because of their transphobia and non-inclusiveness, want to deny trans women entry to a space where they can be safe." Similarly, if you ask, "Do you agree that a rapist should serve his sentence in a women's prison?" the answer will be an overwhelming *no,* but if, using linguistic manoeuvres, you ask, "Should a female delinquent serve her sentence in a women's prison?" the response of the unwary will of course be *yes.* The truth is that a rapist can say he feels as feminine as he likes, but he is not in the least a woman, and it is deceitful to talk about him as if he were.

Surely more than one will accuse me of claiming that trans women are rapists or, as Mauricio Dimeo is said to have stated in Capital 21, that "trans women and other transfeminities are sexual predators." Anyone who has made it to this page and read what the radical feminist model is all about will know that my assertion is quite different. If some males who describe themselves as trans women (or as some kind of *transfeminity*) are rapists, it is not because they describe themselves as such (or claim to have a female gender identity or feminine gender expression), but because they are males. That they believe themselves to be trans women or describe themselves as such does not cancel that fact.

Identity theft

Experience shows that the beliefs men may have about their identity do not affect their often typically masculine behaviours. As Janice Raymond says:

> When we examine how self-declared women (men) behave towards natal women who challenge their right to usurp a woman's identity, it is clear that such men are indulging in the privileged behavior that we

recognize as male entitlement. The most telling proof that self-declared women are still men is their misogynist conduct.

It is magical thinking to believe that men socialized as male could simply transform themselves and their masculinist behavior when they put on a skirt. [...] This is not to argue that men cannot change their masculinist behavior, but rather to say that declaring yourself a woman doesn't result in a behavioral transformation. To disarm male privilege and male dominant behavior entails a lot of self-reflection and hard work. In spite of all assertions that a gender identity change eliminates the risk of male violence to women, e.g. when men are billeted in women's prisons, self-declared female identification does not outdo years of male socialization to violence or abuse (Raymond, 2022, pp. 152–153).

The data confirm it: rates of violence among *trans women* are no different than among males in general, which should come as no surprise. Regardless of whether they take estrogen or have undergone some kind of feminization surgery, they tend to retain the main attributes of masculinity, and the masculine socialization in which they have been raised comes through very often.

Karen Ingala Smith, a Yorkshirewoman with 30 years of experience in researching men's violence against women and girls, looked at the data about homicide and trans people in England and Wales and arrived at this conclusion:

Women are perpetrators of homicide at 18% lower rates than we are victims. Males are perpetrators of homicide at 8% greater rates than they are victims. Trans people [biologically male] are perpetrators of homicide at 71% greater rates than they are victims (Ingala Smith, 2018).

Also in the UK, in the context of public consultations on proposed changes to the Gender Recognition Act 2004, researchers Rosa Freedman, Kathleen Stock and Alice Sullivan presented a Swedish study to the Women and Equalities Committee of the UK Parliament with the following findings:

The researchers state: 'Male-to-females [...] retained a male pattern regarding criminality. The same was true regarding violent crime'.

Mtf transitioners were over 6 times more likely to be convicted of an offence than female comparators and 18 times more likely to be convicted of a violent offence. The group had no statistically significant differences from other natal males, for convictions in general or for violent offending. The group examined were those who committed to surgery, and so were more tightly defined than a population based solely on self-declaration.

The study provides strong evidence that policy makers cannot safely assume a) that transwomen's offending patterns, including violent offending, will be significantly different than those of the general male population or b) that they will be similar to those of the general female population (Freedman, Stock and Sullivan, 2020, pp. 1–2).

Some feminist news outlets that follow offences against women report on the crimes of these men without hiding the fact that they are males. They refer to the offender in question using the masculine gender, when other media refer to them as women, using feminine pronouns, thus hiding the not insignificant fact that the murderer, rapist or child sexual abuse images collector is a man.

As a very small sample of violence committed by males who say they identify as women, allow me to reproduce below, back to front, a month and a half (11 September 2023 to 25 July 2023) worth of headlines from the *Reduxx* website (reduxx.info): 'Trans-Identified Male Who Murdered His Girlfriend Deemed "Vulnerable" by Oregon Court, Seeking Transfer to Women's Prison'; 'Trans-Identified Male Charged, Released in Portland after Defecating in Teen Girl's Car for "Transphobia"'; 'UK: Transgender Sex Offender with 87 Prior Convictions Sexually Assaulted Two Prison Staff'; 'Trans-Identified Male in Switzerland Facing Charges of Sexually Abusing Stepdaughters, Reportedly Molested Them while Wearing Lingerie'; 'UK: Transgender Pedophile Spared Jail after Being Found in Possession of Child Sexual Abuse Materials'; 'ACLU Files Lawsuit on Behalf of Trans-Identified Male Inmate Who Murdered 11-Month-Old Baby Girl'; 'Trans-Identified Male Coach Used Girls' Locker Room to Undress Multiple Times, Incidents Kept Quiet by Pennsylvania School District'; 'Mexico: Female Inmate Sexually

Assaulted by Trans-Identified Male at Women's Prison in Chalco'; 'California: Trans-Identified Male Charged with Murder in Stabbing Death of Homeless Woman'; 'UK: Prominent Trans Activist Known for Having Opponents Arrested Has History of Indecent Assault on 14-Year-Old Boy'; 'UK: Person Who "Identifies as a Woman" Arrested on Charges of Indecent Exposure, Possessing Child Sexual Abuse Imagery'; 'Wales: Pedophile Announces "Transition" after Being Caught for Second Time with Horrific Child Abuse Images'; 'UK: Trans-Identified Pedophile Sentenced to 4 Years in Prison after Being Caught in Two Separate Predator Stings'; 'Spain: Trans-Identified Male Prisoner Transferred to Women's Prison Impregnated Female Inmate'; 'Ireland: Extremely Dangerous Transgender Inmate Moved out of Women's Prison after Threatening to Rape Female Staff'; 'Canada: Pedophile Male Nurse Who Led Youth Sex Ed Workshops Avoids Prison Despite Possessing over One Million Child Abuse Images'; 'Trans-Identified Male Found Guilty of Rape in Guernsey, Defense Argued Victim Was "Transphobic"'; 'Spain: Man Who Murdered His Cousin and Raped Her Corpse Now Seeking Transfer to Women's Prison under New "Trans Law"'; 'Male Inmate Transferred to Washington Women's Cell Prison Despite History of Cellmate Assault'; 'Man Who Beat Two Babies to Death Allegedly Awaiting Breast Implants at California Women's Prison'.

Clearly, it is far from true that this never happens, as some gender identity proselytes claim. Anyone who reads these stories in media outlets that take care not to *misgender* the offender may be left with the impression that crime rates among women are on the rise. Where do so many female rapists come from, when until recently they were a rarity? Misleading the public is not the only pernicious effect of concealing the sex of perpetrators of violent crime: how can male violence against women be eradicated with the pretense that the perpetrators are men and the victims are women by pure chance? The term *gender-based violence* is a perfect example of this tendency to name social problems while omitting the fundamental fact. It is not about people raping and killing other people, in the abstract: it is, concretely, about males raping and killing females.

The Declaration on Women's Sex-Based Rights explains well why it is necessary to keep collecting data based on sex:

> The CEDAW Committee in its General Recommendation 35 underlines the importance of collecting data and compiling statistics relating to the prevalence of different forms of violence against women in relation to developing effective measures to prevent and redress such violence. 'Sex-disaggregated data is data that is cross-classified by sex, presenting information separately for men and women, boys and girls. Sex-disaggregated data reflect roles, real situations, general conditions of women and men, girls and boys in every aspect of society. [...] When data is not disaggregated by sex, it is more difficult to identify real and potential inequalities' (UN Women, Gender Equality Glossary). The conflation of sex with 'gender identity' leads to the collection of data on violence against women and girls which is inaccurate and misleading because it identifies perpetrators of violence on the basis of their 'gender identity' rather than their sex. This creates a significant impediment to the development of effective laws, policies, strategies and actions aimed at the elimination of violence against women and girls (Declaration on Women's Sex Based Rights, 2019: Introduction).

Without this disaggregation of data we would not be able to know, for example, that in Mexico "more than two fifths of men married or united with women aged 15 or older (10.8 million) have exercised some type of violence against their partners throughout their relationship," or that 76 per cent of victims of domestic violence, 80 per cent of rape victims and 91 per cent of victims of incest or child sexual abuse are women (INEGI, 2015). Nor would we have any way of concluding that about 90 per cent of all homicides recorded worldwide are committed by male perpetrators (see UNODC, 2019). Or how could the UN Secretary General conclude that the Covid-19 pandemic "led to a horrifying increase in violence against women" because many women were "trapped at home with their abusers"? (Guterres, 2020).

Regardless of the high rates of male violence, and not giving a damn about women's safety or what women think, the transgender lobby seeks to impose some males' access to women's spaces by portraying it as part of their right to gender expression and self-determined gender identity. However, if women need bathrooms where there are no men, it is not to express their gender, but for far more pressing reasons (they can express their gender elsewhere, but only in a bathroom can they urinate or change their tampon). Similarly, women's and girls' need for male-free toilets has nothing to do with how men dress or what name they want to give to their identity.

A bathroom of one's own

Materially speaking, there is no difference between a man who, considering himself trans or non-binary, wears a skirt and high-heels, and a man who, without considering himself trans or non-binary, wears the same skirt and high heels. Nor is there any difference between a *cis man* wearing a tie and a moustache and a *trans woman* wearing a tie and a moustache. Remember that in the radical feminist model, gender identity is a fiction, so a trans woman is no less male than a cis man. How a man dresses (some would call this gender expression) makes no difference to his manhood – a man in the bathroom is a man in the bathroom.

The bathroom issue is especially politicized. The administrative departments of universities, theatres, cinemas and government offices have come up with an easy way to announce to the world that they are very progressive and on the right side of history. It is to convert women's toilets into *gender-neutral* ones (for this they just have to put up a new sign) and leave the men's toilets untouched.

Recent events at the top Mexican university show that interest in the toilets is not due to men with a female identity just wanting to pee, as is falsely alleged. Nuria Muíña García, a women's and girls' rights advocate based in Switzerland, reports:

> On 24 August 2022, feminist students at the National Autonomous University of Mexico (UNAM) were confronted by trans activists as they painted a lesbian pride symbol on a wall near the Samuel Ramos Library. Speaking to *Reduxx,* a witness who prefers to remain

anonymous said that the activists began hurling verbal abuse at the women who were painting the lesbian labrys.

'They called them TERFs, colonial fascists and transphobes', the source says, noting that shortly after, additional activists from the queer groups on campus joined in to harass the female students. [...]

Shortly after, as a result of the lesbian symbol that had been painted, the trans students reportedly declared that they 'did not feel safe' on campus and went to administrators to demand a gender-neutral washroom be established in that area.

While administrators agreed to create one, the students did not wait for it to be designated. Less than 24 hours later, the activists took over the largest female restroom, which was on the second floor of the Faculty of Philosophy.

As part of their symbolic coup, the activists vandalized the walls outside the washroom with anti-feminist and pro-sex trade graffiti (Muíña, 2022).

Symbolic coup indeed. The existence of a group of lesbians who don't believe in gender identity makes some men feel insecure. And how do they react? By occupying, because they damn well want to, the washroom that until then the female students considered the safest space on campus; by writing on the door of a cubicle, "If the macho or the TERF touches you, break their mouth," and opening it up to anyone who wants to go in there. It is worth mentioning that, three years earlier, female students of the Faculty of Sciences in the same university had reported that they were being filmed in the bathrooms in order to upload videos to pornographic internet sites (see *24 Horas*, 2019). Sexual assaults in the bathrooms of Ciudad Universitaria became so common that panic buttons were installed in them.

On 10 September 2022, a few days after the conquest of the bathrooms of the Faculty of Philosophy and Literature, a queer group celebrated the feat with a musical performance that the user @sairinventada_33 uploaded to his TikTok account and that has been watched, as of 13 September 2023, 611,900 times. It features a young man in a blue dress and wig dancing to Lady Gaga's *Born*

This Way. The act closes with this Ru Paul disciple showing, in a half-triumphant, half-displeased gesture, a basket of feminine sanitary towels. The toilets are completely defaced with slogans such as "We are the trans resistance and here we are," "Dissidence exists and resists" and "Drag is art." What for the female students is an authentic physiological necessity, for their male peers is a self-indulgent performance; what should be a safe space for women is, for men, an opportunity for exhibitionism.

If the reader thinks that the authorities erased graffiti like the one that says "Rape and death to TERFs," giving the women back their bathrooms or done anything to stop lesbian feminists from fearing for their lives, I am afraid I must disappoint you. Under their indifferent gaze, intimidation against women has increased, and drag queens do little protest dances "to get the macho apes and TERFs out of UNAM" (note that, in the eyes of these protesters, they themselves, with their grotesque parody of femininity, are not macho at all).[78]

But that's not all: the faculty council issued a communiqué that made it very clear which side they were on:

> This council agreed to categorically condemn any expression of hatred, violence or discrimination towards gender diversity. There is no room in our faculty for speech that undermines the human rights of the people who make up our community.

We already know that, in Newspeak, *expression of hatred* means thinking that women need some spaces without men, and that

---

78 Several feminists have criticized the misogyny of the supposed art form that is drag, including Sheila Jeffreys, who says:
> The practice of drag could be usefully referred to as 'womanface', meaning men imitating women, because of its similarity to the practice of white people seeking to imitate black people for entertainment which is commonly called 'blackface'. Blackface, though, is universally condemned as a politically unacceptable practice in a way that womanface is not. White people in blackface would not be acceptable in any publicly provided settings (Jeffreys, 2022, p. 280).
At UNAM, however, nobody raises an eyebrow – another sign of how normalized contempt for women is in one of the largest universities in Latin America.

gender diversity does not include feminist lesbians, but does include heterosexual men who claim to be women. For this body, made up of teachers and students, a lesbian symbol and the message, "Only women will save women" are an expression of hatred against *trans* people. But an open call to rape and murder female students does not seem to bother them much. Besides giving too much power to aggressive demonstrators whose stance they uncritically adopt without further enquiry, the faculty council's actions prove that the human rights whose members are concerned about is not those of women for a life free of violence, but those of men for not ever being contradicted.

Denying women their own bathrooms is not a position native to Mexican queers who accuse lesbians of being colonial fascists. In cities like San Francisco, campaigns to make these bathrooms neutral date back to at least 2005. Before that, there was no need because, when the predominant model to understand the trans phenomenon was the medical-sexological explanation and it was common for men who dreamed of being women to make some changes to their appearance, the presence of a few of them who genuinely just wanted to pee was not a serious problem. But the situation has changed. No small matter for the toilet issue is the exponential increase in males identifying as women now that the only requirement is to have woken up one morning thinking "I feel feminine today."

Gender-fluid people are not only teenagers on TikTok; they can also be found in more serious settings and at a more mature age. For example, English sexagenarian comedian Eddie Izzard called himself gender-fluid until late 2020, when he announced: "I just want to be based in girl mode from now on" (Seddon, 2020). And indeed, he now wears more make-up and fuchsia coats because he is campaigning to become a parliamentary candidate for the Labour Party in the next election. Another 'inspiring' profile is that of 40-year-old Swiss man Pips Bunce, a senior manager at Credit Suisse bank in England, who in 2018 appeared in the *Financial Times'* champions of women in business list. "I identify as gender-fluid and non-binary and so decide how I choose to express my gender expression on a given day," said this senior executive (see WATC Content Team, 2021). Accordingly, some days he goes to the office in a suit and tie – and goes by the name of Phillip – and other days he is in a blonde wig, short dress and fishnet tights – and goes by the name of Pippa.

The increased presence of these men in the ladies' toilets wasn't going to go unnoticed by the women, so it was necessary to transform their desire to pass through that door as an inalienable right. Says Sheila Jeffreys in an article on the politics of the toilet:

> The goal of transgender toilet activism is not always clear and may include the desegregation of facilities and/or the admission of transgenders to facilities associated with the 'gender' they identify with, or the creation of 'gender-neutral' toilets as well as sex-segregated ones, but always includes the demand that no 'women's' toilets that exclude men who transgender should exist (Jeffreys, 2014a, p. 44).

One of their arguments is that trans women are not safe in men's toilets, so they must be allowed to use the women's toilets. But in order to let them use the women's toilets it would be necessary to admit both women and men, no questions asked. How can you guarantee that *trans women* are safe from male harassment in toilets that at their request have a male presence? It is very difficult to find the logic in their reasoning, but what is demonstrated time and time again is that women's safety is of no concern to them and that their real interest is to deny women the possibility of setting boundaries. Of course, if a man who honestly believes he is a woman can cross them, any man who falsely claims to believe he is a woman can do so too, for there is no way of distinguishing which is which.

The toilet warriors fail to take into account that the very existence of public bathrooms that women can use is a more or less recent achievement of the feminist movement in western countries. There was a time when women literally had nowhere to urinate. They had to campaign for separate toilets, which, by the way, also met with male opposition. Women's right to a bathroom of their own relates to their right to occupy a public space that was not meant for them. And in an important way, it still is not.

Anyone who has ever compared the queues in women's toilets with those in men's toilets at the theatre or cinema, at a concert hall or at a book fair will know that they are always longer for the women's toilets, despite the fact that they usually have the same number of square metres. It is not taken into account that women's needs are different. Going to the toilet takes them more time because they are often accompanied by children, they always need a cubicle with a door, they may be menstruating, and some women need to urinate more often … In other words, this is a simple urban and architectural planning issue that is biased in favour of men (see Criado Perez, 2019, pp. 47–66). But it is hard to imagine that the demand for space for women's toilets more suited to their needs would gain as much traction as the transgender demand to do away with them altogether.

In India today, there are campaigns (e.g. Right to Pee) for the creation of segregated toilets: women and girls are not safe in mixed toilets, and special toilets for women and girls are a condition for equal access to work, education and public spaces. There are also demands for the creation of toilets specifically for girls in schools, so that they stop missing school when they are menstruating (in India, the stigma of menstruation is another very serious problem that affects only women):

> The attitude amongst civil society groups and social reformers in India to the issue of sex-segregated toilets, which is that they are vital for women's rights, is very different from that being adopted by queer theorists in the west who argue for degendering. Jairam Ramesh, the Minister for Rural Development, is quoted on the *One India News* website as saying, in relation to the importance of toilets for women, 'Toilets are women's fundamental right, for their privacy and their dignity'. The news article comments that 'a society in which men and women have separate toilets, all well-maintained and well-accessible, is, by far, more progressed than a society in which everyone owns a mobile phone' (Jeffreys, 2014a, p. 47).

The risk, in the case of UNAM, is not only theoretical – instances of a male peeping through a hole in the door or filming women while they are sitting on the toilet have already occurred. Voyeurism is one of the main motivations of some men who enter women's toilets, while others are driven more by exhibitionism. Anyone interested in confirming this can type a few key words into Google and they will be presented with multiple options to watch videos of males who cross-dress or claim to identify as women entering ladies' toilets for the purpose of masturbating, but not as an end in itself – the most stimulating thing for them is to film themselves doing it and then upload to social media the visual record of their exploits.

Changing rooms in clothing stores, schools and sports clubs are also a land to be conquered for transgenderism. Women are expected to accept the presence of men in places where they are naked and more vulnerable. In countries where the penetration of this men's rights movement is even more pronounced than in Mexico, it is already common for men to enter women's locker rooms as if they owned the place, much to the discomfort and shock of the women who are there. Under the pretext of not wanting a few people to feel excluded, they throw all women under the bus, regardless of how women might feel.

In 2014, a woman wrote to the *Toronto Star*'s advice column:

> I am a senior woman. Recently, a 'man' claiming to be transgender, who had not yet begun physical treatments, was permitted by our local Y to use the women's locker room. There are no secure change rooms. The person they allowed in was not courteous and stared at me whilst I struggled out of a wet bathing suit. He was naked, had an erection and playfully asked 'Do you come here often?' (quoted in Jeffreys, 2014a, p. 49).

The columnist answered that the *transgender woman* had every right to be there, surgery or no surgery, confirming that, in institutions that have bought into gender identity ideology, the whim of a few men matters more than the needs of all women.

Middle and high school female students have also been made aware that their male peers acquire the right to see them naked if they utter the magic words "I am a woman." In November 2019, an Illinois school district decided that *transgender* students should have unrestricted access to the locker room of their choice. When the voting took place, someone brought a camera and microphone up to the *trans girl* bent on marking territory and to the female swimmer who wanted to be able to dress and undress without males next to her. Asked how they felt, he, ecstatic, felt like a hero for having won such a huge victory for his own. She, on her part, could barely hold back her tears, incredulous at a school board that blithely ignored the privacy of women and girls (see Leventis, 2019).

In discussions of these issues, it is common to hear opponents of this male occupation say that women don't want to see penises in gym locker rooms, citing the example of women who may have PTSD from rape. I have no doubt that many do indeed not want to see penises, and these stories show that schools and companies care more about virtue signalling and projecting a trans-friendly image than they do about women. But in these cases, the male gaze is as intimidating and unwanted a presence as the male sexual organ. In fact, if the man in question is clothed, it makes no difference. Women need, for safety reasons and in order not to feel extremely uncomfortable, spaces free from objectifying male gazes. Not even in toilets and changing rooms will they be granted this?

Blessed among women

Another very serious problem brought about by self-ID is that now in some places male offenders who claim to be female (or non-binary or gender-fluid) are entitled to serve their sentences in women's prisons, without any requirement for hormones or surgery. Most of them, as with males who say they are transgender outside of prison, have intact genitalia. This is a great example of how these policies were decided and implemented without those responsible consulting women or pausing to think for a moment about the multiple implications, and now their hands are tied by their own negligence. "Decades of research have demonstrated that female offenders fare best in rehabilitative environments away from men" (Chandler et al. v. CDCR, p. 4), but for some reason they don't join the dots.

The US feminist organization Women's Liberation Front (WoLF), which is currently representing a group of women prisoners in a lawsuit against the California Department of Corrections and Rehabilitation, reports that in California, as of January 2021, when Senate Bill SB 132, the Transgender Respect, Agency and Dignity Act, came into effect,

> hundreds of men have applied for transfers to women's prisons, and dozens have already been transferred. These transfers have resulted in intimidation, sexual harassment, physical assaults and sexual assaults committed by the men against female inmates. [...] Sharing intimate space with male offenders has exacerbated women's symptoms of depression, anxiety, and PTSD; diminished their quality of life due to increased security measures for male offenders; and reduced their access to appropriate trauma-informed care and rehabilitative programs (Women's Liberation Front, n.d.).

One of the inmates they represent is Tomiekia Johnson, a wrongfully imprisoned survivor of domestic violence who was forced to share a cell with a "vicious and dangerous biological male inmate." As she put it:

> I feel like I can't trust anyone. No one cares about my interests, no one cares about my mental health, no one cares about my safety. So, my whole quality of life is damaged. I have physical symptoms, I have emotional distress, panic, anxiety attacks. I'm triggered by different things, and I have nightmares, insomnia and like, I'm totally affected. I've never felt like this before. Even when I was living with my abusive husband, I've never felt like I feel today (Women's Liberation Front, 2021).

Numerous variables contribute to the loss of quality of life and mental health of Tomiekia and other inmates because of this dangerous and inhumane law. Another complainant, Krystal Gonzalez, was raped by a male transferred to the prison where she was held. She filed a complaint, asked to be housed with other women, and the response was to correct her and tell her that the man who raped her was *a transgender woman with a penis.* But

> Krystal does not believe that women have penises, and the psychological distress caused by her assault is exacerbated by the prison's refusal to acknowledge the sex of her perpetrator (Chandler et al. v. CDCR, p. 18).

Some women who share a cell with a man decided to organize their sleep schedules so that there would always be one woman on watch, lest they shared Krystal's fate and be raped by their male cellmate. This would not be unheard of, given that 33.8 per cent of inmates who identify as trans in Californian prisons are sex offenders (see Slatz, 2022b). In fact, at least one other rape has been reported since these events: that committed by Jonathan Robertson/Siyaah Skylit (who knocked his victim unconscious and she had to be carried out on a stretcher). This rapist with a *female identity* was in the women's prison after intensive transactivist campaigns for his transfer (see Slatz, 2022b).

There are other situations which, without being as severe, also illustrate the institutional violence against these women, who are already particularly vulnerable. In one of the Californian prisons there are some trees in the exercise yard. These shade trees and the birds that live among their branches are one of the inmates' scarce contacts with nature and provide them with some of the few pleasures and moments of relaxation they can enjoy. But as their fellow male inmates could use the trees as weapons, or because they could cause visual blind spots that pose security risks, cutting them down has been considered. The very prospect of being left without these trees and birds because of the presence of males has already caused many women distress (see Chandler et al. v. CDCR, pp. 12–13). Inmate Mimi Le told WoLF lawyers in a sworn declaration:

> Men get to transfer to women's prison because the prison fails to keep them safe from rape by other men in men's prison [...]. But now the prison is protecting [them] by getting [them] out of the men's prison

only to let [them] terrorize women with rape and violence threats, (quoted in Slatz, 2022b).

Observes US feminist lawyer Kara Dansky:

> Women in prison, the majority of whom have not committed a violent offense, are often themselves victims of physical and/or sexual abuse, and many of them struggle with addiction. A disproportionate number of these women are black or Latina. These women are terrified (Dansky, 2021b, p. 63).

In Mexico, a very high proportion of women in prison who have not committed violent crimes have been victims of male violence. In addition, in this country,

> women face significantly more violence when they are accused of a crime, when they are arrested, when they are sentenced, and their life inside prisons seems to be designed as if they were not women (García, 2022).

The Political Constitution of the United Mexican States establishes in Article 18: "Women shall serve their sentences in places separate from those destined for men for this purpose." However, according to various reports of the National Human Rights Commission on the situation of women inmates in Mexican prisons, in several of them there is no

> strict separation between men and women, despite the special situation of vulnerability in which female inmates find themselves, which makes them susceptible to all kinds of abuse (González Pérez, 2015, p. 39).

There is no ambiguity in these words and there is no way to misinterpret them; in Mexico, the need for prisons to be segregated by sex is recognized in order to respect "the human rights of women deprived of their liberty, relating to social reintegration, equality, dignified treatment, health protection, legality and judicial security," and "it is unacceptable that there are prisons in which [...] male and female inmates are allowed to live together in common areas such as dining rooms and yards" (Plascencia, 2013, pp. 10 and 35).

If it is considered unacceptable in the dining room, all the more so in dormitories and showers. But it is hard to imagine that Mexican institutions, having clearly been captured by transgenderism, will not make an exception to the constitutional mandate when an offender arrives who claims to identify as transgender. Claiming that such an offender belongs there because *she* is a woman (since "trans women are women") would be misplaced, since, as has been amply demonstrated, a supposedly female identity has no effect on male socialization or propensity for violent behavior.

Transactivists argue that *trans women* offenders should serve their sentences in women's prisons to protect them from dangerous males ... "which is the same reason why many women are arguing that trans-identified women (men) should *not* be housed in women's prisons" (Raymond, 2021, p. 143). Like these activists, the California law challenged by WoLF expressly claims to seek to protect the dignity of trans or non-binary inmates, but it does so, say the female prisoners' advocates,

> by removing the agency and dignity of inmates who belong to (not by self-identity, but by virtue of material fact) the category 'women', who are disproportionately subjected to violence, harassment, and discrimination on the basis of belonging in the class of humans who are of the female sex, and such harms are inflicted upon women overwhelmingly by men (humans of the male sex) (Chandler et al. v. CDCR, p. 5).

Now, if males who identify as transgender or non-binary are at greater risk of violence at the hands of other males, "the solution cannot be to lower the vulnerability of that subset of men by increasing the vulnerability of women" (Chandler et al. v. CDCR, p. 6).

Everyone knows that men are much more violent and dangerous than women. Even women who identify as men know this. They do not ask to serve their sentences in the prisons of the *gender they identify with,* but the other way around, as happened in Argentina in 2018. A *trans man* "committed a crime in Entre Ríos and now resists being housed in the men's ward." The head of the Penitentiary Service concluded:

> Taking into account the so-called gender identity law, he has done the procedure at the Civil Registry where he made the change of identity, with a man's name, and what we work with is always in accordance with the will that he has expressed in the Registry, therefore he must be housed in a men's sector (*La Voz*, 2018).

The fully justified fear of this detainee brings to light the reality that so many people refuse to openly admit: *trans women* are not women and *trans men* are not men.

When radical feminists are accused of being trans exclusionary, there is a simple way to refute it: radical feminists argue that feminism has a place for all women, even women who identify as trans men. Any woman can understand another woman's utter terror at the prospect of being locked up among male criminals, to whom her gender identity won't matter. As it is much rarer for *a trans man* to commit a crime than for *a trans woman,* for those very few cases a solution can surely be found in the women's prison.

But with toilets it's different. If a woman who identifies as a man has a beard and passes reasonably well (as so many of them do), I tend to think that she should go to the men's toilet, where she will not bother or startle anyone; otherwise, with her apparently masculine presence, she would be inviting men to enter women's toilets. And I say *passing reasonably well* because, sometimes, when faced with a woman with short hair and no make-up, others think at first glance that she is a man. This belief can be seen in the moment when they are startled or because they point out, "This is a ladies' room." Needless to say, *masculine* women still have every right to enter women's toilets and changing rooms, because what qualifies for this is not how much femininity a woman projects outwardly.

Among the many collateral damages of transgenderism, one worth mentioning, albeit briefly, is that now many people, when they see a *masculine* woman or a *feminine* man, the first thing they think is no longer "This person is a masculine woman" or "This person is a feminine man," but "This person is a trans man" or "This person is a trans woman," another sign that this ideological fashion, contrary to what it boasts to do, is not normalizing a rebellion against sexist stereotypes, but does quite the opposite. What happened to Mexican boxer Alejandra *Tigre* Jiménez illustrates this. She recently announced her retirement

> because of the systematic violence she has suffered since 2016, with physical, economic and emotional effects due to ignorance or taboos that still exist, especially against women who stand out in sporting disciplines and do not meet the canons of feminine appearance set by the market. […] Likewise, she said, she has also suffered harassment from some of her opponents and the sports media who have even questioned whether she is a transgender man and for this reason has been so successful (*El Financiero,* 2022a).

We are sure to see more of these cases in the years to come.

No shelter for you

It is cruel enough to house men in women's prisons, but allowing them into women shelters, which were created by the feminist movement to provide housing, food, security and recovery space for women fleeing their homes to safety from a violent partner, is the height of insensitivity and shows an utter lack of what some call a gender perspective. As Ingala Smith explains,

> refuges are single-sex largely, but not only, in recognition of the fact that it is males who pose a threat to women's safety and one of the most effective means by which we can keep women and children in refuges safe is by keeping males out of them (Ingala Smith, 2023, p. 51).

Of course, this includes males who claim to be females. A series of events in Canada make transparent the motivations and methods of gender identity activism and show that the welfare of the most vulnerable women is far from being a priority.

The Vancouver Rape Relief and Women's Shelter, founded in 1973 to house women who were victims of rape and women who needed to get away from violent males in their immediate environment, was at the centre of a legal dispute in 1995. A man who called himself Kimberly Nixon wanted to volunteer, but was turned down because the shelter only served women and accepted only female staff. He claimed that this amounted to discrimination. The verdict of the British Columbia Human Rights Tribunal was that the shelter should give Nixon compensation of 7,500 Canadian dollars. Several appeals by Vancouver Rape Relief followed until the Court of Appeal ruled that the rape crisis centre was entitled to a policy that excluded *trans women* or men in general. In 2007, the Supreme Court of Canada upheld the verdict (see Fein, 2020).

But this did not sit well with gender identity activists, who also found it unbearable that Vancouver Rape Relief's temporary shelter houses were exclusively for women and their young children. It was, at that point, the only shelter that had not yet become mixed sex at the behest of the aggressive trans lobby.[79] In retaliation, transactivists mobilized to have the Vancouver City Council withdraw any possibility of public funding for the shelter. Those in charge of the centre explained in a thousand ways that their motivation was not transphobia, but the safety and peace of mind of the women they cared for; they wrote communiqués to the *transgender community* to remind them that their telephone services did cater to trans women, and they were very empathetic and understanding about their situation because they knew that "people whose behaviour is not consistent with the patriarchal socially imposed definition of manhood or womanhood, including trans people, suffer discrimination and violence" (quoted in Fein,

---

79 Sure it wasn't easy, but it was the right thing to do:
There is not enough refuge provision available to meet the needs of women who need it, and yet some groups are making their services, in some cases their most comfortable accommodation, open to males. I'm aware that this can come about as a result of pressure from commissioners, but I think feminist organisations focused on supporting women should do just that and resist this pressure. And if they are making a choice, then I think they have their priorities wrong (Ingala Smith, 2023, p. 53).

2020). It was in vain. In February 2019, the council decided that it could no longer provide financial support to the organization. This delighted men's rights activists who are determined to destroy every space that women want for themselves.

But defunding was not enough. In August 2019, militants nailed a dead rat to the office door and shortly afterwards scrawled threats and messages such as "Kill TERFs" and "TERFs go home, you are not welcome" on the windows. Yes, you read that right: gender identity activists, those who ask us to be nice and use people's preferred pronouns, left intimidating messages and painted death threats on the premises of a shelter for female victims of male violence.

The shelter is supported by donations from the public and feminists. It continues to do its job, providing services for women in need and defending our sex-based rights. But as mentioned, successful pressure from activists means that now, with the exception of Vancouver Rape Relief, there is no other Canadian shelter that maintains a policy of having exclusively female staff and serving only women. Episodes in other centres show that there are compelling reasons for such a policy.

In 2017, in the city of Kelowna, Tracey, a woman in her 60s living in a shelter for homeless women, was assigned a roommate – a man who was *transitioning into a woman*. "Sorry, if a person identifies themselves as female, then we have to go with that," the staff told her when she complained. In an interview for local television, this woman gave a perfect summary of what was already happening six years ago in the country which is perhaps the most committed to transgender ideology:

> I was kicked out of a women's shelter because I was uncomfortable with my roommate being transgender. If he wants to become a woman, that's his choice, but when a man comes into a women's shelter who still has a penis and genitals, he has more rights than we do (Van Emmerick, 2017).

Housed in the same place was Blaine, a young woman who had recently fled an abusive relationship. "Some women have bad experiences with men," she explained, "so they are there to flee men, and now we have a man living there" (Van Emmerick, 2017).

There is no shortage of examples of how women's discomfort and fears are fully justified. Shane Jacob Green, a reoffender who had already been convicted of sexual assault, arrived on 22 August 2022 at a women's shelter in Parry Sound, Ontario, where all he had to do to be admitted was declare himself a woman. As if it had not been clear from the outset that he was a man, he immediately engaged in behaviour that is, shall we say, unusual for women: "making sexually inappropriate comments to staff and residents." Just two days later he committed a rape:

> Green sometimes uses the name 'Stephanie' when claiming to be trans-gender. Staff at the women's shelter where the rape allegedly occurred may have been too afraid to turn Green away due to the risk of running afoul of Canada's notoriously pro-trans human rights law (Seiland, 2022).

In other words, the Vancouver Rape Relief experience has served as a lesson: now, in order not to be seen as transphobic and risk losing State support, shelters are committing unforgivable oversights and putting the women they are obliged to protect at risk.

Proponents of these anti-women policies seek to justify them by saying that trans people should not be discriminated against, but they demonstrate a misunderstanding of what does and does not constitute discrimination. The society that runs the Kelowna shelter says that their shelters "welcome people without regard to age, race, religion and gender identity" (Van Emmerick, 2017). But what is actually happening with this flaunting of fake progressivism is that fundamental specificities are being disregarded; all the measures that were intended precisely to eliminate discrimination against women are being overturned. These do not consist in acting as if women were identical to men and have the same needs (this assumption has in fact led to many injustices), but in counteracting the disadvantages women face in a society that in practice considers them to be an inferior class of human beings. As Karen Ingala Smith puts it, because of structural inequality, providing equitable services to women who have been abused by men "doesn't mean treating everyone the same; it means recognising that some must have different services because of particular inequalities" (Ingala Smith, 2023, p. 48).

Indeed, ending discrimination requires making distinctions and taking into account the specific needs of each vulnerable group, not pretending that sex or age are irrelevant. As the examples of prisons and shelters show, denying women's sex-based rights, such as when spaces meant to protect them are closed down, makes it difficult for women to access a life free of violence and constitutes a tragic form of discrimination against them.

As stated in the Declaration on Women's Sex-Based Rights (a document that reaffirms the rights of women set out in the Convention on the Elimination of All Forms of Discrimination against Women and other international treaties), endorsed by women from different parts of the world who "oppose all forms of discrimination against women and girls that result from replacing 'sex' with 'gender identity' in law, policy and social practice," it is of great concern that policies based on this concept are being used "in ways which threaten the survival of women-only service provisions, including victim support and health care services" and "to justify the intrusion of men and boys into single-sex spaces aimed at protecting the safety, privacy and dignity of women and girls who have been subject to violence" (WDI, 2019, Preamble).

In countries as steeped in gender identity doctrine as England, in order to fulfill some men's desire to have the world speak to them in the feminine, women are even being robbed of the right to be cared for by people of their own sex in a hospital setting. In October 2022, an alarming sequence of events unfolded at the Princess Grace Hospital in London. Teresa Steele, a retired solicitor, was scheduled to undergo major surgery there and requested that only female nurses attend her, a right recognized by British law. Having been a victim of rape in the past, she feared for her safety in her particularly vulnerable circumstance of being bedridden and unable to move.

She also warned that she would not answer questions on the forms about her gender identity or use female pronouns to refer to men, because, as was confirmed after Maya Forstater's trial, gender-critical beliefs, such as hers, are "worthy of respect in a democratic society" (see Forstater, 2021). But then something happened that suggests that this woman's requests reached the ears of a hospital employee who identified as transgender, and who wanted to teach her a lesson.

She recounts that when she went for her clinical pre-op assessment, which involved intimate procedures, someone knocked on the door and entered without waiting for an answer: a person in a blonde wig, scarlet lipstick and heavy make-up opened the door and made eye contact with her. It turned out he was a *trans woman* nurse, but a nurse who had nothing to do with Steele's care:

> The whole situation was just peculiar, most unnatural. The nurse who was already in the room with me indicated that the room was occupied. [...] Instead of just backing out or saying 'Oh, sorry', as you'd expect, the person lingered and made eye contact, which again I found odd and disconcerting (quoted in Johnston, 2023).

Naturally, Steele was shocked that a male hospital employee would have such disregard for her privacy, given that she was naked and had also made an express request to be seen only by women:

> I began to wonder if it was just a coincidence that this member of staff with a *gender identity* had made their presence felt to me in such an inappropriate way during my first visit. I began to suspect that I had been targeted because my patient records showed that I refused to use pronouns and wanted single sex facilities, although I have no evidence of this (quoted in Sales, 2022).

She panicked as she imagined an entire week in the hospital, after a major surgery, in the care of male nurses and staff. It is normal for a woman to prefer sponge baths to be given by a woman rather than a man, regardless of his gender identity.

> It was a slow, dawning realisation. I felt sick. Alarm bells were ringing in my head. I cannot describe the fear that I felt. I cannot rationalise it (quoted in Sales, 2022).

That evening, she wrote to the Health Care Aide to underline her concerns and to confirm her request to be attended only by women during her post-operative stay. The response from the hospital's chief executive, three days before the date of the operation, reads: "We do not share your beliefs and are not able to adhere to your requests and we have therefore decided that we will not proceed with your surgery at Princess Grace Hospital."

So, the problem is not the male employee who, having no business being there, walked into the room where a woman was undergoing intimate examinations and stared at her. The problem is the patient's gender-critical beliefs, despite the fact that the UK Employment Appeal Tribunal has already ruled that they are valid and respectable, and are not unique to a few people, but are shared "by others who consider that it is important to have an open debate about issues concerning sex and gender identity" (Forstater, 2021). Because of her beliefs, her right to privacy was violated; because of her political stance, a major surgery necessary for her health was cancelled at the last minute and her life was put at risk. His pronouns over her life.

This story is yet another example of how people trample over the fundamental rights of more than 50 per cent of the population and break social norms and agreements that are there for a reason, in order to accommodate the desires of less than one per cent of men, a large proportion of whom do nothing to conceal their contempt for people of the sex to which they say they would like to belong. It also shows how a persecutory atmosphere is developing in supposedly democratic countries in which dissidents from the regime had better think twice before opening their mouths and revealing what they think.

In Canada, the women at the Kelowna shelter suffered repercussions for having spoken to the media: they were thrown out under the pretext that they had broken a confidentiality agreement. That's right, that very day they were asked to leave the shelter for good (see Van Emmerick, 2017). This action confirmed that, in the eyes of this homeless women's shelter, a man has more rights than all women put together, to be sure.

"We'll stick together," Tracey tells Blaine, trying to comfort and reassure her in the face of the distressing prospect.

Blaine answers with her voice cracking: "Yeah, hopefully we'll stay safe."

Discriminated against in your own category

Besides their different roles in reproduction, sport is another area where the physical differences between women and men are most obvious and undeniable. However, some people are indeed determined to deny they even exist – and some people believe it, or rather claim to believe it. It has come to the point that the burden of proof is placed on those who have not lost all touch with reality and understand that female and male categories exist because on average men are heavier than women, have more muscle mass, are much stronger and faster, have a greater ability to kick, a 160 per cent advantage in ability to punch (see Blade, 2020); also greater bone density, larger hearts and lungs and therefore greater aerobic capacity.

Everyone knows this, even if they don't know the precise figures. Without needing to be shown the studies and graphs that demonstrate that they have 33 per cent more explosive power, we know that a man can kill a woman with his fists, but not the other way around. It didn't take male transgender mixed martial arts fighter Fallon Fox giving his female opponent Tamikka Brents a concussion for us to know who was going to win, and we can bet that on the night of 13 September 2014, no one was betting on the female. Writes Linda Blade, a Canadian coach committed to saving women's sport:

> Male-bodied athletes who self-identify as women have become adept at what might be called a form of 'gaslighting': an attempt to conceptually manipulate us into questioning our own reality and perceptions. When damage inflicted by transwomen athletes in contact

sports is too serious to ignore by sports authorities, the perpetrators of the injuries typically deflect attention from the physical victim and proclaim themselves as the real victims – of intolerance – with the greater claim on society's compassion (Blade, 2021).

And, as expected, there were those who cast Fox as the victim when, after his victory over Brents, criticism was made of a man beating women in the ring for entertainment value (see, for example, Calderon, 2021). Soon after, he announced his retirement citing "the negativity" that had surrounded that fight, the most controversial in the history of mixed martial arts (see BJJ World, n.d.).

One newspaper account describes the brutal beating that took place 44 seconds into the first round as follows:

> Fox threw her knees to Brents' face and torso early on, to start the fight. Brents ultimately turned to avoid further damage, and withstood nearly a minute of hard elbows and punches from Fox before the referee stopped her (Vasquez, 2015).

Beaming with joy, Fox bragged about the beating of his opponent. On 16 June 2020, he tweeted:

> For the record, I knocked two [women] out. One woman's skull was fractured, the other not. And just so you know, I enjoyed it. See, I love smacking up TERFs in the cage who talk transphobic nonsense. It's bliss! Don't be mad (quoted in Blade, 2021).

This was followed by winking and kissing emojis. For her part, Tamikka Brents, making sure to use female pronouns to refer to the man who had broken her orbital bone, stated:

> I've fought a lot of women and have never felt the strength that I felt in a fight as I did that night. I can't answer whether it's because she was born a man or not because I'm not a doctor. I can only say, I've never felt so overpowered ever in my life and I am an abnormally strong female in my own right. Her grip was different; I could usually move around in the clinch against other females but couldn't move at all in Fox's clinch (quoted in Purohit, 2021).

So effective has gaslighting become and so far has it gone that some women doubt themselves and what they experience firsthand, to the extent of thinking that only experts and scholars can know something which, in reality, babies and even dogs know without a shadow of a doubt. Until before the transgender wave swept over us, every adult could tell the difference between a man and a woman.

Female categories did not always exist, because for many years women were denied participation in sports. They competed for the first time at the Paris 1900 Olympics, the second of the modern era: out of a total of 997 athletes, 22 were women, in five disciplines. Almost a hundred years later, at Barcelona 1992, there were still 35 countries with all-male delegations. It was not until London 2012 that female representation from all participating countries was reached and women were admitted in all disciplines. But very soon after those goals, which took so many decades to achieve, a reverse path began when in Tokyo 2020 males were openly allowed into the female category. Of course, some media portrayed this as good news and a great triumph in the fight for equality and non-discrimination:

> The Tokyo 2020 Games will go down in history as the Games where transgender athletes have found their chance: on Monday, New Zealand's Laurel Hubbard made history by making her debut in the weightlifting +87kg category as a woman. It is the first time in her life, after thirteen years competing as Gavin Hubbard, that she has competed as Laurel.[80] And with this, a new era begins (Mundi, 2021).

Transgender athletes have never been barred from participating in the category which belongs to them by virtue of their sex (Bruce Jenner knows this and so does Caitlyn Jenner),[81] but transgender

---

80 Referring to Hubbard as a woman is not the only falsehood in the story: nor is it true that he never competed as Laurel. New Zealand women had long objected to the injustice of this specific man usurping places that belong to women; see, for example, Reuters (2019).

81 Incidentally, Jenner, a man who presents himself as a woman, is interested in the protection of women's sport and argues that it is unfair for trans women to compete in the female category. Living your life authentically, he says, "also comes with responsibility and some integrity" (in Edwards, 2022). On the other hand, he thinks that some males, including himself, belong in women's toilets: "I do use the women's bathroom, I've never had a problem whatsoever in eight years. [...] The ladies rooms are much nicer! They smell much better, you don't have pee on

rhetoric never misses an opportunity to characterize the quest for fair play as discrimination. No wonder the press is so enthusiastic about women's achievements when those women are men. The sports pages usually devote far more space to men's competitions than to women's. When they do talk about women, it is not always to praise their performance on the track or in the gym, but to show how sexy they look in bathing suits and to hold them up as examples of beauty, not of sporting greatness. Sometimes the women's uniforms seem designed not for greater freedom of movement, but so that the spectator can gaze at the bodies and the television cameras can show buttocks close-ups (beach volleyball is a telling example).

There is a lot of work to be done in terms of equal opportunities for women in sport, but now, because identity politics has reached the courts, the changing rooms and the International Olympic Committee, we are going backwards. We cannot say that the aim is to kill the female category, but that is what they are achieving as a collateral effect. They are also demoralizing the female competitors, who lose all hope of winning gold as soon as a male invades their category. As female high school runner Alanna Smith says:

> Mentally and physically, we know the outcome before the race even starts. That biological unfairness doesn't go away because of what someone believes about gender identity (Associated Press, 2020a).

Giving women and girls equal opportunities to participate in sport and physical education requires single-sex teams and competitions:

> To ensure fairness and safety for women and girls, the entry of boys and men who claim to have female gender identities into teams, competitions, facilities, or changing rooms, inter alia, set aside for women and girls, should be prohibited as a form of sex discrimination (WDI, 2019, Article 7).

In US high schools, it is increasingly common for a boy who identifies as trans to rob one teammate of her place in the competition and another of her place on the podium. This also leads to several of the

the wall, they got flowers in there... [...] It's a much better environment in the ladies rooms, thank you very much for letting me use them" (Sky News, 2023).

girls losing the athletic scholarship that would have allowed them to pursue a college degree. Veteran sportswomen have come to the defense of these young women and have organized themselves into groups such as Save Women's Sports, in the US, and Fair Play for Women, in the UK, which seek to raise public awareness of the full implications of this male takeover of still another women-only space. The parents of the teenage girls concerned are not happy either.

In September 2022, at a student volleyball tournament in North Carolina, a boy on the Highlands High female team hit a player on the opposing Hiwassee Dam High team in the forehead with the ball and, because of the severe blow (so severe that a 40-year coach said he had never seen one like it), she

> suffered severe head and neck injuries, resulting in long-term concussion symptoms, including vision problems. The girl has not yet been cleared to play again by her primary care physician or a neurologist (Rachmuth, 2022).

Her name, it was later known, is Payton McNabb, and she declared her life "changed forever" when that male student hit her in the face: "My ability to learn, retain, and comprehend, has also been impaired" (quoted in Dedaj, 2023).

As has been demonstrated, it is not only unfair but dangerous to put men in competition with women, most obviously in contact sports, but also in relatively safe sports as volleyball or tennis. If we want to protect women and give them a level playing field and fair play, males have absolutely no business there. Some seek to justify it because *transgender* male athletes have their testosterone levels capped, as if hormone therapy will wipe out all the effects of going through puberty and all the characteristics that give a male body a sporting advantage over women.

Those who demand that everyone play along with people who believe they have a gender identity that does not correspond to their genitalia and their testosterone levels also claim that there are very few of them and that they will not cause any major damage. On the one hand, the truth is that a single man can cause a lot of damage and demoralize everyone. This case constitutes a very concrete example: it was decided to cancel all matches for the rest of the season that the Cherokee County teams were going to play against the Highlands High girls' team with a male member, thus affecting all the young female volleyball players in that territory (see Karnbach, 2022).[82] On the other hand, they are not so few, and they will become more and more: several men have already realized that, thanks to the magic of self-ID, they can quickly go from being a mediocre athlete to the top of the rankings. If men who refuse to participate in the male category – because their internal and individual experience of gender doesn't feel so comfortable among other men – continue to be allowed to participate in the female category, in a few years the women's competitions will be dominated by men, and all the medals and records will go to them.

Finally, there are those who take one of the very few examples of a *transgender man* who beats a *cis man*, and hold it up as compelling proof that there is no physical difference between males and females. This is what Mexican journalist Láurel Miranda does when he makes this hasty generalization:

> If people assigned male at birth are 'by biology' stronger than people assigned female at birth, how do you explain the triumph of trans man Patricio Manuel over cis man Hugo Aguilar? (@laurelyeye, 2022).

As the Spanish sports law specialist Irene Aguiar rightly recalls, Patricio Manuel,

> who was a five-time US national amateur female boxing champion, even competing in Olympic trials, and after more than three years

---

82 Note how requiring the team to expel the male player, which was the obvious solution, seemed unthinkable. Moreover, games not played would count as Highlands High victories (see Lofthouse, 2022). It is also worth mentioning that neither the mainstream news about the case, nor many of the smaller local papers, mention the male teenager who injured his opponent; nobody brings up the fact of a *transgender girl* playing on a female team. People in the county were upset about the cancellations, but they were attributed to a girl being seriously hurt, not to a boy hurting her. This difference in approach is not minor, and not raising the main fact (the sex of the player responsible) means playing on the transgender court.

on testosterone, has only been able to win two bouts, one against an 18-year-old boy, out of four. No titles. The inherent advantages of the male biological sex do not mean that *all* men always beat *all* women: it means that *most* men beat *most* women (@IreneAguiarG, 2022).

When British former Olympic swimmer Sharron Davies was interviewed to talk about Lia Thomas, the University of Pennsylvania male swimmer who in the 2021–2022 season was breaking all records in the female category,[83] she observed that women are now being discriminated against in their own sporting category and all sorts of ethical concerns are being overlooked. "We spend millions around the world to stop people cheating with drugs," she says (quoted in Ball, 2022), but everyone turns a blind eye to the blatant cheating that is males' participation in the female category. Davies knows a thing or two about cheating, by the way: she is still owed a gold medal taken from her in Moscow 1980 by an East German swimmer who several years later admitted doping. It is well known that athletes from East Germany were given testosterone and other anabolic steroid drugs to win medals in international competitions (see Ball, 2022).

There is no doubt that men's bodies, regardless of their personality, gender identity or Zodiac sign, give them an upper hand over women in strength and speed activities where the body takes centre stage. In addition to the abundant empirical evidence always close by (for example, when it comes to carrying a refrigerator or opening a jar), there is no shortage of studies demonstrating the unfair advantage of boys competing against girls, and men competing against women. To philosophize about whether trans women athletes have an advantage is acting dumb (e.g. Corti, 2022).

---

83   The last season Thomas swam on his university's male team, 2018–2019, he ranked 554th in the US in the 200-yard freestyle and 65th in the 500-yard freestyle; when he joined the female team, in 2021–2022, his ranking rebounded to fifth and first, respectively (see Lohn, 2022). Ross Tucker, a sports physiologist, argues that Thomas "is the manifestation of the scientific evidence: the reduction of testosterone did not remove her [*sic*] biological advantage" (in Powell, 2022).

It is another effect of language games, because no headline would ask the question of whether males are stronger and faster than females.

All this discussion must also be very discouraging for female athletes because, in addition to taking away their places, it is as if men's supposed *superiority* by virtue of being stronger is being hammered home. "Look, you're really not that good," or "You're not trying hard enough." Indeed, that very thing was implied, give or take a word or two, by Terry Miller, a male runner who in 2018, along with his fellow Andraya Yearwood, also male, was breaking records in the 100m and 200m dash, not in the male category, but in the female one. Between the two of them they were taking first and second place, race after race. In an interview, speaking of the female competitors who resented this injustice, Miller said that instead of complaining, the girls should try harder (quoted in Robertson, 2020).

It wasn't until 2011 that Fallon Fox was known to be a male: in a sport where women tend to be heavily muscled and have a distinctly masculine appearance, he managed to go unnoticed. Arrogating to himself the supposed right to deceit that underlies transgender claims, he fought several women without it being known that he was not one. That does not stop many from considering him a hero, the first transgender mixed martial arts fighter, the pride of the LGBTQ+ community, a groundbreaking woman, one of a kind, the holder of an impressive record, someone whose story "could help save the lives of so many LGBTQ+ young people who suffer in silence" (Barrie, 2015). Their complacency makes them lose sight of the fact that he was a man committing fraud and beating women for money and medals.

Linda Blade points out:

> The threat to female athletes from self-identified transwomen doesn't exist in a vacuum. Clearly, it requires compliance and assistance from other participants in sports: fellow players, coaches, administrators, news media, government policymakers and the community at large (Blade, 2021, Chapter 1).

There is, however, one area in which there is less willingness on the part of all these actors to take self-ID to its ultimate consequences and give in to the demands of transgenderists.

On 20 January 2021, the date of his inauguration as President of the United States, Joe Biden signed Executive Order 13988 on Preventing and Combating Discrimination on the Basis of Gender Identity or Sexual Orientation, which in practice implied, as Kara Dansky points out, an abolition of sex: eliminating it as an important category without even providing an opportunity for the measure to be publicly discussed (see Dansky, 2021a).

There is one thing, however, that Biden left intact. The US Government's Selective Service, which provides the Defense Department with troops in the event of a military draft, requires all male US citizens and male immigrants between the ages of 18 and 25 to register, "including US citizens or immigrants who are born male and have changed their gender to female," while "individuals who are born female and have changed their gender to male" do not have to register (see George, 2022).

This seems to indicate that at least some bureaucrats, administrators and government policymakers do know that gender identity does not affect someone's speed, strength and ability to punch.

Hello, parity; goodbye, parity

Quotas for women are affirmative action measures aimed at improving their representation in elected office. They are necessary because sexist stereotypes still rule in mindsets and many people think that women do not have the necessary qualities to be in politics. This is consistent with a society where a girl who is averse to femininity is believed to be a boy who was born in the wrong body.

When the representation of both sexes is equal, so-called parity is achieved: a full inclusion of women, which is nowadays considered an indicator of the degree of democracy in a country. As Drude Dahlerup, Professor at the Department of Political Science at Stockholm University, writes:

It is a universal claim today, that elected political assemblies in principle should reflect the composition of society in terms of gender, majority and minorities (Dahlerup, 2021, p. 132).

Gender parity is a constitutional principle in Mexico. Since 2019 it is mandatory

that half of the decision-making positions be held by women in the three branches of the State, in the three orders of government, in autonomous bodies, in the candidacies of political parties for popularly elected positions, as well as in the election of representatives in municipalities with indigenous populations (Instituto Nacional de las Mujeres, 2020).

Gender parity was not graciously granted to us. It is the consequence of a long struggle by Mexican women for the right to vote and be voted for. Challenging "the traditional male-dominance or even male-monopoly in politics" has been "an important result" (Dahlerup, 2021, p. 135). Parity also serves to advance "towards the consolidation of a truly representative, participatory and inclusive democracy" (Inmujeres, 2020).

A great achievement indeed. But it is clear that the principle of parity conflicts with self-identification rules. If it turns out that any man who claims to be a woman is legally a woman, how do you ensure that half of all decision-making positions are held by adult human females? Or does anyone who claims that their deeply felt internal and individual experience of gender is feminine counts as a woman for the purposes of political representation? The answer is yes. Let us say it again: in today's unusual situation, it is not sex that counts for legal purposes, but gender identity – not the material body, but the spiritual soul; not what can be empirically proven, but the dogma of faith.

Under these conditions there is no way to guarantee the political representation that women have fought for. Half of the seats are reserved for women, who for centuries have been excluded from decision-making. Men who identify with femininity have never been denied the vote but now they are taking the places rightfully reserved for women. Why didn't policymakers stop to think about these implications of self-ID? When feminists warned of this risk, the answer was, "It's not going to happen." But it is happening.

In May 2018, in the state of Oaxaca, 17 male candidates pretended to be trans in order to gain access to women's candidacies. Then a group of muxes, indigenous Zapotec men, usually homosexuals, who adopt women's clothing and attitudes, something that isn't frowned upon in their community, denounced this fraud to the electoral authorities. They claimed that, in order to avoid gender quotas, those 17 were lying and trying to "usurp trans identity" (*SDP Noticias,* 2018).

Queer activists have had a strong influence on new generations of muxes and often brandish the existence of this indigenous group, whom they call a third gender, as an example that transsexuality has existed since time immemorial. This is a biased and inaccurate interpretation. To better understand what the muxes represent, Zapotec lesbian poet Yadira del Mar debunks several of the myths that have circulated about them ever since anthropology, sociology and other social sciences set eyes on them:

> The migration of young people to big cities to attend university has put them in contact with gender studies [...], theories that co-opted the reality of the indigenous communities [...], leaving aside our ethnicity's worldview, colonizing again our ways of seeing and understanding the world. [...] There is a division between older muxes and the new muxe generations. The first muxes were aware of their biological reality, meaning they accepted their male body and opposed hormone treatments, *sex reassignment* surgeries, and did not want to be called women, but be understood in their own way of inhabiting the world. It is not [...] that they did not know they were men or that the idea of being a man or a woman came with the arrival of colonizers to the territories of Abya Yala. The ancestors of these territories knew they were men or women and they did not believe someone could have been born in the wrong body. Even though it is true that within their communities gender stereotypes are still being reproduced, there was an awareness between muxes of having been born as biological males. It was also understood that they, according

to this worldview, had inherited the best of both sexes: a masculine body and the *feminine sensibility,* and with it, everything that care work entailed. They accepted that they were cross-dressing in order to imitate a reality that did not change them in a biological, historical, or cultural way. The old muxes did not cross-dress on a daily basis – only in big celebrations like the *velas,* which are the community's patron saint festivities (Del Mar, 2021).

Behind the muxe protest in 2018 there is a transcendental assumption: not just anybody is muxe for simply saying so. Given the possibility of lies, fraud or deception, certain criteria are needed; for example, to have lived for a certain time *as a woman* and to be recognized as muxe in their community. And, as Yadira del Mar confirms, for them living as a woman means wearing beautiful embroidered frocks and flower headdresses, and fulfilling traditionally feminine roles.

The criteria for recognizing someone as muxe has little to do with passing but more to do with a history of living in a community. It is difficult to imagine that someone in their 50s or 60s would one day discover themselves to be muxe, as happened to Bruce Jenner and so many other mature men who in Blanchard's typology would fall into the category of autogynephiliacs when they *discovered themselves to be trans.* For the muxes, self-ID is a useless concept, because they have the recognition that matters, which is that of their own people and their village. Of course, it was going to attract attention that suddenly some men would call themselves trans in a place where today being trans means being muxe.

Alongside the fraudulent candidates were two valid ones: Kristel and Grecia. The activists behind the protest stated that Kristel and Grecia,

> besides affirming themselves as muxes and naming themselves as such in their daily lives, are publicly and widely known by their women's names in their community and, additionally, their sayings and daily actions reaffirm and consolidate this muxe identity as part of *the free development of their personality* (SDP Noticias, 2018; italics mine).

It is interesting to note the presence in their discourse of a term that was being used in Mexico City at the time to defend the existence of *trans children* – but here, speaking about already fully developed adult men, seems somewhat decontextualized.[84]

In the end, the Oaxacan electoral authorities suspended the candidacy of the 17 fake transgender candidates, and two years later the electoral law was amended to include the crime of gender identity usurpation, which is defined as

> the act by which a citizen or person mendaciously self-ascribes to a gender different from their own, in order to benefit from affirmative actions to comply with the requirement of gender parity and alternation (Ulises, 2020).

This "law against faux trans and muxes" is a stitch. The Oaxacan laws contemplated gender self-ID, but the problems that arose with it forced the introduction of exceptions in case *cisgender men* wanted to benefit from electoral quotas. It is a way of recognizing that legal self-ID is problematic and that ultimately some criteria are needed because there can be real trans and fake trans … Not because there can be real women and fake women. It is understood that this reform will serve to protect the political and electoral rights, not of persons of the female sex, but "of muxes and trans persons in the face of the trickery of individuals who usurp this type of identity in order to obtain candidacies for public office" (Ulises, 2020).

A similar fraud occurred in Tlaxcala in May 2021. The Fuerza por México party needed 18 women to cover their quota and resorted to the route of legal self-ID. Overnight, 18 men became women with the power of their word (see Morán, 2021). Don't forget: no one can deny a person their self-perceived gender identity … Moreover, it would be useless, as it is an attribute whose existence is impossible to prove – or disprove. According to the current transgenderist

---

84   The state of Oaxaca, by the way, has recognized *trans children* since 12 September 2021: from the age of 12, they can request a change of sex on their birth certificate. The other places in Mexico where this can be done are Mexico City, Jalisco and Morelos. Next in the transactivists' sights is Puebla. See Ulises (2022).

model, any request for evidence, any requirement at all, is invasive and pathologizing, so that the very laws that allow self-ID with the simplest of procedures have served up the option of committing fraud and telling lies on a silver platter.

Arussi Unda, spokeswoman for the influential Veracruz feminist collective Las Brujas del Mar, said at the time:

> It cannot be said that this was not going to happen. Feminists had already warned of this and the response was to silence us, to violently attack us and to attribute phobias to us when all we pointed out were the legal loopholes and ambiguity in the identity laws that could allow what is happening, that the necessary spaces of representation for women are being usurped, after a long struggle to achieve them. It was too much to presume that we had already achieved equity in decision-making positions (quoted in Morán, 2021).

The authorities in charge of enforcing gender parity are concerned when *trans* people report that men have usurped their identity, but all men who identify as trans are usurping women's identities and occupying places reserved for women. However, the usurpation of women's identity cannot be reported. As "trans women are women" is an unquestionable dogma and to call oneself a woman is to be a woman, gender self-ID is a dead end for women's rights. But for men who identify as women a solution is always found. This double standard is confirmed by the president of the National Institute for Women, Nadine Gasman, with her misleading statements about what happened in Tlaxcala:

> The cases of usurpation of identity to occupy spaces that belong to trans women and indigenous women are a clear violation of the rights of women, indigenous peoples and the LGBTI community. Women in their broadest diversity must be present in the construction of democracy (quoted in Morán, 2021).

In her view, these 18 men were not usurping women's spaces, which is what was happening, but those of *trans women* ... and *women in their broadest diversity* – which is a common way of saying, in a somewhat disguised manner, that trans women are women.

The word *gender* has been instrumental in allowing some men, a little less blatantly than the faux muxes, to occupy women's seats without anyone bothering. Since, by virtue of the euphemistic use of the word, the Constitution speaks of *gender parity* and not *sex parity,* a male who claims to have a feminine gender counts as a female. This has also brought about a censorious effect in the legislature. Despite the fact that the Constitution itself guarantees freedom of belief and expression, congressmen who call themselves congresswomen must be played along with, and those who do not humour them will have to deal with the Electoral Tribunal. What happened to Partido Acción Nacional's (PAN) Deputy Gabriel Quadri for *misgendering* Salma Luévano, a transgender male deputy from the Morena party, is a warning to radical feminists and gender-critical women.

A bit of context. Quadri, who has an engineering degree and, we can deduce, a scientifically-inclined mind, does not believe that men can be women and is concerned about the actions of what he calls "the powerful trans lobby," which, in his view, ends up affecting children, young people and women. His stance has led to repeated accusations of transphobia and hate speech. Salma Luévano has tried to ridicule him and has even gone so far as to take the podium at the Palacio de San Lázaro disguised as him. After a group of *trans women* demonstrated in the Chamber of Deputies on 1 February 2022 to demand his removal from office, Quadri wrote some tweets. Let a reporter from *El País* explain them to us:

> Twitter has been the main megaphone for the congressman's transphobic attacks. In a now-deleted post from 1 February, he wrote: 'Trans-fascism gets its claws into the Chamber of Deputies'. A day later, he continued: 'A prominent feature of fascism is to silence, repress, lynch any different opinion [...]. That is what Trans-fascism is trying to do'. And, on 3 February, he insisted: 'The Trans-fascism of Morena and Trans ideology takes over the Congress. It represses freedom of speech, it is intolerant, it tries to subjugate those who have a different opinion, it does not dialogue, it does not argue (it has neither the capacity nor the inclination to do so), it insults. They go against women ...' (T. de Miguel, 2022).

Teresa de Miguel and much of the press have renounced all pretense of impartiality. Quadri's statements are "transphobic attacks," he writes "transphobic tweets" and he will have to "pay for his transphobia," but anyone who has seen with their own eyes and without a journalistic or ideological filter the actions of the people he refers to, knows that Quadri is not lying when he accuses this political lobby of being intolerant of those who think differently from them. Everything that happened next confirms his words.

On 31 March 2022, almost two months after the tweets of discord, during the debate on the General Health Law in the Chamber, Quadri presented a motion

> to prevent children and adolescents from being subjected to hormonal procedures, puberty suppression or genital mutilation procedures without the consent of their parents and without a court order (Rangel and López, 2022b).

Quadri added: "These types of interventions should be taken exclusively by adults fully aware of the consequences on health, as well as on family, reproductive and sexual life" (Guillén, 2022).

This caution and interest in protecting children seemed unacceptable to the trans deputies – the aforementioned María Clemente García Moreno and Salma Luévano, who called Quadri a "murderous scoundrel" and continued:

> As a proud trans woman, I want to tell the gentleman that he is very wrong and that he should also remember that he has children and family, and that hopefully, hopefully, that will shut his mouth.

In response, Quadri said:

> I want to draw attention to the fact that Mr Luévano is threatening me in the plenary and that he does not provide any argument to the issue we are dealing with: he only insults and disqualifies.

The PAN member was not lying, but "indignation took over the Chamber," in the words of reporter Beatriz Guillén. Partido Revolucionario Institucional (PRI) deputy Cynthia López Castro said that Quadri was "violating article 10 of the Constitution, on non-discrimination," that calling him *Mister* was disrespectful because Luévano "decided to be a woman," and demanded a public apology "because he is disrespecting all women, all deputies and all Mexicans, who have fought for many years in this country against discrimination" (Divany, 2022). For this politician, as for any trans ally worthy of the name, imitating a woman is a human right, but saying *Mister* to a man is disrespectful *to all women.*

This diversionary tactic of the transgender deputies proved to be very effective. Everyone present immediately forgot, or didn't care, that the health and bodily integrity of children was at stake. The fact that Luévano had called Quadri a murderer – because "he is killing her and her community with his hate speech" (Rangel and López, 2022a) – also faded into the background. Nor was the fact that the Morena deputy made a veiled threat to the PAN member a major problem. Everything was overshadowed by the unforgivable misgendering, and the newspapers did not talk about the dangers of suppressing puberty, but about Quadri calling Luévano *Mister.*

Later, in a tweet, Luévano issued a warning:

> Calling me *Mister* and ignoring my gender identity as a woman is clearly gender violence and also hate speech and for that, they are killing us and I will not rest until I see him in the list of sanctioned politicians and [make sure] that he never appears on the ballot again (@SalmaLuevano, 2022).

He did not have to wait long to get his wish. On 26 April, the Electoral Tribunal ruled that Quadri

> committed political violence against women on the basis of gender in the modalities of psychological, sexual and digital violence, by making destructive comparisons and causing rejection by referring to trans women as different from cisgender women and using discriminatory language (T. de Miguel, 2022).[85]

---

85   One year later, congresswoman Teresa Castell was similarly condemned as having committed gender-based political violence for "not respecting" Salma Luévano's identity (see Tribunal Electoral, 2023).

The magistrates of this body, charged with protecting the political and electoral rights of citizens, deny that *transgender women* are different from *cisgender* women. In other words, they uphold the main dogma of transgender faith in its reinforced version: trans women are literally women in every possible sense. They also religiously adhere to the commandments of the good trans ally, such as "A trans ally must actively support trans women and help them meet their needs" and "A trans ally must condemn anyone who talks about trans women without themselves being trans." For his *transphobic* tweets and for calling Luévano *Mister,*

> the court ordered the National Electoral Institute to register the PAN deputy on the list of political aggressors against women on the basis of gender for four years, so he will not be able to be part of the electoral ballot during that time. The magistrates unanimously decided that Quadri will also have to take courses on political violence against women, offer a public apology and publish a summary of the sentence on his Twitter account (T. de Miguel, 2022).

As plain as day. This is a message especially for radical and gender-critical feminists. It is an exemplary measure that makes it impossible to discuss on the legislative floor any bill around gender identity and any measure that violates women's sex-based rights. The transactivist lobby is effectively banning the presence of feminist and dissident voices on issues in which women are the main stakeholders. Everything that radical feminists have warned might happen with gender self-ID has happened and proved them right, but anything they have to say about it is still considered hate speech and moral panic. Mind you, when someone approved by transactivism says the same thing, then it is a valid concern; the case of the muxes is evidence of this double standard.

Time and again, the fears of feminists around the world that self-ID undermines special policies to increase women's political representation have been shown to be true. Being legally recognized as someone of the desired sex without any criteria or requirements is incompatible with parity and gender quotas aiming to warrant it. However, gender identity activists want quotas because it is in their interest to have men who identify as women occupying women's places in spheres of power. Thus, they can live with this contradiction. In the current transgenderist model, there is conceptually no such thing as a fake trans person, since being trans is saying that one is trans, and the possibility of someone lying is, on principle, excluded, but, as it turns out, they are willing to make the exception when the deceit affects their own interests.

Maybe in a city like Juchitán, Oaxaca, land of the muxes, where people know each other, it is possible to detect those who only want to declare themselves women for electoral purposes. But how do you do it in a city of nine million inhabitants? Be that as it may, in most cases fraud is not recognized. Strictly speaking, every time a man assigns a female identity to himself, he is taking the place of a woman, whether in the Chamber of Deputies, in a women's shelter, in a toilet or in a sporting competition. But to say this is sacrilege. Such fraud is not recognized as such.

What happened in Oaxaca and Tlaxcala leaves us with another lesson worth taking into account: there are times when it is not the individual who determines whether he or she is trans or not, but someone else, namely transactivists. If transactivists say, "Those people are not trans," then they are not trans. Feminists will never be asked to give a verdict on whether a man who calls himself trans – and therefore a woman, because trans women are women – actually is a woman. The verdict has to be given by other men who also call themselves trans. A trans ally has an obligation to listen to, and believe, what trans women say about themselves, except when trans women are not actually trans, in which case the trans ally must listen to and believe a trans woman who is indeed trans. How can the trans ally be sure who is indeed a trans woman? She has to ask a trans woman who really is a real trans woman … And how does she know if that trans woman is really a trans woman? By asking some other trans woman … and so on ad infinitum.

As I said, gender identity activism does not mind contradicting itself and sustaining the incompatible positions of sex self-identification *and* having more or less arbitrary requirements for a legal sex change so that others do not usurp *from them* a political position reserved for women. But there is a contradiction that is much harder for them to digest.

A man calls himself a woman – and, by the power of his word, he is a woman. Someone calls that person *Sir* or *Mister* – and the power of that word snatches away their deeply felt internal and individual experience of being a woman. That is why misgendering is so serious a crime, that is why refusing to use their preferred pronouns merits exemplary punishment. What they got with their word, someone else's word can take away from them.

Lesbians and LGB

The T was not always there. It is worth noting two reasons why it was added to LGB. One is economic: after the recognition of same-sex marriage, organizations that had received funding to advance that cause needed to find another target to survive. Why not the recognition of gender identity? For most people, transgenders and homosexuals were more or less the same thing anyway.

The second reason is strategic, and is clear and openly expressed in one of the recommendations made in the "Dentons document," a report which sets out the strategy for advancing *transgender rights* across Europe :

> *Tie your campaign to more popular reform.* In Ireland, Denmark and Norway, changes to the law on legal gender recognition laws were put through at the same time as other more popular reforms such as marriage equality legislation. This provided a veil of protection, particularly in Ireland, where marriage equality was strongly supported, but gender identity remained a more difficult issue to win public support for (IGLYO and Dentons, 2019, p. 20).

But this has meant that the L, the G and the B have been pushed into the background. As Susan Hawthorne puts it:

> The LGBTIQ label is useful only to show a combined strength of numbers. It results in prioritising of some groups over others. Although

L is at the beginning, it represents the group that others in the alphabet would rather ignore. In 2019, Angela Wild and other lesbians protested at Pride in London with banners which put lesbians at the centre including 'Lesbian not queer', 'Lesbian = female homosexual' and 'Transgenderism erases lesbians'. The protesting lesbians were saying that 'lesbians have a right to sexual boundaries and self-definition'. But instead of respecting the needs and rights of lesbians, Pride in London referred to them as 'disgusting' 'bigoted' and 'transphobic'. These are much stronger terms than those on the banners (2020, pp. 191–192).

Current LGBTIQ+ activists like to explain in detail the differences between sexual orientation and gender identity, and yet they insist that lesbian, gay and bisexual be always accompanied by transsexual, intersex, queer and all the identities that want to join them later.[86] The groups that have wanted to separate themselves from the transgender agenda that has piggybacked on the LGB are demonized, a strange attitude if, as those same activists say, it is one thing who you sleep with and another how you identify. This is how the US organization Human Rights Campaign defines these two concepts on the Glossary of Terms on its website:

---

86 As seen in Chapter 4, intersex people do not like being used as puppets to push through measures that have little to do with their needs. *Queer* is, like *non-binary*, part of the trans umbrella, or vice versa: sometimes the umbrella is *queer*, which in any case is another invented identity into which homosexuals, bisexuals and heterosexuals alike fall. According to the List of LGBTQ+ terms on the Stonewall website, a powerful British LGBTQ+ lobby group,

> *queer* is a term used by those wanting to reject specific labels of romantic orientation, sexual orientation and/or gender identity. It can also be a way of rejecting the perceived norms of the LGBT community (racism, sizeism, ableism etc.). Although some LGBT people view the word as a slur, it was reclaimed in the late 80s by the queer community who have embraced it (n.d.).

In practice, everyone who consider themselves outside the norm identify as *queer* or *non-binary* and that's it, they automatically belong to a marginalized community. Contrary to what one might think, being under 23 years old is not a precondition: there have been cases of people in their 40s or even 50s labelling themselves as people who reject labels.

Sexual orientation
An inherent or immutable enduring emotional, romantic or sexual attraction to other people. Note: an individual's sexual orientation is independent of their gender identity.

Gender identity
One's innermost concept of self as male, female, a blend of both or neither – how individuals perceive themselves and what they call themselves. One's gender identity can be the same or different from their sex assigned at birth.

So why do they find it unforgivable that some groups want to look after their own interests related to sexual orientation without being saddled with those of other groups related to gender identity? The LGB Alliance, for example, is systematically characterized as transphobic for not including the T in its name and priorities, despite the fact that on its website it explains the following:

> We fully support trans people in their struggle for dignity, respect, and a life lived free from bigotry and fear. We believe that the issues and priorities for people who are attracted to the same sex (homosexual/ bisexual) are different from those of transgender people, and so, with a number of organizations focusing on trans people and trans issues, our focus is simply on lesbians, gay men, and bisexual people instead (n.d.).

LGBTIQ+ groups devote almost all of their resources to the T and their activists are fully committed to pushing the transgender agenda. It is natural for gays, lesbians and bisexuals to want to join groups that take their specific needs into account.

In spite of having attached themselves to a movement centred on lesbians, gays and bisexuals, gender identity activists find most annoying the word *orientation* in combination with *sexual*. It has proven difficult to convince people that they should base their romantic and erotic choices on the gender identity of their prospective lovers, not their sex. They tried to sneak in the term *gender orientation* but it didn't stick. What did stick was to conflate sexual orientation and gender identity as if they were distinct, yes, but inseparable, for example, in *attempts to change sexual orientation or gender identity*. The name brings to mind old efforts to *cure* male homosexuality with electric shock therapy and lesbianism with *corrective rape*, "an abusive term that refers to the rape and battery of lesbians to cure them of lesbian existence," as defined by Susan Hawthorne (2020, p. 186) – unacceptable practices that, although not entirely eradicated, are not as common as they used to be, especially in the western world.[87]

However, this conflation of sexual orientation and gender identity serves to ban something entirely different, and not hideous at all – talk therapies, like the one many detransitioners would have liked to have had in order to accept themselves as they are and not alter their bodies through hormones and surgery. With a linguistic sleight of hand, transactivists and trans allies promote laws that supposedly aim to end conversion therapies – with the sole purpose of opening the door to conversion therapies and taking us back to the 1950s and the early days of the medical-sexological model.

It is worth remembering that the interests of lesbians are often not the same as those of gay men, as lesbian feminists are well aware. The insistence of many gay men on legalizing so-called surrogacy, which to a feminist mind is nothing but reproductive exploitation of women and a modern form of slavery, is a clear example of such discrepancies.[88] There are therefore also groups that seek to focus exclusively on lesbians. Political artist and researcher Angela C. Wild, founder of Get the L Out UK, conducted a survey of lesbians to find out whether they felt social pressure to accept trans ideology in the LGBT community, and her results prove right those who want to separate the L from the T. Among lesbians who were in groups that were not women-only, whether online or offline, several

> reported 'feeling silenced', 'intimidated', 'unable to speak freely', 'uncomfortable' with the group policy and wishing the group was for

---

87 *Corrective rape* is not unusual in South Africa, a country which nonetheless has constitutional protection for gays and lesbians (see Hawthorne, 2020, Chapter 6).

88 A pioneer in this analysis is the radical lesbian feminist Janice Raymond with her 1994 book *Women as Wombs* (Spinifex Press).

women only but 'dare not say it'. Several reported how 'transwomen derail' and monopolise the discussion to be solely about their issues while shutting down discussion about women's or lesbians' issues by calling it 'transphobic'. Group dynamics are described as 'toxic'. Several women explain how 'transwomen are behaving just like men'. Lesbians constantly report being told their sexuality is 'wrong' if they openly state they are solely attracted to women.

Women reported 'threats', 'intimidations' and 'abuse' by 'trans women' and allies. Several respondents explained they understand and respect the need for 'transwomen' to meet exclusively amongst themselves, but cannot understand the lack of reciprocity accorded to women and lesbians by the trans community (Wild, 2019, p. 16).

Respondents answered the following questions thus: "Do you believe transwomen are women?": NO, 87.5 per cent; "Do you believe transwomen can be lesbians?": NO, 95 per cent; "Would you yourself consider a transwoman as a potential sexual partner?": NO, 98.8 per cent (Wild, 2019, p. 15).

There are also, of course, lesbian feminist groups that have always been independent of the G as much as the T, as they were in the 1970s, when it began to be understood that "the practice of separating from men to create political and social space was fundamental to feminism" (Jeffreys, 2014b, p. 181). These lesbian groups are constantly harassed by men who claim to have a female gender identity who, eager to be allowed in, pressure lesbians to include them in their political struggle and in their beds. This male assault of lesbianism, the ultimate women-only space, was not entirely new back in 1979, when Janice Raymond devoted a chapter of *The Transsexual Empire* to those she called "the transsexually constructed lesbian-feminists." They already represented a typically masculine threat to lesbians and feminism:

> While regarded by many as an obscure issue that affects a relatively minute proportion of the population, transsexualism poses very important feminist questions. Transsexually constructed lesbian-feminists show yet another face of patriarchy. As the male-to-constructed-female transsexual exhibits the attempt to possess women

in a bodily sense while acting out the images into which men have molded women, the male-to-constructed-female who claims to be a lesbian-feminist attempts to possess women at a deeper level, this time under the guise of challenging rather than conforming to the role and behavior of stereotyped femininity. As patriarchy is neither monolithic nor one-dimensional, neither is transsexualism (Raymond, 1979, pp. 99–100).

Some young lesbians have ended up ceding to this attack, giving up their spaces and thus contributing to the end of a political movement that was created by women who came before them for their sake and the following generations. A sad example is the Marcha Lencha, an organization in Mexico City that proudly defines itself as follows: "A space of trans-inclusive *lenchitudes*. We celebrate sex-affective relationships of all kinds between cis, trans, les, bi, pan, non-binary and queer girls, & so on" (@MarchaLencha, Twitter bio). *Lencha* is a derogatory term for *lesbian*. A few years ago, some lesbians rescued it; immediately some men appropriated it for themselves and made it inclusive. That is how the plural *lenchitudes* was born. Including *trans* and *non-binary girls* in a supposedly lesbian march means that men who claim to be women are welcome – and that sometimes they are the ones who take the lead.

Even though the determination to conquer the last territory denied to males has a decades-long history, there's a relatively new term, *cotton ceiling*, put forth by male transgender porn actor Drew Deveaux, that carries their resolve still further. It alludes to the lesbian's knickers, understood as the barrier between these men's penises and the vaginas of women who do not want them. As Susan Hawthorne explains:

By 2012, the term 'cotton ceiling' had entered the language. You would think in an era of #MeToo that concerns about rape would be taken seriously. The term 'cotton ceiling' puts a lie to that. It was invented 'to describe the difficulties faced by men who identify as *trans lesbians* in being accepted as a *real lesbian*, finding lesbians reluctant to choose them as sexual partners'. And, as Angela Wild points out, the norm today is that most transgenders who grew up male 'remain genitally intact males'. The men who still have a 'lady dick' [...] consider it transphobic to refuse their sexual advances. Rape is rape. How is it that when a trans activist says that he is offended, this counts for more than the rape of women? (Hawthorne, 2020, p. 222).

Sheila Jeffreys considers this "an extraordinary example of what political scientist Carole Pateman calls the male right of access" (2014b, p. 180). Since these intruders are not gay, but straight men, thus attracted to women, almost all of them fall into the category of autogynephiliacs, if Blanchard and Bailey's observations are anything to go by.

Today, lesbians cannot devote themselves to rebuilding their movement, their spaces and their own culture[89] (which was already beginning to suffer male incursions in 1973, when Robin Morgan gave that lecture in Los Angeles), distracted by having to constantly spell out that there are no lesbians with penises and to resist the relentless male invasion. The harassment of lesbians in UNAM's Faculty of Philosophy and Literature since the labrys sign was painted on a wall in September 2022 is an example of the challenges faced by those women who in this day and age want to create spaces without men.

Besides music festivals, ball rooms, galleries, nightclubs, bookstores, coffee shops, something else has been snatched from us. Writing 20 years ago, Sheila Jeffreys lamented:

In the late 1980s and 1990s an epidemic of female-to-male (FTM) transsexualism began in Western countries. Women who had

---

89 The Michigan Womyn's Music Festival is perhaps the most iconic of the lesbian cultural losses of the last decades. Sheila Jeffreys writes about this and other lesbian-only places which have disappeared due to transgender entryism in Australia, UK, US and Canada (2014b, pp. 165–169). For lost lesbian spots in Mexico City, see Lecuona (2022). LGB Alliance Australia designed an interactive map which shows the lesbian-only places lost in the past 40 odd years, mainly in Melbourne and Victoria; three examples among dozens: Pemberton Books, a lesbian-owned bookshop that existed in the early 1990s; Pigtail Pottery, a gallery of lesbian and feminist ceramic artists active in the 1990s; and the Women's Ball, which held regular lesbian comedy nights and social dances in the 1980s and 1990s (<https://www.lgballiance.org.au/lost-lesbian-space>).

previously identified as butch lesbians, or been afraid to identify as lesbians despite loving women, began to opt for surgical mutilation. I call this the destruction of lesbians, because lesbians are physically destroyed in this surgery, and their lesbianism is removed along with female body parts. [...] This issue has become, I suggest, an emergency for lesbian politics. In the 1970s, when radical lesbian and gay movements began, there was a strong awareness of the barbaric methods by which the medical profession in the twentieth century had sought to eradicate lesbianism, such as incarceration in mental hospitals, electric shock treatment and lobotomies. At that time it was thought that a brand new day had dawned, in which these cruel forms of control would be ended, so that lesbians could live happily in their lesbian bodies. Transsexual surgery on lesbians, as a burgeoning practice, clearly shows that this optimism was unrealistic. In the twenty-first century the methods being used to get rid of lesbians are very much more cruel than we could have imagined thirty years ago (Jeffreys, 2003, p. 122)

And in 2023, the epidemic is full blown. As I detailed in Chapter 4, between 2009 and 2019 there was a 5,337 per cent increase in girls seeking help in the Tavistock Clinic in England who thought, or wished, they were boys. There have certainly been many possible lesbians amongst them. It is no coincidence that the very first child experimented upon with puberty blockers was a 13-year-old girl who was sexually attracted to other girls (see Chapter 2, section 'The transgenderist model').

Throughout this book, I have shown that lesbians and gay men are groups that are particularly affected by gender identity evangelism. As has been seen, many of the children who are now considered trans kids are, in fact, potential future lesbians and gays. The testimonies of Tavistock Clinic staff, the experiences of detransitioners, accounts by young girls being heterosexualized by transgender charities, and the life stories of lesbians and gays who are now adults bear this out. It is no coincidence that among the leading voices speaking out against gender identity proselytizing are so many lesbian feminists. There are also some gay men, of course. They are not as harassed as lesbians, and harassment of them is less virulent, but they too are targeted for their *genital fetishism*, and one would expect to see more of their involvement since so many children and adolescents like the ones they were end up being seduced by the transgenderist sirens.

It is frustrating to see that it is precisely lesbian voices that are among those to be expelled from mainstream media and roundtables because "we must not give a platform to transphobe bigots." Heterosexual men and women, posing as virtuous LGBTIQ+ allies, set themselves up as censors of lesbians who have a much better grasp of the issue than they do. Lesbian activists were discriminated against long before many of these allies were born in times when being a lesbian meant being marginalized even in progressive circles. Well, what we are seeing now is that, deep down, this is still the case and that those circles are much less progressive than they appear to be. Susan Hawthorne points out:

> Lesbians have been on the front line of this conflict for more than two decades. Two decades in which we noticed how the media picked up the trans side and ignored concerns of lesbians and of its impact on women more broadly (2020, p. 221).

There is a very simple explanation for the phenomenon of LGBTIQ+ allies refusing to listen to lesbians. It comes from Yan María Yaoyólotl Castro, co-founder of some of the groups that initiated Mexican lesbian feminism. She, by the way, was among the very first in that country to see what the onslaught of transgenderism meant for the feminist movement; in 2008 she resigned from the organizing committee of the 11th Encuentro Feminista Latinoamericano y del Caribe precisely because it was not going to be a feminist meeting, "but a genderist/queer one" – which entailed a profound contradiction. She recalls in a letter written 14 years ago:

> Us Mexican lesbians have been fighting for more than 35 years for the feminist movement to assume the defence of lesbianism as a political principle, but we have not succeeded. For many heterosexual feminists it is easier to accept a transvestite, transgender or transsexual man,

because he is a man, than a lesbian woman, because she is a woman. This is an act of misogyny deep down (Yaoyólotl Castro, 2008).

This is confirmed by the actions of all those dutiful female trans allies who, in their failed attempts to understand this debate, adopt the points of view of males who claim to have a feminine gender identity. Because they decided it was hate speech, they exclude the points of view of radical feminists and lesbians. They do not even listen to those whom, in the height of irony, and thanks to the misleading acronym, they pretend to be defending when they advocate for LGBTIQ+ rights and the criminalization of so-called conversion therapy. Trapped in their progressive bubbles, convinced of their moral superiority and unable to understand that opinions other than their own exist, they see transphobia in their neighbour's eye but do not notice lesbophobia in their own eye.

CHAPTER 6

OTHER COLLATERAL DAMAGES

C ontrary to what the intensive propaganda would have us believe, transgenderism does not work to defend the human rights of an oppressed minority group. It is anything but a struggle to end discrimination against people who do not fit sex stereotypes; it does not even seek to normalize what some of its proponents call gender dissidence. They say that being trans is not a pathology, but they turn non-conformity with sexist roles into an abnormal condition that supposedly justifies bodily interventions that are often quite drastic. But not only do people who consider themselves trans lose out, as bad as that is, but gender identity proselytizing leaves a trail of destruction in its wake. In some cases we could say that this is collateral damage, but in others it seems that wreaking havoc is precisely the aim.

Children

Children are the victims of transgenderism that hurt the most. In Chapter 4 it was argued that the transgendering of children has been instrumental in pushing for the exchange of the category of sex for that of gender identity in laws and policies. But lo and behold, the vast majority of *transgender* children and young people are female, while the vast majority of those who acquire a *transgender identity* in adulthood are male. Consequently, and to put it bluntly, there are young girls and pre-teens going to plastic surgeons Giancarlo McEvenue, Sidhbh Gallagher and their ilk to have their "teets yeeted" because it suits some men.

How much cognitive dissonance does it take to think that one contributes to the free development of a prepubescent girl's personality by convincing her that her body needs to be corrected or that there is a mismatch between her sex and her interests in life? As we have seen, the idea that sex is determined not by the body but by tastes in clothing, hair accessories, inclinations and sporting activities is a principle of transgenderism that is spreading like wildfire through schools, TikTok and the television shows that children and teens watch. Judging by the stories of *trans kids,* that the tabloid press is so fond of, and by the speeches of groups that present themselves as experts on the subject, these outward features, however trivial they may seem, are the only criteria for determining that someone is trans. No child would want to change their sex if they knew they did not need to in order to play whatever they want, dress however they like, and aspire to whatever they want to do and be.

More and more people are convinced that so-called gender dysphoria is caused by social influence, particularly among teenage girls, as Lisa Littman has argued. In an important sense, this rejection of the body is enabled by the increasing sexualization of women, which finds its ultimate and most violent expression in pornography ... now always just a click away from every boy and man of their acquaintance. It is impossible to overestimate the damage this does to the adolescent psyche and to men's treatment of women. Gail Dines, Professor Emerita of Sociology and Women's Studies at Wheelock College, has analyzed in depth the effects of the pornographic industry on sexuality and everyday life. In her book *Pornland,* she writes that, unlike women in the post-war 1940s and 1950s, when a return to traditional family values was being promoted by all means,

> today's women are not being forced back to the home, but that does not mean that they are not similarly affected by cultural constructions of idealized femininity. [...] We are still cultural beings who develop our identities out of the dominant images that surround us. [...] The Stepford Wife image, which drove previous generations of women crazy with its insistence on sparkling floors and perfectly orchestrated meals, has all but disappeared, and in its place we now have the Stepford Slut: a hypersexualized, young, thin, toned, hairless, and, in many cases, surgically enhanced woman with a come-hither look on her face. Harriet Nelson and June Cleaver have morphed into Britney, Rihanna, Beyoncé, Paris, Lindsay, and so on. They represent images of contemporary idealized femininity – in a word, hot – that are held up for women, especially young women, to emulate. Women today are still held captive by images that ultimately tell lies about women. The biggest lie is that conforming to this hypersexualized image will give women real power in the world, since in a porn culture, our power rests, we are told, not in our ability to shape the institutions that determine our life chances but in having a hot body that men desire and women envy (Dines, 2010, pp. 101–102).

This radical feminist interpretation is confirmed by a young detransitioner, Helena, who, when asked what she found most appealing about transitioning, recalls:

> I had a really big problem with the concept that at a certain age as a girl you're just supposed to give up your entire personality and all of your quirks, and all of the things that make you interesting for the ability to be pretty, and to do make-up well, to be thin. All of these different things were so suffocating, and being trans felt like a way to escape that (Pique Resilience Project, 2019).

Young women who reject hypersexualization and resist this fate – no less repellent than that faced by their grandmothers and great-grandmothers – are offered the false promise of a sex change. If you are being told that you can save yourself from objectification and the male gaze by simply taking testosterone and having your breasts removed as if they were wisdom teeth, who is going to say no? Non-conformity to sexist stereotypes is not a disease, but the pornification of culture and transgender propaganda are working in unison to create a mental health crisis among adolescents. Heather Brunskell-Evans summarizes this worrying state of affairs:

> Despite the current societal aspiration for gender equality, the culture is still highly sexualised. It signifies to girls that to be female is to be an object of male desire and male entitlement, and girls today are under ever more pressure to capitulate to the 'pinkification' and 'pornification' of culture. Lesbian girls who eschew feminine signifiers can often be lonely and isolated in their apparent idiosyncrasy, acutely aware that their same-sex attraction would be unacceptable to their family and friends. Dawning same-sex attraction occurs against a backdrop of homophobia, as well as a dearth of everyday, run-of-the-mill lesbian visibility. Autistic girls can find the idea of being 'transgender' helpful to make sense of their experiences of always feeling weird, not fitting in, struggling to understand social interactions and cues, being bullied, and feeling themselves to be outside the norm and 'girl' culture. The same is true for girls with eating disorders.
>
> For some girls, the fear of leaving childhood behind, and the terror of becoming women, is overwhelming. [...] Their sexual feelings awaken amidst a culture of sexual predation where not only is there embarrassment, for example, in growing breasts, but fear that they will be pejoratively commented on and, worse, groped. For other girls, their bodies become the site onto which they can project their perceived failure to live up to society's expectations of femininity.
>
> Teenage girls have long recruited their bodies as ways of expressing misery and self-hatred. Alighting on a trans identity can be 'the ultimate act of self-harm hardly noticeable to many because it is so aligned with ... the ever-present attack on gender non-conforming women that exists throughout society' (Anonymous Clinicians, 2020) (Brunskell-Evans, 2020, pp. 43–44).

The dangers of gender identity and the powerful machinery that has set its sights on taking it to the farthest corners of the earth are not limited to children who for whatever reason end up believing they are the other sex or neither. All the other children who, through watching television, at home, from social media or conversations with friends, are internalizing this extreme reinforcement of stereotypical masculinity and femininity, are also victims. Not only that – in addition to inculcating these anti-scientific and sexist notions, by telling them that it is violent to question or seek out the logic of these beliefs, their capacity for critical thinking is impaired.

Detransitioners

The existence of the medical diagnosis of gender dysphoria and the social category of transgender is largely responsible for the problem and the desire (conceptualized as a need) to seek treatment. Before psychiatry and sexology gave shape to transsexualism as a problem to be corrected, there were no transsexuals or transgender people: there were men and women trying to fit as best they could into a strict society that curtailed their freedom to love someone of the same sex or to pursue interests considered unbecoming to women or men.

Living proof that the radical feminist model offers the best explanation of the trans phenomenon are the so-called desisters and detransitioners: people, mostly young and mostly women, who give up a transgender identity and who, having made the medical *transition*, reverse gear (as far as that is possible, since transition leaves damages that are irreparable). They realize that when they embarked on this path of medicalization, they lacked information, analysis and a feminist perspective. Their voices have become fundamental in this debate. Unfortunately, much of the fury of gender identity activism, which does not tolerate the slightest dissent, falls on them. Anyone who desists or detransitions shows a blatant disavowal of their position, and is therefore a traitor to the cause. As Janice Raymond observes in her book *Doublethink*:

> Detransitioners report they have been harassed by trans activists who claim that detransitioning is a danger to trans rights. One detransitioner stated that for her, 'detransitioning has resulted in

the most harassment she has ever faced in her life' (Raymond, 2021, p. 108).

A particularly sad example of this commitment to stamping out heresy is the treatment of Ariel and Han of Detransición Chile. In 2020, these two young Chilean lesbians formed a group to help people who decided, as they had done, to detransition. In interviews and webinars they talked about their experience, about "what they don't tell us about the problems and consequences of transitioning." But before long, just as they had arrived, they left, overwhelmed by the relentless and merciless harassment by the gender identity militia. In their months of activity they made invaluable contributions to this debate and many of us still miss them. Their simple and important message can be summed up in these words from Han: listening to radical feminists, she says, "I realized that being a woman was not a bad thing" (Las Hipopótamas, 2020).

Transactivists' mistreatment of those who once fell for trans-activism's lies and then chose to walk away is yet another example of the double standard that is so characteristic of them. And if someone detransitions, they accuse, it is because they were not really trans in the first place. Let's see if we are understanding correctly: do they mean to say that at the end of the day, declaring oneself to be a man or a woman because that is how one perceives oneself in the depths of one's being is not the infallible and definitive criterion that they themselves told us? Is it possible to believe that one is trans *and still be wrong*?

Helena, from Pique Resilience Project, another short-lived detransitioning group, resents this estrangement from a community of people with whom she was until recently in the same boat. She observes:

> If you detransitioned, you probably know just how frustrating it is to be in a conversation with somebody, sharing your experiences and your concerns, just to be told that, after everything you've been through, you were never really trans. But what does it mean to be 'really trans'? Is there a standard definition of what a trans person is, or will that definition depend on who you're talking to? Some people will say

that a trans person is anyone who says they're a trans person. Other people will say a trans person is someone who has gender dysphoria and medically transitioned to alleviate that dysphoria. Now, obviously, if you transitioned, you definitely at least said you were trans at some point. So, by that definition, you were definitely trans. [...] People who have detransitioned believed we were trans; we lived the trans experience, and most of us had diagnosable gender dysphoria, but the standard treatment still didn't work for us. The fault in this case doesn't rest on the people who were suffering from gender dysphoria and were then led to believe that medical transition would cure them of that dysphoria; it lies with the fact that gender dysphoria is not a well-understood condition, and yet the most invasive treatment possible is prescribed as a one-size-fits-all solution (Pique Resilience Project, 2020).

Although Miquel Missé is not a detransitioner, the following words from her perfectly reflect the feelings of many of these people who consider themselves deceived by what was once their own community:

I ask myself why no one told me that I could have left my body the way it was, why nobody ever explained that sexuality in that body was possible. There was no violence involved, no threats were made. But I feel that I was robbed of the possibility to experience my body any other way (Missé, 2018, Chapter 1).

We could reply to Missé that she was warned – feminists, for a start, have been saying it for years and years in every possible way. The fact that she had not read or heard their voices is a sign of how effective it is for gender identity propaganda to silence, threaten, intimidate, misrepresent and demonize everyone who opposes their ideology. They succeed in their purpose of keeping people from accessing the radical feminist and the gender-critical viewpoints first-hand, even those who most need to know them.

The group of detransitioners is growing, perhaps almost as fast as the group of transgender children grew when it first became fashionable. It is logical that they are numerous, because the detransitioners are the very same *trans* children, only a few years later.

Listening to them confirms what is being said by so many women, both straight and lesbian, who remember being averse to dolls, bows, butterflies and anything that smacked of femininity when they were little girls – and know all too well that nowadays girls like they themselves were would be considered transgender boys. In almost every account of detransitioning, from both women and men, the role of social media and peer influence in their transgender identification emerges, as well as the need for someone to tell them that their bodies were not the problem. A rejection of sexist stereotypes is also a constant, but with no clarity about how these work – clarity that feminism would have provided. @TullipR noted that several detransitioners had had, like him, confusions about masculinity and what it means to be a man. He notes:

> Our stories are eerily similar with themes of overpowering shame and confusion for being male. Autism, ADHD, OCD, anxiety, delayed puberty, high academic intelligence but low social intelligence.
>
> We were *all* bullied.
>
> Many of us are same-sex attracted and even those who aren't, all experienced fear and confusion over our developing sexualities. […]
>
> It feels bitter every time I see the *same* injustice reoccurring. Almost *every single one of us* had a much older trans person grooming us and some of us are still in that situation.
>
> We are lost boys, who are faced with the insurmountable task of rebuilding ourselves as men, when we never knew how to be that in the first place (@TullipR, 2022).

These young men and women eventually matured and realized that this idea of having the wrong body made no sense and that their anxieties came from elsewhere, but now they face new problems. For a start, they have very specific psychological but above all medical needs – because, as we have already seen, puberty interruption and cross-sex hormones are not harmless measures. However, there is not much research on these young people. UK detransitioner Charlie Evans thinks she knows why:

> There's a lack of interest in detransitioner studies and outcomes and data, because it doesn't really suit the people who are pushing this

[gender identity] ideology to know about the bad outcomes [...]. Detransitioners are the rejects ... they're not the good examples from the production line of bodies that transition. In a sense, they're the damaged goods nobody wants to acknowledge (quoted in Raymond, 2021, pp. 107–108).

Another detransitioner interested in talking about what she went through in order to prevent more teenagers from experiencing the same thing is Sinead Watson, from Scotland. She says that in the years before she decided to medically *transition* she was depressed, had problems with alcohol, had had a psychiatric hospitalization, resented the fact that she was attracted to women and resisted her sexuality, was uncomfortable with having breasts, felt she would be safer as a man ... Anyone who had listened to her, she says, could have joined the dots, but no one asked her. None of the people at the gender identity clinic who had her medical records in hand said to her:

> Before we start you on a path with irreversible treatment, we want to talk to you about these things. So, [...] why do you not like that you're attracted to women, why is it that you feel uncomfortable with your breasts, why is it that you feel that you would be safer as a man? [...] Maybe you don't hate being a woman because you have this condition, maybe you hate being a woman because you have been abused for being a woman? (Bindel, 2022).

The age at which these young women typically detransition is close to 25,[90] which coincidentally is around the age at which the development and maturation of the prefrontal cortex is fully accomplished. If we point this fact out to any proponent of the transgendering of children, they will accuse us of adultcentrism. Remember that transgender children laws are based on the premise that the stages of psychological development are an arbitrary invention.

---

90   The first peer-reviewed study with a large sample of self-identified detransitioners found that the average age of detransition was 23 years (22 for women and 30 for men); see Society for Evidence-Based Gender Medicine (2021a).

Detransition is the other side of the coin of *trans children*. To demand effective safeguarding, you don't need to be from the far right, nor a middle-aged white *cis* woman, as so many social justice warriors scornfully call concerned feminists (and then we wonder why girls don't want to become women). Promoting and guaranteeing the rights of children is the duty of all societies, and all adults are obliged to respect them regardless of their political affiliations. To those within transgender children's associations, supreme courts of justice, chambers of deputies, equality ministries, gender studies departments, schools, women's parliaments, media or social networks, who set themselves up as saviours of *gender diverse children*, the very existence of detransitioners says loud and clear: "You failed miserably. If you wanted to protect me, you achieved the exact opposite."

Families

Many families also suffer collateral damage from the *trans children* deception and the blackmail of the transgender movement. Adolescents who consider themselves *trans* find on social media the influence and misinformation that end up making them adopt that identity, and there they learn that, if their parents do not support them in their self-perception, it is because they are transphobes and so they hate and reject them. In environments where sexual diversity is supposedly celebrated, among the most demonized of all are the mothers who, precisely because they support their lesbian daughters, are reluctant to endorse the transgender belief system that these girls have imbibed from the internet. They are expected to unconditionally approve of what their teenage daughters think and decide, and if they don't, they are conservative bigots, like the good middle-aged cisgender women they are.

What is a mother like Chiara's supposed to do? When Chiara was a teenager, she rejected her lesbianism and wanted to adopt a masculine identity and transition. She says:

I began to envision myself as a straight guy (rather than a gay girl), which alleviated a large amount of the discomfort I felt with my sexuality. I begged my mother to let me take testosterone and wanted to schedule 'top surgery' (a double mastectomy) right away (Canaan, 2022).

Today, what Chiara's mother is expected to do is not to help her daughter accept herself as a lesbian, but to share Chiara's own interpretation of her sexuality, with all its implications. Not supporting her daughter in her medical transition would be strong evidence of her transphobia.

Many women are at these kinds of crossroads – do they allow their daughters to go down the path of self-mutilation by proxy and watch helplessly as they make decisions they are likely to regret, or resist, try to care for their daughters, support them and be there for them, prevent them from making a serious mistake but risk their leaving home and losing them? Chiara's mother, despite taking this second path, fortunately did not lose her daughter, who eventually gave up on the idea of transitioning and never left her family. Chiara reflects:

Looking back, I finally understand how much of my desire to transition was a reaction to the homophobia I experienced and witnessed throughout my early life – a universal, unpleasant experience shared amongst almost all gay and lesbian people (Canaan, 2022).

But not all mothers and daughters reach this positive conclusion, and many women do not have the knowledge and strength to stand up for their daughters.

In these stories, the well-tried threat or hint of suicide turns out to be effective. It is not difficult to understand the anguish of a family in which a child claims they will commit suicide if their parents do not affirm their belief that they are trans, or that of a family reading on the Chrysallis website the tragic story of a *transgender boy* – who was actually a young lesbian – who took her own life due to bullying at school.[91] The Mexican family seeking advice from the materials published by the Asociación por las Infancias Transgénero will bump into this reckless statement from its co-chair, Salvador Robles:

> The average life expectancy of a trans woman in Latin America is half that of a cis person: 35 years. The main reasons: gender-based violence, dangerous jobs and suicide. This staggering figure is the epicentre of our work [...]. We must start by addressing the needs of children first, because the violence and discrimination they suffer does not start at the age of 18, but in the first years of life (Robles, 2021, pp. 16–17).

Of course, the source is not cited, nor is it detailed how the calculation was made to obtain the figure that constitutes nothing less than the epicentre of their work. In Chapter 2, we saw where this gimmicky number comes from, which on this occasion serves to make the parents, in anguish and weighed down by uncertainty, believe that, in order to avoid the death of their child, it will be important to act as soon as possible and follow the advice of experts,

---

91 The wretched suicide in December 2015 of a 17-year-old Spanish lesbian due to years of brutal bullying at school is presented by the newspaper *El Mundo* and the association Chrysallis as a transphobia-motivated suicide, despite the fact that the news story reads:

> There [...] Alan found the last links in the chain of mockery that stoned his [*sic*] puberty to death. 'It was the straw that broke the camel's back of a lifetime of bullying', says his mother. 'My son always had a very unladylike appearance, and at the age of 14, when he was in fourth grade, Alan openly and publicly confessed being a lesbian. Alan was holding hands with another girl and at home we thought it was great. But at school things were not the same. He was called 'dyke', 'fucking lesbian' and stuff like that. But he was strong and he put up with it'. Then the harassment intensified. They told Alan that she was no longer a girl, that she should go to the boys' bathroom, that she was a fucking lesbian (Álvarez, 2015).

What drove Alan to despair was not that she was *misgendered*, but something much more serious and cruel. Yet, sad stories like this one are often used to convince us of the importance of preferred pronouns. It is worth mentioning that this poor girl had decided "to be Alan" eight months before her tragic death, but the bullying did not stop. Any rigorous study of youth *transition* and its consequences should consider whether selling it as a magic bullet against problems might not be raising false expectations that could, in the end, cause more suffering than relief. This story also shows that the solution to bullying is not for the bully-victim to *transition*, but rather having a firm school policy against this type of violence, whoever it is perpetrated against, regardless of their identity.

such as Tania Rocha, doctor in Social Psychology, who invites families to reflect:

> The important thing here is to recognize that children and adolescents can give an account of their experience of identity; they are autonomous beings and subjects of rights who can account for what they feel. Let us reflect: why do we believe them when they say that they are in pain or that they are happy or sad, but not when they say that they are a boy, a girl or none? We must recognize that they are legitimate and that far from being sanctioned or repressed, they require recognition and accompaniment. [...] As a result of the restrictions experienced by trans children and adolescents and external rejection, there are problems of self-esteem, self-harm or self-mutilation, an impoverished self-image, substance and drug abuse and suicide. For this reason, strength, support and a watchful eye at home are crucial (Rocha, 2021, pp. 27–28).

What the mother in search of guidance takes this to mean is that if the child says they are trans, they are trans, full stop, because they can "account for what they feel," since the experience of identity is analogous to an earache. Therefore, in order that they do not self-mutilate, their parents have to recognize that "they are legitimate." This kind of paternalistic message, a mixture of lies, fallacies and truisms, is the first thing one finds when typing *trans children* into a search engine. It is difficult for these families, already overwhelmed by not understanding what their children are going through, to have access to reliable and understandable information. The answers they'll come up with on Google will be likely as verbose and manipulative as these displays of a total lack of understanding of what drives a person to the point of suicide and what lies behind a teenager's sudden adoption of a transgender identity.

If they go to sources such as the websites of the discredited English organization Mermaids (which offered binders to girls without their parents' knowledge), the Spanish Chrysallis (with its celebrations of sexist stereotypes), or the Mexican Asociación por las Infancias Transgénero (which accompanies "families with transgender children and adolescents" in their *transition* process), they will find nothing but stories that support the version that, for the child to lead a free, full and happy life, it is necessary to recognize their gender identity. In laypersons' terms, this means supporting them in all steps of the mysterious process by which their daughter will become their son or vice versa.

These same groups are contributing, with their fairy tales and rhetoric, to children convincing themselves of something that is not true and believing they are sick or special and at risk of dying before the age of 35 if others do not participate in the lie that keeps them in a bubble separate from reality. As Lisa Marchiano says, "much mental suffering results from being stuck in a story about ourselves" (Marchiano, 2018). And this American Jungian analyst elaborates on the idea:

> When we construe normal feelings as illness, we offer people an understanding of themselves as disordered. This has the unintended consequence of encouraging people to be stuck in a limited narrative […].
>
> The belief given to [a young patient convinced she had had a panic attack] by the psychiatric establishment and our culture's enthusiasm for reductive diagnoses made her construe [a good experience she had gone through], not as the success that it was, but as a confirmation that she was, in fact, ill. Here was a case in which the process of diagnosis and treatment had concretized the story, arguably making transformation less likely (in Marchiano, 2018).

A *transtimony* of a boy whom the Asociación por las Infancias Transgénero "assisted in her transition" shows how this schoolboy, haunted by a "suffocating sense of sadness that comes into my mind all the time, the anger of knowing that no matter what I do, people will still see me as a boy," is convinced that a *wrong pronoun*, misgendering or deadnaming may well be causes of suicide:

> A few days ago I had problems with my headmistress when I told her not to call me Axel, to please call me Sara, as I felt it was disrespectful for her not to speak to me by my name. She told me that this was not my real name, and therefore it was not disrespectful. It is legally true, and that seems to matter a lot to adults, but is it worth it? To cause

psychological harm to a person because they don't want to use their real name? For anyone reading this, let me tell you I have had countless suicidal thoughts based on that and more (Asociación por las Infancias Transgénero, n.d.).

This boy concludes his story by asking those who have read it: "For my mental health and my personal well-being, give me my name." On the internet and in certain associations that receive money to watch over their rights, children like him learn that if the rest of the world does not participate in their illusion, it can cause them psychological damage and drive them to suicide. It is clear that they also learn to wield this as blackmail.

It's odd that they insist that being trans is not an illness, while at the same time pretending that all the people around them engage in a big lie so that they won't get upset. Is someone for whom *misgendering* can be fatal an example of sound mental health? How does it further a young person's psychological well-being to be told that her emotional stability is totally dependent on what others think of her and how they perceive her? How helpful can it be to deceive someone into believing that falsifying their birth certificate will "help others perceive their gender identity correctly," as Ian Fragoso claims on the website of the association led by Tania Morales?

Perhaps these children need psychological care other than the so-called affirmative therapy offered by transgender children's organizations, whose main objective does not seem to be the mental health of their clients, but to promote self-ID for underage people. It is not enough to claim that a social transition will automatically result in better mental health; it is necessary to present serious studies and hard evidence of such hypothetical causal relationship, not just more ramblings in *inclusive language.*

Traditional families are the best breeding ground for the reductionist diagnosis of transgender children, because they have rigid notions of sexist roles and of what is befitting for women and for men. In these families lesbianism is not accepted, as it is in Chiara's, whose mother, ironically, is nowadays considered an anti-rights conservative for not having given her daughter the top surgery she so desperately wanted for her birthday – in short, for not being more like Jackie Green's mother.

In the educational treasure trove of the Asociación por las Infancias Transgénero, we also find the story of a young woman, Ignacio Narán, who claims to be non-binary. As a child, she liked to ride her bicycle, dismantle appliances and put them back together again, but she had problems with her family, who, despite her unfeminine tastes, insisted on buying her flowery things. Dresses were like a costume for her:

> Almost all of the conflicts I had with my mother were over clothes, especially when we started going to social events, because she wanted me to wear dresses, skirts, blouses and girls' shoes. We fought and fought for weeks on end, and the fights got more serious each time. As much as I told her that I didn't want to wear any of those things, she didn't understand (Asociación por las Infancias Transgénero, n.d.).

And then happened what we see repeated in many stories of girls with an aversion to cutesy and gaudy things:

> In the fourth year of elementary school I found out that I liked girls and learned that it was a bad thing, because in one class they made us do presentations on taboo subjects and, along with drugs and AIDS, there was homosexuality. It was equated to a vice, a disease.
>
> When my breasts started to grow, it was like torture, like a mockery of destiny: not only did I not want them, but I was also insulted all the time. Something similar happened with menstruation, and this was a blow to my self-esteem, so I stopped seeing myself. I ended up coming to terms with it by force – I had to do it, I had to conform and I ended up accepting it before it really hurt me. The way to cope was to avoid it. [...]
>
> I liked the girls so much that the only way I could get close to them was being friends with them, walking them home, making them laugh.
>
> But, of course, I felt bad all the time, because I was seen as just another friend, so that affected me too. I hated even more the fact that I had to wear a skirt and the hideous ruffled blouse of the uniform. All of that meant minimizing me, violating me, attacking me, denigrating

me; I lost hope of being able to do anything to change it (Asociación por las Infancias Transgénero, n.d.).

It is not surprising that Ignacio's family, who found it hard to digest that a girl could be unfeminine, and who imposed flowers and ruffles against their daughter's will, were relieved when someone told them that she was not, in fact, a woman. A masculine soul in a feminine body perfectly explains the attraction to girls and the aversion to pastel colors. Nor is it surprising that this young woman felt different, because she was, or, like many lesbians, she felt "that the role of a girl didn't suit me very well." She alludes to some drama classes, but the truth is that on the big stage of compulsory heterosexuality we are very bad actresses: if you don't want a fiasco, better not ask us to play the role of femininity. Loving someone of the same sex is the behaviour most at odds with sexist stereotypes there could be. Although Ignacio's story reveals some understanding of how society arbitrarily assigns different roles to men and women, something got in the way of her coming to terms with being a disobedient lesbian:

> In retrospect, and had I had the knowledge, I would have changed sex at an early age. If someone around me had the vocabulary and I had the opportunity, I would have done it without a thought, without hesitation. I would have liked to have had the possibility of deciding it in third grade, at the latest, so that by the end of my elementary, middle and high school I would not have been a total disaster in so many emotional ways (Asociación por las Infancias Transgénero, n.d.).

Lesbian, by the way, is a non-existent word in Ignacio's vocabulary, because what got in her way was gender identity ideology and an association that, far from helping her to accept herself just as she is, pushed her towards heterosexualization.

Finally, there are other families in which a trans or non-binary child comes as no surprise. They do not face any dilemmas or disjunctions; everything is already in place to celebrate the gender diversity of the new being, as this other transtimony reveals:

> Ever since I was pregnant with my first child I knew I would have a rainbow. And yes, it was like that when Pau arrived. [...] I remember

that the first thing we got our hands on was the book *I Am My Own Wife*, which tells the wonderful story of Charlotte von Mahlsdorf […], who was a transvestite who lived in the 1940s as an informer for the Stasi (Germany's secret police). We fell in love with her story. This is how art touched our hearts to try to be and do the wonderful work of mum and dad (Asociación por las Infancias Transgénero, n.d.).

We can conclude that there is a lot of magic in the fact that a mother, by reading the memoirs of a man who liked to wear dresses since childhood, has so much insight that, even before her baby is born, she knows a piece of information about its identity that not even the most advanced brain imaging could reveal. Or, less given to fantasy, we can think that there are people who are very easily influenced or very eager to have a special child who might one day break a Guinness world record or even make the cover of *People*.

Although it is more difficult to find them because the algorithms do not favour them, there are associations that offer families with children who assume a transgender identity less politicized and biased information, with a more solid scientific basis. In the Spanish-speaking world we have, in Spain, the Agrupación de Madres de Adolescentes y Niñas con Disforia Acelerada (Mothers of Teenagers and Girls with Sudden Dysphoria, AMANDA), "a support group with a non-partisan and secular vocation" and a position

of caution about irreversible medical and surgical solutions as a response to rapid-onset gender dysphoria, as we consider that exploring sexuality and gender roles is part of a normal child development (AMANDA, official website).

In England, Transgender Trend, which also has no political or religious affiliation and is "concerned about the current trend to diagnose children as transgender, including the unprecedented number of teenage girls suddenly self-identifying as *trans*," has done invaluable work in informing and accompanying families and teachers. In the United States, 4th Wave Now has since 2015 been a vital resource for families who have found nowhere else to quench their thirst for reliable information and their need to understand.

Denise, its founder (who, by the way, is Chiara's mother), created the website,

> because mine is a viewpoint that is seldom publicly heard: that of a left-leaning parent who is critical of the dominant paradigm regarding transgender politics and treatment. My primary concern is children, teens, and people in their early 20s, particularly girls who are contemplating medical transition (4th Wave Now, n.d.).

What these last three groups have in common is that they present themselves as gender-critical, that they have no religious or fundamentalist stance on sexuality, and that they support lesbians, gays and bisexuals; the latter is, in fact, part of what guides and inspires them. It is a big lie that its members are anti-rights bigots, as is now reflexively said of anyone who does not subscribe to transgenderist dogmas.

Both in groups that adopt the transgenderist model (e.g. Chrysallis) and groups that follow something closer to the radical feminist model (e.g. AMANDA), one constant is striking: their presidents or founders are, yes, middle-aged women, usually mothers of teenagers who one day decide that they are not girls, but boys, or vice versa. They are all concerned about their children and it may be that their struggle stems from a genuine interest in helping and doing good. Time will tell which of them knew how to do this in a more sensible way.

In Britain, in October 2022, Susie Green, Chief Executive of Mermaids – a group that is much-praised by celebrities and to which actress Emma Watson, UN Women Goodwill Ambassador and spokesperson for the HeForShe campaign, donated money and invited her followers to do the same – is falling from grace after being implicated in a series of scandals in which serious safeguarding failures have come to light. On the 12th of that same month, Miriam Cates MP, as part of the weekly Prime Minister's Questions, raised with Liz Truss that the organization, which has had "unfettered access to vulnerable children," promotes medical and surgical procedures that are harmful to them. She asked,

Does my right honourable friend agree that it's taken far too long for these concerns to be taken seriously and does she also agree that it is high time for a police investigation into the activities of Mermaids?

The Prime Minister replied:

It's very important that underage teens are able to develop their own decision-making capabilities and not be forced into any kind of activity. What would I say on the subject of the investigation she raises, of course those matters should be raised and should be properly looked at (ITV News, 2022).

Four months earlier, in June 2022, Stephanie Davies-Arai, founder of Transgender Trend, was awarded the British Empire Medal for her services to children, a fitting vindication after the attacks she has received:

I hope [this award] indicates a change of opinion about the treatment of children with gender dysphoria and is a recognition of my work, which has been wrongly called transphobic or bigoted. What I saw was a one-size-fits-all approach to dealing with these children, which risks sending them towards a medical pathway. One of my concerns was the alternative wasn't talked about. Everyone should be open to debate; it's healthy. Silencing debate by calling evidence-based approaches 'bigoted or transphobic' is very dangerous (quoted in Rayner, 2022).

This lack of debate has been the cause of the institutional capture that is becoming clearer every day. Perhaps what we are now seeing in countries like England or Sweden – another country that is reversing the transgenderization of children – heralds the definitive end of this horrifying form of homophobia and child abuse. Now, as more people know what is behind transgenderism, it is more difficult to see it as a progressive stance and virtue-signal saying "I support trans kids," which, as I argue in this book, is nothing more than a cover for the medicalization of healthy children, the vast majority of whom might be lesbians and gays in the near future. Let us hope that it will soon be recognized that, like lobotomy and skull trepanning, puberty blockers, cross-sex hormones and *gender affirmation* surgeries on minors are irresponsible and unscientific medical practices that should never have been allowed.

Trans widows

Another group directly affected by transgenderism are straight women married to men who one day start believing that their internal and personal experience of gender indicates that they are women and thus begin exploring their feminine side. They are, one could say, the other side of the *cotton ceiling*. In the previous case it is lesbians on whom men want to impose themselves in order for them to feel lesbian, and in this case it is heterosexual women whom their husbands want to turn into lesbians so that they can say that they are lesbians too.

As Sheila Jeffreys and Lorene Gottschalk observe:

> The phenomenon of transgenderism is generally written about as if those who transition are engaged in an individual heroic quest and the persons who surround them – partners, wives, girlfriends, mothers, children, workmates – are mentioned only to stress the importance of their giving unqualified support. In fact transgenderism inflicts serious harms on the family members of transgenders (Jeffreys, 2014b, p. 80).

One name these women have chosen for themselves is *trans widows,* reflecting their sense of having lost their husband, that he died in becoming someone else. Calling themselves by this name is also enabling them to find each other to share their experiences (see Trans Widows Voices), which have much in common and offer a very different perspective on transgenderism from that presented to us by its propagandists.

There are some effects on their lives that are worth noting here. The first is that, if the statement "Trans women are women" is taken to its ultimate consequences, they cease to be married to a man and become married to a woman. That is supposed to turn them into lesbians – but without anyone having asked them if that's what they want.

In a much smaller number, there are also lesbians whose partners suddenly identify as trans men and transition. And now these women are supposed to stop being lesbians because their partner has supposedly changed into a man? It also bears mentioning that, as Susan Hawthorne points out, not only men who now claim to be women reinforce sexist stereotypes: "Among *transmen,* similar behaviours result and some women partners or *transmen* express their anger at the misogynist behaviours some *transmen* take on" (2020, p. 224).

Donna Chapman and Benjamin Caldwell, who have studied these dynamics, explain that the partner of someone who trans-genders "experiences a role and identity change that is 'unplanned and uncontrolled'" (Jeffreys, 2014b, p. 83). Another effect in trans widows is that they now have to take on new caregiving tasks. Their husbands, in addition to psychological support in their difficult adventure of getting to know themselves, expect their wives to be their coaches of femininity. Femininity reduced, of course, to clothing, gesticulations and other inconsequential outward features. They are not interested in being taught how to mop up and put the washing machine on, but how to put on make-up and walk in high heels:

> Feminist research on the unpaid work of wives suggests that support-ing men's hobbies and leisure activities, e.g. by washing the football outfit, is an under-recognised aspect of housework. In the case of transgenderism, the work required is rather more extensive. It may be that wives find that, far from taking on a more equal share of the household chores now in their female persona, their husbands may engage in a form of acquired helplessness they think is suited to femininity and place even more burdens on their wives (Jeffreys, 2014b, p. 89).

It is clear from these women's accounts that witnessing their husbands' transformations is not a pleasant experience. In many cases it brings with it various forms of psychological and sometimes sexual violence. The parody of femininity they attempt can even be offensive to their partners; Helen Boyd says she felt like she was living with Britney Spears:

> The more I encouraged him to find an identity that felt comfortable and natural to him, the more unnatural he seemed to me. His manner changed, as did the way he used his hands. He flipped his hair and started using a new voice (quoted in Jeffreys, 2014b, p. 93).

Christine Benvenuto had the feeling that her husband did not want to be with her, but wanted to *be* her.

These women, moreover, have the heavy responsibility of being the permanent audience for men whose female identity depends on external validation and is very much a theatrical role. "The wife's place in relation to the hero is to be a servant, not a critic or an obstacle" (Jeffreys, 2014b, p. 82).

Many of them end up wanting to divorce, a decision that for different reasons (e.g. economic) is not always easy to make. Some of them also face the same fate as so many abused women: leaving is a risk. Sometimes, it seems, the prospect of being left alone brings out the worst in these men. As Christine Benvenuto recounts in her memoir, *Sex Changes*: "If Tracey was becoming a woman, he had never seemed so male – a tyrannical bully he had never been in our marriage" (2012, p. 69).

Another factor that emerges from numerous accounts of trans widows is very striking: several of them confirm from first-hand experience the observations that led Ray Blanchard to propose his distinction between *homosexual transsexuals* and *autogynephilic transsexuals*. Their husbands show strong signs of almost invariably falling into the second category. Says Tsevea: "Then came the autogynephilia. First it was him wanting silky underwear." Then he shaved his pubic hair, underarms and legs. Then he got acrylic nails. Then "he wanted to know what it felt like to have breasts." On the weekends he wanted make-up, but she was the one who had to apply it:

He didn't want to buy his own stuff: he *wanted mine*. He liked *my* things. He wanted to look like me. Wear my clothes. Wear my shoes. Have me put my make-up on him. [...]

Then I broke. I will never forget that night. He wanted to wear my lingerie. He wanted me to wear a strap on, to get on top of me and ride me. I let it happen, feeling numb. I will never forget the look on his face as he straddled me riding the dildo, wearing my red corset, hurting my pelvis with his bouncing (Tsevea, n.d.).

Wives, then, are not only spectators in the show of femininity, but co-stars, even against their will. Writes Jeffreys:

Most of the accounts by wives are explicit about the fact that their husbands' cross-dressing is a sexual practice that wives are now being expected to tolerate, or take part in, on the grounds that it is some kind of biological condition that the men cannot control. [...] It continues to be a problem that as men's sexual interests change – often through their consumption of pornography and other elements of the sex industry, the demands upon wives escalate. [...] In the case of transgenderism, it may be even harder for women to object because the practice is framed as inevitable and uncontrollable (2014b, p. 97).

Indeed, in several stories of women who were partners of these men, pornography is present and they point out that on many occasions its consumption has had an important influence on the acquisition of a supposedly female identity.[92] Sometimes they themselves confirm this and say the quiet part out loud, like the American Pulitzer Prize-winning essayist Andrea Long Chu, who is not shy about revealing his own fondness for pornography:

Almost every night, for at least a year before I transitioned, I would wait till my girlfriend had fallen asleep and slip out of bed for the bathroom with my phone. I was going on Tumblr to look at something called sissy porn. [...] In the right corner of Reddit you can find a whole genre of posts concerned that sissy porn has irreversibly altered

---

92 Feminist researcher and essayist Genevieve Gluck has extensively studied the relationship between transgenderism and pornography, in particular so-called *hypno sissy porn*. See Gluck (2020, 2021a and 2021b).

the course of their lives. 'Did sissy porn make me trans or was I trans all along?', asks one concerned user (2019, pp. 55–56).

The digital age is prodigal in scenes that undisguisedly flaunt this kind of influence; a particularly sad sight are the Instagram accounts of men in their 60s or 70s fond of posting selfies of themselves with painted lips, in sexy poses – or so they seem to believe – and in (skimpy) ultra-feminine clothing. Brain plasticity can play heavily against us; just as, to recall Gina Rippon's words, "a gendered world will produce a gendered brain," an addiction to pornography will produce a brain convinced that women are what porn shows us – a mind for which, as Long Chu thinks, "getting fucked makes you female because fucked is what a female is" (2019, p. 59).[93]

The relationship between porn and some aspects of transgenderism forces us to look at a reality which is much more crude than the aseptic definition of *gender identity* that emerged from Yogyakarta. Turning some men's paraphilic fantasy into a human right to be recognized worldwide was no easy task. Such a project required a massive propaganda campaign and lots of money.

Indeed, American investigative journalist Jennifer Bilek found hard evidence of something that those observing the institutionalization of transgender doctrine at unprecedented speeds and its near-universal imposition already assumed:

> I found exceedingly rich, white men with enormous cultural influence are funding the transgender lobby and various transgender organizations. These include but are not limited to Jennifer Pritzker (a male who identifies as transgender), George Soros, Martine Rothblatt (a male who identifies as transgender and transhumanist), Tim Gill (a gay man), Drummond Pike, Warren and Peter Buffett, Jon Stryker (a gay man), Mark Bonham (a gay man) and Ric Weiland (a deceased gay man whose philanthropy is still LGBT-oriented). Most of these

---

93 For an estimate of the magnitude of the effects of pornography on culture and on our relationships, not only concerning the topics of this book, see Dines (2010), Tankard Reist (2022) and Jeffreys (2022).

billionaires fund the transgender lobby and organizations through their own organizations, including corporations (Bilek, 2018).[94]

Every workshop on how to be a better trans ally, every new trans law passed somewhere in the world, every new TV series featuring trans characters, every invitation to male influencers who call themselves women to talk about feminism, every panel discussion cancelled because of *transphobia*, every *marcha lencha*, every plastic surgeon who opens a clinic to treat transgender children in need of their services, every new celebrity who comes out as transgender, every human interest story on trans kids, every teenage girl proudly flaunting her new flat chest and scars, every women's bathroom transformed into a gender-neutral bathroom, every harassment campaign against radical feminists or gender-critical people, every media outlet that reports on these issues while renouncing impartiality, every trans rights organization that receives funding, can be traced back to the fortunes of white male billionaires with shares in big pharma and tech giants.

Transgenderism in the twenty-first century is not a genuine grassroots movement that emerged from a marginalized minority population seeking recognition of their fundamental rights. It is not driven by people interested in abolishing sexist roles and in need of our empathy: it is driven by some of the most powerful men on the planet who want to make more money and gain more power. To achieve their ends, they have the enthusiastic support of a part of society that is more eager to be on what is believed to be the right side of history than to really inform itself and analyze the issue in depth.

For women convinced that by being trans allies they are serving a progressive cause and supporting a small and discriminated group in need of protection, such a revelation must be very hard to swallow.

---

94 In addition to the aforementioned article, Jennifer Bilek maintains a blog with a wealth of information about the money and powerful men behind transgenderism: <the11thhourblog.com>.

Freedom of speech

The gender identity movement makes extensive use of a strategy to silence its opponents that has worked like a charm. It consists of accusing them of transphobia and hate speech or thoughtcrime before they even open their mouths. It is a perfect tactic, because if someone asks – either out of curiosity or to force the accusers to produce some evidence – "What transphobic things did they say?" or "Why is this hate speech?" they will also be accused of transphobia and hate speech. This is how every possible discussion is settled before it gets started, with a point in favour of the accuser. In the thirteenth century it was possible to ask what evidence there was for the existence of God and to write treatises on the subject; we have moved on and now, in the twenty-first century, anyone who asks for evidence that certain ideas meet the definition of *hate speech* will be condemned for simply asking for it.

According to the UN, hate speech is

> any kind of communication in speech, writing or behavior, that attacks or uses pejorative or discriminatory language with reference to a person or a group on the basis of who they are; in other words, based on their religion, ethnicity, nationality, race, color, descent, gender or other identity factor (United Nations, 2019, p. 2).

We can argue about this definition, ask ourselves how accurate and useful it is, whether we should not need to take into account other criteria, whether it runs the risk of ending up characterizing as hate speech communicative acts that have another motivation, or whether, on the contrary, it leaves out others that are indeed motivated by hatred, and we will certainly find problems with it. Let us not rule out the possibility that definitions such as this one, which are so broad, imprecise and trapped in their good intentions, are conducive to the habit of producing an accusation of hate speech as soon as one feels offended in their beliefs. But in any case, it is the one given by the UN and can be the starting point for a necessary conversation.

The tactic of automatically accusing someone of hate speech is not only employed in the context of disagreements between transgenderism and feminism: there is a pervasive climate in the world against the free expression of ideas, and attributing hatred or malice to the interlocutor can have the desired effect of bringing the dialogue to a crashing stop.[95] With regard to the topics covered in this book, it is routine for gender identity activists to accuse radical feminists or people critical of transgenderism of using discriminatory language and attacking these people on the basis of who they are. In their minds, any idea contrary to theirs is a thought crime and should therefore be banned.

Another notable feature is that the accuser rarely backs up their accusation. No one has been able to point to a time when J. K. Rowling, the most prominent in the group of alleged *transphobes,* has attacked trans people orally or in writing on the basis of who they are, but instead many complainants attack Rowling, using pejorative language, on the basis of her sex and age (and the evidence is there for all to see; see Reilly-Cooper, 2020, and TERF Is a Slur, n.d.). On social media, very often the response to alleged hate speech are words that certainly look like hate speech, but are launched en masse, so that the original alleged hate speech gives rise to tens, hundreds or thousands of hate speeches in response. So maybe it's not really hate speech they're worried about.

In other cases, the accusers, in the absence of evidence, repeat the accusation over and over again. An example of this rhetorical device are these words by congressman Salma Luévano in an interview about his disagreements with Gabriel Quadri:

---

95   Another example is the debate surrounding Covid vaccination. Doctors and scientists like Robert Maloney, Peter McCullough, Pierre Kory, Bret Weinstein, Heather Heying and others who are sceptical about the safety and effectiveness of a kind of inoculation that has never been tested are called *anti-vaxxers,* and their observations and reflections are branded as *misinformation.* Critics insult and disqualify them without bothering to listen to or understand what they are saying or analyze the data they present. *Misinformation,* like *hate speech,* is dangerous and should also be censored.

Words are a double-edged sword, and when one of the edges is directed or channeled at a person, a population or a sector with hatred, we know that the speeches are the prelude to hate crimes. [...] Since the beginning of December, this man has been making these transphobic remarks that he has not wanted to acknowledge and yet he has gone on. I pointed out to him that he was wrong and [...] he continued; instead of stopping his hate speeches, he continued, continued, kept going with these hate speeches. [...] When you direct these speeches in what he determines [*sic*], it unleashes this whole situation. I had to file the corresponding complaints and also, as a form of protest, as a way of saying 'Enough is enough', and as a way of showing sisterhood with respect to these [...] hate crimes, these sisters, brothers, siblings who have died precisely because of this type of person, I shaved my head.[96] [...] He is a murderer and a hypocrite because he is killing us. Hate speech is the prelude to hate crimes. We know exactly what it is triggered by. [...] Hate speech is not just anything, and let's not confuse it [...] with freedom of speech. I support freedom of speech, but not in that way, because that is not freedom of speech. That's why he is a murderer! (in Rangel and López, 2022a).

Why is it hate speech? Because it is hate speech. Why is it not free speech? Because it is not free speech. What more evidence do you need?

Even in the hypothetical case that a feminist's position qualifies as hate speech, it turns out that addressing it,

does not mean limiting or prohibiting freedom of speech. It means keeping hate speech from escalating into something more dangerous, particularly incitement to discrimination, hostility and violence, which is prohibited under international law (United Nations, 2019, p. 1).

Combating hate speech must be "in line with the right to freedom of opinion and expression" and should support "more speech, not less, as the key means to address hate speech" (United Nations, 2019, p. 3).

---

96   He alludes to the fact that in January 2022 he shaved his head to, as a *Forbes Mexico* headline puts it, "condemn transphobic speeches by Quadri."

However, in this atmosphere of intolerance disguised as support for diversity, the defendants are not allowed to speak even to explain themselves, and the audience is not given the opportunity to judge for themselves the content of the speech and determine its value. Characterizing them as Nazis and painting them as worse than the devil with the help of the TERF epithet is the masterstroke. What they say is hate speech and they are also Nazis and trans exclusionary, so to prevent them from inciting violence and being murderers, there is no choice but to shut them up and deny them freedoms. Janice Raymond writes:

> In degrading the meaning of *hate speech* and *violence* to *misgendering* (using the *wrong* pronouns) and *deadnaming* (identifying one's pre-transition status), trans activists have corrupted free speech into hate speech demonizing critics as bigots.
>
> The glue that binds trans activists together is the smothering of dissent. At the heart of trans censorship is a discrediting of feminists, lesbians, academics who are gender-critical, therapists and medical personnel who won't prescribe puberty blockers for children, and journalists who publish any mild criticism of transgender ideology and practices (Raymond, 2021, p. 185).

In a democratic society such as Mexico's, it should be possible to organize a panel discussion at, say, UNAM's Feria Internacional del Libro de las Universitarias y los Universitarios bookfair, in which participants could freely discuss whether any of the following expressions could be considered hate speech, and elaborate on the reasons why or why not:

1. Referring in the masculine to a man who claims to be a woman.
2. Writing in a women's bathroom: "Rape and death to TERFs."
3. Utter the words: "If sex has become so problematic, how come in Afghanistan they know exactly who should be banned from school?"
4. Send a writer the message: "Bitch suck my dick you are so pressed and insecure about trans women. Your womanhood

should not feel threatened unless you come for us which you did, you old tired bitch."

5. Post the tweet: "There's no such thing as a trans kid: there are children who rightly resist restrictive definitions of what a girl or boy should look like. Feminists support those children, of course. What we don't support are those definitions: we want to put an end to them."

6. Repeatedly calling the editorial staff of a magazine to demand that they apologize for having published an article by a certain allegedly transphobe author and that they never again publish her contributions or any opinion like hers in their pages.

7. Writing: "I am concerned about the huge explosion in young women wishing to transition and also about the increasing numbers who seem to be detransitioning (returning to their original sex), because they regret taking steps that have, in some cases, altered their bodies irrevocably, and taken away their fertility. Some say they decided to transition after realizing they were same-sex attracted, and that transitioning was partly driven by homophobia, either in society or in their families."

8. Going to a feminist demonstration with a t-shirt that says "I punch TERFs" or painting "Death to radfem" on a wall.

9. Nailing a dead rat to the door of a women's shelter and scrawling across the windows and walls messages such as "Kill TERFs. Trans power."

10. Shouting "Nazi," "bigot," "TERF" and "scum" at a woman and lunging at her.

11. Leaving cards in a queer bar with the captions: "A woman is someone with a female body and any personality, not a female personality and any body. Any other definition is sexism. Source: women-don't-have-dicks" and "Defend women's rights. Get involved! NO to self-ID. A woman is born not worn."

12. Interrupting a feminist colloquium by throwing glitter towards a speaker with a pistol-like explosive device and shouting slogans such as "TERFs go home" and "No more transphobia in safe spaces."

13. Placing a billboard with the dictionary definition: "Woman: adult human female."
14. Ramming and beating up a group of lesbians holding banners with the lesbian symbol of the labrys and phrases such as "Lesbian: homosexual, not queer," and putting one of them in a headlock.
15. Posting a tweet with the suggestion of setting fire to the venue where a feminist conference will take place.
16. Writing: "My main point is to show how so-called health values of therapy, hormonal treatment, and surgery have replaced ethical values of choice, freedom, and autonomy; how these same 'health' values have diffused critical awareness about the social context in which the problem of transsexualism arises."
17. Assuring that no one is born in the wrong body.
18. Telling a lesbian that her "genital preferences" are transphobic.
19. Standing in front of the bar where two feminists are having a beer, shouting slogans with a megaphone to express their rejection of their presence.
20. Shouting one's head off at a protest rally yelling at a mediator, "Which of your loved ones do you want me to kill for you to calm down?"[97]

---

97 Point 1 is what they call *misgendering*; 2, a graffiti scrawled in the bathroom of UNAM's Faculty of Philosophy and Literature; 3, words by Amelia Valcárcel in the forum 'Necessary Clarifications on the Categories Sex and Gender'; 4, one of the multiple responses of transactivists to J. K. Rowling after her tweet criticizing the use of the term *people who menstruate* instead of simply *women*; 5, tweet by @laura_lecuona; 6, common practice in cancel culture; 7, quote from Rowling (2020); 8, common practice of transactivists and trans allies; 9, one of the protest actions against the women-only Vancouver Rape Relief shelter; 10, what they did to Julie Bindel on 4 June, 2019; 11, like those found at The Queer Emporium in October 2022 (fun fact: the man who a few weeks earlier had written the message mentioned in point 15 tagged Cardiff Police in the tweet about the cards and wrote, not exactly in jest, "I'm pretty certain this counts as a hate crime. You should be doing something about this and finding out who did it"); 12, what Eme Flores did on 21 November 2019 at the colloquium 'Retos del Feminismo Actual Mexicano', organized by the grassroots group Feministas UAM Xochimilco, when it was my turn to speak; 13, such as the one that in September 2018, Kellie-Jay Keen paid for and that was withdrawn due to Adrian Harrop's protests; 14, what happened

In 2023, it is difficult to imagine that the National Autonomous University of Mexico, or for that matter any other university or cultural institution captured by transgenderist intolerance, would host such a debate, because anyone who expresses, defends or allows 1, 3, 5, 7, 11, 13, 16 or 17 faces the possibility of a group of people supporting or committing 2, 4, 6, 8, 9, 10, 12, 14, 15, 18, 19 or 20. At UNAM, there have already been signs that, in order to stay out of trouble, some administrative staff prefer to avoid such controversial issues, as they did by cancelling the roundtable on masculinities (as reported in Chapter 2). Of course, it could be argued that the organizing office, by accepting a priori the version of those who pointed the finger at the panellists and obeying those who demanded the roundtable's cancellation, were engaging in prior censorship and violated the university's code of ethics, which establishes the principles of freedom of thought and expression.

This current tendency of rejecting the diversity of ideas by people who claim to be pro-diversity has the effect of inhibiting debate, impoverishing discussion and curbing critical thinking. Stories like that of Capital 21 (recounted in Chapter 2) have become an everyday occurrence. The public, with no time to investigate the substance of the matter, tends to believe the simplistic versions of those who shout the loudest and have more loudspeakers. But undoubtedly the most serious thing is that a large part of the media is also left with only a superficial version of the facts and embraces one of the voices in the debate, and always the same one, as *Animal*

---

in Cologne on 2 July 2022 at a march of *transinclusive* lesbians; 15, as two tweeters did in October 2022 referring to the FiLiA Women's Rights Conference; 16, Janice Raymond's words in the introduction to *The Transsexual Empire*, 1979; 17, as the radical feminist model has held since the days when the transgenderist model was based on the idea of having been born in the wrong body (since they began to abandon that image, less than six years ago, it is transphobic to imply that anyone has ever thought that there is such thing as a wrong body); 18, a usual form of sexual pressure, coercion and shaming inaugurated by *youtuber* Dennis J. Riley; 19, as 20 people did to Helen Joyce and Maya Forstater on the night of 21 October 2022 in the capital of Wales; 20, shout of one of the demonstrators who on 28 March 2022 demanded the removal of the recording of the forum 'Necessary Clarifications on the Categories Sex and Gender' from UNAM's YouTube channel.

Político, El País, The Guardian, The New York Times and many other influential media outlets do.

In October 2022, the Mexican senators were discussing proposed amendments to the criminal code and the health law to impose prison sentences from two to six years to

> anyone who performs, imparts, applies, forces or finances any type of treatment, therapy, service or practice that hinders, restricts, prevents, impairs, undermines, annuls or suppresses the sexual orientation, gender identity or gender expression of a person (*Animal Político*, 2022).

These are so-called conversion therapies. Mexican reporter and TV talk host Luisa Cantú commented she found it unbelievable that there was a diversity of positions in the Senate and that some legislators thought differently from her. She was also surprised to learn that such therapies were not already banned and that the issue was being debated at this stage. She attributed her utter astonishment to living in "these circles of privilege where we assume that the rights are already there":

> When we validate a debate, when we put the anti-rights argument with the rights arguments on the same plane, we assume that either one can win. To bring it up in a plenary, for example, and put pro and con arguments, is to validate that there are pro and con arguments, [whereas] when it comes to rights there aren't – there are only rights (Cantú, 2022).

Later, in response to the criticism of communicologist Dana Corres on Twitter for this call to censor those who do not think like her, and especially gender-critical feminists, she reiterated her position, in case the public had any doubts or considered it a small slip of the tongue:

> I am calling to silence and dismantle your hate speech. Otherwise no one is censoring you. There are no 'counter-arguments' or 'freedom of speech' in the denial of rights because they are not up for debate. There is no place in media for trans exclusion (@luigicantu, 2022).

Wherever does this journalist imagine that rights come from? Are they revealed to us by some authority? What would be the equivalent of the Tables of the Law in a democratic, secular society? If a feminist wanted to explain to her that women's sex-based rights are seriously endangered by laws and policies that replace the category of sex with that of gender identity, how would she propose to address the issue if, when it comes to rights, there are no arguments, only rights? In a case of competing rights, how do we determine which should predominate? Since "trans women are women," are we going to put Fallon Fox's right to fight in the female category above the right to health of the women who are going to confront him? And by what criteria? Shouldn't one of the two rights take precedence? Isn't the right to health fundamental and the right to be seen as you want to be seen less so? Shall we debate and argue, or shall we let our prejudices guide us?

Cantú believes that members of Congress like those who opposed these reforms are "resolving without the slightest effort to look into what we are talking about." The bad news is that she, so convinced that her positions are right and everyone else is wrong, also failed to see what we talk about in 2022 and 2023 when we talk about *conversion therapies*. A feminist trying to tell her the history of the concept of *attempts to change sexual orientation or gender identity* would have hit the wall. In vain would she try to explain to Cantú that simple talk therapies for girls who say they want to be boys and vice versa are misleadingly considered conversion therapies. To no avail would she invite her to read what the Cass Review in England found about the harms of the categorical gender affirmative model (the opposite of what they call *conversion therapies*) and what happened in Spain to the psychologist Carola López Moya. It would be pointless to tell her about the experiences of detransitioners and trying to make her see that these legislative moves (driven by the transgender agenda, by the way, and that's precisely why it was being debated – she was absolutely right in saying that it was not necessary to legislate about it) actually open the door to real conversion therapies consisting of turning, via hormones and surgery, possible future lesbians into supposedly heterosexual men and possible future gays into supposedly heterosexual women.

Of course, feminists know better than anyone that there is nothing to cure, like transactivists disingenuously like to say. Feminists know that homosexuality is not a disease and that children who reject sexist roles should be supported and accompanied in their rejection of the status quo, not repressed. However, experiences in several countries show that the conversion therapy that those pushing for these reforms and many of those who applaud them have in their sights are not puberty blockers and double mastectomies, but the work done by psychologists like the one who made me understand, when I was six years old, that I did not need to be a boy to dress the way I liked. They are not concerned with the conversion therapy undergone by Jazz Jennings from the age of six as an entertainment for the masses, but with the supposed conversion therapy consisting in not following to the letter the affirmative model that begins in social *transition* and usually ends in surgery. Conversion therapies have no raison d'être, that we agree on, but we have not sufficiently discussed what is to be understood by *conversion therapy*. As the women of FiLiA say:

> Feminist analyses of sex and gender in this context have been suppressed or labelled hateful. The Government should be sensitive to the fact that what gets called *conversion therapy* when it comes to gender dysphoria may be in the eye of the beholder, particularly in the absence of clear definitions or sufficient evidence on this subject (FiLiA, 2022).

However, that necessary discussion is unlikely to take place, because Cantú, like her colleagues and her circle-of-privilege-fellows, was told that all positions other than her own fall into the hate speech category and any questioning of measures that vaguely sound pro-LGBTIQ+ is bigoted right-wing extremism … and she bought it. The stance of others is hate speech and therefore dangerous, so it shouldn't be given a platform or listened to. Carolina Sanín alludes to this tendency when she writes:

For many years now, I have been uncomfortable with the feeling that liberals – or progressives, or whatever you call people who defend human rights and freedom over prosperity or economic interests – are compelled to think in packages. If we believe in the social State and the preservation of public space, then we must also be against the State of Israel, for example, as if one thing entailed the other. If we believe in the right of all adult citizens to live and share their sexuality as they wish, then we must also celebrate the alleged pregnancy of a man (Sanín, 2017).

This crude Manichaeism pervades debates. Many people do not want to go deeper: they are better off sticking to the ideological packages pre-approved by their sources, and end up subrogating their capacity for thought. In their haste to show the world how woke they are, they remain at the superficial level of slogans and 280 characters, without analyzing or making the effort to understand their opponents – on the contrary, there is an active effort to not allow their words to penetrate the brain. Those women are *anti-rights* and that's all they need to know. "They are bad, I am good."

Spanish journalist Rocío Benavente also showed signs of this impermeability when she tweeted: "I swear that I read it a thousand times and a thousand times I don't understand what's the danger or the problem that trans people pose for women and feminism. I just don't see it," and in response to numerous attempts to explain to her the harms of the trans law in her country, she concluded:

I just see some women, who have undeniably been fighting for their rights for decades, turning against another, much smaller and discriminated group, who they should be embracing and supporting, for reasons that are either minuscule or in no way a threat to them, I think. I think there are moments when you choose which side of history you stand on, and this is one of them. And for some reason they have chosen to stand with those who always stand on the wrong side (@galatea128, 2022).

In that conviction of belonging to the pro-rights group, they deny those who think differently the right to express themselves, and, in the process, they also affect everyone's right to information.

Someone like Cantú also deprives herself of the possibility of broadening her horizons and understanding a subject that interests her, an attitude that seems antagonistic to the journalistic profession.

Jack Appleby proposes that people attending the show 'Feminists vs Trans' ask themselves a simple question:

> What's more likely: that a load of life-long left-leaning LGBT-supporting women have inexplicably and uncharacteristically all suddenly become bigots or that one might be missing something here? (@j4ppleby, 2019).

Grasping this paradox might arouse a very fertile curiosity, but not everyone is willing to recognize that, if they can't join the dots, it is because they are missing some information or because, if they do have the information, they need to process it better.

In February 2018, a panel discussion on diversity took place in Portland, Oregon (with a heavy police presence, as the organizers had received threats of violence if they didn't cancel it). The event was disrupted by students who stormed out of the auditorium and kicked the sound system immediately after biologist Heather Heying uttered these words: "Anatomically and physiologically speaking, men and women are different." These protesters justified their gesture as follows: "We should not listen to fascism, it should not be tolerated in civil society, Nazis are not welcome in civil society." Heying soon afterwards wrote about the incident and stated:

> It is true that the authoritarian left is denying biology, but the deeper truth of the situation is perhaps even more concerning. The incoherence of the protesters' responses and the fact that the walkout was scheduled in advance suggests something darker: the protesters are 'read-only' people, like a computer file that cannot be altered. They will not engage with ideas – they will not even *hear* ideas – because their minds are already made up. They have been led to believe that exposure to information is in and of itself dangerous.
>
> Scientists, philosophers and scholars of all sorts have effectively been accused of thoughtcrimes before it is even known what we're going to say. The very concept of thoughtcrime, as Orwell himself well

understood, is the death knell to discourse, to discovery, to democracy (Heying, 2018).

Along with censorship practices, the determination not to listen to dissent is a constant feature of transgender politics. Mention has already been made of groups of organized feminists in Spain who have long been standing up to the government's repeated attempts to push through the "bill for real and effective equality for trans people and for the guarantee of the rights of LGBTI people." They argue that the proposal is contrary to "the feminist agenda, science and law," and to approve it

> would mean a serious violation of the rights of women and children, homosexuals and people affected by gender dysphoria or incongruence, as well as constituting a serious setback for the exercise of critical thinking and freedom of expression (Confluencia Movimiento Feminista 2021b, pp. 2, 29).

When it was still a preliminary draft, these women pointed out the anomaly that critical positions had not been taken into account and claimed that it was not possible

> to initiate its parliamentary procedure without having taken into consideration the critical positions it has raised and without a transparent and democratic social debate that includes, in accordance with political responsibility and the principles of plurality and neutrality of information in the media, the following actors: the feminist movement, health [...] and psychology professionals, teachers, as well as families and family associations not linked to transactivist organizations (Confluencia Movimiento Feminista, 2021b).

One of the measures the government wanted to introduce without an indispensable transparent and democratic debate is

> the criminalization of people who, in the exercise of their fundamental right to freedom of expression, defend the use of the words *woman, mother* or *vulva,* or 'err' in the use of pronouns, imposing fines of up to 150,000 euros (Confluencia Movimiento Feminista, 2021a).

There is a report that lays bare transgender strategies for their social engineering project that aims to make society as a whole submit to their demands and capture one institution after another (see Still, 2021). Popularly known as the Dentons Document because the powerful law firm was involved in its drafting, it proposes a series of good practices to civil society groups engaged in lobbying European governments for the approval of self-ID laws. One is to "avoid excessive coverage in the media." The reason is that if the public knows what is being cooked up, reforms are less likely to be passed:

> In certain countries, like the UK, information on legal gender recognition reforms has been misinterpreted in the mainstream media, and opposition has arisen as a result. [...] Against this background, many believe that public campaigning has been detrimental to progress, as much of the general public is not well informed about trans issues, and therefore misinterpretations can arise. [...]
>
> The major lesson NGOs drew from the UK experience is the importance of avoiding, where possible, excessive and negative press coverage. Largely as a result of such press coverage, legal gender recognition continues to be an incredibly divisive issue in the UK (IGLYO and Dentons, 2019, pp. 20, 62).

In other words, the best way to push for the replacement of the category of sex with that of gender identity in legislation in different parts of the world is to prevent people from knowing about and participating in the discussion, especially those who might have a critical position and interest in the issue, i.e. feminists. Democratic procedures and debates are very inconvenient for this woman-hating activism.

There is another factor that comes into play when a draft law comes before an assembly that proposes measures that to outsiders may seem positive and very pro-rights. It is very likely that legislators who have faced bills that take up the non-binding Yogyakarta Principles are participating in what Cass Sunstein, a Harvard Law School professor, calls *cascades:* "large-scale social movements in which many people end up thinking something, or doing something, because of the beliefs or actions of a few early movers" (Sunstein, 2019, p. 35). He adds:

The system of legal precedent also produces cascades, as early decisions lead later courts to a certain result, and eventually most or all courts come into line, not because of independent judgement but because of a decision to follow the apparently informed decisions of others. The sheer level of agreement will be misleading if most courts have been influenced, even decisively influenced, by their predecessors, especially in highly technical areas (Sunstein, 2019, p. 37).

Put differently, many momentous decisions for society at large are made by merely imitating what others did, in the belief that they did know what they were doing and understood the implications.

Let us imagine that members of a certain legislature receive a reform bill that includes the concept of gender identity. They read the familiar definition, according to which gender identity is "each person's deeply felt internal and individual experience of gender," and so on and so forth. They know that similar laws have already been passed in other countries. In Canada, for example, which is a progressive country, and we cannot lag behind. Besides, who could object to the legal recognition of an individual's experience of gender? Remember, too, opposing same-sex marriage brought us bad publicity. We have to support women in all their diversity. People are already more tolerant of the LGBT+ population, so trans women are women and, careful, we don't want to seem to be right-wing extremists. Trans children exist and resist; we must recognize that they are legitimate and we should not deny them their identity. We also have these other problems of low self-esteem and suicide. As the Court Justice said, we all have the right to freely pursue happiness. And this binarism, which is also imposed, because in the end everything we live has been imposed by someone, is a form of violence. We need more gender perspective. Trans women have an average lifespan of 35 years. Binarism also has to do with colonial oppression, and in New Zealand they have a third gender and so do we here in Oaxaca. Rights are not up for debate.

One reason why people sometimes prefer to support what others support is because they attribute more authority on the matter to these other people. Many are scared to ask questions so as not to appear foolish, or are afraid to speak out because they don't want to be contrarians … It gets worse if they know that raising an objection can turn them into alleged transphobes, anti-rights bigots and even murderers. Several circumstances are then mixed together: insufficient information, confusing verbosity that is difficult to refute, the desire to be on the right side of history, fear of appearing moralistic, lack of time, etc. You don't need a conspiracy theory to understand how single thought is imposed: you just need some basic psychology. Add to that a determined effort to prevent some people from speaking out, precisely those who have analyzed the subject the most.

For transgenderism, information and dissidence are dangerous in more than one sense. Its theoretical basis is fragile and better not not be subjected to the counterargument of theories and positions that have proven to be solid and have been confirmed by reality. But there is a deeper and more serious implication, which explains its passionate commitment to the gagging of opponents. It is one thing to have one's gender identity legally recognized, but it is quite another to have the validating gaze of others.[98] Their ID card might say *woman*, but they very well know that in the eyes of others they are not. Radical feminists and gender-critical people are a reminder of this truth. It is understandable that they accuse those who allegedly misgender them of denying them their identity – an identity that is acquired with a performative speech act crumbles with speech acts that challenge it.

Having achieved legal self-ID without any requirement whatsoever, it is now necessary to take over the gaze of others, to make everyone participate in their illusion, even forcibly. Now everyone will have to experience the world from their perspective, until

---

98 Andrea Long Chu recognizes the fundamental importance of the other for the validation of a gender identity:

If there is any lesson of gender transition – from the simplest request regarding pronouns to the most invasive surgeries – it's that gender is something other people have to *give* you. Gender exists, if it is to exist at all, only in the structural generosity of strangers (2019, p. 32).

transphobic speech ceases to exist, and in the end they "shall make thoughtcrime literally impossible, because there will be no words in which to express it."

CONCLUSION

The reality of transgenderism is very different from the progressive façade that its propagandists show us. Transgender activists have tried to sell us as just and protective of minorities a movement against women's and children's rights, based on falsehoods, wrath and violence, which responds to corporatist interests. Many people don't know who they work for, but they certainly make a good job of it, precisely because they believe what the attractive publicity brochure says. With their perhaps well-intentioned but misinformed actions and with the aim, according to them, of allowing the free development of the personality of trans kids, preventing hate speech, supporting the rights of LGBTIQ+ people, transgressing sexist roles, they are achieving the opposite of what they set out to do: they are enriching unscrupulous people with an anti-feminist and anti-social agenda, and being participants in collateral damage.

There is no need to invent conspiracies: just follow the money, see how many lines point to big pharma and remember also that a very common human motive is selfishness. If nothing else, in a fiercely competitive market, virtue signalling presents a mind prone to self-deception with a noble reason to eliminate the competition. Do I want the attention of the reading public for myself? Don't read the transphobe! Do I crave one of the few teaching positions available? Transphobia cannot be allowed in the classroom. How do I express my contempt for feminists but in a concealed way? By shouting at them that they are wretched TERFs. Am I among the finalists for a job promotion? I'll accuse this other one of refusing to use preferred pronouns. Am I looking for their votes? I'll tell them I'm the best choice for women in all their diversity. Am I interested in pleasing? I tweet "Trans people have a right to exist." Do I need to keep my job? To show them I'm with the good guys I'm going to point to the bad guys. I have a desk full of to-dos and these people came to me to demand I cancel the roundtable? I'm doing it to get them off my back without stopping to see if it's fair. Do we require funding? Don't fund those others – they liked a tweet from a transphobe. It's as crass and as mundane as that.

While so many people have bought into the single, manipulative version presented by the mainstream media and the social media accounts with the most followers, there are many other sources of information available to us today. The facts and analyses, as well as the actions and daily harassment that show the gender identity advocates for what they are, are at hand for anyone with access to the internet. But there is also a need for critical thinking and a sceptical attitude that make us less vulnerable to naively believing everything we are told. It is urgent to disprove the justification that rights are not up for debate and to put an end to the easy way out that "we must be intolerant of intolerance." The pages in this book call for dialogue. But an honest one. And one that leads to action.

The picture I have presented is extremely serious and something has to change if we want to prevent it from getting worse. The adjustment of beliefs in the face of the evidence of facts and analysis must lead to changes in behaviour. It is not automatic, but it is important to find the necessary motivation and to organize. Feminism has rarely faced such a brutal onslaught, and never have so many women who consider themselves feminists had such a decisive role in the war against themselves. Women's rights are on the line, and so is our freedom to come together as a movement to watch over those rights and to speak out in their defense.

The onslaught of gender identity militancy against the rights of women and girls should alarm us. It is necessary for us all to speak out and stand up to it. Among those who are concerned and who do realize this, many do not dare speaking their mind because they have seen what transgenderists are capable of. But as long as they keep silent, this will continue to happen. It is necessary to overcome fear and defy this backlash. Opinions contrary to transgenderism are less unpopular than the active silencing of dissent makes it seem – some people are silent because others are silent. For others to speak out and discover that they are not alone, it is encouraging when one finds others with the courage to speak frankly. These attacks will not stop without more people who dare to take a stand against them. The tide is beginning to turn and it is a little less risky now than it was a few years ago: remember England and all that has been stopped thanks to feminist campaigns. Keep in mind that the more of us there are, the harassment will be distributed among more people and it will be less overwhelming. It can start with small groups of friends or one-on-one conversations. Everyone, from their own place and under their own circumstances, can do something; no action is too small. Let's set an example and start rebuilding the feminism that was taken from us.

EPILOGUE

This book, in its original Spanish edition, was to be presented at the Guadalajara International Book Fair on 28 November 2022, published by Siglo XXI Editores, but there was a change of plans.

Gender identity activists, identical to those who star in so many examples of intolerance and closed-mindedness narrated in these pages, upon learning I was going to be there, mounted a campaign of harassment in networks that brought them good dividends. In the face of threats to set fire to the publisher's stand and other veiled threats of violence, an important cultural event that boasts of being based on free speech didn't face up to them. As I detailed in the chapter 'In the Beginning Was the Pronoun', by publishing the book *Gender-Critical Feminism* by Holly Lawford-Smith, Oxford University Press acted in a way that "seemed impossible in a climate of transgender censorship and institutional capture," while Siglo XXI, by postponing indefinitely the publication of *Cuando lo trans no es transgresor* in response to the usual accusations on social media, did something that would have seemed unthinkable to the Mexican intellectuals who founded this publishing house in 1965 as a response to an act of government censorship. Today, censorship is exercised by other actors with other mechanisms: in that editorial decision, three minutes of a spiteful fast-motion video on TikTok carried more weight than 120,000 words of patient and sustained argumentation on paper.

In 2014, Sheila Jeffreys closed *Gender Hurts* with the words "There will be interesting times ahead." We cannot say that nobody warned us.

BIBLIOGRAPHY

24 Horas (18 February 2019). 'Alumnas de la UNAM denuncian ser grabadas en los baños; videos circulan en sitios para adultos'. <www.24-horas. mx/2019/02/18/alumnas-de-la-unam-denuncian-ser-grabadas-en-los-banos-videos-circulan-en-sitios-para-adultos>

4th Wave Now (n.d.). 'About'. Official website. <4thwavenow.com>

Adams, Richard (3 November 2021). 'Kathleen Stock Says She Quit University Post Over "Medieval" Ostracism'. *The Guardian*. <www.theguardian.com/education/2021/nov/03/kathleen-stock-says-she-quit-university-post-over-medieval-ostracism>

Adauy, Arlette, Jorge Sandoval, Rafael Ríos, Alejandra Cartes and Hugo Salinas (2018). 'Terapia hormonal en persona transgénero según World Professional Association for Transgender Health y guías clínicas de la Endocrine Society'. *Revista Chilena de Obstetricia y Ginecología*, 83(4), pp. 426–441. <https://www.scielo.cl/scielo.php?script=sci_arttext&pid=S0717-75262018000400426>

Administración de la Comunidad Autónoma del País Vasco (2016). *Guía de atención integral a las personas en situación de transexualidad. Actuaciones recomendadas desde los ámbitos educativo, social y sanitario*. Vitoria-Gasteiz: Servicio Central de Publicaciones del Gobierno Vasco. <https://www.euskadi.eus/informacion/guia-de-atencion-integral-a-las-personas-en-situacion-de-transexualidad/web01-s2osa/es/>

Agence France-Presse (22 May 2022). 'Female TV Presenters in Afghanistan Cover their Faces to Go on Air'. <www.swissinfo.ch/spa/presentadoras-de-tv-en-afganist%C3%A1n-se-cubren-el-rostro-para-salir-al-aire/47614016>

AMANDA (Agrupación de Madres de Adolescentes y Niñas con Disforia Acelerada) (n.d.). Official website. <amandafamilias.org>

Allen, Garland E. (1997). 'The Double-Edged Sword of Genetic Determinism. Social and Political Agendas in Genetic Studies of Homosexuality, 1940–1994'. In Vernon A. Rosario (ed.) *Science and Homosexualities*. New York and Oxford: Routledge.

Álvarez, Rafael J. (30 December 2015). 'Acosaron a Alan desde los 14 años, su suicidio es un crimen social'. *El Mundo*. <https://www.elmundo.es/sociedad/2015/12/30/5682ca5322601d8c0f8b4632.html>

AMDA (Asociación Mexicana de Defensorías de las Audiencias) (n.d.). 'Derechos de las audiencias'. <amda.unam.mx/derechos-de-las-audiencias>.

American Psychiatric Association (2013). *Diagnostic and Statistical Manual of Mental Disorders*, fifth edition, Washington, D.C.: American Psychiatric Association.

American Society of Plastic Surgeons (2017). *Plastic Surgery Statistics Report*. <www.plasticsurgery.org/documents/News/Statistics/2017/plastic-surgery-statistics-full-report-2017.pdf.>

AMS of UBC (2019). 'AMS Statement on Jenn Smith's Talk at UBC', June. <www.ams.ubc.ca/news/ams-statement-on-jenn-smiths-talk-at-ubc>

Animal Político (11 October 2022). 'Senadores prohíben las terapias de conversión sexual; se castigará con hasta con 12 años de cárcel a quien las realice'. <www.animalpolitico.com/2022/10/el-senado-prohibe-las-terapias-de-conversion-sexual>

Anonymous (18 December 2016). 'Teaching Transgender Doctrine in Schools: "A Bizarre Educational Experiment"'. *Transgender Trend*. <www.transgendertrend.com/teaching-transgender-doctrine-in-schools-a-bizarre-educational-experiment>

Anonymous Clinicians (17 February 2020). 'The Natal Female Question', *Woman's Place UK*. <https://womansplaceuk.org/2020/02/17/the-natal-female-question/>

Aquino, Eréndira (28 September 2022). 'Activistas protestan frente a Capital 21 por discurso transfóbico y exigen renuncias; gobierno recibe demandas'. *Animal Político*. <www.animalpolitico.com/2022/09/capital-21-protesta-discurso-transfobico>

Arena Pública (9 November 2018). 'Cirugías a niños intersexuales violan derechos humanos, pero en México son la norma'. <www.arenapublica.com/politicas-publicas/cirugias-ninos-intersexuales-violan-derechos-humanos-pero-en-mexico-son-la-norma>

Artemisia (24 April 2019). 'Susie Green, Under-18 SRS, and Thai Law'. *4th Wave Now*. <4thwavenow.com/2019/04/24/susie-green-under-18-srs-and-thai-law>

Asociación por las Infancias Transgénero (n.d.). 'Transtimoniales'. <https://infanciastrans.org/transtimoniales/>

Asociación por las Infancias Transgénero (2018). *Protocolo de actuación para escuelas con casos de niñas, niños y adolescentes trans.* Updated August 2020. <infanciastrans.org/wp-content/uploads/2020/08/Protocolo-educaci%C3%B3n.pdf>

Asociación por las Infancias Transgénero (27 March 2020). 'Mitos y realidades de la iniciativa de infancias trans'. <infanciastrans.org/mitos-y-realidades-de-la-iniciativa-de-infancias-trans>

Asociación por las Infancias Transgénero (2021). *Súmate. Infancias trans* en México.* Mexico. <https://infanciastrans.org/wp-content/uploads/2021/04/SUMATE-infancias-trans-mexico.pdf>

Associated Press (13 February 2020a). 'Teen Runners Sue to Block Trans Athletes from Girls' Sports'. *The Guardian.* <https://www.theguardian.com/us-news/2020/feb/13/transgender-athletes-girls-sports-high-school>

Associated Press (7 June 2020b). 'JK Rowling's Tweets about Transgender People Spark Anger'. *Los Angeles Times.* <https://apnews.com/article/entertainment-jk-rowling-us-news-media-7338b2b262090c00f04deafe2e6689c2>

Austin, J. L. (1975). *How to Do Things with Words.* (J. O. Urmson and Marina Sbisà, eds.) 2nd. ed., Cambridge, Mass.: Harvard University Press.

Ávila, Fernanda (8 July 2021). 'Ophelia Pastrana, la mujer transgénero que apuesta por la diversidad en los negocios'. *El Sol de México.* <www.elsoldemexico.com.mx/finanzas/ophelia-pastrana-la-mujer-transgenero-que-apuesta-por-la-diversidad-en-los-negocios-6940293.html>

Badenoch, Kemi (30 July 2022). 'The Tavistock Scandal Shows the Dangers of Civil Service Groupthink'. *The Times.* <www.thetimes.co.uk/article/the-tavistock-scandal-shows-the-dangers-of-civil-service-groupthink-5bj2z26c7>

Bailey, J. Michael (2003). *The Man Who Would Be Queen: The Science of Gender-Bending and Transsexualism.* Washington, D.C.: Joseph Henry Press. Kindle edition.

Ball, Elliot (20 March 2022). 'Former Plymouth Olympian Sharron Davies Compares Trans Athletes to Doping Cheats'. *Plymouth Live.* <www.plymouthherald.co.uk/news/plymouth-news/former-plymouth-olympian-sharron-davies-6833459>

Barrie, Zara (28 July 2015). 'How Fallon Fox Became the First Openly Transgender Fighter in MMA'. *Elite Daily.* <www.elitedaily.com/sports/fallon-fox-became-first-openly-transgender-fighter-mma-video/1143650>

Bartosch, Jo (3 March 2021). 'The TERF War down under'. *Spiked.* <www.spiked-online.com/2021/03/03/the-terf-war-down-under>

Bazelon, Emily (15 June 2022). 'The Battle over Gender Therapy'. *The New York Times Magazine.* <www.nytimes.com/2022/06/15/magazine/gender-therapy.html>

BBC (2017). *Transgender Kids, Who Knows Best?* Documentary directed and produced by John Conroy.

BBC Newsnight (19 June 2020). 'NHS Child Gender Clinic: Staff Welfare Concerns "Shut Down"'. <https://www.bbc.com/news/health-51806962>

BBC Stories (16 August 2017). *Girl Toys vs Boy Toys: The Experiment.* <https://www.bbc.co.uk/programmes/p05cfsym>

Beal, James (4 October 2022). 'Trustee of the Transgender Charity Mermaids Quits after Speech to Paedophile Aid Group'. *The Times.* <www.thetimes.co.uk/article/trustee-of-the-transgender-charity-mermaids-quits-over-speech-to-paedophile-aid-group-jkjn2jrk9>

Beijing Declaration and Platform for Action (1996). UN Women. <https://www.un.org/womenwatch/daw/beijing/pdf/BDPfA%20E.pdf>

Bell, Diane and Renate Klein (eds.) (1996). *Radically Speaking: Feminism Reclaimed.* North Melbourne: Spinifex Press.

Benvenuto, Christine (2012). *Sex Changes: A Memoir of Marriage, Gender, and Moving On.* New York: St. Martin's Press.

Biggs, Michael (2020). *The Tavistock's Experimentation with Puberty Blockers.* A collection of articles by Dr Michael Biggs for Transgender Trend. <https://www.transgendertrend.com/product/the-tavistocks-experimentation-with-puberty-blockers/>

Biggs, Michael (2022). 'The Dutch Protocol for Juvenile Transsexuals: Origins and Evidence'. *Journal of Sex & Marital Therapy,* 49 (4), pp. 348–368.

Bilek, Jennifer (20 February 2018). 'Who Are the Rich, White Men Institutionalizing Transgender Ideology?'. *The Federalist.* <thefederalist.com/2018/02/20/rich-white-men-institutionalizing-transgender-ideology>

Bindel, Julie (2014). *Straight Expectations.* London: Guardian Books.

Bindel, Julie (9 June 2019). 'The Man in a Skirt Called Me a Nazi, then Attacked'. *The Times.* <https://www.thetimes.co.uk/article/julie-bindel-the-man-in-a-skirt-called-me-a-nazi-then-attacked-8dfwk8jft>

Bindel, Julie (26 August 2020). 'Stop Searching for the Gay Gene'. *UnHerd.* <unherd.com/2020/08/stop-searching-for-the-gay-gene>

Bindel, Julie (18 August 2022). 'Close down Sandyford Gender Clinic! A chat with Sinead Watson'. <https://juliebindel.substack.com/p/close-down-sandyford-gender-clinic?utm_source=twitter&utm_campaign=auto_share&s=w#details>

BJJ World (n.d.). 'Fallon Fox, Transgender MMA Fighter Who Broke the Skull of Her Opponent'. <https://bjj-world.com/transgender-mma-fighter-fallon-fox-breaks-skull-of-her-female-opponent/>

Blade, Linda (22 December 2020). 'La absurda muerte del deporte femenino'. Women's Declaration International. <www.youtube.com/watch?v=rbBEt0ixcGM>

Blade, Linda and Barbara Kay (2020). *Unsporting: How Trans Activism and Science Denial Are Destroying Sport*. Toronto: Rebel News. Kindle edition.

Bob Cut Magazine (7 September 2021). 'What Are the 78 Gender Pronouns?'. <bobcutmag.com/2021/09/07/what-are-the-78-gender-pronouns>

Boskey, Elizabeth (15 July 2022). 'Different Types of Vaginoplasty'. *Verywell Health*. <https://www.verywellhealth.com/different-types-of-vaginoplasty-4171503>

Brill, Stephanie and Rachel Pepper (2022). *The Transgender Child: A Handbook for Families and Professionals*. Revised and expanded edition. New Jersey: Cleis Press.

Brite, Joey (2 October 2020). 'The Four Horsemen of the Gender-Critical Apocalypse'. *Uncommon Ground Media*. <uncommongroundmedia.com/the-four-horsemen-of-the-gender-critical-apocalypse>

Brown, Lauren (6 May 2022). 'OUP Stands by Book on Gender-Critical Feminism after Author Backlash'. *The Bookseller*. <www.thebookseller.com/news/news/oup-stands-by-book-on-gender-critical-feminism-after-author-backlash>

Brownmiller, Susan (1984). *Femininity*. New York: Simon & Schuster. Digital edition: 2013. New York: Open Road.

Brunskell-Evans, Heather (2019). 'The Tavistock: Inventing "The Transgender Child"'. In Michele Moore and Heather Brunskell-Evans (eds.) (2019). *Inventing Transgender Children and Young People*, Newcastle: Cambridge Scholars Publishing.

Brunskell-Evans, Heather (2020). *Transgender Body Politics*. Mission Beach: Spinifex Press.

Bunge, Mario (7 July 2017). 'Elogio del cientificismo'. *El País*. <elpais.com/elpais/2017/07/02/02/ciencia/1499008570_546858.html>

Calderón, Emilio (17 February 2021). 'Tamikka Brents: la luchadora que la transfobia reemplazó'. *Noticias en la Mira*. <https://noticiasenlamira.com/sociales/tamikka-brents-entre-la-transfobia-y-invizibilizacion/>

Cámara de Diputados (6 July 2022). VII Congreso Latinoamericano y Caribeño sobre Trata de Personas y Tráfico de Migrantes. <www.youtube.com/watch?v=tDZj1OK7O-k>

Canaan, Chiara (21 March 2019). 'Girlhood Interrupted. Path of Desistance'. *The Velvet Chronicle*. <https://thevelvetchronicle.com/path-of-desistance-childhood-interrupted/>

Canadian Press (7 October 2018). 'CAMH Reaches Settlement with Former Head of Gender Identity Clinic'. *CBC*. <https://www.cbc.ca/news/canada/toronto/camh-settlement-former-head-gender-identity-clinic-1.4854015>

Cantor, James (11 January 2016). 'Do Trans Kids Stay Trans When They Grow up?'. *Sexology Today!* <www.sexologytoday.org/2016/01/do-trans-kids-stay-trans-when-they-grow_99.html>

Cantú, Luisa (13 October 2022). Rompeviento TV. <www.youtube.com/watch?v=91dSTU2lJyU>

Capital 21 (21 September 2022). 'Conversamos Braulio Luna, Mercurio Cadena, Itzel Suárez y Mauricio Dimeo. Y la entrevista a Juan Pablo Morales. Conduce Renata Turrent'. <www.youtube.com/watch?v=M6XsDT9m770>

Carlisle, Madeleine (15 July 2021). '"A Serious, Violent Incident." Promotion of an "Anti-Trans" Paperback Stirs Criticism of Amazon, American Booksellers Association'. *Time*. <time.com/6080670/irreversible-damage-trans-book-amazon>

Carrasco, Silvia (23 June 2022). 'El secuestro de la coeducación' Hoy por Hoy Las Palmas (*Cadena Ser*). <dofemco.org/blog/2022/06/23/el-secuestro-de-la-coeducacion>

Carroll, Lee, and Jan Tober (eds.) (1999). *The Indigo Children: The New Kids Have Arrived*. Carlsbad: Hay House. Kindle edition.

Carter, Matilda (2022). 'Trans Women Are (or Are Becoming) Female: Disputing the Endogeneity Constraint'. *Hypatia*, 37, pp. 384–401. <https://www.cambridge.org/core/journals/hypatia/article/trans-women-are-or-are-becoming-female-disputing-the-endogeneity-constraint/090DEAA53EA17414C5D3E8D76ED5A75C>

Cass, Hilary (February 2022). *The Cass Review. Independent Review of Gender Identity Services for Children and Young People: Interim Report*. <cass.independent-review.uk>

Castellanos, Rosario (1973). 'La mujer y su imagen'. In *Mujer que sabe latín …* Mexico: Fondo de Cultura Económica.

CEIICH (Centro de Investigaciones Interdisciplinarias en Ciencias y Humanidades) (24 March 2022). 'Aclaraciones necesarias sobre las categorías sexo y género'. <www.youtube.com/watch?v=EpiyXz1fO-8>

Chandler, Janine, Krystal Gonzalez, Tomiekia Johnson, Nadia Romero, et al. v. California Department of Corrections and Rehabilitation (17 November 2021). Case no. 1:21-cv-01657-NONE-HBK.

Channel 4 News (11 March 2017). 'Chimamanda Ngozi Adichie Interview'. <www.youtube.com/watch?v=KP1C7VXUfZQ&t=204s>

Chiappe, Doménico (18 June 2022). 'El porno ya afecta a la conducta en secundaria'. *Canarias 7*. <www.canarias7.es/sociedad/porno-afecta-conducta-20220619192926-ntrc.html>

Chu, Andrea Long (2019). *Females*. Brooklyn: Verso.

Clark, Lucy (26 February 2021). 'The Trouble with Boys: What Lies behind the Flood of Teenage Sexual Assault Stories'. *The Guardian*. <www.theguardian.com/society/2021/feb/27/the-trouble-with-boys-what-lies-behind-the-flood-of-teenage-sexual-assault-stories>

Clínica de Atención Transgénero Integral (5 September 2022). 'Preguntas frecuentes'. <clinicatrans.org.mx/preguntas>

Clínica Saint Paul (23 March 2021). 'Cirugías estéticas más comunes en mujeres'. <clinicasaintpaul.com/cirugias-esteticas-mas-comunes-en-mujeres>

Cobo, Rosa (2017). *La prostitución en el corazón del capitalismo*. Madrid: Catarata.

Colapinto, John (2000). *As Nature Made Him: The Boy Who Was Raised as a Girl*. New York: HarperCollins.

CDHCM (Comisión de Derechos Humanos de la Ciudad de México) (29 August 2021). 'CDHCM se congratula del avance en la protección del derecho a la identidad de adolescentes en la Ciudad de México'. News bulletin 163/2021.

CDHCM (Comisión de Derechos Humanos de la Ciudad de México) (15 June 2022). 'CDHCM celebra el criterio de la SCJN que permite el acceso de NNYA al procedimiento administrativo para el reconocimiento de la identidad de género autopercibida en la Ciudad de México'. News bulletin 75/2022.

Christian Institute (15 June 2020). 'Children's Author Retires after Abuse from Trans Activists'. <www.christian.org.uk/news/childrens-author-retires-after-abuse-from-trans-activists>

Confluencia Movimiento Feminista (26 June 2021a). *Feminist Manifesto: In Support of the Feminist Agenda, Against So-Called Trans Laws*. <https://movimientofeminista.org/manifesto-26j-english-version/>

Confluencia Movimiento Feminista (10 August 2021b). *Alegaciones al anteproyecto de ley para la igualdad real y efectiva de las personas trans y para la garantía de los derechos de las personas LGBTI*. <movimientofeminista.org/wp-content/uploads/2021/08/Alegaciones-CMF-Ley-Trans-LGTBI.pdf>

Congreso de la Ciudad de México (14 November 2019). 'Proyecto de dictamen en el sentido positivo con modificaciones de las iniciativas con proyecto de decreto por las que se reforman y derogan diversas disposiciones del Código Civil y del Código de Procedimientos Civiles, ambos para el Distrito Federal'. Comisiones Unidas de Igualdad de Género y de Administración y Procuración de Justicia. <www.congresocdmx.gob.mx/archivo-acfd1a5 0fd9e0fd63a9d6da95503747a1098693e.pdf>

Copred (Consejo para Prevenir y Eliminar la Discriminación de la Ciudad de México) (31 March 2020). 'Día Internacional de la Visibilidad Trans; reconocimiento a las infancias trans, un pendiente'. Pronouncement 009. <www.copred.cdmx.gob.mx/comunicacion/nota/dia-internacional-de-la-visibilidad-trans-reconocimiento-las-infancias-trans-un-pendiente>

Copred (Consejo para Prevenir y Eliminar la Discriminación de la Ciudad de México) (9 August 2021). 'Copred llama a reconocer a las infancias trans y permitir el cambio de acta por la vía administrativa'. <bit.ly/3TQr70n>

Coronado, Nuria (4 July 2022). 'Ahora deshacerse del género, de aquello que nos oprime, es hacer terapia de conversión'. *La Hora Digital.* <www.lahoradigital.com/noticia/32007/igualdad/ahora-deshacerse-del-genero-de-aquello-que-nos-oprime-es-hacer-terapia-de-conversion.aspx>

Corti, Delfina (28 March 2022). 'Qué se sabe hasta el momento sobre si existe o no una ventaja deportiva en atletas transgénero'. *Chequeado.* <https://chequeado.com/hilando-fino/que-se-sabe-hasta-el-momento-sobre-si-existe-o-no-una-ventaja-deportiva-en-atletas-transgenero/>

Criado Perez, Caroline (2019). *Invisible Women: Data Bias in a World Designed for Men.* New York: Abrams Press.

Crocker, Catherine (21 November 1993). 'Ginsburg Explains Origin of Sex, Gender'. *Los Angeles Times.* <www.latimes.com/archives/la-xpm-1993-11-21-mn-59217-story.html>

Cultura UNAM (2019). Presentación del número 'Feminismos' de la *Revista de la Universidad.* (<facebook.com/watch/live/?ref=watch_ permalink&v=77716272929413708>: accessed November 2022; site inactive on 29 October 2023)

Dahlerup, Drude (2021). *Género, democracia y cuotas. ¿Cuándo funcionan las cuotas de género.* (Laura Lecuona, translator) México: Instituto Nacional Electoral.

Dansky, Kara (11 May 2021a). 'The Biden Administration Is Obliterating Women and Girls'. <www.karadansky.com/read/the-biden-administration-is-obliterating-women-and-girls>

Dansky, Kara (2021b). *The Abolition of Sex: How the 'Transgender' Agenda Harms Women and Girls.* New York: Bombardier Books.

Dawkins, Richard (5 January 2022). 'Race is a Spectrum. Sex is Pretty Damn Binary'. *Areo Magazine*. <areomagazine.com/2022/01/05/race-is-a-spectrum-sex-is-pretty-damn-binary>

de Beauvoir, Simone (6 April 1975). 'Why I am a feminist'. *Questionnaire*. <https://www.youtube.com/watch?v=g6eDMaDWquI>

de Beauvoir, Simone (2011). *The Second Sex*. (Constance Borde and Sheila Malovany Chevallier, translators) New York: Vintage Books.

De Miguel, Ana (1985). *Neoliberalismo sexual: El mito de la libre elección*. Madrid: Cátedra.

De Miguel, Teresa (26 April 2022). 'Gabriel Quadri, sancionado por sus ataques transfóbicos contra la diputada Salma Luévano'. *El País*. <elpais.com/mexico/2022-04-26/gabriel-quadri-sancionado-por-sus-ataques-transfobicos-contra-la-diputada-salma-luevano.html>

Dedaj, Paulina (21 April 2023). 'High School Volleyball Player Says She Suffered Concussion After Being Injured by Trans Athlete, Calls for Ban'. *Fox Sports*. <https://www.foxnews.com/sports/high-school-volleyball-player-says-suffered-concussion-being-injured-trans-athlete-calls-ban>

Del Mar, Yadira (19 April 2021). 'The Queer Paradise'. Women's Declaration International. <www.youtube.com/watch?v=588OqoFzBDo>

Di Ceglie, Domenico (November 2000). 'Gender Identity Disorder in Young People'. *Advances in Psychiatric Treatment*, 6 (6), pp. 458–466. <https://doi.org/10.1192/apt.6.6.458>

Dines, Gail (2010). *Pornland: How Porn Has Hijacked Our Sexuality*. Boston: Beacon Press.

Divany, Javier (31 March 2022). 'Piden juicio contra diputado Gabriel Quadri, por violencia política en razón de género'. *El Sol de México*. <www.elsoldemexico.com.mx/mexico/politica/piden-juicio-contra-diputado-gabriel-quadri-por-violencia-politica-en-razon-de-genero-8074676.html>

Docentes Feministas por la Coeducación (9 July 2022). 'Comunicado de Dofemco ante el proyecto de "Ley Trans" del Consejo de Ministros'. <dofemco.org/blog/2022/07/09/comunicado-de-dofemco-ante-el-proyecto-de-ley-trans-del-consejo-de-ministros>

Donnelly, Laura (12 December 2019). 'Children's Transgender Clinic Hit by 35 Resignations in Three Years as Psychologists Warn of Gender Dysphoria "Over-Diagnoses"'. *The Telegraph*. <www.telegraph.co.uk/news/2019/12/12/childrens-transgender-clinic-hit-35-resignations-three-years>

Dreger, Alice (2015). *Galileo's Middle Finger: Heretics, Activists, and the Search for Justice*. New York: Penguin.

Edwards, Jonathan (20 January 2022). 'In Fox Interview, Olympian Caitlyn Jenner Says Record-Breaking Transgender Swimmer Shouldn't Compete with Women'. *The Washington Post.* <https://www.washingtonpost.com/nation/2022/01/20/caitlyn-jenner-transgender-athletes-womens-sports/>

EFE and Telemundo (4 August 2022). 'Muertes tras cirugías estéticas en Tijuana alertan de turismo médico de EEUU'. *Telemundo San Diego.* <bit.ly/3WhbWic>

Ekman, Kajsa Ekis (2023). *On the Meaning of Sex: Thoughts About the New Definition of Woman.* (Kristina Mäki, translator) Mission Beach: Spinifex Press.

El Financiero (10 October 2022a). 'Alejandra "Tigre" Jiménez demanda al Consejo Mundial de Boxeo por discriminación y lesbofobia'. *El Financiero.* <https://www.elfinanciero.com.mx/deportes/2022/10/10/alejandra-tigre-jimenez-demanda-al-consejo-mundial-de-boxeo-por-discriminacion-y-lesbofobia/>

El Financiero (8 November 2022b). 'Capital 21 ofrece disculpa por discursos transfóbicos en uno de sus programas'. <https://www.elfinanciero.com.mx/cdmx/2022/11/08/capital-21-ofrece-disculpa-por-discursos-transfobicos-en-uno-de-sus-programas/>

El Universal (2 August 2019). 'Ophelia y Ofelio: tendencia en redes'. <www.eluniversal.com.mx/nacion/sociedad/por-que-es-tendencia-en-redes-ophelia-y-ofelio>

El Universal (24 July 2022). 'México lidera en embarazo infantil, alertan'. <www.eluniversal.com.mx/nacion/mexico-lidera-en-embarazo-infantil-alertan>

Ellery, Ben (18 June 2022). 'Cambridge Academics Reject Trans "Thought Control"'. *The Times.* <www.thetimes.co.uk/article/cambridge-academics-reject-trans-thought-control-7w25jv8jq>

Evans, Martin, Kate McCann and Olivia Rudgard (6 September 2018). 'Transgender Person Accused of Rape is Remanded into Female Prison and Sexually Assaults Inmates Within Days'. *The Telegraph.* <https://www.telegraph.co.uk/news/2018/09/06/transgender-person-accused-rape-remanded-female-prison-sexually/>

Fair Play for Women (27 May 2022). 'Press Regulator is Failing Women with Approach to Transgender Coverage'. <fairplayforwomen.com/ipso-failing-women-with-transgender-rules>

Favaro, Laura (15 September 2022). 'Researchers Are Wounded in Academia's Gender Wars'. *Times Higher Education.* <www.timeshighereducation.com/depth/researchers-are-wounded-academias-gender-wars>

Faye, Shon (2021). *The Transgender Issue: Trans Justice Is Justice for All.* London: Allen Lane / Penguin Random House.

Faye, Shon (2022). 'Prólogo a la edición en castellano'. *Trans. Un alegato por un mundo más justo y más libre.* (Rosa María García, translator) Barcelona: Blackie Books.

Fein, Luba (21 April 2020). 'Vancouver Rape Relief and Women's Shelter'. <www.filia.org.uk/latest-news/2020/4/21/vancouver-rape-relief-and-womens-shelter>

Feminario Valencia (23–24 September 2022). 'Mujer, feminismo y democracia'. <www.youtube.com/watch?v=lkFLstSwq-g&t=5s>

FiLiA (2 February 2022). 'FiLiA Responds to the Conversion Therapy Consultation'. <www.filia.org.uk/latest-news/2022/2/19/filia-response-to-conversion-therapy-consultation>

Film Underground Corporation (4 August 2021). 'Sarah Robles "No thank you" Refuses Question about Transgender Athlete Laurel Hubbard'. <www.youtube.com/watch?v=UhZjmpWBlnk>

Fine, Cordelia (2010). *Delusions of Gender: How our Minds, Society and Neurosexism Create Difference.* New York: Norton & Company.

Finlay, Karen (16 June 2019). 'UK Courts Ordered to Address "Transgender" Defendants as the "Gender" of their Choice'. *Women Are Human.* <www.womenarehuman.com/uk-courts-ordered-to-address-transgender-defendants-as-the-gender-of-their-choice>

Flores, Ana (24 March 2021). 'Ella es Tania Morales, activista por las infancias trans'. *Homosensual.* <www.homosensual.com/lgbt/activismo/ella-es-tania-morales-activista-infancias-trans>

Fondo Semillas (n.d.). 'Voz manifiesta'. <semillas.org.mx/pdf/Manifiesto.pdf>.

Forstater, Maya (10 June 2021). 'Press Release: Gender-Critical Beliefs are Worthy of Respect in a Democratic Society'. <sex-matters.org/wp-content/uploads/2021/06/Maya-Forstater-press-release-final-.pdf>

Freedman, Rosa, Kathleen Stock and Alice Sullivan (November 2020). *Evidence and Data on Trans Women's Offending Rates. Written Evidence Submitted by Professor Rosa Freedman, Professor Kathleen Stock and Professor Alice Sullivan (GRA 2021).* <committees.parliament.uk/writtenevidence/18973/pdf>

Frye, Marilyn (1983). 'Lesbian Feminism and the Gay Rights Movement: Another View of Male Supremacy, Another Separatism'. In *The Politics of Reality: Essays in Feminist Theory.* New York: Crossing Press.

Fundación Huésped (n.d.). Official website. <www.huesped.org.ar>

Gaetano, Phil (15 November 2017). 'David Reimer and John Money Gender Reassignment Controversy: The John/Joan Case'. *The Embryo Project Encyclopedia.* <embryo.asu.edu/pages/david-reimer-and-john-money-gender-reassignment-controversy-johnjoan-case>

Gallego, Juana (2 April 2021). 'Mujeres molestas en la universidad'. *Público*. <https://blogs.publico.es/cuarto-y-mitad/2021/04/02/mujeres-molestas-en-la-universidad>

García Arenales, María (18 January 2022). '"Sara tenía 30 perforaciones en varios órganos, lesiones más propias de una reyerta con armas": la muerte en España de una mujer tras una operación de cirugía estética'. *BBC Mundo*. <www.bbc.com/mundo/noticias-60033092>

García, Ana Karen (19 June 2022). 'Las mujeres y los niños: los más olvidados e invisibles dentro de las cárceles en México'. *El Economista*. <www.eleconomista.com.mx/politica/Las-mujeres-y-los-ninos-los-mas-olvidados-e-invisibles-dentro-de-las-carceles-en-Mexico-20220617-0083.html>

George, Liz (10 October 2022). 'Biden Admin: Trans Women Must Register for Draft; Trans Men Don't Have to'. *American Military News*. <https://americanmilitarynews.com/2022/10/biden-admin-trans-women-must-register-for-draft-trans-men-dont-have-to/>

Gervais, Ricky (2022). *Supernature*. Netflix special.

Gianini Belotti, Elena (1975). *Little Girls: Social Conditioning and Its Effects on the Stereotyped Role of Women During Infancy*. (Lisa Appignanesi, translator) Toronto: Writers and Readers Publishing Cooperative.

Gluck, Genevieve (29 November 2020). 'Why Isn't Anyone Talking about the Influence of Porn on the Trans Trend?'. *Feminist Current*. <www.feministcurrent.com/2020/11/29/why-isnt-anyone-talking-about-the-influence-of-porn-on-the-trans-trend>

Gluck, Genevieve (26 March 2021a). 'The Truth About Sissy Hypno Porn'. *Whose Body Is It*. <www.youtube.com/watch?v=QpeHOHe6yT0>

Gluck, Genevieve (30 May 2021b). 'Sissy Porn at Princeton University'. *Women's Voices*. <genevievegluck.substack.com/p/sissy-porn-at-princeton-university>

Gluck, Genevieve (4 July 2022). 'Lesbians Assaulted by Trans Activists at Dyke March in Cologne'. *Reduxx*. <reduxx.info/lesbians-assaulted-by-trans-activists-at-dyke-march-in-cologne>

Gobierno de la Ciudad de México (27 August 2021a). 'Lineamientos para Garantizar los Derechos Humanos en el Procedimiento Administrativo de Reconocimiento de Identidad de Género en la Ciudad de México de las Personas Adolescentes'. *Gaceta Oficial de la Ciudad de México*, núm. 671 bis.

Gobierno de la Ciudad de México (1 October 2021b). 'Inaugura Gobierno capitalino Unidad de Salud Integral para Personas Trans y el Centro Especializado en Medicina Integrativa'. News bulletin 534/2021. <https://www.obras.cdmx.gob.mx/comunicacion/nota/inaugura-gobierno-

capitalino-unidad-de-salud-integral-para-personas-trans-y-el-centro-especializado-en-medicina-integrativa>

Goldberg, Michelle (9 December 2015). 'The Trans Women Who Say that Trans Women Aren't Women'. *Slate*. <slate.com/human-interest/2015/12/gender-critical-trans-women-the-apostates-of-the-trans-rights-movement.html>

González Pérez, Luis Raúl (18 February 2015). *Informe especial de la Comisión Nacional de los Derechos Humanos sobre las mujeres internas en los centros de reclusión de la República Mexicana*. Mexico: Comisión Nacional de los Derechos Humanos. <https://www.cndh.org.mx/sites/all/doc/Informes/Especiales/2015_IE_MujeresInternas.pdf>

González, Georgina (26 August 2020). 'Niñeces trans necesitan protección y el Congreso de CDMX se la niega'. Agencia Presentes. <agenciapresentes.org/2020/10/08/el-congreso-de-ciudad-de-mexico-frena-proteccion-para-nines-y-jovenes-trans-2>

Gottschalk, Lorene (2003). 'From Gender Inversion to Choice and Back: Changing Perceptions of the Aetiology of Lesbianism over Three Historical Periods'. *Women's Studies International Forum*, 26 (3), May-June, pp. 221–233. <https://doi.org/10.1016/S0277-5395(03)00052-9>

Graham, Claire (1 August 2019). 'Why Do Trans Activists Claim to Be Intersex?'. <https://mrkhvoice.com/index.php/2019/08/01/why-do-trans-activists-claim-to-be-intersex/>

Graham, Claire (2021). Interview. In Lime Soda Films, part 2.

Graham, Dee (1994). *Loving to Survive: Sexual Terror, Men's Violence and Women's Lives*. New York: New York University Press.

Grand View Research (n.d.). *U. S. Sex Reassignment Surgery Market Size, Share & Trends Analysis Report by Gender Transition (Male to Female, Female to Male) and Segment Forecasts, 2022–2030*. <www.grandviewresearch.com/industry-analysis/us-sex-reassignment-surgery-market>

Green, Susie (13 December 2017). 'Transgender: A Mother's Story'. Ted Talk. (<www.ted.com/talks/susie_green_transgender_a_mother_s_story>, accessed November 2022; site inactive on 29 October 2023.)

Greer, Germaine (22 July 1989). 'On Why Sex-Change is a Lie'. *The Independent Magazine*. <twitter.com/terfcitations/status/1550465693073567744>

Greer, Germaine (2000). *The Whole Woman*. New York: Anchor Books.

Guichard Bello, Claudia (2015). *Manual de comunicación no sexista. Hacia un lenguaje incluyente*. México: Instituto Nacional de las Mujeres. <http://cedoc.inmujeres.gob.mx/documentos_download/101265.pdf>

Guillén, Beatriz (1 April 2022). 'Transfobia en el Congreso mexicano: el día en que el panista Quadri llamó "señor" a la diputada Salma Luévano'. *El País*.

<elpais.com/mexico/2022-04-01/transfobia-en-el-congreso-mexicano-el-dia-en-que-el-panista-quadri-llamo-senor-a-la-diputada-salma-luevano.html>

Guterres, António (1 April 2020). 'Put Women and Girls at the Centre of Efforts to Recover from COVID-19'. <https://www.un.org/en/un-coronavirus-communications-team/put-women-and-girls-centre-efforts-recover-covid-19>

Hamedani, Ali (5 November 2014). 'The Gay People Pushed to Change Their Gender'. *BBC News Magazine.* <https://www.bbc.com/news/magazine-29832690>

Hands Across the Aisle (14 March 2018). 'Mother Interrogated by the Police for Gender-Critical Tweets'. <handsacrosstheaislewomen.com/?s=Mother+interrogated+by+the+police+for+gender-critical+tweets>

Hastings, Chris (28 August 2021). 'Bestselling Author Who Accuses the Trans Lobby of Trying to "Supplant Biology" Says She Has Been Cancelled by the BBC and Waterstones'. *Daily Mail.* <www.dailymail.co.uk/news/article-9936523/Author-accused-trans-lobby-trying-supplant-biology-says-cancelled.html>

Hawthorne, Susan (2020). *Vortex: The Crisis of Patriarchy.* Mission Beach: Spinifex Press.

Hayton, Debbie (18 February 2020). 'I May Have Gender Dysphoria. But I Still Prefer to Base My Life on Biology, Not Fantasy'. <debbiehayton.com/2020/02/18/i-may-have-gender-dysphoria-but-i-still-prefer-to-base-my-life-on-biology-not-fantasy>

Herzog, Katie (23 September 2019). 'Is the Life Expectancy of Trans Women in the U. S. Just 35? No'. *The Stranger.* <www.thestranger.com/slog/2019/09/23/41471629/is-the-life-expectancy-of-trans-women-in-the-us-just-35-no>

Heying, Heather (2 March 2018). 'On the Dangers of Read-Only Activism'. <medium.com/@heyingh/on-the-dangers-of-read-only-activism-e4891ebacaac>

Hodson, Nathan (2019). 'Sex Development: Beyond Binaries, Beyond Spectrums'. In Michele Moore and Heather Brunskell-Evans (eds.) (2019). *Inventing Transgender Children and Young People.* Newcastle: Cambridge Scholars Publishing.

Holmes, Martin (24 May 2022). 'Ricky Gervais Slammed for Mocking Trans People in New Netflix Special'. *TV Insider.* <www.tvinsider.com/1045749/ricky-gervais-slammed-for-mocking-trans-people-in-new-netflix-special>

IACHR (Inter-American Commission on Human Rights) (2015). *Violence against LGBTI persons in the Americas.* <https://www.oas.org/en/iachr/reports/pdfs/violencelgbtipersons.pdf>

IGLYO, Thomson Reuters Foundation and Dentons (2019). *Only Adults? Good Practices in Legal Gender Recognition for Youth: A Report on the Current State of Laws and Advocacy in Eight Countries in Europe, with a Focus on Rights of Young People,* November. <www.iglyo.com/wp-content/uploads/2019/11/IGLYO_v3-1.pdf>

Ingala Smith, Karen (3 October 2018). 'Amnesty International and the Gender Recognition Act Consultation'. <https://kareningalasmith.com/2018/10>

Ingala Smith, Karen (2023). *Defending Women's Spaces.* Cambridge, UK: Polity Press.

INB (Instituto de Neurobiología) (n.d.). 'Activa tu cerebro: efecto Stroop'. <inb.unam.mx/semanadelcerebro/?page_id=1397>

INEGI (Instituto Nacional de Estadística y Geografía) (2015). 'Víctimas, inculpados y sentenciados registrados'. <www.inegi.org.mx/temas/victimas>

Inmujeres (Instituto Nacional de las Mujeres) (21 September 2020). 'La paridad de género, un asunto de igualdad y de justicia'. <www.gob.mx/inmujeres/articulos/la-paridad-de-genero-un-asunto-de-igualdad-y-de-justicia>

International Olympic Committee (n.d.). 'When Did Women First Compete in the Olympic Games?'. Official website. <olympics.com>

Intersexunicorn (n.d.). 'FAAB, MAAB, CAMAB, FAMAB, and Intersex Erasure'. <thatswhatkentsaid.tumblr.com/post/11187424315/faab-maab-camab-famab-and-intersex-erasure/amp?>

ITV News (13 October 2022). 'Conservative MP Miriam Cates Calls for Police to Investigate Trans Charity Mermaids'. <www.itv.com/news/calendar/2022-10-12/mp-calls-for-police-to-investigate-trans-charity>

Izea (14 March 2022). 'Ten Trans Influencers Telling Their Stories'. <izea.com/resources/trans-influencers>

Jeffreys, Sheila (1993). *The Lesbian Heresy: A Feminist Perspective on the Lesbian Sexual Revolution.* North Melbourne: Spinifex Press.

Jeffreys, Sheila (2003). *Unpacking Queer Politics: A Lesbian Feminist Perspective.* Cambridge, UK: Polity Press.

Jeffreys, Sheila (2005). *Beauty and Misogyny: Harmful Cultural Practices in the West.* Oxford: Routledge.

Jeffreys, Sheila (1990, 2011). *Anticlimax: A Feminist Perspective on the Sexual Revolution.* London: The Women's Press; North Melbourne: Spinifex Press.

Jeffreys, Sheila (July–August 2014a). 'The Politics of the Toilet: A Feminist Response to the Campaign to "Degender" a Women's Space'. *Women's Studies International Forum,* 45, pp. 42–51. <doi.org/10.1016/j.wsif.2014.05.003>

Jeffreys, Sheila (2014b). *Gender Hurts: A Feminist Analysis of the Politics of Transgenderism*. Oxford: Routledge.

Jeffreys, Sheila (2020). *Trigger Warning: My Lesbian Feminist Life*. Mission Beach: Spinifex Press.

Jeffreys, Sheila (2022). *Penile Imperialism: The Male Sex Right and Women's Subordination*. Mission Beach: Spinifex Press.

Jensen, Robert (2017). *The End of Patriarchy: Radical Feminism for Men*. North Melbourne: Spinifex Press.

Johnston, Jenny (11 August 2023). 'Retired Solicitor Left at Death's Door When Her Surgery Was Cancelled Because She Dared to Object to a Trans Woman Nurse in Her Hospital Room Tells Her Full Shocking Story'. <https://www.dailymail.co.uk/news/article-12398959/Retired-solicitor-left-deaths-door-surgery-cancelled-dared-object-trans-woman-nurse-hospital-room-tells-shocking-story-vowing-cancel-Im-not-scared-speak-out.html>

Joyce, Helen (2021). *Trans: When Ideology Meets Reality*. London: Oneworld Publications.

Justice Centre for Constitutional Freedoms (4 July 2019). 'UBC Commended for Allowing Jenn Smith Presentation but Warned that Security Fees Illegally Undermine Free Speech on Campus'. <www.jccf.ca/ubc-commended-for-allowing-jenn-smith-presentation-but-warned-that-security-fees-illegally-undermine-free-speech-on-campus>

Karnbach, Jordan (4 October 2022). 'After Player Injury, Cherokee Co. Schools Forfeit All Volleyball Games Against 1 School'. *ABC 13 News*. <wlos.com/news/local/after-player-injury-cherokee-co-schools-forfeit-all-volleyball-games-against-1-school>

Kerr, Barra (4 June 2019). 'Pronouns Are Rohypnol'. <fairplayforwomen.com/pronouns>

Klein, Renate (1983). 'The 'Men-Problem' in Women's Studies: The Expert, the Ignoramus and the Poor Dear'. *Women's Studies International Forum,* 6 (4), pp. 413–421. <https://doi.org/10.1016/0277-5395(83)90034-1>

Kornick, Lindsay (18 July 2022). 'Rachel Levine Blasted for Call to "Support and Empower" Youth with Transgender Treatments: "Unserious Regime"'. Fox News. <www.foxnews.com/media/rachel-levine-blasted-call-support-empower-youth-transgender-treatments-unserious-regime>

Kraus, Arnoldo (26 June 2017). '*Desmedicalizar* la vida'. *Nexos*. <www.nexos.com.mx/?p=46261>

La Voz (11 July 2018). 'Nació mujer e hizo la transición de género a varón: cometió un delito en Entre Ríos y se resiste a ir a la cárcel de hombres'. <https://www.lavoz.com.ar/ciudadanos/nacio-mujer-e-hizo-la-transicion-de-genero-varon-cometio-un-delito-en-entre-rios-y-se-res/>

Lane, Bernard (13 August 2023). 'Doubt in Denmark'. *Gender Clinic News.* <https://www.genderclinicnews.com/p/doubt-in-denmark>

Langston, Nancy (2011). *Toxic Bodies: Hormone Disruptors and the Legacy of DES.* New Haven: Yale University Press.

Las Hipopótamas (28 August 2020). 'Entrevista a Detransición Chile. Lo que no nos cuentan. Problemas y consecuencias de transicionar'. <www.youtube.com/watch?v=PpQUW0tc2Wo>

Lecuona, Laura (24 June 2022). 'En recuerdo de algunos lugares exclusivos para lesbianas'. *Tribuna Feminista.* <https://tribunafeminista.org/2022/06/en-recuerdo-de-algunos-lugares-exclusivos-para-lesbianas-ciudad-de-mexico/>

Lee, Georgina (23 November 2018). 'How Many Trans People Are Murdered in the UK?'. Channel 4 News. <www.channel4.com/news/factcheck/factcheck-how-many-trans-people-murdered-uk>

Leland, John (12 January 2006). 'Are They Here to Save the World?'. *The New York Times.* <www.nytimes.com/2006/01/12/fashion/thursdaystyles/are-they-here-to-save-the-world.html>

Lerner, Gerda (1986). *The Creation of Patriarchy.* New York: Oxford University Press.

Lesbians United (2022a). *Puberty Suppression: Medicine or Malpractice?* <lesbians-united.org/cgi-sys/suspendedpage.cgi>

Lesbians United (21 August 2022b). 'Statement on Puberty Suppression'. <https://thelesbianpost.substack.com/p/statement-on-puberty-suppression>

Leventis Lourgos, Angie (15 November 2019). 'After Four Years of Controversy, Embattled Palatine-Based School District Grants Transgender Students Unrestricted Locker Room Access'. *Chicago Tribune.* <bit.ly/3t7yhBH>

LGB Alliance (n.d.). 'Myths'. <https://lgballiance.org.uk/facts/>

Lime Soda Films (2021). *Dysphoric.* Documentary directed by Vaishnavi Sundar. <www.youtube.com/watch?v=w8taOdnXD6o>

Littman, Lisa (16 August 2018). 'Parent Reports of Adolescents and Young Adults Perceived to Show Signs of a Rapid Onset of Gender Dysphoria'. *Plos One.* <journals.plos.org/plosone/article?id=10.1371/journal.pone.0202330>

Lloyd, Lin Alexander (13 October 2020). 'Jenn Smith: What LGBTQ+ Allies Need to Know'. <medium.com/@linalexanderlloyd/jenn-smith-what-lgbtq-allies-need-to-know-ec63f5fb2701>

Lobo, Ariadna (21 June 2022). 'Las infancias trans aún tienen obstáculos para cambiar su identidad de género'. *La Lista.* <la-lista.com/derechos-humanos/2022/06/21/las-infancias-trans-aun-tienen-obstaculos-para-cambiar-su-identidad-de-genero>

Lofthouse, Brittney (28 September 2022). 'Cherokee County Schools Forfeits All Volleyball Games against Highlands Citing "Safety Concerns"'. *The Southern Scoop*. <thesouthernscoopnews.com/education/cherokee-county-schools-forfeits-all-volleyball-games-against-highlands-citing-safety-concerns>

Lohn, John (5 April 2022). 'A Look at the Numbers and Times: No Denying the Advantages of Lia Thomas'. *Swimming World Magazine*. <www.swimmingworldmagazine.com/news/a-look-at-the-numbers-and-times-no-denying-the-advantages-of-lia-thomas>

Long, Julia (12 May 2020a). 'A Meaningful Transition?'. *Uncommon Ground Media*. <uncommongroundmedia.com/a-meaningful-transition-julia-long>

Long, Julia (16 August 2020b). 'The Importance of Language When Talking About Transgenderism'. Women's Declaration International. <www.youtube.com/watch?v=MlwKCfB5FVs>

Maldonado, Lorena G. (9 March 2021). 'Elizabeth Duval: "El putero es una lacra social: la agenda trans no ha de regular la prostitución"'. *El Español*. <www.elespanol.com/cultura/20210309/elizabeth-duval-putero-social-no-regularprostitucion/564444892_0.html>

Mandel, Michele (11 November 2021). 'Decision Upheld Against Surgeon's Social Media Posts on Transgender Top Surgery'. *Toronto Sun*. <torontosun.com/news/local-news/mandel-decision-upheld-against-surgeons-social-media-posts-on-transgender-top-surgery>

Mañero, Iván (n.d.). Official website. <www.ivanmanero.com>

Mañero, Iván (16 May 2019). 'Complicaciones de la faloplastia: la mayoría son menores'. Interview. MedsBla. <noticias.medsbla.com/noticias-medicas/cirugia-plastica-estetica-y-reparadora/complicaciones-de-la-faloplastia>

Manning, Sanchez (29 July 2017). 'How 800 Children as Young as 10 Have Been Given Sex Change Drugs'. *Daily Mail*. <www.dailymail.co.uk/news/article-4743036/800-children-young-10-puberty-blockers.html>

Marchiano, Lisa (7 August 2018). 'No, You Don't Have a Disorder. You Have Feelings'. *Areo*. <areomagazine.com/2018/07/08/no-you-dont-have-a-disorder-you-have-feelings>

Marqués, Josep Vicent (1982). *No es natural. Para una sociología de la vida cotidiana*. (Julio A. Máñez, translator) Barcelona: Anagrama.

Mata, Haniel (18 July 2020). 'Qué significa ser una persona no binaria? Te decimos'. *El Heraldo de México*. <www.heraldodemexico.com.mx/tendencias/2020/7/18/que-significa-ser-una-persona-no-binaria-te-decimos-193548.html>

Mayo Clinic (n.d.) 'Feminizing surgery'. <https://www.mayoclinic.org/tests-procedures/feminizing-surgery/about/pac-20385102>

Mederes, Nayely (2022). 'Lenguaje incluyente es una forma de protestar ante el odio: Arturo Zaldívar'. NRT, 27 September. <noticiasnrt.com/2022/09/27/lenguaje-incluyente-es-una-forma-de-protestar-ante-el-odio-arturo-zaldivar>

Medina, Andrea (2022). 'Participation'. In CEIICH (2022).

Membrado, Zahida (20 December 2015). 'Gays in Iran: Surgery or Death'. *El Mundo*. <www.elmundo.es/sociedad/2015/12/20/5675869f46163f324b8b45f4.html>

Meyer, Len (30 June 2021). 'Why Pronouns Are So Important?'. Planned Parenthood of Illinois. <https://www.plannedparenthood.org/planned-parenthood-illinois/blog/why-are-pronouns-so-important-2>

Missé, Miquel (2018). *A la conquista del cuerpo equivocado*. Barcelona: Egales. Kindle edition.

Miyares, Alicia (2021). *Distopías patriarcales: Análisis feminista del 'generismo queer'*. Madrid: Cátedra.

Moore, Michele, and Heather Brunskell-Evans (eds.) (2019). *Inventing Transgender Children and Young People*. Newcastle: Cambridge Scholars Publishing.

Morán Breña, Carmen (15 May 2021). 'Paridad electoral con falsas trans en México'. *El País*. <elpais.com/mexico/2021-05-16/paridad-electoral-con-falsas-trans-en-mexico.html>

Moreno, Montserrat (1986). *Como se enseña a ser niña: El sexismo en la escuela*. Barcelona: Icaria.

Morgan, Robin (1973). 'Lesbianism and Feminism: Synonyms or Contradictions?' In Morgan (2014). *Going Too Far: The Personal Chronicle of a Feminist*. New York: Open Media.

Morgan, Robin (1996). 'Light Bulbs, Radishes, and the Politics of the 21st Century'. In Diane Bell and Renate Klein (eds.) *Radically Speaking: Feminism Reclaimed*. North Melbourne: Spinifex Press.

Morgan, Robin (2014). *Going Too Far: The Personal Chronicle of a Feminist*. New York: Open Media.

Moss, Julie (21 June 2018). 'Maria MacLachlan on the GRA and the Aftermath of Her Assault at Speaker's Corner'. *Feminist Current*. <www.feministcurrent.com/2018/06/21/interview-maria-maclauchlan-gra-aftermath-assault-speakers-corner>

Muíña García, Nuria (10 September 2022). 'México: Trans Activists Stage "Coup" of Women's Washroom at University, Issue Rape Threats'. *Reduxx*.

<https://reduxx.info/exclusive-trans-activists-stage-coup-of-womens-washroom-at-university-paint-whore-graffiti>

Mundi, Carolina (2 August 2021). 'La "era Laurel Hubbard": las atletas transgénero encuentran su sitio en los Juegos Olímpicos'. RTVE. <www.rtve.es/deportes/20210802/laurel-hubbard-transgenero-nueva-era-tokio-2021/2147300.shtml>

Murphy, Meghan (21 September 2017). '"TERF" Isn't Just a Slur, It's Hate Speech'. *Feminist Current.* <www.feministcurrent.com/2017/09/21/terf-isnt-slur-hate-speech>

Murphy, Meghan (18 July 2019). 'Women Warned You: Yaniv's Human Rights Case Is the Inevitable Result of Gender Identity Ideology'. *Feminist Current.* <www.feministcurrent.com/2019/07/18/women-warned-you-yanivs-human-rights-tribunal-case-is-natural-result-of-gender-identity-ideology>

Murphy, Meghan (4 October 2022). 'The "Transing Kids" Racket Gets Evermore Creepy'. *Feminist Current.* <www.feministcurrent.com/2022/10/04/the-transing-kids-racket-gets-evermore-creepy>

NHS England (9 June 2023). 'Implementing Advice from the Cass Review'. <england.nhs.uk>

Nochebuena, Marcela (23 June 2022). 'Corte deja abierta la puerta a que se pidan peritajes a infancias que quieran cambiar identidad de género; es regresivo: expertas'. *Animal Político.* <www.animalpolitico.com/2022/06/infancias-trans-corte-peritajes-medicos-regresion>

Nolan, Ian T., Christopher J. Kuhner and Geolani W. Dy (27 June 2019). 'Demographic and Temporal Trends in Transgender Identities and Gender Confirming Surgery'. *Translational Andrology and Urology,* 8 (3). <https://tau.amegroups.org/article/view/25593/24252>

Noticias IMER (14 August 2020). 'Ley de Infancias Trans, el derecho de menores a elegir su identidad de género'. <bit.ly/3TY8APB>

Noticieros Televisa (19 November 2021). 'Mujer trans: te explicamos qué es'. <noticieros.televisa.com/historia/mujer-transexual-que-es>

Nutt, Amy Ellis (5 April 2017). 'Long Shadow Cast by Psychiatrist on Transgender Issues Finally Recedes at Johns Hopkins'. *The Washington Post.* <www.washingtonpost.com/national/health-science/long-shadow-cast-by-psychiatrist-on-transgender-issues-finally-recedes-at-johns-hopkins/2017/04/05/e851e56e-0d85-11e7-ab07-07d9f521f6b5_story.html>

OAS (Organization of American States) (2020). *Panorama of the Legal Recognition of Gender Identity in the Americas.* <https://www.nodal.am/wp-content/uploads/2020/06/PANORAMA-DEL-RECONOCIMIENTO-LEGAL-DE-LA-IDENTIDAD-DE-GENERO-EN-LAS-AMERICAS.pdf>

O'Hara, Maureen (3 January 2022). 'The New Interim Version of the Equal Treatment Bench Book'. Legal Feminist. <www.legalfeminist.org.uk/2022/01/03/the-new-interim-version-of-the-equal-treatment-bench-book>

Orwell, George (1961). *1984*. New York: Signet Classics.

Osborne, Matt (30 November 2022). 'Here Are a Few of the Tweets that Jackie Green Deleted'. <https://www.thedistancemag.com/p/here-are-a-few-of-the-tweets-that>

Osorio Zuluaga, Daniela (18 May 2022). 'Han asesinado a 46 mujeres trans entre 2021 y 2022'. El Colombiano. <www.elcolombiano.com/colombia/han-asesinado-a-46-mujeres-trans-entre-2021-y-2022-OA17534974>

Ostertag, Bob (2016). *Sex Science Self: A Social History of Estrogen, Testosterone, and Identity*. Amherst: University of Massachusetts Press. Kindle edition.

Peterson, Jordan (12 November 2016). 'I Discuss Chaos and Order with Theryn Meyer, Reasonable Transperson'. <www.youtube.com/watch?v=a5sl4wbMT5g>

Pillard, Richard C. (1997). 'The Search for a Genetic Influence on Sexual Orientation'. In Vernon A. Rosario (ed.) *Science and Homosexualities*. New York and London: Routledge.

Pique Resilience Project (27 September 2019). 'Dagny Interviews Helena'. <www.youtube.com/channel/UCmGEMjyAwk6R1lTmG_JjLUA>

Pique Resilience Project (20 February 2020). 'Detransitioners were *never* trans?'. <www.youtube.com/channel/UCmGEMjyAwk6R1lTmG_JjLUA>

Pisano, Margarita (3 March 1995). 'La regalona del patriarcado'. *La Correa Feminista*, pp. 10–11.

Plascencia Villanueva, Raúl (25 June 2013). *Informe especial de la Comisión Nacional de los Derechos Humanos sobre el estado que guardan los derechos humanos de las mujeres internas en centros de reclusión de la República Mexicana*. Comisión Nacional de los Derechos Humanos. <https://www.cndh.org.mx/sites/default/files/doc/Informes/Especiales/informeEspecial_CentrosReclusion.pdf>

Portella, Anna (14 June 2022). 'Hablan las víctimas de la cirugía estética letal en Colombia'. *Ara*. <en.ara.cat/internacional/america/hablan-victimas-cirugia-estetica-letal-colombia_1_4401986.html>

Powell, Michael (29 May 2022). 'What Lia Thomas Could Mean for Women's Elite Sports'. *The New York Times*. <www.nytimes.com/2022/05/29/us/lia-thomas-women-sports.html>

Pressly, Linda (19 August 2021). 'México: cómo la narcoestética está cambiando el cuerpo de las mujeres de Sinaloa'. *BBC News*. <www.bbc.com/mundo/noticias-america-latina-57942206>

Purohit, Bavesh (30 September 2021). 'When Transgender Fighter Fallon Fox Broke Her Opponent's Skull in MMA Fight'. *Sportskeeda*. <www.sportskeeda.com/mma/news-when-transgender-fighter-fallon-fox-broke-opponent-s-skull-mma-fight>

Quintana, Carlos A. (2007). *Los niños índigo: fraude or realidad*. North Carolina: Self-published.

Rachmuth, Sloan (11 October 2022). 'HS Volleyball Player Injured by Transgender Competitor in North Carolina'. Education First Alliance. <www.edfirstnc.org/post/female-hs-volleyball-player-seriously-injured-by-alleged-trans-competitor-in-north-carolina>

Ramsey, Gerald (1996). *Transsexuals: Candid Answers to Private Questions*. Freedom, CA: The Crossing Press.

Rangel Laguna, Raymundo, and Manuel López Sanmartín (1 April 2022a). '"Gabriel Quadri es un asesino e hipócrita": Salma Luévano'. *MVS Noticias*. <https://mvsnoticias.com/autos-mas/2022/4/1/gabriel-quadri-es-un-asesino-hipocrita-salma-luevano-547421.html>

Rangel Laguna, Raymundo, and Manuel López Sanmartín (1 April 2022b). '"Yo no odio a las personas"': Gabriel Quadri'. *MVS Noticias*. <https://mvsnoticias.com/autos-mas/2022/4/1/yo-no-odio-las-personas-gabriel-quadri-547422.html>

Raymond, Janice G. (1979). *The Transsexual Empire: The Making of the She-Male*. Boston: Beacon Press.

Raymond, Janice G. (1993/1994). *Women as Wombs: Reproductive Technologies and the Battle over Women's Freedom*. New York: Harper Collins; North Melbourne: Spinifex Press.

Raymond, Janice G. (1994). Introduction to the 1994 edition of *The Transsexual Empire*. New York: Teachers College Press.

Raymond, Janice G. (n.d.). 'Fictions and Facts about *The Transsexual Empire*'. <janiceraymond.com/fictions-and-facts-about-the-transsexual-empire>

Raymond, Janice G. (2021). *Doublethink: A Feminist Challenge to Transgenderism*. Mission Beach: Spinifex Press.

Raymond, Janice G. (3 May 2022). 'FiLiA Interview'. <www.filia.org.uk/latest-news/2022/5/3/filia-interview-janice-raymond>

Rayner, Gordon (1 June 2022). 'Vindication for "Transphobic" Gender-Critical Campaigner Named in Queen's Birthday Honours List'. *The Telegraph*. <www.telegraph.co.uk/royal-family/2022/06/01/vindication-transphobic-gender-critical-campaigner-named-queens>

Red de Resistencia y Disidencia Sexual y de Género (28 September 2022). 'A la comunidad LGBT+ de la Ciudad de México y de todo el país'.

<docs.google.com/document/d/157Q01jjTsveziyoesgRlgd7sXIqzz2ccoYw
euwRGslc/mobilebasic>

Reduxx (21 September 2022). 'Forbes Highlights Recently Transitioned Male at Women's Summit'. <reduxx.info/forbes-highlights-recently-transitioned-male-at-womens-summit>

Registro Nacional de Población e Identidad (2 November 2020). 'Derecho a la identidad, la puerta de acceso a tus derechos'. <www.gob.mx/segob/renapo/acciones-y-programas/derecho-a-la-identidad-la-puerta-de-acceso-a-tus-derechos>

Reilly-Cooper, Rebecca (2015). 'Trans issues and gender identity'. In *Sex and Gender: A Beginner's Guide*. <https://sexandgenderintro.com/>

Reilly-Cooper, Rebecca (20 March 2016a). 'Critically Examining the Doctrine of Gender Identity'. <www.youtube.com/watch?v=QPVNxYkawao>

Reilly-Cooper, Rebecca (28 June 2016b). 'Gender Is Not a Spectrum'. *Aeon*. <https://aeon.co/essays/the-idea-that-gender-is-a-spectrum-is-a-new-gender-prison>

Reilly-Cooper, Rebecca (9 June 2020). 'J. K. Rowling and the Trans Activists: A Story in Screenshots'. <medium.com/@rebeccarc/j-k-rowling-and-the-trans-activists-a-story-in-screenshots-78e01dca68d>

Reuters (30 July 2019). 'Weightlifter Hubbard Becomes Lightning Rod for Criticism of Transgender Policy'. *Reuters*. <www.reuters.com/article/us-weightlifting-newzealand-hubbard-idUSKCN1UP0F0>

Rich, Adrienne (1980/2018). 'Compulsory Heterosexuality and Lesbian Existence'. In *Essential Essays: Culture, Politics, and the Art of Poetry*. New York and London: W. W. Norton & Company.

Rippon, Gina (2019). *Gender and Our Brains: How Neuroscience Explodes the Myths of the Male and Female Minds*. New York: Pantheon Books.

Robertson, Julia Diana (27 November 2018). 'Twitter Bans Meghan Murphy, Founder of Canada's Leading Feminist Website'. *After Ellen*. <bit.ly/3zxAHwN>

Robertson, Julia Diana (26 March 2020). 'DOJ Sides with 3 Connecticut HS Girls about Fairness in Sports'. *The Velvet Chronicle*. <thevelvetchronicle.com/doj-sides-with-three-connecticut-hs-girls-about-fairness-in-sport>

Robinson, Max (2021). *Detransition: Beyond Before and After*. North Melbourne: Spinifex Press.

Robles, Salvador (2021). 'Introducción'. In Asociación por las Infancias Transgénero (2021), pp. 14–17.

Rocha, Tania (2021). 'Relevancia del papel de las madres en el acompañamiento de infantes y adolescentes trans'. In Asociación por las Infancias Transgénero (2021), pp. 26–28.

Rodríguez Magda, Rosa María (2019). *La mujer molesta. Feminismos postgénero y transidentidad sexual.* Madrid: Ménades Editorial.

Rooney, Rachel (3 June 2020). Twitter. <twitter.com/RooneyRachel/status/1268188762938449923>

Rooney, Rachel (9 December 2021). 'Rachel Rooney's Exit Interview from Publishing'. Wild Woman Writing Club. <https://wildwomanwritingclub.wordpress.com/2021/12/09/rachel-rooneys-exit-interview-from-publishing>

Rosario Sánchez, Raquel (7 March 2018). 'Cómo Boko Haram supo a quién secuestrar?'. <8rosariosanchez.wordpress.com/2018/03/07/como-boko-haram-supo-a-quien-secuestrar>

Rosario, Vernon A. (ed.) (1997). *Science and Homosexualities.* New York and London: Routledge.

Rowling, J. K. (10 June 2020). 'J. K. Rowling Writes about Her Reasons for Speaking out on Sex and Gender Issues'. <www.jkrowling.com/opinions/j-k-rowling-writes-about-her-reasons-for-speaking-out-on-sex-and-gender-issues>

Rowling, J. K. (20 September 2022). Twitter. <twitter.com/jk_rowling/status/1572293140882788353>

Rubin, Gayle (2007). 'Thinking Sex: Notes for a Radical Theory of the Politics of Sexuality'. In Richard Parker and Peter Aggleton. *Culture, Society and Sexuality: A Reader.* London: Routledge.

Sales, Dan (19 October 2022). 'Hospital Refuses to Operate on Sex Attack Victim after She Requests All-Female Care because She Fears Mixed Sex Facilities Are Unsafe for Women'. *Daily Mail.* <www.dailymail.co.uk/news/article-11316141/Hospital-bans-sex-assault-victim-op-female-care-request.html>

Sanín, Carolina (30 June 2017). 'El mundo sin mujeres'. *Vice.* <www.vice.com/es/article/qvppa7/el-mundo-sin-mujeres>

Sanín, Carolina (26 August 2022). Twitter. <twitter.com/SaninPazC/status/1563157326558662659>

Sarkeesian, Anita (2012a). 'LEGO & Gender, Part 1: Lego Friends'. *Feminist Frequency.* <feministfrequency.com/video/lego-gender-part-1-lego-friends>

Sarkeesian, Anita (2012b). 'LEGO & Gender, Part 2: The Boys Club'. *Feminist Frequency.* <feministfrequency.com/video/lego-gender-part-2-the-boys-club>

Sastre, Noelia (12 May 2015). 'Clases de feminidad para mujeres transexuales'. *Vanity Fair.* <www.revistavanityfair.es/sociedad/celebrities/articulos/

monica-prata-clases-feminidad-mujeres-transexuales-nueva-york-bruce-jenner-kim-kardashian/20811>

Schemmel, Alec (18 July 2022). 'Rachel Levine Says Youth Access to "Gender-Affirming Care" Should Not Be Limited'. KATV. <katv.com/news/nation-world/rachel-levine-says-youth-access-to-gender-affirming-care-should-not-be-limited>

Scott, Joan Wallach (2018). 'Gender: A Useful Category of Historical Analysis'. In *Gender and the Politics of History,* 30th anniversary edition. New York: Columbia University Press. Kindle edition.

SDP Noticias (7 May 2018). '17 candidatos fingen ser trans para simular paridad de género, denuncian'. *SDP Noticias.* <www.sdpnoticias.com/local/oaxaca/candidatos-simular-fingen-trans-17-2.html>

Seddon, Dan (31 December 2020). 'Eddie Izzard Speaks about Being Gender-Fluid'. *Digital Spy.* <www.digitalspy.com/showbiz/a35103871/eddie-izzard-gender-fluid-she-pronouns>

Seiland, Jennifer (18 October 2022). 'Sex Offender Identified as Woman to Access Women's Shelter, Allegedly Raped a Female Resident'. *Reduxx.* <https://reduxx.info/male-sex-offender-identified-as-woman-to-access-womens-shelter-allegedly-raped-a-female-resident>

Shrier, Abigail (2020). *Irreversible Damage: The Transgender Craze Seducing Our Daughters.* Washington, D.C.: Regenery Publishing.

Singal, Jesse (13 January 2017). 'You Should Watch the BBC's Controversial Documentary on the Gender-Dysphoria Researcher Kenneth Zucker'. *The Cut.* <www.thecut.com/2017/01/you-should-watch-the-bbcs-kenneth-zucker-documentary.html>

Skirt Go Spinny (16 January 2022a). *The Call is Coming from Inside the House.* <www.youtube.com/watch?v=PBInNGgdF2M&t=152s>

Skirt Go Spinny (19 May 2022b). *This is Not a Drill: The Indoctrination of Gender Ideology in Schools.* <www.youtube.com/watch?v=kc90Set-640>

Sky News (26 September 2018). 'Woman Billboard Was "Transphobic" and "Dangerous"'. <www.youtube.com/watch?v=y8nViKYmEhU>

Sky News (4 October 2023). 'Caitlyn Jenner Says She Would Not Feel Safe Using Men's Toilets and "Never Had a Problem" Using Women's'. <https://news.sky.com/video/caitlyn-jenner-says-she-would-not-feel-safe-using-mens-toilets-and-never-had-a-problem-using-womens-12976939>

Slatz, Anna (16 December 2021). 'TikTok Doctor Performed Breast Removal on 'Trans' 13-Year-Old Girl'. *4W.* <4w.pub/tiktok-gender-doctor-per-breast-removal-on-13-year-old-girl>

Slatz, Anna (24 January 2022a). 'John Money: The Pro-Pedophile Pervert Who

Invented "Gender"'. *Reduxx*. <reduxx.info/john-money-the-pervert-who-invented-gender>

Slatz, Anna (31 May 2022b). 'Female Inmate Reports Rape Occurred in California Women's Prison'. *Reduxx*. <reduxx.info/exclusive-female-inmate-reports-rape-occurred-in-california-womens-prison>

Slatz, Anna (8 July 2022c). 'Mexico: Trans Politician Interrupted Anti-Trafficking Conference, Screamed "Sex Work Is Work"'. *Reduxx*. <https://reduxx.info/mexico-trans-politician-interrupted-anti-trafficking-conference-screamed-sex-work-is-work/>

Smith, Jenn (n.d.). Official website. <transanityca.wordpress.com>

Smith, Jenn (13 August 2017). 'Synanon, the Brainwashing "Game" and Modern Transgender Activism: The Orwellian Implications of Transgender Activism'. <archive.org/stream/Synanon00/SynanonTransgender_djvu.txt>

Society for Evidence Based Gender Medicine (30 May 2021a). 'Detransition: A Real and Growing Phenomenon'. <segm.org/first_large_study_of_detransitioners>

Society for Evidence Based Gender Medicine (2 July 2021b). 'One Year Since Finland Broke with WPATH "Standards of Care"'. <https://segm.org/Finland_deviates_from_WPATH_prioritizing_psychotherapy_no_surgery_for_minors>

Sorto, Gabrielle (2 October 2019). 'A Teacher Says He Was Fired for Refusing to Use Male Pronouns for a Transgender Student'. CNN. <edition.cnn.com/2019/10/02/us/virginia-teacher-says-wrongfully-fired-student-wrong-pronouns-trnd/index.html>

Still, Tish (23 July 2021). 'That Dentons Document'. <gendercriticalwoman.blog/2020/07/23/that-dentons-document>

Still, Tish (11 January 2022). 'The Truth about Trans Murders'. *UnHerd*. <unherd.com/2022/01/the-truth-about-trans-murders>

Stock, Kathleen (2021). *Material Girls: Why Reality Matters to Feminism*. London: Fleet.

Stonewall (16 October 2019). 'It's International Pronouns Day, and It's Time for All of Us to Step as Trans Allies'. <www.stonewall.org.uk/about-us/blog/it%E2%80%99s-international-pronouns-day-and-it%E2%80%99s-time-all-us-step-trans-allies>

Stonewall (n.d.). 'List of LGBTQ+ Terms' <https://www.stonewall.org.uk/list-lgbtq-terms#:~:text=Queer%20is%20a%20term%20used,orientation%20and%2For%20gender%20identity>.

Stryker, Susan (2017). *Transgender History: The Roots of Today's Revolution*. Revised edition. New York: Seal Press. Kindle edition.

Sunstein, Cass R. (2019). Conformity: The Power of Social Influences. New York: New York University Press.

Suprema Corte de Justicia de la Nación (SCJN) (17 October 2018). 'Reconocimiento de la identidad de género de personas trans en documentos oficiales', amparo en revisión 1317/2017. <www.scjn.gob.mx/derechos-humanos/sites/default/files/sentencias-emblematicas/resumen/2020-12/Resumen%20AR1317-2017%20DGDH.pdf>

Tankard Reist, Melinda (5 September 2022). 'Melinda Tankard Reist, Australia, Discusses Her New Book *He Chose Porn Over Me*'. Women's Declaration International. <https://www.youtube.com/watch?v=pUIMp4zRtBk>

Teen Line (12 December 2018). '13 Trans Influencers & Activists that Inspire Us'. <teenlineonline.org/13-trans-influencers-activists-that-inspire-us>

Terf Is a Slur. Documenting the Abuse, Harassment and Misogyny of Transgender Identity Politics (n.d.). Official website. <terfisaslur.com>

The Guardian (30 September 2022). 'Trans Charity Mermaids Investigated over "Breast Binders Given to Children"'. <www.theguardian.com/society/2022/sep/30/transgender-charity-mermaids-investigated-breast-binders-given-to-children>

Tirado Morales, Luis (30 August 2021). 'Y aquí seguimos las infancias y adolescencias trans'. *Animal Político*. <www.animalpolitico.com/de-generando/y-aqui-seguimos-las-infancias-y-adolescencias-trans>

Tomsons, Kira (4 June 2020). 'Lying to Children and the Cultivation of Epistemic Virtue'. *Canadian Journal of Practical Philosophy*. <https://scholar.uwindsor.ca/cgi/viewcontent.cgi?article=1023&context=csspe>

Transgender Trend (18 February 2019a). 'Severe Pain at Orgasm: Effect of Testosterone on the Female Body'. <www.transgendertrend.com/severe-pain-orgasm-effect-testosterone-female-body>

Transgender Trend (1 July 2019b). 'The Surge in Referral Rates of Girls to the Tavistock Continues to Rise'. <www.transgendertrend.com/surge-referral-rates-girls-tavistock-continues-rise>

Transgender Trend (30 July 2022). 'The Tavistock Gender Clinic to be Closed Down: Our Response'. <www.transgendertrend.com/tavistock-gender-clinic-closed-down>

Transgender Trend (n.d.). 'Do Children Grow Out of Gender Dysphoria?' <www.transgendertrend.com/children-change-minds>

TransLine. Transgender Medical Consultation Service (9 September 2022). 'Surgical Options for Trans Masculine (FTM) Individuals'. <https://transline.zendesk.com/hc/en-us/articles/229372808-Surgical-Options-for-Trans-Masculine-FTM-Individuals>

Transrespect Versus Transphobia (9 November 2016). 'TMM Update Trans Day of Remembrance 2016'. <https://transrespect.org/en/tmm-trans-day-remembrance-2016/>

Trans Widows Voices (n.d.). Official website. <transwidowsvoices.org>

Tribunal Electoral del Poder Judicial de la Federación (4 May 2023). 'La diputada federal Salma Luévano sufrió violencia política contra las mujeres en razón de género: Sala Especializada'. <https://www.te.gob.mx/front3/bulletins/detail/194321/6>

Tsevea (2022). 'Tsevea's Story: The Man in the Mirror'. <https://www.transwidowsvoices.org/post/tseveas-story-the-man-in-the-mirror>

Ulises, Édgar (13 August 2020). 'Aprueban en Oaxaca ley contra trans y muxes "cachirules"'. *Homosensual.* <www.homosensual.com/uncategorized/aprueban-oaxaca-ley-trans-muxes>

Ulises, Édgar (6 April 2022). 'México: Estados que reconocen a las infancias trans'. *Homosensual.* <www.homosensual.com/lgbt/trans/mexico-estados-que-reconocen-a-las-infancias-trans>

UNODC (United Nations Office on Drugs and Crime) (2019). *Global Study on Homicide: Executive Summary.* <www.unodc.org/documents/data-and-analysis/gsh/Booklet1.pdf>

UN Women, 'Gender Equality Glossary'. <trainingcentre.unwomen.org/?lang=en>

United Nations (1996). *Report of the Fourth World Conference on Women.* <https://www.unwomen.org/en/digital-library/publications/2015/01/beijing-declaration>

United Nations (May 2019). *The United Nations Strategy and Plan of Action on Hate Speech.* <https://www.un.org/en/hate-speech/un-strategy-and-plan-of-action-on-hate-speech>

Uwujaren, Jarune (14 March 2017). 'Why Chimamanda Ngozi Adichie's Comments on Trans Women Are Wrong and Dangerous'. Coalition. <coalition.org.mk/archives/8188?lang=en>

Valcárcel, Amelia (2019). *Ahora, feminismo. Cuestiones candentes y frentes abiertos.* Madrid: Cátedra.

Valero, Ian (9 June 2020). 'Top 10: influencers LGBT+ mexicanos que puedes seguir en Instagram'. *BrandMe.* <brandme.la/blog/top-10-influencers-lgbt-mexicanos-que-puedes-seguir-en-instagram>

Valle, Norma, Bertha Hiriart and Ana María Amado (1996). *El abc de un periodismo no sexista.* Santiago: Fempress.

Van Emmerick, Klaudia (9 March 2017). 'Concerns over Transgender Client at Okanagan Shelter'. *Global News.* <globalnews.ca/news/3300518/concerns-over-transgender-client-at-okanagan-shelter>

Vargas, Aabye (6 October 2021). 'Clínica para personas trans inicia con 20 terapias hormonales'. *El Sol de México*. <www.elsoldemexico.com.mx/metropoli/cdmx/clinica-para-personas-trans-inicia-con-20-terapias-hormonales-7302364.html>

Vasquez, Ricardo (23 July 2015). '"Mujer" transgénero lesiona brutalmente a oponente mujer'. *Noticias MMA*. (<mma.uno/mujer-transgenero-lesionada-brutalmente-a-opponente-mujer>: accessed November 2022; site inactive on 30 October 2023)

Veloz, Estefanía (14 October 2022). '¿Qué es una terf y cómo identificarla?'. *La Lista*. <la-lista.com/opinion/2022/10/14/que-es-una-terf-y-como-identificarla>

Vigo, Julian (10 March 2017). 'The Invisible Woman: Gender Identity in the Age of Neoliberalism'. *Feminist Current*. <www.feministcurrent.com/2017/03/10/invisible-woman-gender-identity-age-neoliberalism>

Vigo, Julian (7 August 2020). 'What's Driving Authoritarianism Today?'. *Savage Minds*. <savageminds.substack.com/p/whats-driving-authoritarianism-today>

Vigo, Julian (1 April 2021). Interview with Lisa Littman. *Savage Minds*. <savageminds.substack.com/p/lisa-littman#details>

Vikander, Tessa (21 June 2019). 'UBC Staff and Students Want Presentation Cancelled over Concerns of Hatred towards Trans People'. *Toronto Star*. <www.thestar.com/vancouver/2019/06/21/students-and-staff-feel-betrayed-by-ubc-for-allowing-talk-on-harms-of-transgender-politics-in-school.html>

Wadman, Meredith (30 August 2018). 'New Paper Ignites Storm over Whether Teens Experience "Rapid Onset" of Transgender Identity'. *Science*. <www.science.org/content/article/new-paper-ignites-storm-over-whether-teens-experience-rapid-onset-transgender-identity>

WATC Content Team (16 February 2021). 'Inspirational Profile: Pips Bunce, Director, Credit Suisse'. *We Are the City*. <wearethecity.com/inspirational-profile-pips-bunce-director-credit-suisse>

WDI (Women's Declaration International) (2019). Declaration on Women's Sex-Based Rights. <www.womensdeclaration.com/es/womens-sex-based-rights-full-text-es>

WDI (Women's Declaration International) (8 May 2022). '*Gender Critical Feminism* by Holly Lawford-Smith discussed by the author, Caroline Norma and Jo Brew'. <www.youtube.com/c/WomensDeclarationInternationalWDI>

WDI-México (Women's Declaration International-Mexico) (6 May 2022). 'Amago de linchamiento al representante del rector de la UNAM'. <www.youtube.com/watch?v=LwytonhcC7k&t=1s>

Weinberg, Justin (12 April 2022). 'OUP'S Decision to Publish "Gender-Critical" Book Raises Concerns of Scholars and OUP Employees'. *Daily Nous*. <dailynous.com/2022/04/12/oups-decision-to-publish-gender-critical-book-raises-concerns-of-scholars-and-oup-employees>

Wild, Angela C. (2019). *Lesbians at Ground Zero: How Transgenderism Is Conquering the Lesbian Body*, Get the L Out, March. <https://www.gettheloutuk.com/attachments/lesbiansatgroundzero.pdf>

Winkler, Claudia (19 June 2000). 'Boy, Interrupted. A Tale of Sex, Lies, and Dr. Money'. *The Weekly Standard*. <www.washingtonexaminer.com/weekly-standard/boy-interrupted>

Withers, Robert (2019). 'Be Careful What You Wish for: Trans-Identification and the Evasion of Psychological Distress'. In Michele Moore and Heather Brunskell-Evans (eds.) *Inventing Transgender Children and Young People*. Newcastle: Cambridge Scholars Publishing.

Witkin, Rachel (1 May 2014). 'Hopkins Hospital: A History of Sex Reassignment'. The Johns Hopkins Newsletter. <www.jhunewsletter.com/article/2014/05/hopkins-hospital-a-history-of-sex-reassignment-76004>

Women's Liberation Front (17 November 2021). 'Incarcerated Women Speak! Tomiekia's Story'. <www.youtube.com/watch?v=gJoKAPJe9m4>

WLRN (Women's Liberation Radio News) (3 August 2017). 'Money Behind the Transgender Movement and Impact on Lesbians. <womensliberationradionews.com/2017/08/03/edition-16-the-money-behind-the-trans-movement-and-impact-on-lesbians>

WPATH (World Professional Association for Transgender Health) (2012). *Standards of Care for the Health of Transsexual, Transgender, and Gender Nonconforming People*, 7th version. <https://www.wpath.org/media/cms/Documents/SOC%20v7/SOC%20V7_English.pdf>

––– (2022). *Standards of Care for The Health of Transgender and Gender Diverse People*. London: Taylor & Francis, 8th version. <https://www.tandfonline.com/doi/pdf/10.1080/26895269.2022.2100644>

Woulahan, Shay (4 October 2022). 'Trustee of Trans Youth Charity Resigns over Speech at Pro-Pedophile Event'. *Reduxx*, <reduxx.info/trustee-of-trans-youth-charity-resigns-after-pro-pedophile-revelations>

Wright, Colin (4 February 2022). 'When Asked "What Are Your Pronouns?", Don't Answer'. *The Wall Street Journal*. <https://www.wsj.com/articles/asked-your-pronouns-dont-answer-lgbtqia-sogie-gender-identity-nonbinary-transgender-trans-rights-sexism-misogyny-feminism-11643992762>

Yaoyólotl Castro and María Yan (2008). 'Renuncia al comité impulsor del XI Encuentro Feminista Latinoamericano y del Caribe'. Unpublished manuscript.

Yardley, Miranda (9 August 2017). 'Common Threads and Narratives of Transgender Children and What This Means for Our Lesbian and Gay Populations'. <medium.com/@mirandayardley/common-threads-and-narratives-of-transgender-children-and-what-this-means-for-our-lesbian-and-gay-210726e2336>

Yogyakarta Principles (2007). *Principles on the Application of International Human Rights Law in Relation to Sexual Orientation and Gender Identity.* <https://yogyakartaprinciples.org/principles-en/>

Yogyakarta Principles Plus 10 (2017). *Additional Principles and State Obligations on the Application of International Human Rights Law in Relation to Sexual Orientation, Gender Identity, Gender Expression and Sex Characteristics to Complement the Yogyakarta Principles.* <https://yogyakarta principles.org/principles-en/yp10/>

Yoon, JeongMee (n.d.). Official website. <www.jeongmeeyoon.com>

Zobnina, Anna (17 August 2020). 'Where Did Gender Identity Ideology Come from?'. Women's Declaration International. <www.youtube.com/c/WomensDeclarationInternationalWDI>

@galatea128 (21 Oct 2022a). Twitter. <twitter.com/galatea128/status/158345332797453926>

@galatea128 (23 October 2022b). Twitter. <twitter.com/galatea128/status/158370630955555635>

@IreneAguiarG (24 March 2022). Twitter. <twitter.com/IreneAguiarG/status/1507070648243704709602>

@j4ppleby (8 July 2019). Twitter. <twitter.com/j4ppleby/status/1148425600954241024>

@laurelyeye (23 March 2022). Twitter. <twitter.com/laurelyeye/status/1506781209682190341>

@luigicantu (13 October 2022). Twitter. <twitter.com/luigicantu/status/1580671718603259909>

@MariaClementeMx (6 October 2022). Twitter. <twitter.com/MARIACLEMENTEMX/status/1577995612745867271>

@SalmaLuevano (31 March 2022). Twitter. <twitter.com/SalmaLuevano/status/1509756846952919079>

@TheAttagirls (3 October 2022). Twitter. <twitter.com/TheAttagirls/status/157688734112142950>

@TullipR Detrans Male (23 March 2022). 'Lost Boys. Speaking Up for Detrans Males'. <tullipr.substack.com>

INDEX

Doublethink: A Feminist Challenge to Transgenderism
Janice Raymond

In an age when falsehoods are commonly taken as truth, Janice Raymond's book illuminates the 'doublethink' of a transgender movement that is able to define men as women, women as men, he as she, dissent as heresy, science as sham, and critics as fascists.
ISBN 9781925950380

Detransition: Beyond Before and After
Max Robinson

In this brave and thoughtful book, Max Robinson goes beyond the 'before' and 'after' of the transition she underwent and takes us through the processes that led her, first, to transition in an attempt to get relief from her distress, and then to detransition as she discovered feminist thought and community.
ISBN 9781925950403

On the Meaning of Sex:
Thoughts about the New Definition of Woman
Kajsa Ekis Ekman
Translated by Kristina Mäki

A brilliant examination of the intellectually incoherent and anti-feminist character of gender identity theory.
ISBN 9781925950663

Not Sacred, Not Squaws: Indigenous Feminism Redefined
Cherry Smiley

This book is a refreshing feminist contemporary challenge to the patriarchal ideology that governs our world and a vigorous and irreverent defence against the attempts to silence Indigenous radical feminists.
ISBN 9781925950649

From the 'Neutral' Body to the Posthuman Cyborg:
A Critique of Gender Ideology
Silvia Guerini

The idea of the 'neutral' body and body modification pave the way for the construction of the post-human cyborg and the genetic engineering of bodies. Is the last bioethical barrier about to be breached to give way to transhumanist demands? And at what cost?
ISBN 9781925950885

*If you would like to know more about
Spinifex Press, write to us for a free catalogue, visit our
website or email us for further information
on how to subscribe to our monthly newsletter.*

Spinifex Press
PO Box 105
Mission Beach QLD 4852
Australia

www.spinifexpress.com.au
women@spinifexpress.com.au